21世纪英语专业系列教材

英语构词法实用教程

（第二版）

夏洋 李佳 / 主　编
孟健 高婷婷 / 副主编
孙美秀 刘君 张婉婷 史月 齐磊 / 编　委

图书在版编目 (CIP) 数据

英语构词法实用教程 / 夏洋，李佳主编. -- 2版. 北京：北京大学出版社，2024.10.
--21世纪英语专业系列教材. -- ISBN 978-7-301-35479-7

I. H314.1

中国国家版本馆 CIP 数据核字第 2024M6J860 号

书　　　名	英语构词法实用教程（第二版）
	YINGYU GOUCIFA SHIYONG JIAOCHENG（DI-ER BAN）
著作责任者	夏　洋　李　佳　主编
责 任 编 辑	李　颖
标 准 书 号	ISBN 978-7-301-35479-7
出 版 发 行	北京大学出版社
地　　　址	北京市海淀区成府路 205 号　100871
网　　　址	http://www.pup.cn　　　　　新浪微博：@ 北京大学出版社
电 子 邮 箱	编辑部 pupwaiwen@pup.cn　　总编室 zpup@pup.cn
电　　　话	邮购部 010-62752015　发行部 010-62750672　编辑部 010-62754382
印 刷 者	河北博文科技印务有限公司
经 销 者	新华书店
	787 毫米 ×1092 毫米　16 开本　25.25 印张　846 千字
	2019 年 10 月第 1 版
	2024 年 10 月第 2 版　2024 年 10 月第 1 次印刷
定　　　价	79.00 元

未经许可，不得以任何方式复制或抄袭本书之部分或全部内容。
版权所有，侵权必究
举报电话：010-62752024　电子邮箱：fd@pup.cn
图书如有印装质量问题，请与出版部联系，电话：010-62756370

目 录

- 第一篇　英语词汇构词法简介 ··· 1
- 第二篇　派生法:英语词缀与构词 ·· 7
  - 第1章　常用英语词汇前缀 ··· 8
    - 第1单元　表示"数字"的前缀 ··· 8
    - 第2单元　表示"空间"的前缀(一) ··································· 16
    - 第3单元　表示"空间"的前缀(二) ··································· 23
    - 第4单元　表示"否定"的前缀 ·· 31
    - 第5单元　表示"大小多少"的前缀 ··································· 39
    - 第6单元　表示"新旧好坏"的前缀 ··································· 46
    - 第7单元　表示"正误异同"的前缀 ··································· 53
    - 第8单元　决定词性的前缀 ·· 61
    - 第9单元　多义前缀(一) ·· 69
    - 第10单元　多义前缀 (二) ·· 77
  - 第2章　常用英语词汇后缀 ·· 84
    - 第1单元　表示"人"的名词后缀 ······································ 84
    - 第2单元　表示"缩小的名词"的后缀 ································ 92
    - 第3单元　表示抽象意义的名词后缀 ·································· 100
    - 第4单元　表示集合名词的后缀 ·· 108
    - 第5单元　常用形容词后缀 ··· 116
    - 第6单元　常用副词后缀 ·· 126
    - 第7单元　常用动词后缀 ·· 133
- 第三篇　派生法:英语词根与构词 ··· 141
  - 第1章　表示"看"的词根 ·· 142
  - 第2章　表示"听"的词根 ·· 149

1

第3章	表示"说"的词根	153
第4章	表示"喊叫"的词根	160
第5章	表示"吃喝"的词根	166
第6章	表示"推拉"的词根	171
第7章	表示"投掷"的词根	178
第8章	表示"上升"的词根	185
第9章	表示"写画"的词根	192
第10章	表示"走"的词根	199
第11章	表示"坐"的词根	206
第12章	表示"伸展"的词根	213
第13章	表示"引导,汇集"的词根	220
第14章	表示"信任"的词根	228
第15章	表示"心智"的词根	236
第16章	表示"人"的词根	246
第17章	表示"父母"的词根	254
第18章	表示"身体"的词根	262
第19章	表示"手足"的词根	269
第20章	表示"生死"的词根	277
第21章	表示"光热"的词根	287
第22章	表示"水"的词根	293
第23章	表示"土地"的词根	299
第24章	表示"动植物"的词根	304
第25章	表示"流动"的词根	310
第26章	表示"声音"的词根	317
第27章	表示"重量"的词根	323
第28章	表示"真假"的词根	329
第29章	表示"相同"的词根	334

第30章	表示"时间"的词根	339
第31章	表示"方位"的词根	345
第32章	表示"名字"的词根	351

第四篇 英语其他构词法 357

第1章 复合法 358
- 第1单元 复合名词 358
- 第2单元 复合形容词 361
- 第3单元 复合动词 363

第2章 词类转化法 365
- 第1单元 名词转化成动词 365
- 第2单元 形容词转化成动词 368
- 第3单元 动词转化成名词 370
- 第4单元 形容词转化成名词 372

第3章 缩略法 375
- 第1单元 截短词 375
- 第2单元 首字母缩略词 379
- 第3单元 首字母拼音词 382
- 第4单元 拼缀词 385

第4章 逆生法 388

第5章 拟声法 391

第6章 专有名词普通化 394

第一篇　英语词汇构词法简介

英语虽然只有26个字母，但却有极强的构词能力。据称英语的总词汇约有50万个，实际远不止于此。如此庞大的英语词汇要想全部记住是不可能的。我们知道英国大文豪莎士比亚掌握的词汇非常丰富，使用也最为纯熟和美妙，但有研究者借助电子计算机统计出莎士比亚使用的全部词汇只有29066个，与英语的总词汇量比较起来，不过是冰山一角而已。尽可能多地掌握大量词汇的有效途径就是学习和利用英语构词法。英语中有相当一部分词汇是符合构词法的。掌握了基本词汇，运用构词知识，不仅可以大大提高记忆效率，而且在阅读中还可以逆向利用构词知识分解单词、破解词义、消除阅读障碍。就英语词汇而言，有派生法、复合法、词类转化法三种主要的构词法和首字母缩略法、拼缀法、逆生法、拟声法、截短法和专有名词普通化等次要的构词法。

1. 复合法（compounding）：把两个或两个以上的词按照一定的次序排列构成新词，可以构成复合名词、复合动词、复合形容词等。多数复合词可以通过其组成部分猜测到词义。例如，electrocardiograph这个词就是由 electro（电）、cardio（心）和graph（图）三个部分复合而成的，这种复合词是理据词（motivated word）。复合词往往使语言表达言简意赅，形象生动。只要稍加注意，就会发现复合词的使用比比皆是。如：greenhouse，homepage，breakthrough，blackboard和round-the-clock等。

2. 派生法（derivation）：通过在原有词或词根的基础上加前缀或后缀而构成新词。前缀通常用以修饰或改变词义。例如：词根comfort 加前缀un-和加后缀-able 构成新词uncomfortable。派生法可以进一步分为加前缀法（prefixation）和加后缀法（suffixation）两种。英语中常见前缀有：in-（il-，im-，ir-），non-，dis-，a-，un-，de-等表示"否定""相对"；super-，arch-，out-，over-等表示"等级"；co-，counter-，anti-，pro-，trans-，sub-，fore-，pre-，post-，re-等表示态度、位置、时间、顺序等。后缀通常显示词性，常见的名词后缀有：-er，-ar，-or，-ent，-an，-ist，-tion，-ment，-al，-ence，-ing，-ness，-(i)ty，-hood，-ship，-dom，-ocracy，-ful，-age等；形容词后缀有：-ful，-ly，-like，-ish，-y，-al，-ic，-ous，-ive等；动词后缀有：-fy，-ize，-en，-ate等；副词后缀多以-ly，-wards常见。掌握派生法，单词记忆就可由一及多，省时省力。比如与nation这一基本词相关的派生词有：national，nationalize，nationality，nationalization，international，internationalization。

3. 词类转化法（conversion）：这种构词法实际上是一种特殊的派生，无须借助词缀即由一种词类转化为另一种词类，也叫作零位派生。词性转化后其意义与原义有着密切联系。如: His smile could not very well mask his anger. 其中 mask即由名词转化为动词，而动词意义是名词意义的衍生。这种构词法灵活多变，如名词转化为动词：He bused to the city. 动词转化为名词: He likes a quiet smoke after supper. 形容词转化为名词：There is only one black in my class.

4. 首字母缩略法（initialism）：将几个单词的首字母以大写形式缩合到一起构成的一个新词，叫作首字母缩略词。这种构词法多用于专有名词，方便易记。这种构词法使用相当频繁，一个典型例子是BBC，指British Broadcasting Corporation（英国广播公司）。早在罗马帝国时期，罗马远征军旗帜上的四个拉丁文字母SPQR就可算作一个首字母缩略词，它代表Senatus Populusque Romanus（The Senate and the Roman People，意思是"为元老院和罗马人民而战"）。但是，现代快节奏的生活才是促成首字缩略词大量产生的沃土。从结构来看，首字缩略词可以用字母代表整个词，如：

  IOC ← International Olympic Committee　国际奥委会
  ISBN ← International Standard Book Number　国际标准书号
  GEM ← Ground-Effect Machine　气垫船
  GMT ← Greenwich Mean Time　格林尼治标准时间

字母也可以代表词的一部分，例如：

  TV ← television　电视
  MTV ← Music TV　音乐电视
  GHQ ← General Headquarters　总司令部
  TB ← tuberculosis　肺结核

有的缩略词还可以和其他词连用，如：

  E-mail ← electronic mail　电子邮件
  H-bomb ← hydrogen bomb　氢弹
  V-Day ← Victory Day　第二次世界大战胜利日

5. 拼缀法（blending）：拼缀法是一种析取法，即对两个或多个词进行剪裁，取舍其中的首部或尾部，然后组合在一起构成新词，其意义则是两个单词意义的组合。用这种构词方法构成的词叫作拼缀词或合成词（blend），也叫作"混成词"（telescopic word）或"紧缩词"（portmanteau word）。利用这种构词法创造的新词在英语中的比例相当大，例如：

  brunch = breakfast + lunch
  motel = motor + hotel
  smog = smoke + fog
  helipad = helicopter + pad
  stagflation = stagnation + inflation
  kidult = kid + adult
  Eurasian = Europe + Asian
  sitcom = situation + comedy

6. 逆生法（back-formation）：这种构词法的产生最初基于对某些词的错误判断。它与派生法（derivation）恰好相反，派生法借助词缀构成新词，而逆生法则去掉被误认为是后缀的部分构成新词，如laze由lazy逆生而成，televise则由television逆生而成，新词语gobsmack（使完全不知所措）即由gobsmacked逆生而成；一个典型的例子是来自于德语的英语词汇Schwindler原意是"使产生梦幻的人"，又泛指"骗子"。这个词被引入英语后便成为swindler（骗子，诈骗犯）。它的词尾与施事名词后缀-er一致，人们就错误地类推出to swindle这个动词，作"行骗"的意思使用。这样，一个新动词swindle就逆生而成了。现在人们也往往有意识地从已有的名词中去掉词尾产生新的动词，这种方法就是逆生法。

一个有趣的例子是动词escalate（逐步升级），它是由名词escalation逆生而来的，第一次使用是1955年，由于这个词出现的历史比较短，我们比较容易追寻其发展的踪迹。对于英语学习者来说，escalator（自动扶梯）跟lift（电梯）一样是一个熟悉的词语。动词escalate（逐步升级）在新闻用语中的普及却是20世纪后半期的事情。近年来，escalate的使用范围已经逐渐扩大，物价的迅速上升和开支的急剧增加都可以用这个动词来表示：escalating price和escalating costs。但是，这个动词主要用于表示某种令人不快的事情不断恶化（greater in size, seriousness or intensity），既可以用作不及物动词又可以用作及物动词。

因为在英语中以动词为词根派生出来的名词种类多、数量大，所以人们最容易把一些名词错当成有动词词根的派生词。逆生法形成的词也以动词为主，也有些是以形容词逆生出来的。

    to automate (使自动化) ← automation (*n.*)
    to donate (捐献，赠送) ← donation (*n.*)
    to negate (否定) ← negation (*n.*)
    to beg (行乞) ← beggar (*n.*)
    to appreciate (欣赏) ← appreciation (*n.*)
    to diagnose (诊断) ← diagnosis (*n.*)
    to enthuse (使热心，表示热心) ← enthusiasm (*n.*)
    to reminisce (追忆往事) ← reminiscence (*n.*)
    to audit (审计，查账) ← auditor (*n.*)
    to edit (编辑) ← editor (*n.*)

也有几个逆生而成的名词，如greed（贪婪） ← greedy(*a.*)，pup(小狗) ← puppy(*n.*)；而形容词difficult是由名词difficulty逆生出来的。许多复合动词都是由逆生法形成的，例如：to housekeep（管理家务）来自名词housekeeper（管理家务的主妇）；to baby-sit（代人临时照看婴孩）来自名词baby-sitter（代人临时照看婴孩者）；to henpeck（使怕老婆）来自由过去分词构成的复合形容词hen-pecked（怕老婆的）；to eavesdrop（偷听）来自由动名词构成的复合名词eavesdropping（偷听）。

7. 截短法（clipping）：为了方便使用，把英语中一个较长的单词裁减为一个较简单易懂的词。例如：

    zoological garden→zoo
    automobile→auto
    laboratory→lab
    aeroplane→plane
    memorandum→memo
    exposition→expo

截短法产生的新词一般具有与原词相同的意义或概念，但也有个别截短词词义发生了一定的变化，如miss现在指未婚女子，特别是未婚的青年女子，它的前身mistress却是"女主人"的意思。有的截短词跟原词同时存在，但截短词是通用的词，而原词却不常用，甚至带有书卷气，例如：lunch（← luncheon 午餐），movie（← motion picture 电影），pram（← perambulator 童车）。也有的时候，截短词跟原词同时存在，但词义有分工，例如：cute ← acute, mend ← amend, peal ← appeal。

8. 专有名词普通化（new words from proper names）：在人们长期的语言实践过程中，作为英语词汇的重要组成部分，专有名词毫不例外地一直处于普通化的过程中。专有名词的普通化，对丰富英语词汇、使其形象化起着积极作用。一般来讲，专有名词向普通名词的转化要经历一个漫长的过程。这些已经或者可能被普通化的专有名词来自各个领域，从科学家、作家、公众人物、小说人物的名字到地名以及商标等等，不胜枚举。

为人熟知的一个例子就是curie，它被用做放射强度单位，相当于一秒钟内发生 3.7×10^{10} 次裂变，而这个词正是为了纪念伟大的化学家居里（Curie）夫妇，因为他们是镭元素的发现者。与此类似的词还有：newton, ampere, hertz等等。再如，spoonerism这个词来自于一位叫作William Archibald Spooner的牧师。他曾任牛津新学院院长，经常会表现出一种特殊的语言混乱现象，例如他会把a well-oiled bicycle说成a well-boiled icicle，把dear old queen说成queer old dean。后来人们便以他的名字命名这种特殊的首音互换现象。John Hancock（1737—1793）是美国的一位革命领袖，他是第一个在《独立宣言》上签名的人，现John Hancock用来指"亲笔签名"。

在英语中还有许多形象、生动的词是从神话故事、圣经故事及历史和文学故事中的人物名字发展而来的。比方说，在神话故事中，我们有Midas（一位国王，爱财，能点石成金），常用做wealth和avariciousness的同义词；Apollo（太阳神），象征着完美的青年男子。圣经故事中，我们有Judas（叛徒），形容那些出卖朋友的人；Delilah（大力士 Samson 的情妇，把 Samson出卖给腓力斯人），指那些勾引男人又背叛他们的女人。莎士比亚作品中一些人物的名字也成为现代英语中的普通词汇。最典型的要算《威尼斯商人》中奸商Shylock了，此外还有Hamlet，Romeo和Juliet等。离我们的时代稍近一些的有Frankenstein，它源自玛丽·雪莱的一部小说 *Frankenstein*，现代的人们把它用做"作法自毙的人"的同义词。

与此类似的是由于该地具有特殊的意义或在该地曾经发生过意义重大的事件转变而来的一些词汇。Copper源出塞浦路斯，该地以产铜著称。英语中不少商品名字原为出产地的地名。如java来自印度尼西亚地名Java（爪哇岛），指"爪哇咖啡"；cologne来自德国城市Cologne，指"科隆香水"；bourbon来自美国肯塔基州的Bourbon，指"一种烈性威士忌酒"。Watergate一词出现于20世纪70年代，它原是华盛顿的一建筑群，是美国民主党的总部，然而它却由于1972年的"水门事件"而经常与共和党滥用职权、违背公众信任、贿赂、蔑视国会及企图妨碍司法的丑闻联系起来。从此，人们在日常生活中常用Watergate一词，如今它已经发展了多种形式Watergater，Watergatish和Watergatism等。此类词汇常用来描述现实生活中和某一历史事件具有相似特点的事或人。

　　另外，许多商标由于其非常著名而常被人们用来指称同类产品，换句话说就是把某一商标转变为普通名词来表示由不同公司生产的产品。Xerox（施乐牌复印机），现泛指复印机；Cadillac（卡迪拉克），现泛指质量极好的产品；Kodak（柯达相机），现泛指小照相机。类似的词还有Ford（福特牌汽车）、Vaseline（凡士林矿脂）、Coca-Cola（可口可乐饮料）、Pepsi-Cola（百事可乐饮料）等。有的商标名词还有派生词，如xeroxer和xeroxable。另外有的商标名词还可以用作形容词，如Micky Mouse指"小的""小规格的""微不足道的"（petty）。

　　以上列举的是英语词汇内部的主要构词法，构词法的学习和掌握有助于英语学习者认清英语词汇的内部结构，掌握基本的构词规则，最终通过分析词汇的结构达到理解词汇确切含义的目的。

第二篇 派生法:英语词缀与构词

第1章 常用英语词汇前缀

第1单元 表示"数字"的前缀

Words in Context

The Dilemma of a College Student

Accidentally having failed in the entrance examination, I was just one step away from a famous university I had been dreaming of. What else could be more miserable than one's dream turning out to be an illusion? For a long time, I was deeply frustrated, wondering whether I would be ranked "inferior" in the rest of my life. One day, a sparkle flashed across my mind. "Why should my life be determined just by one exam? Why should I acknowledge beaten?" Encouraged by parents and friends, I was ignited again. Later I was accepted as a Japanese-English **bilingual** major by a second-class university. Soon, I became the top student in class and got the first prize scholarship every semester. I can feel the great confidence I'd never felt before. But behind the fruitful achievements, there's much bitterness only myself know.

One day, a friend of mine asked me "Hey bookworm, except high mark, what else can you show me?" For the first time in my life, I felt the overwhelming embarrassment bursting inside me. Some say, life in university should be colorful, but mine is so **monotonous**. I guess that's the price I have to pay, for everyone who sets his sights for the postgraduate admission test should work at it whole-heartedly, leaving everything behind. "Leaving everything behind," sometimes it turns out to be so cruel.

I discussed it with my classmates, but we cannot arrive at a **unanimous** agreement on this issue. Then I turned to my teachers, and I got nothing but **ambiguous** answers. I just keep going, though, sometimes, with a little bit hesitation.

Word Building

More Words with the Prefixes

前缀	释义	例词
mono- , uni-, un-	一，单一的	monologue, monogamy, monotonous, unilateral, unanimous, unify

（续表）

前缀	释义	例词
bi-, di-, ambi-, amphi-	二，双的	bilingual, bicycle, bilateral, dialogue, dilemma, dioxide, ambiguous, amphibian
tri-	三	triangle, trinity, trigonometry
quadri-	四	quadrangle, quarterly, quartet
penta-	五	pentagon, pentagram
hexa-	六	hexagon
hepta-	七	heptagon
octa-	八	octagon, octopus
nona-	九	nonary
deca-, deci-	十，十分之一	decade, decimal, decimeter
hecta-, centi-	百	hectoliter, centigrade, centipede
kilo-, mili-	千	kilowatt, kilovolt, milligram
mega-	百万，大量	megahertz, mega-death

1. monologue: ['mɒnəlɒg] *n.* 独白

　　分解记忆法：mono- (一) + logue(说，说话) = 独白

　　【例句】He writes dialogue by cutting monologue in two.

　　　　　他把独白切成两截来写对白。

　　　　　Henry looked up at the sky, and then continued his monologue.

　　　　　亨利抬头看了看天空，又继续自言自语起来。

2. monogamy: [mə'nɒgəmi] *n.* 一夫一妻制

　　分解记忆法：mono- (一) + gam(marriage 婚姻) = 一夫一妻制

　　【例句】Monogamy is rare in most animal groups, but is common among birds.

　　　　　在大多数动物群体中一夫一妻制比较少见，但是在鸟类中比较常见。

　　　　　It is highly impossible to impose monogamy on them.

　　　　　对他们强行实施一夫一妻制是非常不现实的。

　　常用派生词：monogamy → monogamous

3. monotonous: [mə'nɒtənəs] *a.* 单调的；无变化的；无聊的

　　分解记忆法：mono- (一，单一的) + ton(声音) = 声音单一的，单调的

　　【例句】The explorer lived on a monotonous diet of bean and rice.

　　　　　探险者靠吃豆子和米饭这些单调的食物为生。

　　　　　This musical instrument produces a monotonous rhythmical drumbeat or similar sound.

　　　　　这种乐器发出一种单调而有节奏的敲鼓声或类似的声音。

常用派生词：monotone → monotony → monotonous

4. unilateral: [ˌjuːniˈlætərəl] *a.* 单边的；单方面的；片面的

分解记忆法：uni- (一，单一的) + lateral(边)=单边的

【例句】The candidates had to state their position on unilateral disarmament.
候选人须表明他们对单方面裁军所持的立场。
Nobody really expected that the announcement of a unilateral ceasefire would bring an immediate end to the fighting.
没有人真的指望单方面停火能够迅速结束这场争斗。

常用派生词：unilateral → unilateralism → unilaterally

5. unanimous: [juːˈnænɪməs] *a.* 全体一致的；一致同意的

分解记忆法：uni- (一，单一的) + anim(心智，精神)=统一精神的

【例句】Politicians from all parties were completely unanimous in condemning his action.
所有党派的政治家们一致谴责他的行为。
The committee was unanimous that the application should be turned down.
委员会一致同意拒绝这项申请。

常用派生词：unanimous → unanimity

6. bilingual: [baɪˈlɪŋgwəl] *a.* 能使用两种语言的

分解记忆法：bi- (两个的) + lingua(语言)= 两种语言的

【例句】He is bilingual in French and Chinese.
他会法语和汉语两种语言。
The report proposed bilingual education in middle schools.
报告提出在中学实施双语教育。

常用派生词：bilingual → bilingualism

7. dilemma: [dɪˈlemə] *n.* 进退两难

分解记忆法：di-(两个)+lemma(假设)= 在两个假设之间

【例句】He was in a dilemma.
他陷入进退两难之境。
I don't know how to deal with my dilemma.
我不知道如何处理我进退两难的处境。

常用派生词：dilemma → dilemmatic

8. duplicate: [ˈdjuːplɪkɪt] *v.* 复制

分解记忆法：du- (两个) + plic(折叠)+ate(动词后缀)= 复制

【例句】The research is duplicating work already done before.
这项研究正在重复已经做过的工作。
He is duplicating the form.
他正在复制表格。

常用派生词：duplicate → duplication

9. **ambidextrous:** [ˌæmbiˈdekstrəs] *a.* 两手都很灵巧的；搞两面派的；非常灵巧的；非常熟练的

分解记忆法：ambi-(两个)+ dext(e)r(右手)+ -ous(形容词后缀)=两个手都像右手一样灵活

【例句】The woman can use both of her hands equally well and she is ambidextrous.
这个妇女左右手使用一样好，她两只手都很灵巧。
I cannot carry heavy things with my left hand. I am not ambidextrous.
我不能用左手拿重物。我两只手不是一样灵活。

常用派生词：ambidextrous → ambidexterity

10. **ambiguous:** [æmˈbigjuəs] *a.* 含糊的

分解记忆法 ambi-(两个)+ igu- (驱使)+-ous (形容词后缀) = 踌躇的

【例句】She wears an ambiguous smile.
她笑容含糊。
The sentence in the composition is ambiguous.
作文里的这句话意思含糊。

常用派生词：ambiguous→ ambiguity

11. **amphibian:** [æmˈfibiən] *a.* 水陆两栖的

分解记忆法：amphi- (两方面的) + bi-(生活)+ -an(形容词后缀) = 生活在水中和陆地上的

【例句】Frogs are amphibian animals.
青蛙是水陆两栖动物。
What's the definition of amphibian animals?
水陆两栖动物的定义是什么？

常用派生词：amphibian → amphibious

12. **triangle:** [ˈtraiæŋgəl] *n.* 三角形

分解记忆法：tri-(三) + angle(角) = 三角

【例句】There is a triangle of grass beside the path.
路边有一块三角形的草地。
You can see benches arranged in a triangle.
你可以看到排成三角形的长凳。

常用派生词：triangle → triangular

13. **trigonometry:** [ˌtrigəˈnɔmətri] *n.* 三角学

分解记忆法：tri-(三)+ gono(角) + metry(测量) = 三角法则

【例句】Some students are not good at trigonometry.
一些学生不擅长三角学。
Students who major in architecture should study trigonometry.
学建筑的学生要学三角学。

常用派生词：trigonometry → trigonometric

14. **quadruple:** [ˈkwɑdrupəl] *v.* 变成四倍

    分解记忆法：quadru-(四) + ple (折叠) = 四倍

    【例句】Their profits have quadrupled in ten years.

    他们的利润十年中增长四倍。

    Twenty is the quadruple of five.

    二十是五的四倍。

    常用派生词：quadruple→ quadruplex

15. **pentagon:** [ˈpentəgən] *n.* 五角形；五边形；五角大楼（指美国国防部）

    分解记忆法：peta- (五) + gon(角) = 五角

    【例句】The flowers are arranged in a pentagon.

    这些花被摆放成五角形。

    The plane crashed into the Pentagon.

    飞机撞到美国五角大楼上。

    常用派生词：pentagon → pentagonal

16. **decimal:** [ˈdesiməl] *a. & n.* 十进制的；小数

    分解记忆法：decima- (十分之一) + -al (形容词后缀) = 十分之一的

    【例句】The currency in the United States has a decimal system.

    美国货币采用十进制。

    0.8 is a decimal.

    0.8是一个小数。

    常用派生词：decimal → decimalize

17. **centipede:** [ˈsentipi:d] *n.* 蜈蚣

    分解记忆法：cent-(百) + pede(脚) = 一百只脚

    【例句】Centipedes are small crawling animals.

    蜈蚣是小型爬行动物。

    If you lift up a heavy rock, you may find a centipede living under it.

    如果你举起一块大石，可能会发现底下有蜈蚣。

18. **kilovolt:** [ˈkiləwɔt] *n.* 千伏特

    分解记忆法：kilo- (千) + volt(伏特) = 千伏特

    【例句】"Kilovolt" is a compound word.

    Kilovolt 是一个合成词。

    It also built up an important supporting role for perfecting the 500-kilovolt electric power grid network.

    它也对500千伏特的电站网络的完善起到了重要支持作用。

19. **kilocalorie:** [kiləˈkæləri] *n.* 一千卡

    分解记忆法：kilo- (千) + calorie(卡路里) = 一千卡

    【例句】Chocolate about 200 grams contains more than one kilocalorie.

200克的巧克力含有超过一千卡的热量。
How much food supplies one kilocalorie?
多少食物可以提供一千卡的热量？

20. mega-death: [ˈmegəˌdeθ] *n.* 百万人的死亡

分解记忆法：mege-(百万，大量)+death (死亡)=百万人的死亡

【例句】The massacre caused mega-death.
这次屠杀死了百万人。
World War II led to mega-death.
第二次世界大战导致了百万人的死亡。

Words in Use

1. There is a need for constructive _____ between leaders.
   A. catalogue   B. monologue   C. dialogue   D. prologue
2. Jody would fly to San Francisco for the _____ coaches meeting twice a year.
   A. annually   B. biannual   C. yearly   D. bicentennial
3. Green, who has five wives and 30 children, had been charged with four counts of _____.
   A. bilingualism   B. bipolar   C. bigamist   D. bigamy
4. Danny left this _____ message on my answering machine: "I must see you. Meet me at twelve o'clock." Did he mean noon or midnight?
   A. amphibian   B. ambidextrous   C. ambivalent   D. ambiguous
5. Few of us are naturally _____, but this can be achieved through training.
   A. amphibian   B. ambidextrous   C. ambivalent   D. ambiguous
6. I want to buy a _____ thermometer to measure the temperature of the room.
   A. centipede   B. centimeter   C. centigrade   D. centennial
7. Most soldiers can't bear the _____ life on the island.
   A. peaceful   B. starved   C. colorful   D. monotonous
8. The lecture is _____. You should understand both English and French.
   A. bilateral   B. bilingual   C. bicycle   D. dioxide
9. The air-conditioning system maintains a _____ temperature throughout the building.
   A. unilateral   B. unanimous   C. uniform   D. unify
10. The _____ of Italy resulted in a single country instead of several kingdoms.
    A. unilateral   B. unanimous   C. uniform   D. unity
11. The scarf is made of a _____ of blue silk.
    A. triangle   B. trinity   C. trigonometry   D. trial
12. The man was rescued from the sea by a _____.
    A. hectoliter   B. helicopter   C. heliport   D. heliotrope

13. He is accused of _____.
    A. bigot	B. bigamy	C. bilingual	D. bilateral
14. Auto-exhaust releases much carbon _____.
    A. dinosaur	B. dialogue	C. dilemma	D. dioxide
15. He is an _____ young manager.
    A. ambitious	B. amble	C. ambivalent	D. ambiguous
16. Much British humor depends on _____.
    A. ambitious	B. ambition	C. ambiguity	D. ambidextrous
17. We reached a _____ agreement.
    A. bigot	B. bigamy	C. bilingual	D. bilateral
18. Most plays are written in _____.
    A. dialogue	B. dilemma	C. climax	D. dioxide
19. Three _____ ago, he immigrated to Australia.
    A. time	B. ages	C. decades	D. centuries
20. Corn contains 8.5 grams of protein each _____.
    A. pentagon	B. hectogram	C. heptagon	D. hexagon
21. The company is trying to _____ the supply of oil.
    A. monopolize	B. monologue	C. monogamy	D. monotonous
22. This is a _____ dictionary. You can see words are explained both in English and Chinese.
    A. monolingual	B. bilingual	C. monogamy	D. multilingual
23. The same routine every week may become _____, so you can set some goals to stay focused.
    A. monotonous	B. monosyllabic	C. monolingual	D. monogamy
24. The villagers are _____ in their opposition to the building of a bypass.
    A. unanimous	B. unilateral	C. unify	D. monotonous
25. The output of the televisions in the factory has _____ since last year.
    A. quadrangled	B. triangled	C. quadriplegia	D. quadrupled
26. I receive _____ bank statements.
    A. quartet	B. quarterly	C. quadriplegia	D. quadruple
27. A _____ person speaks three languages.
    A. monolingual	B. bilingual	C. trilingual	D. multilingual
28. I was hurt by the _____ of my ex-boyfriend who cheated on me.
    A. duplicity	B. dioxide	C. dilemma	D. duplicate
29. If something is produced in septuplicate, there are _____ copies of it.
    A. five	B. six	C. seven	D. eight
30. Mother became aware of the _____ relationship between Maggie and two men.
    A. trinity	B. trilogy	C. triangle	D. triangular

Key to *Words in Use*

1. C	2. B	3. D	4. D	5. B
6. C	7. D	8. B	9. C	10. D
11. A	12. B	13. B	14. D	15. A
16. C	17. D	18. A	19. C	20. B
21. A	22. B	23. A	24. A	25. D
26. B	27. C	28. A	29. C	30. D

第2单元 表示"空间"的前缀(一)

Words in Context

Overweight Children

There are some **overweight** children today than ever before. Many children eat too many calories from high fat foods, sweets and large portion sizes. And the children usually lack exercise. Children today get less exercise than ever before in history.

Being overweight can also cause your child to be self conscious about his looks or be teased or ignored by his classmates. An overweight boy student **recalled**: "Nobody wanted to play with me because they thought I was awkward." As a result, they may think too much about weight and set the stage for an eating disorder. Another problem is that overweight children often become overweight adults. Studies show that half of overweight children stay fat throughout adulthood, which is severely harmful for their health.

Most parents don't take the weight of their children seriously and often **overlook** the problem. But when they notice that their children are becoming fatter and fatter, they begin to feel anxious. Therefore, parents should cut on the problem as soon as it is noticed and work with your children to follow a healthier lifestyle. The concern is when a child is carrying extra body fat for their ages, parents have much control and influence over their children's habits and eating patterns. If you provide your family with healthy foods and involve yourself and your children in regular physical activity, your kids will also follow these healthy habits and their body weight will **return** to normal.

Word Building

More Words with the Prefixes

前缀	释义	例词
ante-, fore-, pre-, pro-	前	anteroom, antedate, antecedent, foretell, foreword, forefather, prehistoric, prefix, precaution, predict, progress, prolong, prominent, propel, prospect

(续表)

前缀	释义	例词
post-, re-, retro-	后	postwar, postgraduate, regress, recede, retract, return, recall, reclaim, retrospect, retrocede
over-, super-, sur-, hyper-	上	overlook, overcast, overlap, overcome, overwork, overweight, superman, superstar, supersonic, supervise, surface, surpass, surplus, survive, hypercritical, hypertension
sub-, under-, hypo-, infra-	下	subway, subconscious, underline, undercurrent, hypocrisy, hypothesis, infrastructure, infrasound

1. **antecedent:** [ˌænti'siːdənt] *a. & n.* 在先的；祖先

   分解记忆法：ante-(前)+ced(去)+-ent(形容词字尾)=走在前的

   【例句】Those were events antecedent to the revolution.

   这些都是革命前的事了。

   That was antecedent to this event.

   那是在这件事之前。

   常用派生词：antecedent→ antecedence

2. **foretell:** [fɔː'tel] *v.* 预言

   分解记忆法：fore-(前)+tell(告诉)=事先告诉

   【例句】The fortune-teller foretold that he would lose his job.

   算命人预言他将失去工作。

   No one could foretell such strange events.

   没有人可以预言这些奇怪的事。

3. **foreword:** ['fɔːwəːd] *n.* 前言

   分解记忆法：fore-(前)+word(单词)=前言

   【例句】Before I read the book, I often read the foreword first.

   在看书之前，我经常先读前言。

   The famous linguist wrote the foreword for the book.

   这位著名的语言学家为这本书写了前言。

4. **prehistoric:** [ˌpriːhi'stɔrik] *a.* 史前的

   分解记忆法：pre-(前)+historic(历史的)=历史前的

   【例句】His idea on girl education is quite prehistoric.

   他在女孩子的教育问题上所持的观点是老掉牙的。

We are appreciating prehistoric cave paintings.
我们正在欣赏史前洞穴壁画。

常用派生词：prehistoric→ prehistory

5. precaution: [priˈkɔːʃən] *n.* 预防

分解记忆法：pre-(前)+caution(小心)=事前的准备

【例句】Take an umbrella just as a precaution.
带把雨伞，有备无患。
I took the precaution of locking everything important in the safe.
我把一切重要的东西都锁在保险箱子里以防万一。

常用派生词：precaution→ precautionary

6. predict: [priˈdikt] *v.* 预言

分解记忆法：pre-(前)+dict(说)=事先说

【例句】He predicted that the improvement would continue.
他预测情况将继续好转。
It is impossible to predict what will happen in the future.
要预测未来发生什么是不可能的。

常用派生词：predict→ predictive→ predictable

7. progress: [ˈprəugres] *n.* 进步

分解记忆法：pro-(向前)+gress(走路)=向前进

【例句】He has made great progress this semester.
他这个学期取得了很大的进步。
The patient is making good progress after the operation.
病人在手术后病情大为好转。

常用派生词：progress→ progressive

8. prolong: [prəˈlɔŋ] *v.* 延长

分解记忆法：pro-(向前)+long(长)=向前一直延伸

【例句】It is said that the drug can prolong life.
据说这药可延年益寿。
He prolonged his visit by a few days.
他把访问时间延长了几天。

9. prominent: [ˈprɔminənt] *a.* 突出的

分解记忆法：pro-(向前)+min(突出)+-ent(形容词后缀)=向前突出

【例句】The house is in a prominent position in the village.
那房子坐落在村中最显眼的地方。
He was the prominent political figure of the year.
他是当年杰出的政治人物。

常用派生词：prominent→ prominence

10. propel: [prəˈpel] *v.* 推进

　　分解记忆法： pro-(向前)+pel(推动)=向前推动

　　【例句】The boat is propelled by oars.

　　　　　这只船用桨划。

　　　　　His addition to drugs propelled him to a life of crime.

　　　　　吸毒成瘾使他走上了犯罪的道路。

11. postgraduate: [ˌpəustˈɡrædjuit] *n.* 研究生

　　分解记忆法： post-(之后)+graduate(毕业)=毕业后继续研究，研究生

　　【例句】He wants to become a postgraduate after getting the bachelor degree.

　　　　　在获得学士学位之后，他想成为一名研究生。

　　　　　There are about forty postgraduates in the Finance Department.

　　　　　金融学院大约有40位研究生。

12. recede: [riˈsiːd] *v.* 后退

　　分解记忆法： re-(向后)+cede(走)=往后退

　　【例句】As the tide receded, we were able to look for shells.

　　　　　潮水退去，我们就能寻找贝壳了。

　　　　　We reached the open sea and the coast receded into the distance.

　　　　　我们驶抵公海，海岸似乎退到了远方。

13. recall: [riˈkɔ(ː)l] *v.* 回忆

　　分解记忆法： re-(向后)+call(喊)=唤回

　　【例句】I can't recall his telephone number.

　　　　　我想不起他的电话。

　　　　　She recalled that they met each other before.

　　　　　她回忆起他们以前见过。

14. retrospect: [ˈretrəspekt] *n.* 回顾

　　分解记忆法： retro-(向后)+spect(看)=回头看

　　【例句】In retrospect, I found I had a colorful life.

　　　　　回顾过去，我发现我的生活是丰富多彩的。

　　常用派生词： retrospect→ retrospective

　　　　　I went to a retrospective exhibition of the painter's work.

　　　　　我去看了那画家作品的回顾展。

15. overlook: [ˌəuvəˈluk] *v.* 忽视；忽略；远眺

　　分解记忆法： over-(上)+look(看)=越过……看

　　【例句】Although he was reminded of his mistakes, he overlooked them.

　　　　　尽管他被提醒了犯的错误，但是他忽视了。

　　　　　We can afford to overlook minor offences.

　　　　　我们可以不计较小过。

16. overcome: [ˌəuvəˈkʌm] *v.* 击败；克服

分解记忆法：over-(上) +come(来)=压倒

【例句】You can overcome your bad habit.

你可以克服你的坏习惯。

I had to overcome the temptation to give up.

我得克服放弃的诱惑。

17. surpass: [səˈpɑːs] *v.* 胜过

分解记忆法：sur-(上)+pass(通过)=越过

【例句】The car surpassed that car in speed.

这辆车在速度上胜过那辆车。

The beauty of the painting surpassed all my expectations.

我根本没有想到这幅画那么美。

常用派生词：surpass → surpassable

18. subconscious: [sʌbˈkɔnʃəs] *a.* 潜意识的

分解记忆法：sub-(下)+conscious(意识的)=下意识的

【例句】The subconscious self tells me that I'm wrong.

潜意识的自我告诉我，我错了。

I refuted my boss out of my subconscious urges.

由于下意识的冲动我反驳了我的老板。

常用派生词：subconscious → unconsciousness

19. underline: [ˌʌndəˈlain, ˈʌndərlain] *v.* 在……下面画线；加强；强调

分解记忆法：under-(下面)+line(线)=在下面画线

【例句】Please underline the sentence I read just now.

把我刚才读的句子划下来。

He underlined the important language points while reading.

他在读书的时候划下了重点的语言点。

常用派生词：underline→ underlineation

20. hypothesis: [haiˈpɔθisis] *n.* 假说

分解记忆法：hypo-(下面)+thesis(被放置)=作为基础

【例句】We are trying to prove the hypothesis.

我们正在努力证明这种假说是正确的。

He made an experiment to validate the hypothesis.

他做了一个实验来验证这种假说。

常用派生词：hypothesis→ hypothesize

Words in Use

1. The couple had the _____ to plan their retirement wisely.
   A. foresight   B. foreword   C. forearm   D. forefather
2. The mother is fondling the _____ of her baby.
   A. foresight   B. forehead   C. forearm   D. forefather
3. We have been _____ the risk of fire.
   A. foretold   B. forewarned   C. forecast   D. foreseen
4. My mother is used to listening to the weather _____ after CCTV news.
   A. foretell   B. forewarn   C. forecast   D. foresee
5. It often rains in July. Take an umbrella as a _____.
   A. preparation   B. precaution   C. prelude   D. premium
6. The weather is _____.
   A. precise   B. preconscious   C. predictable   D. preconceived
7. She made a _____ record of the events.
   A. precise   B. preconscious   C. predictable   D. preconceived
8. There is a fully _____ health center on the ground floor of the main office building.
   A. equipped   B. projected   C. provided   D. installed
9. It was the first time that such a _____ had to be taken at a British nuclear power station.
   A. presentation   B. preparation   C. prediction   D. precaution
10. Because of a _____ engagement, Lora couldn't attend my birthday party.
    A. pioneer   B. premature   C. prior   D. past
11. It gave me a strange feeling of excitement to see my name in _____.
    A. prospect   B. print   C. process   D. press
12. The _____ of finding gold in California attracted a lot of people to settle down there.
    A. prospects   B. speculations   C. stakes   D. provisions
13. The work was almost complete when we received orders to _____ no further with it.
    A. progress   B. proceed   C. march   D. promote
14. A fire engine must have priority as it usually has to deal with some kind of _____.
    A. precaution   B. crisis   C. emergency   D. urgency
15. In a time of social reform, people's state of mind tends to keep _____ with the changes of society.
    A. step   B. progress   C. pace   D. touch
16. The government is trying to do something to _____ better understanding between two countries.
    A. raise   B. promote   C. heighten   D. increase
17. Ten days ago, the young man informed his boss of his intention to _____.
    A. resign   B. return   C. regress   D. recede

18. I hate people who _____ the end of a film that you haven't seen before.
    A. reclaim		B. recall		C. reverse		D. reveal
19. I try to _____ exactly what happened yesterday evening.
    A. reclaim		B. recall		C. reverse		D. reveal
20. He _____ the car into a tree.
    A. regressed		B. recalled		C. reversed		D. revealed
21. It has been revealed that some government leaders _____ their authority and position to get illegal profits for themselves.
    A. employ		B. take		C. abuse		D. overlook
22. You have _____ some mistakes in your work.
    A. overlooked		B. overhead		C. overseas		D. overworked
23. This boy was _____ for what he had done in class.
    A. scolded		B. overcome		C. multiplied		D. displayed
24. With the help of the government, a large number of people _____ after the flood in 1991.
    A. survived		B. suspended		C. suffered		D. subscribed
25. The glass has a smooth _____.
    A. superstar		B. surface		C. supervise		D. retrospect
26. Research shows that there is no _____ relationship between how much a person earns and whether he feels good about life.
    A. successive		B. sincere		C. significant		D. subsequent
27. Strikes by prison officers _____ the need for reform in our goals.
    A. underlie		B. underlay		C. undermine		D. underline
28. _____ of food can be sold for cash.
    A. Supplies		B. Surpluses		C. Number		D. Amount
29. The submarine _____ to avoid enemy ships.
    A. submerged		B. sank		C. dropped		D. fell
30. We _____ the difficulties and completed the task on time.
    A. overlooked		B. overcast		C. overcame		D. overlapped

Key to *Words in Use*

1. A	2. B	3. B	4. C	5. B
6. C	7. A	8. A	9. D	10. C
11. B	12. A	13. B	14. C	15. C
16. B	17. A	18. D	19. B	20. C
21. C	22. A	23. A	24. A	25. B
26. C	27. D	28. B	29. A	30. C

第3单元 表示"空间"的前缀(二)

Words in Context

American Experience

I used to go on the **Internet** to enjoy the beautiful scenery of America. But, luckily, I have got a chance to go to the country. The thing that first surprises any traveler arriving in America is its size. Everything seems bigger than it is elsewhere. Today, it takes just hours to cross the continent by aircraft. But it is hard not to feel a sense of awe at the size and beauty of the land.

America is home to about 250 million people—making it the third most populous country on the earth. Yet, in spite of this, its natural landscape **impresses** the visitors greatly.

The best way to see much of America is by car. The visitor has the freedom to cross the whole country on the country's **extensive** highway system.

It is easy for the visitor to be dazzled by modern America. It seems that everywhere you go, there is something to celebrate.

The opportunities to be entertained in the US are endless, but there is much more to American cultural life than simply having fun. You will be **introduced** to their arts and heritages, and major cities have world-class museums, art galleries and concert halls. The US leads the way in many of the contemporary arts.

Americans are extremely proud of their history, and a lot of effort has gone into preserving the country's heritage.

Over the last century, Americans have come to realize that their natural environment is one of the greatest assets they have, and that it needs looking after. Today, the amazingly varied landscape and wildlife of America are preserved in thousands of national and state parks, covering millions of square kilometers.

Word Building

More Words with the Prefixes

前缀	释义	例词
in(im)-, intro-	内	indoor, inland, inject immigrate, import, impress, imprison, introduce, introspect introvert

(续表)

前缀	释义	例词
e-, ex-, extra-, ultra-, out-	外	evaluate, emigrate, emerge, evade, exclude, export, extract, expel, extracurricular, extraordinary, ultrasound, outgrow, outlast, outline
inter-, mid-	中间	international, intercontinental, interpersonal, Internet, interpret, interrupt, midday, midstream, midway
circum-	四周	circumspect, circumstance, circumscribe, circumvent

1. **inject:** [inˈdʒekt] *v.* 注射

    分解记忆法：in-(往里)+ ject(扔) =注入

    【例句】The nurse is injecting the patient with drug.

    护士正在给病人注射药物。

    The drug can be injected or taken by mouth.

    这种药可以注射也可以口服。

    常用派生词：inject → injection

2. **immigrate:** [ˈimigreit] *v.* 移民进入

    分解记忆法：im- (进入) +migrate (闲逛) =信步而入

    【例句】They immigrated to China last year.

    他们去年移民到中国。

    They wanted to immigrate from England to Australia to find work.

    他们想从英国移民澳大利亚找工作。

    常用派生词：immigrate → immigration

3. **import:** [imˈpɔːt, ˈimpɔːt] *v.* 输入；进口

    分解记忆法：im- (进入) +port (搬运)=搬入

    【例句】The country imports most of its raw materials.

    这个国家进口大部分原料。

    There are imported foods in the supermarket.

    这家超市有进口食物。

    常用派生词：import → importer

4. **impress:** [imˈpres, ˈimpres] *v.* 铭记

    分解记忆法：im- (进入) +press (压)=押附于心头

    【例句】His words were strongly impressed on my memory.

    他的话我铭记在心。

　　　　The beautiful scenery impresses foreign tourists.
　　　　美丽的风景给外国游客留下了深刻的印象。
　常用派生词：impress→ impressive → impression

5. impoverish: [imˈpɔvəriʃ] *v.* 使贫乏
　分解记忆法：im=em=en(使)+pover(贫穷的)+-ish(动词后缀)=使贫穷
　【例句】The loss of the job impoverished her.
　　　　失去工作使她贫困。
　　　　The failure of her investment made her impoverished.
　　　　投资的失败使她贫困。

6. introduce: [ˈintrəˈdju:s] *v.* 介绍
　分解记忆法：intro-(内部)+duce(指导)=引导
　【例句】Allow me to introduce our new workmate.
　　　　允许我介绍我们的新同事。
　　　　I was introduced to the president at the party.
　　　　在聚会上，有人把我介绍给了总裁。
　常用派生词：introduce→ introduction

7. introspect: [ˌintrəuˈspekt] *v.* 内省
　分解记忆法：intro-(内部的)+spect(看)=向内部看
　【例句】We need to introspect.
　　　　我们需要内省。
　　　　When I make a mistake, I would pause and introspect.
　　　　当我犯错误的时候，我会停下来反省。
　常用派生词：introspect→ introspective→ introspection

8. evaluate: [iˈvæljueit] *v.* 估价
　分解记忆法：e-(向外)+valu(价值)+-ate(动词后缀)
　【例句】The teacher is objective when he evaluates his students.
　　　　这位老师在评价学生的时候很客观。
　　　　I can't evaluate his ability without seeing his work.
　　　　没有看到他的工作，我无法评价他的能力。
　常用派生词：evaluate→ evaluation

9. emerge: [iˈməːdʒ] *v.* 出现
　分解记忆法：e-(出来)+merge(沉入)=从沉没状态中出来
　【例句】The sun emerged from behind the clouds.
　　　　太阳从云后面露出来。
　　　　The boy emerges from the lake.
　　　　小男孩从湖中出来。
　常用派生词：emerge→ emergence

10. evade: [iˈveid] *v.* 逃避

　　分解记忆法：e-(向外)+vade(行走)=逃避在外面

　　【例句】The thief turned around to evade the police.

　　　　　小偷转身为了逃避警察。

　　　　　The student lowered his head to evade answering the question.

　　　　　这个学生低下头逃避回答问题。

　　常用派生词：evade→ evader

11. exclude: [ikˈsklu:d] *v.* 除外

　　分解记忆法：ex-(向外)+clude(关闭)=关闭在外

　　【例句】They excluded people under 18 from joining the club.

　　　　　他们拒绝18岁以下的人加入俱乐部。

　　　　　We cannot exclude the possibility that the child has run away.

　　　　　我们不可排除这孩子离家出走的可能性。

　　常用派生词：exclude→ exclusive

12. extract: [ikˈstrækt, ˈekstrækt] *v.* 摘取；抽出

　　分解记忆法：ex-(向外)+tract(抽取)=抽出来

　　【例句】We had a tooth extracted yesterday.

　　　　　他昨天拔牙了。

　　　　　The poem is extracted from a modern collection.

　　　　　这首诗是从一本当代诗集中摘选的。

　　常用派生词：extract→ extractable

13. expel: [ikˈspel] *v.* 驱逐

　　分解记忆法：ex-(向外)+pel(驱赶)=赶在外面

　　【例句】The naughty boy was expelled from school.

　　　　　这个淘气的男孩被赶出学校。

　　　　　The official at the embassy was expelled from the country.

　　　　　大使馆的一名官员被驱逐出境。

　　常用派生词：expel→ expellable

14. extracurricular: [ˌekstrəkəˈrikjulə] *a.* 课外的

　　分解记忆法：extra-(超出以外)+curri(运行)+-cular(形容词后缀)=课程以外的

　　【例句】What extracurricular activities do you take part in?

　　　　　你参加什么课外活动？

　　　　　She is involved in many extracurricular activities, such as music and sports.

　　　　　她参加了许多课外活动，如音乐和体育。

15. extraordinary: [ikˈstrɔ:dinəri] *a.* 非常的，特别的

　　分解记忆法：extra-(超出以外)+ordinary(普通的)=超出普通的

　　【例句】His talents are quite extraordinary.

他才华出众。
The weather is extraordinary for the time of the year.
一年中这个时间这样的天气很反常。

常用派生词：extraordinary→ extraordinarily

16. international: [ˌintəˈnæʃənəl] *a.* 国际的

分解记忆法：inter-(之间)+national (国家的)=国与国之间的

【例句】We reached an international agreement.
我们达成了国际协议。
The pianist enjoys international reputation.
这位钢琴家享有国际声誉。

常用派生词：international→ internationally

17. interpret: [inˈtə:prit] *v.* 解释

分解记忆法：inter-(之间)＋pret (价值)=在两者之间确定价值

【例句】How would you interpret his silence?
你如何理解他的沉默？
Poetry helps us to interpret life.
诗歌有助于我们解释人生。

常用派生词：interpret→ interpretation

18. interrupt: [ˌintəˈrʌpt] *v.* 中断

分解记忆法：inter-(之间)+rupt(打破)=决裂

【例句】Trade between the two countries was interrupted by the war.
两国之间的贸易因战争而中断。
Don't interrupt while I am busy.
我正忙着，不要打扰我。

常用派生词：interrupt→ interruption

19. circumstance: [ˈsə:kəmstəns] *n.* 环境

分解记忆法：circum-(周围)+stan(站立)+-ce(名词后缀)=周围的东西

【例句】Under no circumstance will I give up.
在任何情况下，我都不会放弃。
She was found dead in suspicious circumstance.
她死的情形可疑。

20. circumspect: [ˈsə:kəmspekt] *a.* 慎重的

分解记忆法：circum-(周围)+ spect(看)=仔细地看看周围

【例句】She is quite a circumspect person.
她是一个相当慎重的人。
She does everything in a circumspect manner.
她做事很慎重。

常用派生词：circumspect→ circumspection

Words in Use

1. These teachers try to be objective when they _____ the integrated ability of the student.
   A. justify　　　　　B. evaluate　　　　　C. indicate　　　　　D. reckon
2. They are trying to _____ the waste discharged by the factory for profit.
   A. expose　　　　　B. export　　　　　C. extract　　　　　D. exploit
3. The university has launched a research center to develop new ways of _____ bacteria which have become resistant to drug treatment.
   A. regulating　　　　　B. halting　　　　　C. interrupting　　　　　D. combating
4. He is a talent for _____ decoration.
   A. internal　　　　　B. inner　　　　　C. indoor　　　　　D. inland
5. Researchers at the University of Illinois determined that the _____ of a father can help improve a child's grades.
   A. involvement　　　　　B. interaction　　　　　C. association　　　　　D. communication
6. I'm sorry to have _____ you with so many questions.
   A. interfered　　　　　B. impressed　　　　　C. interrupted　　　　　D. bothered
7. It's rude to _____ others while they are talking.
   A. interrupt　　　　　B. interpret　　　　　C. withdraw　　　　　D. forbid
8. The nurse _____ penicillin into her arm.
   A. injected　　　　　B. imported　　　　　C. impressed　　　　　D. introduced
9. We were most _____ by your deficiency.
   A. injected　　　　　B. imported　　　　　C. impressed　　　　　D. introduced
10. Most materials in the country are _____.
    A. injected　　　　　B. imported　　　　　C. impressed　　　　　D. introduced
11. She always examines her thoughts and feelings and we call her an _____ person.
    A. introvert　　　　　B. extrovert　　　　　C. introspective　　　　　D. introductory
12. She doesn't like to talk in public and we call her an _____ girl.
    A. introvert　　　　　B. extrovert　　　　　C. introspective　　　　　D. introductory
13. The _____ remarks by the chairman are very remarkable.
    A. introvert　　　　　B. extrovert　　　　　C. introspective　　　　　D. introductory
14. They _____ from China to Australia two years ago.
    A. immigrated　　　　　B. emigrated　　　　　C. emerged　　　　　D. evaded
15. The sun _____ from behind the clouds.
    A. immigrated　　　　　B. emigrated　　　　　C. emerged　　　　　D. evaded

16. The student turned around to _____ meeting his teacher.
    A. evade   B. emerge   C. evaluate   D. expel
17. My leader _____ our ability by work.
    A. evades   B. emerges   C. evaluates   D. expels
18. Women are often _____ from positions of authority.
    A. expelled   B. expanded   C. excluded   D. expected
19. His modest business eventually _____ into a supermarket empire.
    A. expelled   B. expanded   C. excluded   D. expected
20. You can't _____ to learn a foreign language in a week.
    A. expel   B. expand   C. expect   D. explore
21. She had her tooth _____ yesterday.
    A. excluded   B. extracted   C. pulled   D. taken
22. I take part in some _____ activities in my leisure time in college.
    A. extracurricular   B. extravagant   C. extraordinary   D. extraterrestrial
23. It is an _____ film about a highly gifted child.
    A. extracurricular   B. extravagant   C. extraordinary   D. extraterrestrial
24. The man spends too much on food and clothes and he is _____.
    A. extracurricular   B. extravagant   C. extraordinary   D. extraterrestrial
25. He is not good at dealing with _____ relations.
    A. international B. personal   C. internal   D. interpersonal
26. There will be a 15-minute _____.
    A. interlude   B. internal   C. international   D. interpersonal
27. We _____ the program to bring you a new flash.
    A. interplay   B. interrelate   C. interrupt   D. interpret
28. The text is hard to _____.
    A. interplay   B. interrelate   C. interrupt   D. interpret
29. It is said that crime and poverty _____.
    A. interplay   B. interrelate   C. interrupt   D. interpret
30. Under no _____ will I do that.
    A. condition   B. circumstance   C. situation   D. case

Key to *Words in Use*

1. B	2. D	3. D	4. C	5. A
6. C	7. A	8. A	9. C	10. B
11. C	12. A	13. D	14. B	15. C
16. A	17. C	18. C	19. B	20. C
21. B	22. A	23. C	24. B	25. D
26. A	27. C	28. D	29. B	30. B

第4单元 表示"否定"的前缀

Words in Context

The World Without Imagination

Imagine a world in which there was suddenly no imagination—a world in which human beings lost their gift to imagine **nonexistent** substances, to picture the future, to write fantasies. People may not be able to create: looking forward to nothing but the ordinary, they lost hope for the future as well as the motivation to create and to make things better and better.

Without imagination, the fabulous imagined world would soon **disappear**: no matter whether it is, the beautiful Snow White, the lovely Mickey Mouse or even the popular wizard Harry Potter, the cartoon figures could be the first ones to lose their game and be forgotten by the whole world, because people would simply hold with such **nonsense** anymore.

Industries concerned with imagination, such as the Disneyland, will face its biggest ever breakdown. The only good thing may be those children will no longer be frightened by ghosts since they could hardly know what can be called ghosts. The world could transfer to the age of boredom.

In such a world, the chances that society would develop are next to zero, because imagination, which plays an important role in every step of civilization, is the basic ability that helps mankind to think of the impossible, and make it possible. Therefore, science of any field will stop developing. And things can be even worse: inventions like computers and telephones were unlikely to be further developed. History, therefore, may get its way to go back instead of moving forward.

Word Building

More Words with the Prefixes

前缀	释义	例词
dis-, in(im, il, ir)-, a-, un-, non-	否定	disorder, dishonest, disappear, incapable, impossible, illogical, irregular, asymmetry, unreal, unfortunate, uncivilized, nonexistent, nonsense, nonstop

（续表）

前缀	释义	例词
dis-, de-	过程逆转	discourage, disconnect, dispose, disorganize, deforest, defrost, decelerate, decode, decentralize, decompose
anti-, contra-, counter-,	相互对立	antipathy, antithesis, antagonist, contradiction, contraposition, controvert, counteract, counterpart, counterclockwise, counterproductive

1. disorder: [disˈɔːdə] *n.* 无秩序；骚乱

　　分解记忆法：dis-(远离)+order(顺序)=没有秩序

　【例句】Everyone began shouting at once and the meeting broke up in disorder.

　　　　 大家一下子全都喊起来，会议秩序大乱而被迫中断。

　　　　 The continuing disorder has been reported in the city.

　　　　 据报道那座城市有持续的骚乱。

2. disappear: [ˌdisəˈpiə] *v.* 消失

　　分解记忆法：dis-(远离)+appear(出现)=没有出现

　【例句】The plane disappeared behind clouds.

　　　　 飞机飞入云中不见了。

　　　　 His smile disappeared when he heard the news.

　　　　 当他听到这个消息时，他的笑容消失了。

　　常用派生词：disappear→ disappearance

3. incomparable: [inˈkɔmpərəbəl] *a.* 不能比较的，无与伦比的

　　分解记忆法：in-(不)+compare(比较)+ -able(能够……的)=不可比较的

　【例句】These two dresses are incomparable.

　　　　 这两条裙子不能比较。

　　　　 The food in the restaurant is incomparable.

　　　　 这家饭店里的食物无与伦比。

　　常用派生词：incomparable→ comparable

4. impossible: [imˈpɔsəbəl] *a.* 不可能的

　　分解记忆法：im- (不)+possible(可能的)=不可能的

　【例句】It is impossible for him to catch up with the train.

　　　　 他不可能赶上火车。

　　　　 It is impossible to predict the future accurately.

　　　　 精确地预言未来是不可能的。

　　常用派生词：impossible→ impossibility

5. illogical: [iˈlɔdʒik(ə)l] *a.* 不合常理的

分解记忆法：in-(不)+logic(逻辑) + -al(……的)=不合理的

【例句】It is illogical to change the schedule so often.

时间表变动得如此频繁，似乎没有什么道理。

He drew an illogical conclusion.

他得出了一个不合常理的结论。

常用派生词：logic→ logical →illogical

6. irregular: [iˈregjulə] *a.* 不规则的

分解记忆法：ir-(不)+regular(规则的)=不规则的

【例句】He lives an irregular life.

他过着不规律的生活。

The coast is with an irregular outline.

这是一条曲折的海岸线。

常用派生词：irregular→ regular

7. nonexistent: [ˌnɔnigˈzistənt] *a.* 不存在的

分解记忆法：non-(不)+existent(存在的)=不存在的

【例句】She is frightened by the nonexistent danger.

她被不存在的危险吓坏了。

Bread is practically nonexistent.

实际上没有面包了。

常用派生词：exist→ existence→ nonexistent→ nonexistence

8. nonsense: [ˈnɔnsəns] *n.* 没有意义的话

分解记忆法：non-(不)+sense(意义)=没有意义

【例句】This so-called translation is merely nonsense.

这种所谓的翻译仅仅是无意义的词语。

You are talking nonsense.

你在胡说八道。

常用派生词：sense →nonsense

9. discourage: [disˈkʌridʒ] *v.* 使气馁

分解记忆法：dis-(剥夺)+courage(勇气)=剥夺勇气

【例句】Don't discourage her, because she is trying her best.

别泄她的气，因为她正在尽力做呢。

He discouraged me by saying that I was unable to complete the job alone.

他说我不能独立完成这份工作，这使我气馁。

常用派生词：courage → discourage

10. dispose: [diˈspəuz] *v.* 布置；处理；安排

分解记忆法：dis-(分离)+pose(放)=布置，放置

【例句】They disposed the chairs in a semi-circle.

他们把椅子排成半圆形。

The troops were disposed in battle formation.

军队被编成战斗队形。

常用派生词：dispose→ disposal→disposable

11. defrost: [ˌdiːˈfrɔst] *v.* 除霜

分解记忆法：de-(分离)+frost(霜)=除霜

【例句】He is defrosting the fridge.

他在给冰箱除冰。

A frozen chicken should be defrosted before cooking.

冻鸡应该在解冻之后烹调。

常用派生词：frost→ defrost→ defroster

12. decode: [ˌdiːˈkəud] *v.* 解码

分解记忆法：de-(分离)+code(密码)=解码

【例句】Nobody can decode the safe.

没有人可以为保险箱解码。

The man decoded the computer and stole the important information.

这个男人给电脑解码，从中偷取了重要的信息。

常用派生词：code→ decode→ decoder

13. decelerate: [ˌdiːˈseləreit] *v.* （使）减速

分解记忆法：de-(不)+celerate(加速)=不加速

【例句】The car decelerated on the icy road.

那辆轿车在结冰的路面上减速。

Too much rain decelerates the rate of growth.

太多雨水降低了生长速度。

常用派生词：decelerate→ deceleration

14. antipathy: [ænˈtipəθi] *n.* 反感

分解记忆法：anti-(相反)+-pathy(感情)=对立的感情

【例句】She felt antipathy to the beautiful woman.

她对这个漂亮女人感到反感。

They show a marked antipathy to foreigners.

他们对外国人流露出明显的反感。

常用派生词：antipathy→ antipathetic

15. antagonist: [ænˈtæɡənist] *n.* 敌手

分解记忆法：anti-(相反)+agony(斗争)+-ist(表示人的后缀)=对立争斗的人

【例句】We are antagonists in love.

我们是情敌。

34

She treats me as her antagonist in business.

她把我当成商业上的对手。

常用派生词：antagonist→ antagonistic

16. antonym: [ˈæntənim] *n.* 反义词

分解记忆法：anti-(相反)+onym(名称)=反义词(对立的名称)

【例句】The antonym of "old" is "new."

"旧的"的反义词是"新的"。

Can you tell me the definition of antonym?

你能告诉我反义词的定义吗？

17. counteract: [ˌkauntəˈrækt] *v.* 抵消

分解记忆法：counter-(相对)+act(作用)=相对作用

【例句】We must counteract extremism in the party.

我们必须抵制党内的极端主义。

This medicine can counteract the poison.

这种药可以消解毒性。

常用派生词：counteract→ counteraction

18. counterpart: [ˈkauntəpɑːt] *n.* 相对的人或物

分解记忆法：counter-(相对)+part(部分)=相对部分

【例句】The personnel director telephoned her counterpart in the other company.

人事部的主任给另一家公司的人事部主任打了电话。

The Minister of Defence is meeting his American counterpart in Washington.

国防大臣在华盛顿会见美国国防部长。

19. contradict: [ˌkɔntrəˈdikt] *v.* 反驳

分解记忆法：contra-(相对)+dict(说)=说反对的话

【例句】You should not contradict your teacher.

你不应该反驳你的老师。

If you contradict me again, you are fired.

如果你再反驳我，我就开除你。

常用派生词：contradict→ contradiction

20. contraband: [ˈkɔntrəbænd] *n.* 走私货

分解记忆法：contra-(相对，相反)+band(捆绑)=走私

【例句】The man trades in contraband.

这个男人买卖走私品。

Customs officials seized several tons of contraband toys.

海关人员截获了数吨走私玩具。

Words in Use

1. Many a player who had been highly thought of has _____ from the tennis scene.
   A. disposed　　　B. disappeared　　　C. discouraged　　　D. discarded
2. Many people lost their jobs during the business _____.
   A. desperation　　B. decrease　　　C. despair　　　D. depression
3. In the Chinese household, grandparents play an _____ role in raising children.
   A. incapable　　　B. indispensable　　C. insensible　　　D. infinite
4. It is _____ for us to complete the work in time because we don't have enough workers and money.
   A. possible　　　B. likely　　　C. impossible　　　D. able
5. I was offered a decent job all of a sudden, which seemed _____ to me.
   A. unreal　　　B. real　　　C. true　　　D. untrue
6. _____, he lost the chance to work abroad because of his illness.
   A. Luckily　　　B. Happily　　　C. Fortunately　　　D. Unfortunately
7. The food is hard to digest and it is extremely _____ for the children.
   A. fit　　　B. unfit　　　C. suit　　　D. suitable
8. My experience in Canada is so _____ that I will write a book to memorize it.
   A. forgettable　　B. boring　　　C. dull　　　D. unforgettable
9. Our teacher _____ us to speak English as much as possible.
   A. encourages　　B. disconnects　　　C. disorganizes　　　D. discourages
10. We are living in a _____ society now.
    A. civilized　　　B. uncivilized　　　C. civilizing　　　D. uncivilzing
11. We find a better way to _____ of the household waste.
    A. disconnect　　B. disorganize　　　C. dispose　　　D. disappear
12. We'd better _____ the fish before cooking.
    A. decode　　　B. deforest　　　C. defrost　　　D. decelerate
13. She has a _____ foot and can't walk very easily.
    A. deformed　　　B. deform　　　C. deforming　　　D. deformation
14. The car _____ as it overtook me.
    A. accelerated　　B. decelerated　　　C. decoded　　　D. decentralized
15. Don't be afraid of the _____ danger.
    A. existent　　　B. nonexistent　　　C. sense　　　D. nonsense
16. He claimed that he is an _____, denying the existence of God.
    A. antithesis　　　B. atheist　　　C. antipathy　　　D. asocialist

17. Modern human beings feel _____ toward slavery.
    A. antithesis   B. atheist   C. antipathy   D. asocialist
18. The plan sounds good, but I'm afraid it is _____.
    A. practical   B. impractical   C. practicable   D. impracticable
19. I'm afraid that your inference is _____.
    A. practical   B. impractical   C. practicable   D. impracticable
20. The campaign has helped us _____ rich reserves of talent among our employees.
    A. lock   B. unlock   C. code   D. decode
21. I had to ask a locksmith to _____ the chest.
    A. lock   B. unlock   C. frost   D. defrost
22. Many animal protection organizations are against the cruel and _____ use of animals in medical research.
    A. impolite   B. impractical   C. impossible   D. immoral
23. Scientists are making an attempt to reproduce identical offspring of humans _____.
    A. asocial   B. asocially   C. asexual   D. asexually
24. The speaker has got confused, and began _____ himself.
    A. contradict   B. contradicting   C. contradicted   D. contradiction
25. It is _____ to leave litter in public places.
    A. asocial   B. social   C. unsocial   D. antisocial
26. Three hundred rebels were captured and _____.
    A. disarmed   B. armed   C. disorganized   D. organized
27. Even friends sometimes _____.
    A. disconnect   B. disarm   C. disorganize   D. disagree
28. The woman is not able to read and write and she is _____.
    A. illiberal   B. illiterate   C. illegal   D. illicit
29. It is _____ of you not to prepare meals for your children.
    A. irregular   B. irresponsible   C. irreverent   D. irresistible
30. Military intervention is highly _____.
    A. undeveloped   B. unlikely   C. undesirable   D. unsatisfied

Key to *Words in Use*

1. B	2. D	3. B	4. C	5. A
6. D	7. B	8. D	9. A	10. A
11. C	12. C	13. A	14. A	15. B
16. B	17. C	18. D	19. B	20. B
21. B	22. D	23. D	24. B	25. D
26. A	27. D	28. B	29. B	30. C

第5单元　表示"大小多少"的前缀

Words in Context

Television

History and news become confused, and one's impressions tend to be a mixture of skepticism and optimism. Television is one of the means by which these feelings are created and conveyed and perhaps never before has it served so much to connect different peoples and nations as in the recent events in Europe. In Europe, as elsewhere, **multimedia** groups have been increasingly successful groups which bring together television, radio newspapers, magazines and publishing houses that work in relation to one another.

Although most companies have noticed the **magnitude** of the competition, only the biggest and most flexible television companies are going to be able to compete in such a rich and hotly contested market. This alone demonstrates that the television business is not an easy world to survive in, a fact underlined by statistics that show that out of eighty European television networks, no less than 50% took a loss in 1989.

Moreover, the integration of the European community will oblige television companies to cooperate more closely in terms of both production and distribution. And we cannot **underestimate** the power of other television companies.

Creating a "European identity" that respects the **multicultural** backgrounds and traditions which go to make up the connecting fabric of the old continent is no easy task and demands a strategic choice of producing programs in Europe for Europe. This entails reducing our dependence on the North American market, whose programs relate to experiences and cultural traditions which are different from our own.

Word Building

More Words with the Prefixes

前缀	释义	例词
macro-, maga-, magn-	大	macrocosm, macroeconomics, macrometeorology, magnify, megalith, megnate, magnanimous, magnitude

（续表）

前缀	释义	例词
micro-, mini-	小	microphone, microbiology, microeconomics, microcosm, microwave, minibus, minister, minimum, miniature, minimal
multi-, poly-	多	multilateral, multilingual, multinational, multiply, multimedia, polyandry, polygamy, polyphony, polysyllable
under-	少	undercharge, underdeveloped, understaffed, underfed, underpay underestimate

1. macrocosm: [ˈmækrəukɔzəm] *n.* 宏观宇宙；总体

分解记忆法：macro- (大)+cosm (宇宙)=大宇宙

【例句】When we regard the world as a whole, we mean it is the macrocosm.

当我们把世界看成一个整体，我们的意思是它是宏观宇宙。

How do we define the macrocosm?

我们如何定义宏观宇宙？

2. macroeconomics: [ˌmækrəuˌiːkəˈnɔmiks] *n.* 宏观经济学

分解记忆法：macro- (大的, 宏观的)+economics (经济学)=宏观经济学

【例句】We begin to learn macroeconomics this semester.

这个学期我们开始学习宏观经济学。

The professor who studies macroeconomics is giving a lecture.

研究宏观经济学的教授正在做讲座。

3. magnify: [ˈmægnifai] *v.* 放大

分解记忆法：magn-(大)+-fy(使……)=使宽大

【例句】A microscope can magnify these germs.

显微镜会放大这些细菌。

The importance of his lecture has been magnified out of proportion.

他的演讲的重要性被过分夸大了。

常用派生词：magnify→ magnification

4. magnate: [ˈmægneit] *n.* 伟人；大企业家

分解记忆法：magn-(伟大的)+-ate(表示人的名词后缀)=伟大的人

【例句】This is an oil magnate.

这是一位石油大亨。

Many magnates attend the meeting.

很多工商界大亨参与了会议。

5. **magnanimous:** [mægˈnænɪməs] *a.* 心灵高尚的；度量宽大的

   分解记忆法：magn-(伟大的)+anim(心灵)+-ous(形容词后缀)=伟大心灵的

   【例句】It was very magnanimous of you to overlook his impolite behaviors.
   　　　你很宽宏大量，不计较他的无礼行为。
   　　　My parents are magnanimous to my mistakes.
   　　　我的父母对我的错误很宽宏大量。

   常用派生词：magnanimous→ magnanimity

6. **magnitude:** [ˈmæɡnɪtjuːd] *n.* 巨大；重要；（地震）级数

   分解记忆法：magn-(大)+-itude(抽象名词后缀)=大，重要

   【例句】I have realized the magnitude of the problem.
   　　　我已经意识到了问题的严重性。
   　　　The magnitude of the epidemic was scary.
   　　　这种流行病传播范围之广令人惊慌不安。

7. **microbiology:** [maɪkrəʊbaɪˈɒlədʒi] *n.* 微生物学

   分解记忆法：micro-(小)+bio(生命)+logy(名词后缀)=微生物学

   【例句】The book is a brief introduction to microbiology.
   　　　这本书是对微生物学的简单介绍。
   　　　The students majoring in medicine should study microbiology.
   　　　医学专业的学生要学微生物学。

   常用派生词：biology→ microbiology→ microbiological

8. **microeconomics:** [ˈmaɪkrəʊˌiːkəˈnɒmɪks] *n.* 微观经济学

   分解记忆法：micro-(小)+economics(经济学)=微观经济学

   【例句】What's the difference between macroeconomics and microeconomics?
   　　　宏观经济学和微观经济学有什么区别？
   　　　The professor is an expert on microeconomics.
   　　　这位教授是微观经济学方面的专家。

9. **microphone:** [ˈmaɪkrəfəʊn] *n.* 扩音器

   分解记忆法：micro-(小)+phone(声音)= 扩音器

   【例句】Some teachers use microphones in class to make their voice louder.
   　　　一些老师上课使用扩音器使他们的声音更大。
   　　　The singer is singing a beautiful song with a microphone in one hand and flowers in the other.
   　　　这位歌手一手拿着麦克风，一手拿着花，唱着优美的歌曲。

10. **microcosm:** [ˈmaɪkrəkɒzəm] *n.* 小宇宙，缩图

    分解记忆法：micro-(小)+cosm(宇宙)=小宇宙

    【例句】In many ways, Pennsylvania is a microcosm of the United States.
    　　　从许多方面来看，宾夕法尼亚州是美国的一个缩影。

Campus life can be compared to a microcosm of the social life.
校园生活可以比作是社会生活的一缩影。

11. microwave: ['maikrəweiv] *n.* 微波

分解记忆法：micro-(小)+wave(波)=微波

【例句】It is convenient to heat food in a microwave oven.
用微波炉加热食物很方便。
A microwave oven is an oven which cooks food by a kind of radiation rather than by heat.
微波炉是一种用放射物而不是热量做饭的炉具。

12. minimum: ['minimәm] *n.* 最低限度

分解记忆法：mini-(小)+-mum(拉丁文的"最高级"后缀)=最低限度

【例句】This will take a minimum of two hours.
这要花最少两个小时。
Repairing your car will cost a minimum of 100 dollars.
修理你的车最少要100美元。

13. minister: ['ministә] *n.* 牧师；部长

分解记忆法：mini-(小)+-ster(表示人的名词后缀)=小人物

【例句】The Minister of Education is giving a speech on higher education.
教育部部长正在就高等教育发表讲话。
The minister declared that they were legal couple.
牧师宣布他们是合法夫妻。

常用派生词：minister→ ministerial

14. multimedia: ['mʌlti'mi:djә] *n.* 多媒体

分解记忆法：multi-(多)+media(媒介)=多媒介

【例句】Multimedia is the use of television and other different media in class, as well as textbooks.
多媒体教学在课堂教学中，不仅用课本，而且用电视等多种不同手段。
Using multimedia in teaching can make your class colorful and attractive.
运用多媒体教学可以使课堂丰富多彩，有吸引力。

15. multiply: ['mʌltiplai] *v.* 增加；乘

分解记忆法：multi-(多)+ply(重叠)=许多东西重叠在一起

【例句】Her husband multiplied his demands on her time.
她丈夫占用她的时间大大增加了。
Twenty multiplied by five is one hundred.
二十乘五是一百。

常用派生词：multiply→ multiplication

16. polygamy: [pəˈligəmi] *n.* 一夫多妻

　　分解记忆法：poly-(多)+gamy(结婚)=一夫多妻

　【例句】Sudan allows polygamy.

　　　　　苏丹允许一夫多妻。

　　　　　If a man is allowed to have several wives at the same time, that means the country permits polygamy.

　　　　　如果一个男人同时有几个妻子，那就意味着这个国家允许一夫多妻。

　　常用派生词：polygamy→ polygamist

17. polysyllable: [ˈpɔlisiləbl] *n.* （三个音节以上的）多音节字

　　分解记忆法：poly-(多)+syllable(音节)=多音节

　【例句】Polysyllable means a word having several syllables.

　　　　　多音节词是指有多个音节的词。

　　　　　The word "beautiful" is polysyllable.

　　　　　beautiful 这个词是多音节词。

　　常用派生词：polysyllable→ polysyllabic

18. underdeveloped: [ˌʌndədiˈveləpt] *a.* 低度开发的

　　分解记忆法：under-(少)+developed(发展的)=发展不全的

　【例句】Underdeveloped countries don't have modern industries and usually have low standards of living.

　　　　　不发达国家没有现代工业而且通常生活标准很低。

　　　　　The western part of that country is underdeveloped.

　　　　　那个国家的西部地区不发达。

19. underestimate: [ˌʌndərˈestimeit] *v.* 评价过低

　　分解记忆法：under-(少)+estimate(估计)=少估计

　【例句】They have underestimated how much tax would be demanded.

　　　　　他们低估了应付税款的数目。

　　　　　Don't underestimate your opponents.

　　　　　不要低估了你的对手。

20. underemployment: [ˌʌndərimˈplɔimənt] *n.* 就业率低

　　分解记忆法：under-(少)+em(在内部)+ploy(重叠)+ment(表示名词的后缀)=不完全雇用

　【例句】Economics crisis leads to underemployment.

　　　　　经济危机导致就业率过低。

　　　　　Underemployment is one of the social problems for this country.

　　　　　就业率过低是这个国家中的社会问题之一。

Words in Use

1. The meeting of the U.N. must be ____.
   A. monolingual   B. lingual   C. bilingual   D. multilingual
2. We usually take a ____ to go to school in the morning.
   A. truck   B. vehicle   C. minibus   D. plane
3. It will take a ____ of 20 minutes to complete the work.
   A. minimum   B. minute   C. limit   D. miniature
4. I really admire her ____ generosity.
   A. magnificent   B. magnify   C. magnitude   D. megalith
5. Most of us don't realize the ____ of her achievement.
   A. magnificent   B. magnify   C. magnitude   D. megalith
6. The bacteria are magnified to 1000 times their ____ size.
   A. real   B. true   C. actual   D. factual
7. The block becomes ____ when the current is switched on.
   A. magnify   B. magnetic   C. magnitude   D. magnificent
8. We stayed with our parents and so our expenses were ____.
   A. minimize   B. minimum   C. minim   D. minimal
9. To ____ the risk of burglary, install a good alarm system.
   A. minimize   B. minimum   C. minim   D. minimal
10. Our problems ____ since last year.
    A. multitude   B. multiplied   C. mumbled   D. multilateral
11. She always ____ when she's embarrassed.
    A. multitude   B. multiplied   C. mumbled   D. multilateral
12. You can find many languages in the dictionary and it is a ____ one.
    A. monolingual   B. bilingual   C. multilingual   D. multilateral
13. Many countries take part in the organization and it is a ____ one.
    A. bilateral   B. multilateral   C. national   D. multinational
14. Many people believe ____ companies have too much power.
    A. multiple   B. multilateral   C. multilingual   D. multinational
15. He ____ me $1 for the book.
    A. underdeveloped   B. undercharged   C. underbid   D. underestimated
16. The beef was ____ and quite uneatable.
    A. underdone   B. underbid   C. underdeveloped   D. underestimated
17. We ____ the cost of the expedition and we were short of money now.
    A. underbid   B. underestimated   C. underdeveloped   D. underwent

18. They are ____ great hardship during the process of the exploration
    A. undergoing   B. underlying   C. underestimating   D. underdeveloping
19. Most patients complain that our hospitals are seriously ____.
    A. underdone   B. underbid   C. undermanned   D. underdeveloped
20. The child is too thin and he is ____.
    A. underdone   B. underbid   C. undernourished   D. undermanned
21. There are not enough teachers in the school and it is badly ____.
    A. undernourished B. underdeveloped   C. understaffed   D. underestimated
22. People pay much attention to ____ food now.
    A. microcosm   B. macrobiotic   C. macrobiotics   D. macrocosm
23. The ____ means the universe.
    A. microcosm   B. macrocosm   C. macroeconomics   D. microeconomics
24. Most universities adopt ____ education.
    A. multilateral   B. multilingual   C. multimedia   D. multinational
25. He walked out into the snow, heavily ____ in a thick scarf.
    A. muffled   B. multiplied   C. muddled   D. multitude
26. A large ____ assemble under the townhall.
    A. crowds   B. people   C. magnitude   D. multitude
27. The cleaner had ____ the papers and I couldn't find the one I wanted.
    A. muffled   B. multiplied   C. muddled   D. multitude
28. China implements the custom of ____.
    A. polygamy   B. monogamy   C. polyandry   D. polygon
29. Sudan implements the custom of ____.
    A. polygamy   B. monogamy   C. polyandry   D. polygon
30. Nurses are overworked and ____.
    A. underpinned   B. underpants   C. underpaid   D. underpass

Key to *Words in Use*

1. D	2. C	3. A	4. A	5. C
6. C	7. B	8. D	9. A	10. B
11. C	12. C	13. D	14. D	15. B
16. A	17. B	18. A	19. C	20. C
21. C	22. B	23. B	24. B	25. A
26. D	27. C	28. B	29. A	30. C

第6单元　表示"新旧好坏"的前缀

Words in Context

Hunger and Malnutrition

We've all seen news reports about people who are starving in countries plagued by war or drought. Unfortunately, many people in the world go hungry because they can't get enough to eat most of the time.

According to the UN World Food Programme, there are 400 million hungry children in the world — that's more than the entire population of the United States. Children who are starving are at risk of **malnutrition**, and malnourished kids don't develop normally.

We all feel hungry at times. Hunger is the way the body signals that it needs to eat. Once a person is able to eat enough food to satisfy the body's needs, he or she stops being hungry. Teens can feel hungry a lot because their rapidly growing and developing bodies demand extra food.

People with malnutrition lack the nutrients necessary for their bodies to grow and stay healthy. Someone can be **malnourished** for a long or short period of time, and the condition may be mild or severe. Malnutrition can affect a person's physical and mental health. People who are suffering from malnutrition are more likely to get sick; in very severe cases, they may even die from its effects. Many people don't know how to choose exercise means, exercise intensity and which sport game to be **beneficial** for health.

Word Building

More Words with the Prefixes

前缀	释义	例词
neo-	新	neoclassical, neocolonialism, neologism, neophyte
pale-	旧	paleography, paleontology
bene-, eu-	好	benediction, benefaction, beneficent, benevolent eulogy, euphemism
mal-	坏	maladjusted, maladministration, malformation, maleficent, malnutrition, malpractice

1. **neoclassical**: [ˌniːəuˈklæsikl] *a.* 新古典主义的

    分解记忆法：neo-(新) + classic(古典主义的) + al(形容词后缀)= 新古典主义的

    【例句】Alexander Pope was the most important English neoclassical poet in the first half of the 18th century.

    亚历山大·蒲柏是18世纪上半叶英国启蒙运动时期最具代表性的新古典主义诗人。

    The neoclassical theory of distribution teaches us that a person's earnings depend on his or her productivity.

    分配的新古典理论告诉我们，个人的收入依赖于其生产力。

    常用派生词：classic → classical → neoclassical

2. **neocolonialism**: [ˌniːəukəˈləuniəlizəm] *n.* 新殖民主义

    分解记忆法：neo-(新) + colonial(殖民主义) +ism(名词后缀)= 新殖民主义

    【例句】Those African leaders have now fallen victims of neocolonialism and sold their fellow Africans down the river.

    那些非洲领袖现已沦为新殖民主义的牺牲品而将同胞出卖了。

    The problem of neocolonialism is discussed in the history book.

    这本历史书讨论了新殖民主义的问题。

    常用派生词：neocolonial → neocolonialism

3. **neologism**: [niːˈɔlədʒiz(ə)m] *n.* 新字；新义

    分解记忆法：neo-(新) + log(说，说话) + -ism(名词后缀)=新字

    【例句】This article summarizes the main characteristics to the formation of sci-tech neologism.

    本文总结了英语科技新词汇的主要构词特点。

    She caught up a popular neologism from the newspapers.

    她急忙采用了报刊上流行的一种新词语。

    常用派生词：neology → neological → neologism

4. **neophyte**: [ˈniəfait] *n.* 新手；初学者

    分解记忆法：neo-(新) + phyte(植物)= 新手；初学者

    【例句】This is one mistake of judgment often made by the neophyte.

    这是一个初学者经常在判断上出现的问题。

    The neophyte must not despair of mastering the rules and procedures.

    初学的人不必在熟悉规则和程序中感到失望。

5. **paleography**: [ˌpæliˈɔgrəfi] *n.* 古文字学

    分解记忆法：paleo-(旧) + graphy(文字)= 古文字学

    【例句】Based on paleography evidence, he concluded its date was about the end of the third century AD.

    基于古文书学证据，他推论它的日期大约是公元3世纪末。

    It is really regretted in the research on paleography.

这些不能不说是古文字研究的遗憾。

常用派生词：paleography → paleographic

6. paleontology: [ˌpæliɔnˈtɔlədʒi] *n.* 古生物学

分解记忆法：paleo-（一）+ ontology（生物）= 古生物学

【例句】This is big news in the paleontology field, and will rewrite earth-life history.
这个消息是全球古生物学界的大消息，势将改写地球生命史。

As devastating as this volcanic torrent was for the creatures it buried, it would become a boon for paleontology.
破坏力如此强大的火山泥流吞没了动物，必定成为古生物学的宝库。

7. benediction: [beniˈdikʃən] *n.* 祝福；祈祷

分解记忆法：bene-（好）+ dic（说）+ -tion（名词后缀）= 祝祷

【例句】The priest pronounced a benediction over the couple at the end of the marriage ceremony.
牧师在婚礼结束时为新婚夫妇祈求上帝赐福。

I say the benediction to my father's birthday.
我祝福父亲的生日。

常用派生词：benediction → benedictional → benedictive → benedictory

8. benefaction: [ˌbeniˈfækʃən] *n.* 善行；恩惠；施舍

分解记忆法：bene-（好）+ fac（做）+ -tion（名词后缀）= 恩惠；施惠

【例句】The familiar brand name with a life of its own has been proclaimed as a public benefaction by the advertising industry.
为人们所熟悉的牌子有它自己的生命，广告业把它们称为公众的恩惠。

Benefaction should not be done by words but by deeds.
善行不是用嘴来说的而是要用实际行动来做的。

常用派生词：benefaction → benefactive

9. beneficent: [biˈnefisənt] *a.* 仁慈的；慈善的；善行的

分解记忆法：bene-（好）+ fic（做）+ -ent（形容词后缀）= 亲切的；慈善的

【例句】All of us like her for her beneficent behavior.
因为她友善的品行，我们每个人都喜欢她。

She had now a life filled also with beneficent activity.
她目前的生活充满各种仁慈的活动。

常用派生词：beneficent → beneficence

10. benevolent: [biˈnevələnt] *a.* 仁慈的；善意的；慈善的

分解记忆法：bene-（好）+ vol（祝愿）+ -ent（形容词后缀）= 慈善的

【例句】His colleague was amazed at his benevolent nature.
他的同事都惊讶于他仁慈的天性。

Our teachers taught us to be benevolent.
我们的老师教导我们应当以仁慈为怀。

常用派生词：benevolent → benevolently → benevolence

11. eulogy: [ˈjuːlədʒi] *n.* 颂词

分解记忆法：eu-(好) + logy(说，说话) = 颂辞

【例句】His speech made at the opening ceremony serves as an inspiring eulogy.
他在开幕式上演讲真堪称是鼓舞人心的颂词。
This is a eulogy of the eminent naturalist.
这是篇颂扬这位杰出博物学家的致辞。

常用派生词：eulogy → eulogize → eulogist

12. euphemism: [ˈjuːfimizəm] *n.* 婉言

分解记忆法：eu-(好) + phem(说，说话) + -ism(名词后缀) = 委婉的说法

【例句】Euphemism is a very common and complicated linguistic phenomenon.
委婉语是一种十分常见而又非常复杂的语言现象。
"Pass water" is a euphemism for "urinate."
"小便"是"排尿"的委婉语。

13. maladjusted: [ˌmæləˈdʒʌstid] *a.* 失调的；不适应环境的

分解记忆法：mal-(坏) + adjusted(调节的) = 失调的

【例句】A series of ecologically maladjusted problems emerged because of deforestation in recent decades.
几十年来，该地区植被的大量砍伐引起了一系列生态恶化问题。
He suddenly found he bought a maladjusted carburetor yesterday.
他突然发现昨天他买的是一个失调的汽化器。

常用派生词：adjust → maladjusted → maladjustment

14. maladministration: [mælədminisˈtreiʃ(ə)n] *n.* 管理不善

分解记忆法：mal-(坏) + administration(管理) = 管理不善

【例句】This emergency exhibits the maladministration of public office.
这次突发事件表明公共部门中的管理不善。
The maladministration has always been a tough problem for the officials.
对于政府官员来说，管理不善一直以来都是个严重的问题。

15. malformation: [ˌmælfɔːˈmeiʃən] *n.* 难看；畸形

分解记忆法：mal-(坏) + form(形成) + -ation(名词后缀) = 畸形

【例句】This little boy suffers from the malformation of central nervous system
这个小男孩中枢神经系统先天畸形。
This treatment could result in malformation of the arms.
这种处理方法能造成上肢畸形。

常用派生词：formation → malformation

16. maleficent: [məˈlefisnt] *a.* 有害的

分解记忆法：mal-(坏) + fic(做) + -ent(形容词后缀) = 有害的

【例句】Biological immune system prevents the organism from being affected by alien maleficent cells, such as viruses and cells etc.

生物免疫系统保护了生物体不受外来有害细胞(包括病毒、细胞等)的侵袭。

Some TV programs are maleficent to the growth of adolescents.

一些电视节目对青少年成长有害。

17. **malnutrition**: [ˌmælnjuˈtrɪʃən] *n.* 营养不良

分解记忆法：mal- (坏) + nutrition（营养）= 营养不良

【例句】Malnutrition is dangerous to the patient.

营养不良对患者而言是非常危险的。

In the third world, where two out of three people still live by farming, food shortage and malnutrition are common.

在第三世界，有三分之二的人仍然以务农为生，但粮食短缺和营养不良现象却司空见惯。

常用派生词：nutrition →nutritious→ malnutrition

18. **malpractice**: [ˌmælˈpræktɪs] *n.* 失职，行为不当

分解记忆法：mal- (坏) + practice（实践）= 行为不当

【例句】Various malpractices by police officers were brought to light by the enquiry.

警察的各种不法行为经调查已揭露出来。

A doctor who refused to give treatment is on trial for medical malpractice.

一位曾拒绝医疗的医师因有渎医职而在接受审判。

Words in Use

1. ____ scientific ideas about light were changed by Einstein.
   A. Neoclassical   B. Classical   C. Novelty   D. Unique
2. This country becomes independent after many years of British ____.
   A. colonialism   B. neocolonialism   C. anti-colonialism   D. self-colonialism
3. Its title was Utopia, a ____ coined by More from Greek.
   A. eulogy   B. neologism   C. apology   D. prologue
4. He is a 12 year ____ in this league now.
   A. veteran   B. neophyte   C. beginner   D. green hand
5. The novel should be read in conjunction with the author's ____.
   A. paleography   B. biography   C. calligraphy   D. geography
6. He found a piece of ____ of an ancient bird.
   A. paleontology   B. ecology   C. biology   D. fossil
7. The priest pronounced a ____ over the couple at the end of the marriage ceremony.
   A. diction   B. benediction   C. dictum   D. malediction

8. I will repay your ____ one day.
   A. defection   B. confection   C. benefaction   D. malefactor
9. Because of this our experiences seem to verify, and thereby strengthen our self-images and a vicious or a ____ cycle, as the case may be, is set up.
   A. bellicose   B. beneficence   C. beneficial   D. beneficent
10. His ____ nature prevented him from refusing any beggar who accosted him.
    A. benevolent   B. benign   C. austere   D. stoic
11. He needs no ____ from me or from any other man. He has written his own history and written it in red on his enemy's breast.
    A. denounce   B. eulogy   C. stricture   D. defamation
12. The term Rumors is often a ____ for anti-government views in China.
    A. euphemism   B. eupepticity   C. euphemist   D. euphenics
13. However, a series of ecologically ____ problems emerged because of the massive lop and reasonless utilization of vegetation in recent decades.
    A. maladjustment   B. maladies   C. maladroit   D. maladjusted
14. You will need some experience in ____ before you can run the department.
    A. maladministration   B. administration   C. ministry   D. administrative
15. Different congenital ____ has influences on fetal kidneys development to different extents.
    A. information   B. malformation   C. conformation   D. reformation
16. Results have been delayed owing to a ____ in the computer.
    A. malfunction   B. maleficent   C. malediction   D. malefactor
17. The World Health Organization says ____ in children can cause life-long health problems.
    A. maltreat   B. malnutrition   C. malnourished   D. hunger
18. Give up is not to ____ of responsibility, give up is not to abandon heartless and inhospitality, but face the life of and then a chance.
    A. malnutrition   B. error   C. malpractice   D. malaise
19. That's a flat ____ of what you said before.
    A. malediction   B. benediction   C. contradiction   D. interdiction
20. This project is of great ____ to everyone.
    A. boon   B. benefit   C. benefaction   D. bonus
21. Snobs are usually contemptuous of people they feel to be ____ them.
    A. beneficent   B. beneath   C. beside   D. beyond
22. By supporting the work of the ____ Fund through a donation or Deed of Covenant.
    A. Benevolent   B. Benignant   C. Bountiful   D. Bereaved
23. People ask you for criticism, but they only want ____.
    A. praise   B. eulogy   C. euphony   D. euphemism

24. We must learn to master ____ to avoid embarrassment or unpleasant circumstances.
    A. taboo   B. eupepsia   C. dialect   D. euphemism
25. Most of the countries in the region have ____ economies.
    A. unstable   B. maladjusted   C. changeable   D. turbid
26. School life has a great influence on the ____ of a child's character.
    A. formation   B. malformation   C. arrangement   D. formula
27. Food fiber may accelerate increase of good bacteria, and withhold ____ bacteria.
    A. objectionable B. evil   C. maleficent   D. disapproval
28. The scientist generally believed that milk is very ____.
    A. malnutrition   B. nutritious   C. nutriment   D. innutrition
29. The accident was caused by the gross ____ of the driver.
    A. malfeasance   B. negligence   C. malpractice   D. negative
30. It was very ____ of you to lend them your new car for their holiday.
    A. beneficent   B. selfish   C. maladjusted   D. generous

Key to *Words in Use*

1. B	2. A	3. B	4. A	5. B
6. D	7. B	8. C	9. D	10. A
11. B	12. A	13. D	14. B	15. B
16. A	17. B	18. C	19. C	20. B
21. B	22. A	23. A	24. D	25. A
26. A	27. C	28. B	29. B	30. A

第7单元　表示"正误异同"的前缀

Words in Context

What Is a Homonym?

The word **homonym** comes from Greek meaning "the same name" and applies to any pair or group of words that sound the same but mean different things. Homonyms include **homophones**, homographs and complete homonyms. The following are some examples:
- Sale: half-price sale and Sail: to sail a boat
- Pail: to collect water in and Pale: to have no color
- Fair: to be just and Fare: a fee to be paid

Most commonly these words are also spelled differently, although sometimes the spelling remains the same, for instance "fair" can mean "to be just" or it can also mean "to be pale of skin".

Homonyms are quite important to writing, merely because homonyms are crucial to your story. And incorrect use of homonyms can give rise to **misunderstanding** in communication. And some **misprints** in published books are also cases of **misuse** of homonyms. With just one word you can completely change the meaning of a sentence. For instance:
- "Tom wasn't sure, but in the end it proved the right root to take."
- "Tom wasn't sure, but in the end it proved the right route to take."

The first suggests that Tom didn't poison himself, because he chose the right root vegetable to take for his supper. The second suggests Tom didn't get lost because it was the right route home.

Try and become aware of the homonyms you consistently get wrong and double-check when they come up in your writing.

Word Building

More Words with the Prefixes

前缀	释义	例词
ortho-	正确	orthography, orthopedic, orthodox, orthodontics
mis-	错误	mistrial, misprint, misspell, misunderstand, miscalculate

(续表)

前缀	释义	例词
homo-	相同	homocentric, homodont, homogeneous, homograph, homologous, homonym
hetero-	不同	heteroclite, heterocyclic, heterodox, heterogeneous, heteronym

1. orthography: [ɔːˈθɔgrəfi] *n.* 拼字法；拼字式

　　分解记忆法：ortho- (正确) + graphy (字) =拼字法

　【例句】In dictionaries, words are listed according to their orthography.

　　　　　在词典中，词是按照字母拼写顺序排列的。

　　　　　American orthography and English orthography are very much alike.

　　　　　美语与英语的拼写方法非常相似。

　常用派生词：orthography→orthographical→orthographically

2. orthopedic: [ɔːθəuˈpiːdik] *a.* 整形外科的

　　分解记忆法：ortho- (正确) + pedic (儿童的) =整形外科的

　【例句】The boy's father is an orthopedic specialist.

　　　　　男孩的父亲是一位矫形外科医生。

　　　　　She was so eager to become beautiful that she went to an orthopedic hospital.

　　　　　她是如此渴望变得美丽，以至于她走进了一家矫形外科医院。

　常用派生词：orthopedic→orthopedics

3. orthodox: [ˈɔːθədɔks] *a.* 传统的；正统的，正宗的

　　分解记忆法：ortho- (正确) + dox (意见) =正统的

　【例句】The orthodox Thanksgiving dinner includes turkey and pumpkin pie.

　　　　　传统的感恩节晚餐包括火鸡和南瓜馅饼。

　　　　　It was an obvious reaction to the Orthodox strictness of her home.

　　　　　这是对她家里东正教的清规戒律的明显反抗。

　常用派生词：orthodox→orthodoxy

4. orthodontics: [ˌɔːθəˈdɔntiks] *n.* 畸齿矫正学

　　分解记忆法：ortho- (正确) + dont (牙齿) + -ics (名词后缀) =畸齿矫正学

　【例句】Due to shortening much time of treatment, the technique has broad prospects in the field of orthodontics.

　　　　　由于大大缩短了治疗时间，这项技术在口腔正畸领域有着广阔前景。

　　　　　It is most important to master the force and its way of action in orthodontics.

　　　　　在口腔正畸矫治中，最重要的是把握矫治力及其作用方式。

　常用派生词：orthodontics→orthodontist→orthodontic→orthodontically

5. mistrial: [ˌmisˈtraiəl] *n.* 无效审判

　　分解记忆法：mis- (错误) + trial (审讯) =无效审判

【例句】The High Court declared it a mistrial.
高等法院宣布这一审判无效。
At the first trial in last year, jurors could not agree on a verdict and a mistrial was declared.
去年的初次审判中，审查委员未能做出裁决，宣布无效审判。

6. misprint: [misˈprint] *n*. 印错

分解记忆法： mis- (错误) + print (印刷) = 印错

【例句】This misprint led to great confusion.
这个印刷错误造成很大的混淆。
They misprinted John as Jhon.
他们把John印成Jhon了。

常用派生词： misprint→ misprinted

7. misspell: [ˌmisˈspel] *v*. 拼错

分解记忆法： mis- (错误) + spell (拼写) = 拼错

【例句】A domain name—clear, concise and easy to remember. Also be careful with names that people can easily misspell.
域名——清楚、简明、易记的名称。记住，千万不要挑选那些人们容易拼错的域名。
They intentionally misspell the name four times.
他们故意写错那人的名字四次。

8. misunderstand: [ˌmisʌndəˈstændiŋ] *v*. 误解；误会

分解记忆法： mis- (错误) + understand (理解) = 误解，误会

【例句】His remarks show that he misunderstood my position on the question.
他的话说明他误解了我在这一问题上的立场。
He wrote her a letter for fear she misunderstand him.
他给她写了封信,免得她误会。

常用派生词： misunderstand→ misunderstanding

9. miscalculate: [ˈmisˈkælkjuleit] *v*. 误算

分解记忆法： mis- (错误) + calculate (计算) = 误算

【例句】There's too much meat. I must have miscalculated the amount/how much I needed.
肉多了。准是我算错需要的量了。
I missed the train because I'd miscalculated the time it would take me to reach the station.
我误了火车，因为算错了到车站所需要的时间。

常用派生词： miscalculate→ miscalculation

10. **homocentric:** [hɔməuˈsentrik] *a.* 具同一中心的；同心的

    分解记忆法：homo-（相同）+ centr（中心）+ -ic（形容词后缀）=同心的

    【例句】The background was comprised of three homocentric white circles.

    背景由三个同心白色圆形线条组成。

    There were 8 capital English letters in each circle, which formed three homocentric circles.

    每个圆是八个大写英文字母,组成大、中、小三个同心圆。

    常用派生词：homocentric→ homocentrically

11. **homodont:** [ˈhəumədɔnt] *a.* 同型齿的

    分解记忆法：homo-（相同）+ dont（牙齿）=同型齿的

    【例句】Homodont dentition teeth in jaw have the same shape.

    颌内的同型齿有相同的形状。

    Homodont type of dentition where the teeth are all similar is indicative of a uniform diet.

    同型齿的齿形均匀全部相似的，显示食性的单一。

12. **homogeneous:** [ˌhɔməˈdʒi:niəs] *a.* 同种类的；同性质的；有相同特征的

    分解记忆法：homo-（相同）+ gene（种类）+ -ous（形容词后缀）=同种类的

    【例句】It's a dense, homogeneous rock with constituents so fine that they cannot be seen by the naked eye.

    这是一种成分细密肉眼不能看到的致密同质岩石。

    This experiment shows the state or quality of being homogeneous.

    这个实验显示出同质或相似的性质或状态。

    常用派生词：homogeneity→ homogeneous → homogeneously→ homogeneousness

13. **homograph:** [ˈhɔməgrɑ:f] *n.* 同形异义字

    分解记忆法：homo-（相同）+ graph（书写）=同形异义字

    【例句】The noun "record" and the verb "record" are homographs.

    名词record和动词record是同形异义词。

    Two words are homographs if they are spelled the same way but differ in meaning.

    拼写相同但含义不同的两个词就是同形异义词。

    常用派生词：homograph→homographic

14. **homologous:** [həˈmɔləgəs] *a.* 相应的；对应的；一致的

    分解记忆法：homo-（相同）+ log（说，说话）+ -ous（形容词后缀）=一致的

    【例句】The seal's flipper is homologous with the human arm.

    海豹的鳍肢与人类的手臂同源。

    The measures offer useful reference to repair rubbish measure during the construction of the homologous water conservancy project.

    这些措施对其他类似水利工程建设项目的弃渣治理有一定的借鉴意义。

15. homonym: [ˈhɔmənim] *n.* 同音异义词

  分解记忆法：homo-(相同)+nym(名)=同音异义词

 【例句】Two words are homonyms if they are pronounced the same way but have different meanings.

   两个词如果读音相同但意思不同时叫同音异义词。

   There is the Probabilistic Postprocessing Algorithm for Homonym in Chinese Syllable-to-Word Transcription.

   汉语音字转换中，有一种同音字(词)的概率后处理算法。

16. heterocyclic: [ˌhetərəuˈsaiklik] *a.* 杂环的；不同环式的

  分解记忆法：hetero-(不同)+cycl(圆)+-ic(形容词后缀)=不同环式的

 【例句】Biogenic amines are aliphatic, alicyclic or heterocyclic organic bases of low molecular mass, which arise as a consequence of metabolic processes in animal, plants and microorganisms.

   生物胺是动植物和微生物代谢过程中产生的低分子量的脂族、脂环或杂环有机碱。

   The results showed that there were 36 to 131 sorts of benzene and its derivatives, heterocyclic compounds, and polycyclic compounds being detected. Most of them have harmful effect on human health.

   分析结果表明,这些香烟中,含有苯类衍生物、杂环类化合物及多环化合物等,从36种到131种不等,绝大多数有害人体健康。

  常用派生词：heterocyclic→heterocycle

17. heterodox: [ˈhetərədɔks] *a.* 异端的；非正统的

  分解记忆法：hetero-(不同)+dox(观点)=异端的，非正统的

 【例句】His father is a heterodox person.

   他父亲是一位持非正统观点的人。

   It might be, that a Quaker, or other heterodox religionist, was to be scourged out of the town.

   或许是一位教友派的教友或信仰其他异端的教徒被鞭挞出城。

  常用派生词：heterodox→heterodoxy

18. heterogeneous: [ˌhetərəuˈdʒi:niəs] *a.* 混杂的

  分解记忆法：hetero-(不同)+gene(种类)+-ous(形容词后缀)=混杂的

 【例句】It is made up of loosely cemented heterogeneous material.

   这是由不同特质的材料松散黏合而成的。

   It is a heterogeneous, often incongruous mixture of elements.

   这是一种异质的、通常有不协调成分的混合物。

  常用派生词：heterogeneous→heterogeneously

Words in Use

1. The police attributed the increase in the crime rate to the _____ of bystanders who do not help victims.
   A. apathy   B. orthography   C. resonant   D. aura
2. Augmentation of the deficit caused much _____ for the general manager from the board of directors.
   A. adulation   B. orthodontics   C. approbation   D. reprobation
3. The young generation today doesn't like _____ teaching.
   A. orient   B. orthodox   C. overall   D. paradox
4. What they knew for knowledge for so many years was that their grandparents lived under a _____ government.
   A. dexterous   B. orthopedic   C. despotic   D. desultory
5. If prosecutorial misconduct results in a _____, a later prosecution may be barred.
   A. mistrial   B. mistress   C. mistrust   D. missing
6. Be careful about reading health books. You may die of a _____.
   A. misplug   B. misprise   C. misplacement   D. misprint
7. I am very sorry to _____ your name, which is a clerical error.
   A. misspell   B. mistake   C. misspeak   D. misspend
8. Good men make women understand the world; bad men make women _____ the world.
   A. misunderstand   B. misuse   C. mistake   D. mistreat
9. The salesman _____ the discount, so we hardly break even on the deal.
   A. judge   B. misbrand   C. misconceive   D. miscalculate
10. Our relationship ended as I found him rather _____ and aggressive.
    A. bashful   B. boorish   C. homocentric   D. unsullied
11. She described the new criminal bill as a _____ attack on democracy.
    A. pretentious   B. homodont   C. precipitous   D. perfidious
12. From early on Europe was considered a single and _____ area.
    A. homogeneous   B. homodisperse   C. homodont   D. homologous
13. The 200-year-old jail is overcrowded, understaffed and lacking in basic _____.
    A. atrocities   B. amenities   C. armistices   D. homographs
14. The wing of a bat and the arm of a man are _____.
    A. same   B. homologous   C. homocentric   D. similar
15. The Chinese word for "lotus" is "lian," which is, in Chinese, a _____ of "join."
    A. word   B. homograph   C. synonym   D. homonym

16. The warden had a(n) _____ attitude toward his prisoners.
    A. autocratic   B. heterocyclic   C. aristocratic   D. bureaucratic
17. I declined answering Mrs. Dean's question, which struck me as something _____.
    A. orthodox   B. heterodox   C. tacit   D. heterodont
18. The population of the United States is vast and _____.
    A. heterogeneous   B. heteroclite   C. homogeneous   D. homologous
19. The members of the club with lower middle class _____ are numerous.
    A. decadence   B. decency   C. pedigrees   D. heteronym
20. The enemy is liable to make mistakes; just as we ourselves sometimes _____ and give him openings to exploit.
    A. miscalculate   B. miscount   C. misdeem   D. misdirect
21. The doctor warned him that his _____ nature made him susceptible to a stroke and urged him to curb his temper.
    A. orthodox   B. capricious   C. choleric   D. chimerical
22. We sensed a _____ in him that made us feel sick inside.
    A. mischief   B. wickedness   C. misconduct   D. mistrial
23. The offshore oil _____ has become an essential part of the European economy.
    A. spew   B. rig   C. misprint   D. sprout
24. All too often journalists fail to _____ personal privacy.
    A. misunderstand   B. respect   C. regard   D. honor
25. We had to _____ our stay for another week for the contract had not been signed yet.
    A. delay   B. misspell   C. prolong   D. expedite
26. He was _____ and ready to conform to the pattern set by his friends.
    A. homogeneous   B. complacent   C. compliant   D. determined
27. In this land of plenty, we must be ashamed of the _____ and suffering that still exists in the slum areas.
    A. misery   B. homograph   C. anguish   D. penury
28. The electrician was _____ about grounding all the wires in the factory.
    A. scrupulous   B. homologous   C. detrimental   D. infirmity
29. It is a _____ attempt to turn back the pages of history.
    A. inexplicable   B. preposterous   C. heterodox   D. demonstrable
30. The manager considered it _____ to his position to accept the demands of the trade union leaders.
    A. unaccustomed   B. heterogeneous   C. derivative   D. derogatory

Key to *Words in Use*

1. A	2. D	3. B	4. C	5. A
6. D	7. A	8. A	9. D	10. B
11. D	12. A	13. B	14. B	15. D
16. D	17. B	18. A	19. C	20. A
21. C	22. B	23. B	24. B	25. C
26. C	27. D	28. A	29. B	30. D

第8单元　决定词性的前缀

Words in Context

Company and Environment

Nowadays companies contribute money to many worthy causes. In fact many cultural events only become possible through corporate sponsorship and financial support. The choice between supporting the arts and protecting the environment is not an easy one. However, the company should give money to protect the environment because a healthy environment is necessary in order to produce and enjoy the arts and also because every company has an obligation to secure the environment which can **encourage** products either directly or indirectly.

A healthy environment has served as inspiration to artists over the centuries and millennia. On all continents creative people have drawn from the positive effects of natural beauty to produce landmark pieces of art, and painters, writers, and musicians **alike** talk about the stimulating effects that nature has on their work. Furthermore, nature is the focal point of many works of art, for example, landscape painting. Therefore, a healthy environment becomes a prerequisite for art.

Protecting the environment will also **ensure** that people will be able to enjoy the arts in the future. After all, environmental pollution causes and contributes to many diseases and illnesses. Naturally, sick people are not very concerned with high culture but are more worried about getting healthy or staying alive. Thus, money spent on environmental protection will make it possible for people to continue to enjoy art because they will **befriend** with environment and live healthier lives.

Word Building

More Words with the Prefixes

前缀	释义	例词
a-	在特定地点（名词变副词）	ashore, aboard, abed, aside, ahead
	表示动作的状态（动词变形容词）	asleep, alike, awake, awash, adrift, ablaze, apart, ajar

（续表）

前缀	释义	例词
be-	形容词变动词	besiege, behead, becalm, befriend, befool, beguile, belittle, benumb, betroth
en-	使……（名词、形容词变动词）	enable, enlarge, embody, encircle, encourage, enlighten, empower, enrich, enslave, enforce, ensure, entitle

1. ashore: [ə'ʃɔː] *adv.* 在岸上；上岸

　　分解记忆法：a- (在) + shore(岸)=在岸上

　【例句】They have been ashore for two hours.

　　　　　他们上岸已经两个小时了。

　　　　　The little ship was driven ashore by the wind.

　　　　　这只小船被风吹到了岸边。

2. aboard: [ə'bɔːd] *prep. & adv.* 在（船、飞机、车）上；上（船、飞机、车等）

　　分解记忆法：a- (在) + board(木板、甲板)=在船上；在飞机上

　【例句】We travelled aboard the same flight.

　　　　　我们搭乘同一航班。

　　　　　The boat swayed slightly as he stepped aboard.

　　　　　他上船的时候，船轻轻地摇摆起来。

3. abed: [ə'bed] *adv.* 在床上

　　分解记忆法：a- (在) + bed(床)= 在床上

　【例句】Each morning they lay abed till the breakfast bell, pleasantly conscious that there were no efficient wives to rouse them.

　　　　　每天早晨，他们都赖到早餐铃响才起床，愉快地意识到没有管得宽的妻子来催促。

　　　　　She does not, with lying long abed, spoil both her complexion and conditions.

　　　　　她从不因贪睡而糟蹋容颜和身体。

4. aside: [ə'said] *adv.* 在旁边；到（或向）一边

　　分解记忆法：a- (在) + side(旁边)=在旁边

　【例句】I laid my book aside, turned off the light and went to sleep.

　　　　　我把书放在一边，关了灯睡觉。

　　　　　He pushed his half-eaten salad aside and left.

　　　　　他把吃了一半的沙拉推到一旁离开了。

5. ahead: [ə'hed] *adv.* 在前面（头）；向（朝）前；提前

　　分解记忆法：a- (在) + head(前)= 在前面

　【例句】By doing extra homework, he soon got ahead of his classmates.

他靠多做家庭作业，很快在班上名列前茅。
We do not foresee any major changes in the years ahead.
对未来的几年，我们没有预见到任何重大的变化。

6. **asleep**: [əˈsliːp] *a.* 睡着的

   分解记忆法：a- + sleep(睡) = 睡着的

   【例句】He soon fell asleep with weariness.

   他疲倦得很快就睡着了。

   Still half asleep, Jenny began to make the kids' breakfast.

   珍妮睡眼惺忪地开始给孩子做早饭。

7. **alike**: [əˈlaik] *a. & adv.* 同样的；相像的

   分解记忆法：a- + like(像、一样) = 同样的；相像的

   【例句】These kittens look exactly alike. How can you tell which is which?

   这些小猫看上去一模一样，你怎么能分出哪个是哪个？

   I learned a lot from teachers and classmates alike.

   我从老师和同学身上都学到了很多。

8. **adrift**: [əˈdrift] *adv. & a.* 漂流地；漂泊的

   分解记忆法：a- + drift(漂流) = 漂泊地(的)

   【例句】The top of your pen is going adrift and will soon fall.

   你的笔帽松了，很快就要掉了。

   She untied the rope and set the boat adrift.

   她把绳索解开，放开小船。

9. **apart**: [əˈpɑːt] *a.& adv.* 分离（隔）的（地）

   分解记忆法：a- + part(部分) = 分离(隔)的(地)

   【例句】The two villages are three miles apart.

   这两个村子相距三英里。

   A couple of men started fighting and we had to pull them apart.

   几个人打了起来，我们不得不把他们拉开。

   常用派生词：apart→ apartness

10. **ajar**: [əˈdʒɑː] *a.*（门窗等）微开的

    分解记忆法：a- + jar(宽口的瓶) = (门窗等)微开的

    【例句】As soon as the door is left ajar the puppy makes a bid for freedom.

    这门刚开到一半，那条小狗就企图逃跑。

    The door was/stood ajar.

    那扇门半开着。

11. **besiege**: [biˈsiːdʒ] *v.* 围攻；围困

    分解记忆法：be- + siege(包围) = 围攻；围困

    【例句】The city was besieged by the enemy for a few days.

这座城市被敌人围困了几天。

Miller was besieged by press photographers and visitors.

米勒被媒体记者和来宾团团围住。

常用派生词：besiege→ besieged→ besiegement

12. behead: [biˈhed] *v.* 砍……的头

分解记忆法：be- + head（头）= 砍……的头

【例句】Anne Boleyn was beheaded in 1536.

安妮·博林于1536年被斩首。

He was beheaded for high treason.

他因叛国罪被斩首。

13. becalm: [biˈkɑːm] *v.* 使平静；使安静；因无风而停止前进

分解记忆法：be- + calm（平静的）= 使平静

【例句】The ship was becalmed for two weeks.

船由于没有风而停驶了两周。

The crying baby was becalmed by being rocked in her mother's arms.

母亲抱着哭泣的孩子晃动使他平静了下来。

常用派生词：becalm → becalmed

14. belittle: [biˈlitl] *v.* 贬低

分解记忆法：be- + little（小的）= 贬低

【例句】I find it belittling to be criticized by someone so much younger than me.

有个比我年轻许多的人批评了我，我觉得是小看了我。

Her colleagues tend to belittle her devotion and efforts.

她的同事总是轻视她的奉献和努力。

15. betroth: [biˈtrəuð] *v.* 同……订婚

分解记忆法：be- + troth（truth 真实）= 同……订婚

【例句】Her father betrothed her to him at an early age.

她父亲在她年幼时已把她许配给他。

She betrothed herself to him.

她和他订婚了。

16. enable: [iˈneibəl] *v.* 使能够；使可能；使可行

分解记忆法：en-（使）+ able（能够）= 使能够

【例句】I gave him full directions to enable him to find the house.

我向他作了详细说明，好让他能找到那房子。

The collapse of the strike enabled the company to resume normal bus services.

罢工的失败使公司恢复了正常的公共汽车营业。

常用派生词：able → enable → enabled→ enabling

17. enlarge: [inˈlɑːdʒ] *v.* 扩大；增大

　　分解记忆法： en-（使）+ large（大）= 扩大；增大

【例句】I planned to enlarge this photograph.
　　　　我计划放大这张照片。
　　　　I needn't enlarge upon this matter; you all know my views.
　　　　我不需要详述此事；你们都知道我的意见。

　　常用派生词： enlarge → enlargement

18. encourage: [inˈkʌridʒ] *v.* 鼓励；激励；支持

　　分解记忆法： en-（使）+ courage（勇气）= 鼓励；激励；支持

【例句】High prices for farm products encouraged farming.
　　　　农产品价格的提高有助于农业。
　　　　Her success encouraged me to try the same thing.
　　　　她的成功鼓励我试做同样的事。

　　常用派生词： encourage → encouraging → encouragement

19. enlighten: [inˈlaitn] *vt.* 启发；开导

　　分解记忆法： en-（使）+ light（光）+ -en（动词后缀）= 启发；开导

【例句】She was anxious to enlighten me about the events that led up to the dispute.
　　　　她急着要使我明白引起这场争执的那些事情。
　　　　The disciples were greatly enlightened by his words.
　　　　他的话启发了很多门徒。

　　常用派生词： enlighten → enlightening → enlightenment

20. enslave: [inˈsleiv] *v.* 使做奴隶；使处于奴役的状态

　　分解记忆法： en-（使）+ slave（奴隶）= 使做奴隶

【例句】He is enslaved by love.
　　　　他正沉溺于爱情。
　　　　Her beauty enslaved many young men.
　　　　她的美貌倾倒了很多男青年。

21. ensure: [inˈʃuə] *v.* 保证；担保；确保

　　分解记忆法： en-（使）+ sure（确信）= 保证，担保，确保

【例句】We must ensure the purity of drinking water.
　　　　我们必须确保饮用水的纯净。
　　　　People should wash regularly to ensure personal hygiene.
　　　　人们应经常洗澡以保证个人卫生。

　　常用派生词： ensure → ensured → ensuring

22. entitle: [inˈtaitl] *v.* 取名为；使有权利

　　分解记忆法： en-（使）+ title（题目）= 取名为，使有权利

【例句】She read a poem entitled "The Apple Tree".

她读了一首题为《苹果树》的诗。
Full-time employees are entitled to receive health insurance.
正式职员有权获得健康保险。

常用派生词：entitle→ entitlement

Words in Use

1. We went ____ when the boat reached the port.
   A. arouse   B. ashore   C. aboard   D. around
2. The plane crashed, killing all 200 people ____.
   A. aboard   B. abroad   C. broad   D. board
3. The sluggard lies late ____.
   A. bed   B. abed   C. aberrant   D. abduct
4. I gave her a plate of food but she pushed it ____.
   A. aslant   B. assail   C. aside   D. assay
5. The line of cars moved ____ slowly.
   A. beforehand   B. betimes   C. early   D. ahead
6. Still half ____, Jenny began to make the kids' breakfast.
   A. asleep   B. sleep   C. alone   D. alive
7. The climate here is always hot, summer and winter ____.
   A. alike   B. like   C. same   D. likely
8. The survivors were ____ in a lifeboat for six days.
   A. floating   B. adroit   C. adrift   D. adored
9. He tried in vain to keep the two dogs ____ before the neighbor intervened.
   A. apart   B. isolated   C. independently   D. alone
10. She had left the kitchen door slightly ____.
    A. unlocked   B. unwrapped   C. unscrewed   D. ajar
11. When the pop star tried to leave her hotel she was ____ by waiting journalists and fans.
    A. invested   B. besieged   C. bedeviled   D. besmirched
12. He was charged with treason and ____.
    A. beheaded   B. removed   C. cut   D. beheld
13. The size of the office tower ____ the surrounding buildings.
    A. becalms   B. underestimates C. belittles   D. underrates
14. Though she had spent hours fixing the computer he ____ her efforts.
    A. belittled   B. belabored   C. beleaguered   D. belied
15. The pair was later ____.
    A. betoken   B. betrayed   C. bestowed   D. betrothed

16. This dictionary ____ you to understand English words.
    A. enables   B. accredits   C. authorizes   D. entitles
17. Newspapers should not publish material that is likely to _____ discrimination on the grounds of race or color.
    A. cheer   B. discourage   C. encourage   D. inspire
18. Should the function of children's television be to entertain or to ____?
    A. ensure   B. enlighten   C. ennoble   D. explain
19. The company has built an additional factory to ____ its operations.
    A. broaden   B. increase   C. enlarge   D. reduce
20. The early settlers ____ or killed much of the native population.
    A. captured   B. ensnared   C. enthralled   D. enslaved
21. Our precautions ____ our safety.
    A. ensured   B. sure   C. promised   D. undertook
22. Membership ____ you to the monthly journal.
    A. authorizes   B. forbids   C. prohibits   D. entitles
23. Dean refused to join in the game, even though they all did their best to ____ him.
    A. persuade   B. encourage   C. press   D. force
24. When I taught, I would ____ a topic to children which they would write about.
    A. entitle   B. assume   C. assign   D. allow
25. Your passport ____ you to receive free medical treatment.
    A. moderates   B. enables   C. licenses   D. qualifies
26. The doctor ____ her that he would do his best to save the child's life.
    A. vowed   B. assured   C. ensured   D. swore
27. We must ask you to ____ your statement.
    A. amplify   B. enlarge   C. extend   D. magnify
28. The skiing instructor started the lesson by ____ turning techniques.
    A. simplifying   B. enlightening   C. demonstrating   D. setting out
29. It is a pity that he doesn't have enough money to ____ the project.
    A. encourage   B. sponsor   C. urge   D. promote
30. By saying this, I do not mean to ____ the importance of his role.
    A. belittle   B. decry   C. downgrade   D. denigrate

Key to *Words in Use*

1. B	2. A	3. B	4. C	5. D
6. A	7. A	8. C	9. A	10. D
11. B	12. A	13. C	14. A	15. D
16. A	17. C	18. B	19. C	20. D
21. A	22. D	23. A	24. C	25. D
26. B	27. A	28. C	29. B	30. A

第9单元 多义前缀(一)

Words in Context

David Duke as a Malignant Narcissist

He invents and then projects a false, fictitious, self for the world to fear, or to **admire**. He maintains a tenuous grasp on reality to start with and the trappings of power further exacerbate this. Real life authority and David Duke's predilection to surround him with obsequious sycophants support David Duke's grandiose self-delusions and fantasies of omnipotence and omniscience.

David Duke's personality is so precariously balanced that he cannot tolerate even a hint of criticism and disagreement. Most narcissists are paranoid and suffer from ideas of reference (the delusion that they are being mocked or discussed when they are not). Thus, narcissists often regard themselves as "victims of persecution."

But being a-human or superhuman also means being **asexual** and **amoral**. Narcissism is nihilistic not only operationally, or ideologically. Its very language and narratives are nihilistic. Narcissism is conspicuous nihilism and the cult's leader serves as a role model, annihilating the Man, only to reappear as a preordained and **irresistible** force of nature.

This is precisely the source of the fascination with Hitler, diagnosed by Erich Fromm, as a **malignant** narcissist. His unconscious was his conscious. He acted out our most repressed drives, fantasies, and wishes. At first, in a desperate effort to maintain the fiction underlying his chaotic personality, David Duke strives to explain away the sudden reversal of sentiment. When these flimsy attempts to patch a tattered personal mythology fail, David Duke becomes injured. Narcissistic injury inevitably leads to narcissistic rage and to a terrifying display of unbridled aggression.

Word Building

More Words with the Prefixes

前缀	释义	例词
a-	加在动词前变形容词	alive, awake, adrift, asleep, ablaze
	加在名词前变副词	ashore, abed, aside, ahead, aboard
	加在形容词前表否定	atheism, atypical, amoral, asymmetry, apathetic

(续表)

前缀	释义	例词
ad-	朝，面向 (to, forward)	adhere, advent, admit, advocate, adverse, admire, affront
	一再，加强 (again)	accelerate, accentuate, afflict, aggrandize, assiduous
ex-	外，外部	export, exterior, expel, extract, exclude, expatriate
	前任的	ex-wife, ex-president, ex-boyfriend
in-	内，内部	inject, inspire, incorporate, immigrant, include
	表否定	insensitive, incapable, injustice, immoral, illegal, illogical, illiterate, irregular, irresolute

1. **alive:** [ə'laiv] *a.* 活着的；有活力

   分解记忆法：a- + live(生活)=活着的, 有活力

   【例句】You seem very much alive today.

   你今天好像非常活跃。

   Are your grandparents still alive?

   你的祖父母还在世吗？

   常用派生词：alive → aliveness

2. **awake:** [ə'weik] *a.* 醒着的

   分解记忆法：a- + wake(醒)=醒着的

   【例句】He lay awake in his bed.

   他醒着躺在床上。

   I find it so difficult to stay awake during history lessons.

   我发现上历史课总想睡觉。

   常用派生词：awake → awakeable

3. **ablaze:** [ə'bleiz] *a.* 发光的；激愤的；着火的

   分解记忆法：a- + blaze(发光)=发光的

   【例句】The house was ablaze in a few minutes.

   房子几分钟就烧起来了。

   The house was ablaze with lights.

   那屋子灯火通明。

4. **ashore:** [ə'ʃɔ:] *ad.* 在岸上；上岸

   分解记忆法：a- + shore(岸)=在岸上，上岸

   【例句】We went ashore when the boat reached the port.

   船一靠港我们就上岸了。

   He managed to swim ashore.

   他设法向岸边游过去。

5. ahead: [əˈhed] *ad.* 在前面（头）；向（朝）前；提前

　　分解记忆法：a- + head(头)=在前面(头)

　　【例句】Will it still go ahead and explode your dog?

　　　　　　它是否会继续，接着炸死你家的狗？

　　　　　　You'd better plan ahead.

　　　　　　你最好事先计划一下。

6. atheism: [ˈeiθi-izəm] *n.* 无神论；不信神

　　分解记忆法：a- (没有) + the-(上帝) + -ism (表示主义、学说的后缀)=无神论

　　【例句】They are inclined to atheism.

　　　　　　他们倾向无神论。

　　　　　　Atheism is the opinion that there is no God.

　　　　　　无神论认为上帝是不存在的。

　常用派生词：atheism → atheist

7. amoral: [eiˈmɔrəl] *a.* 与道德无关的；超道德的

　　分解记忆法：a- (否定) + moral (道德)=与道德无关的, 超道德的

　　【例句】Young children are amoral.

　　　　　　小孩子是不知好歹的。

　　　　　　Science as such is completely amoral.

　　　　　　科学与道德无关。

　常用派生词：amoral → amorality → amorally

8. apathetic: [ˌæpəˈθetik] *a.* 缺乏感情的；缺乏兴趣的；无动于衷的

　　分解记忆法：a- (没有) + pathetic (悲哀的, 可怜的)=缺乏感情的, 无动于衷的

　　【例句】What is that apathetic being doing?

　　　　　　那无情的东西在做什么？

　　　　　　He felt no warmth towards his comrades but was cold, indifferent and apathetic.

　　　　　　他对同志不是满腔热情，而是冷冰冰，漠不关心，麻木不仁。

　常用派生词：apathy → apathetic → apathetically

9. adhere: [ədˈhiə] *v.* 黏附；附着；遵守，坚持；追随；支持

　　分解记忆法：ad- (朝) + here (粘贴)=附着

　　【例句】A smooth, dry surface helps the tiles adhere to the wall.

　　　　　　光滑干燥的墙面有助于瓷砖的粘连。

　　　　　　We will adhere to our plan.

　　　　　　我们将坚持按计划行事。

　常用派生词：adhere → adherent → adhesion

10. advent: [ˈædvent] *n.* 出现；到来

　　分解记忆法：ad- (面向) + vent (来)=到来

　　【例句】Since the advent of Emilia, his mind was never quiet.

同埃米莉亚交往以后，他的心境从此安静不下来了。

Life in Britain was transformed by the advent of the steam engine.

蒸汽机的问世使得英国人的生活状况大大改观。

11. affront: [əˈfrʌnt] *v. & n.* 侮辱

分解记忆法：af-(朝)+ front(前额)=侮辱

【例句】It was an affront to common decency.

这是对社会礼仪的公然冒犯。

He felt affronted at having his word doubted.

他因自己的诺言受到怀疑而感到难堪。

12. accelerate: [əkˈseləreit] *v.* （使）加快；（使）增速

分解记忆法：ac-(加强)+ celer(加速)+ -ate(动词后缀)=(使)加快，(使)增速

【例句】The driver stepped on the gas and accelerated the car.

司机加大油门,让汽车加速行驶。

He decided to accelerate his advertising.

他决定增加广告的数量。

常用派生词：accelerate→ acceleration

13. afflict: [əˈflikt] *v.* 使苦恼；折磨

分解记忆法：af-(一再)+ flict(斗争)=使苦恼，折磨

【例句】They were much afflicted by the heat.

他们深为暑热所苦。

She was afflicted with conscience.

她受良心责备。

常用派生词：afflict→ affliction

14. exterior: [eksˈtiəriə] *n.& a.* 外部；外部的

分解记忆法：exter-(外)+ ior(表比较级的字尾)=外部的

【例句】Beneath his gruff exterior he's really very kind-hearted.

他外表粗鲁，心地却十分善良。

The film includes some striking exteriors.

这部电影有一些引人注目的外景。

15. expel: [ikˈspel] *v.* 驱逐；逐出；开除

分解记忆法：ex-(向外)+ pel(驱使)=逐出

【例句】He was expelled from the school.

他被学校开除了。

Is that antidote strong enough to expel the poison?

这种解毒药有那么强，能驱散毒素吗？

16. exclude: [ikˈsklu:d] *v.* 把……排斥在外；不包括

分解记忆法：ex-(对外)+ clude(关闭)=把……排斥在外，不包括

【例句】That price excludes accommodation.
那价钱不包括住宿。
Curtains exclude light.
窗帘挡光。

常用派生词：exclude→ excluding → exclusion→ exclusive

17. ex-wife: [ˈekswaif] *n.* 前妻

分解记忆法：ex-(前任的)＋wife(妻子)＝前妻

【例句】George has been up for not paying alimony to his ex-wife.
乔治因没有支付前妻的赡养费而出庭受审。
He said he was framed by his ex-wife.
他说他受到了前妻的诬陷。

18. ex-president: [ˈeksˈprezidənt] *n.* 前总统

分解记忆法：ex-(前任的)＋president(总统)＝前总统

【例句】And yet the ex-president's existential predicament remains.
然而，这位前总统现在的处境依旧尴尬。
US ex-president Nixon's comeback is placed at sixth on the list of fake news.
美国前总统尼克松的复出被评为第六大经典假新闻。

19. inject: [inˈdʒekt] *v.* 注射

分解记忆法：in-(向内)＋ject(注入)＝注射

【例句】The doctor injected the drug into my arm.
医生把药注入我手臂。
We hope to inject new life into our business.
我们希望使我们的业务工作充满朝气。

常用派生词：inject→ injectable→ injection

20. include: [inˈklu:d] *v.* 包括；包含

分解记忆法：in-(内部)＋clude(关闭)＝包括，包含

【例句】The price includes both house and furniture.
价钱包括房子和家具。
He had included a large number of funny stories in the speech.
他在讲话中加进了许多引人发笑的故事。

常用派生词：include→ including → inclusion→ inclusive

21. immigrant: [ˈimigrənt] *n.* 移民；侨民

分解记忆法：im-(内部)＋migr(迁居)＋-ant(人)＝移民，侨民

【例句】Canada has many immigrants from Europe.
加拿大有许多欧洲移民。
He admitted that he was an illegal immigrant.
他承认他是非法移民。

常用派生词：immigrate→ immigrant→ immigration

22. insensitive: [inˈsensitiv] *a.* 对……没有感觉的，感觉迟钝的

　　分解记忆法：in- (不) + sensitive (敏感的) =对……没有感觉的，感觉迟钝的

　　【例句】The plates are insensitive to red light.

　　　　　这些感光片均对红光感觉迟钝。

　　　　　It is insensitive of you to mention that.

　　　　　你提那件事是愚钝的。

　　常用派生词：insensitive→ insensitivity

23. incapable: [inˈkeipəbəl] *a.* 无能力的；不能的

　　分解记忆法：in- (不) + capable (有能力的) =无能力的，不能的

　　【例句】As a lawyer she's totally incapable.

　　　　　她当律师完全不合格。

　　　　　That child seems incapable of keeping out of mischief.

　　　　　那个孩子不调皮捣蛋简直就受不了。

　　常用派生词：incapable→ incapability

24. immoral: [iˈmɔrəl] *a.* 不道德的；淫荡的

　　分解记忆法：im- (不) + moral (道德) =不道德的，淫荡的

　　【例句】She lives off immoral earnings.

　　　　　她靠赚肮脏钱生活。

　　　　　It is immoral to strip him when he was down.

　　　　　一旦他倒下了，去剥他的衣服是不道德的。

　　常用派生词：immoral→ immorally→ immorality

25. illegal: [iˈli:gəl] *a.* 不合法的；非法的

　　分解记忆法：il- (不) + legal (合法的) =不合法的，非法的

　　【例句】It is illegal to steal things.

　　　　　偷东西是违法的。

　　　　　It is illegal to sell alcohol to children.

　　　　　卖酒给儿童是违法的。

　　常用派生词：illegal→ illegally→ illegality

26. illiterate: [iˈlitərit] *a.* 文盲的；一窍不通的

　　分解记忆法：il- (不) + literate (受过教育的) =文盲的；一窍不通的

　　【例句】He is musically illiterate.

　　　　　他对音乐一无所知。

　　　　　Her powers had received no aid from education: she was ignorant and illiterate.

　　　　　教育对她的能力毫无助力：她依然蒙昧无知。

Words in Use

1. Nobody can keep _____ forever.
   A. alive　　　　　B. live　　　　　　C. life　　　　　　D. living

2. Too few people are _____ to the dangers of noise pollution.
   A. wake　　　　　B. award　　　　　C. awake　　　　　D. awful

3. During the riot, many cars and buses were set _____.
   A. ablaze　　　　B. flame　　　　　C. light　　　　　D. abhor

4. Cats are _____; they can't be censured for killing birds.
   A. amorous　　　B. moral　　　　　C. asexual　　　　D. amoral

5. Young people today are so _____ about politics.
   A. detached　　　B. apathetic　　　C. interested　　　D. aperture

6. We must strictly _____ to the terms of the contract.
   A. adhere　　　　B. grip　　　　　　C. adieu　　　　　D. adjoin

7. With the _____ of the new chairman, the company began to prosper.
   A. adventure　　B. advent　　　　C. advance　　　　D. advantage

8. He regarded the comments as an _____ to his dignity.
   A. affront　　　　B. afford　　　　　C. affright　　　　D. afraid

9. Inflation is likely to _____ this year, adding further upward pressure on interest rates.
   A. fast　　　　　B. race　　　　　　C. dart　　　　　　D. accelerate

10. He's badly _____ with a skin disorder.
    A. attacked　　　B. cursed　　　　C. afflicted　　　　D. consoled

11. Beneath that calm _____, he has a fierce will to win.
    A. exterior　　　B. inside　　　　　C. interior　　　　D. external

12. That country was _____ from the organization after it refused to withdraw its troops.
    A. deserted　　　B. expelled　　　　C. fired　　　　　D. resigned

13. You don't have to pay for your flights; they're _____ in the price of your holiday.
    A. contained　　B. included　　　　C. covered　　　　D. excluded

14. She was on a special diet which _____ dairy products.
    A. excluded　　　B. presided　　　　C. omitted　　　　D. prescribed

15. Phil's a diabetic and has to _____ himself with insulin every day.
    A. interpose　　B. introduce　　　C. put in　　　　　D. inject

16. When I brought up the question of funding, he quickly _____ that it had been settled.
    A. interjected　　B. implanted　　　C. injected　　　　D. inserted

17. She thought about the offer for a while, but in the end decided not to _____ it.
    A. include　　　B. receive　　　　C. accept　　　　　D. contain

18. The ship's captain was arrested for transporting illegal _____.

    A. foreigners   B. aliens   C. expatriates   D. immigrants

19. I'm sorry it was _____ of me to phone so early.

    A. insensitive   B. unsympathetic   C. inconsiderate   D. hard-hearted

20. My boss is so _____ that he never notices when I am feeling tired.

    A. unkind   B. uncharitable   C. unfair   D. insensitive

21. He seemed _____ of understanding how she felt.

    A. unable   B. incapable   C. inadequate   D. unqualified

22. Without her glasses she found ordinary newsprint almost _____.

    A. indecipherable   B. illegible   C. illiterate   D. scrawling

23. The Senator launched a(n) _____ attack on the former President.

    A. vicious   B. insensitive   C. inconsiderate   D. thoughtless

24. For many _____ people, television is the one means of getting news.

    A. illiterate   B. legible   C. literate   D. readable

25. Most West European countries have _____ the concept of high-speed rail networks with enthusiasm.

    A. included   B. contained   C. embraced   D. involved

26. It's _____ to be rich while people are starving and homeless.

    A. amoral   B. unmoral   C. moral   D. immoral

27. It is _____ to drive a car that is not taxed and insured.

    A. illegible   B. illiberal   C. evil   D. illegal

28. There's nothing _____ about wanting to earn more money.

    A. evil   B. immoral   C. shocking   D. moral

29. She _____ all offers of help.

    A. expelled   B. disgusted   C. offended   D. repelled

30. She was _____ by his sudden appearance at the party.

    A. agitated   B. aghast   C. afflicted   D. agreed

Key to *Words in Use*

1. A	2. C	3. A	4. D	5. B
6. A	7. B	8. A	9. D	10. C
11. A	12. B	13. B	14. A	15. D
16. A	17. C	18. D	19. C	20. D
21. B	22. B	23. A	24. A	25. C
26. D	27. D	28. B	29. D	30. A

第10单元 多义前缀(二)

Words in Context

Humans and the Earth

The environment is usually changed to benefit human life. Cars and roads make **transportation** fast and easy, factories make products that make our lives more comfortable, public services in cities like water treatment, electricity, and waste disposal make our lives more convenient. All of these advances, however, come with a significant environmental cost. Human activity does **dispassionate** damage to the Earth.

One of the main effects of human activity on an area is water pollution. Dumping waste materials from human activity into rivers and streams is popular because the waste seems to **disappear** downstream. The main sources of water pollution are factory waste, oil and gas runoff from highways, and untreated human waste. When this waste dumped into rivers, the water downstream and **underground** becomes undrinkable and unusable for agriculture, and also kills plant and animal life in the rivers.

Clean air and water is a prerequisite not only for human life, but also for all life on the planet. But air is now being polluted by modern transportation, notably gas-powered automobiles, as well as electrical generators that burn fossil fuels and pour polluting chemical waste into the air. This makes the air much less healthy to breathe. The air-borne pollution also falls back to the earth in the form of acid rain, which destroys plant life and human buildings.

Word Building

More Words with the Prefixes

前缀	释义	例词
dis-	表否定	dishonest, disorder, disappear, dispassionate, disorganized
	表过程逆转	discourage, disconnect, disarm, disproof
	表脱离，分开	disseminate, distract, discard, dismantle

（续表）

前缀	释义	例词
trans-	跨越两地	transect, transmit, transplant, transport, transatlantic, transcribe, transfer, transcontinental
	穿透	transparent, translucent
	改变，转变	transfigure, transform, transsexual, transvestite
under-	在……之下	underline, underground, undercurrent, undergraduate, underpass
	过低，不足	underestimate, undersized, underfed, underdevelopment, underage, undernourishment

1. dishonest: [dis'ɔnist] *a.* 不诚实的

分解记忆法：dis- (不) + honest (诚实的) = 不诚实的

【例句】The dishonest government official was publicly disgraced.

那个不诚实的政府官员被公开贬斥。

Inconsistencies in his testimony made it obvious that he was dishonest.

他证词不一致，很明显，他并不诚实。

常用派生词：dishonest→ dishonestly

2. disappear: [ˌdisə'piə] *v.* 不见；消失

分解记忆法：dis- (不) + appear (出现) = 不见，消失

【例句】All at once Phil disappeared.

菲尔突然不见了。

The sun disappeared behind a cloud.

太阳消失在云层后面。

3. discourage: [dis'kʌridʒ] *v.* 使气馁；阻碍

分解记忆法：dis- (表逆转) + courage (勇气) = 使气馁，阻碍

【例句】They tried to discourage their son from marrying the girl.

他们企图阻止儿子和那女子结婚。

His parents discouraged him from joining the air force.

他的父母亲劝他不要参加空军。

常用派生词：discourageable→ discourager→ discouragingly

4. disarm: [dis'ɑ:m] *v.* 解除武装；裁军

分解记忆法：dis- (表逆转) + arm (武装) = 解除武装

【例句】I felt angry, but her smile disarmed me.

我动气了，但她一笑，又将我的气儿给消了。

It is difficult to persuade them to disarm.

要说服他们放下武器是很难的。

5. **distract:** [diˈstrækt] *n.* 转移；分心

   分解记忆法：dis-（分开）+ tract（拉）= 转移，分心

   【例句】He was distracted between two objects.
   他被这两件东西所迷惑。
   Noise distracted the writer from his work.
   吵闹声使这位作者工作时注意力分散。

   常用派生词：distract→distractingly →distractive

6. **discard:** [disˈkɑːd] *vt.* 丢弃；抛弃

   分解记忆法：dis-（脱离）+ card（纸牌）= 掷出无用的纸牌

   【例句】She discarded a four, and picked up a king.
   她打出一张四点的牌，抓起一张K。
   Discarded food containers and bottles littered the streets.
   街上到处是丢弃的食品包装。

7. **transmit:** [trænzˈmit, træns-] *vt.* 播送；传送

   分解记忆法：trans-（跨越两地）+ mit（发送）= 播送，传送

   【例句】I'll transmit the money by special messenger.
   我将派专人前来送交该款。
   Parents transmit some of their characteristics to their children.
   父母把一些特有的素质遗传给儿女。

   常用派生词：transmit→ transmittable → transmission

8. **transport:** [ˈtrænspɔːt] *v. & n.* 运输

   分解记忆法：trans-（跨越两地）+ port（携带）= 运输

   【例句】Bicycles are a cheap and efficient form of transport.
   自行车是一种便宜但有效的交通工具。
   On hearing of the victory, the nation was transported with joy.
   听到胜利的消息，全国人民一片欢腾。

   常用派生词：transport→ transportable → transportability

9. **transfer:** [trænsˈfəː] *v.& n.* 迁移；调转；调任

   分解记忆法：trans-（跨越两地）+fer（带来）= 迁移

   【例句】He has transferred from the warehouse to the accountant's office.
   他已由仓库调到会计室任职。
   Her father transferred her to a better school.
   她父亲把她转到了一所更好的学校。

10. **transparent:** [trænsˈpeərənt] *a.* 透明的；明显的；清晰的

    分解记忆法：trans-（穿透）+ parent（出现）= 透明的

    【例句】No material is perfectly transparent.
    没有一种物质是完全透明的。

Her mother disapproves of her wearing transparent raincoat.

她母亲不赞成她穿透明的雨衣。

11. transfigure: [træns'figə] *v.* 使变形；使改观

分解记忆法：trans- (改变) + figure (形状) =使变形

【例句】As she gazed down at the baby, her face was transfigured with tenderness.

当她眼光落在孩子身上时，脸上现出慈爱的神态。

Hearing the news, she had a face transfigured with joy.

听到那个消息，她的脸因喜悦而容光焕发。

12. transform: [træns'fɔːm] *v.* 变形；变质

分解记忆法：trans- (转变) + form (形式) =变形

【例句】He knew that he could not transform society by one bugle blast.

他知道改造社会不能一蹴而就。

The situation has been greatly transformed.

形势已经大大改观。

常用派生词：transform→transformer→transformation

13. underline: [ˌʌndə'lain, 'ʌndərlain] *v.* 在……下面画线；强调；使突出

分解记忆法：under- (在……之下) + line (线) =在……下面画线

【例句】Strikes by prison officers underline the need for reform in our goals.

监狱工作人员罢工一事，突出地表明我们的目标亟须改革。

Underline all the sentences you do not know.

在你不懂的句子下面画一条线。

常用派生词：underline→ underlined→ underlining

14. underground: [ˌʌndə'graund] *a. & adv.* 地下的；秘密地

分解记忆法：under- (在……之下) + ground (地面) =地下的

【例句】He joined the underground to fight against the fascists.

他参加了地下组织与法西斯作战。

There is an underground room in the old house.

在老房子里有一个地下室。

15. underestimate: [ˌʌndər'estimeit] *v. & n.* 估计不足，低估

分解记忆法：under- (过低 不足) + estimate (评价) =估计不足 低估

【例句】Don't underestimate people.

别把人看扁了。

Don't underestimate him. He looks stupid but he has great intelligence.

别低估他，他看起来愚笨，其实很聪明。

常用派生词：underestimate→ underestimation

Words in Use

1. Inconsistencies in his testimony made it obvious that he was _____.
   A. lying   B. honest   C. untruthful   D. deceitful

2. Even when she is not being overtly _____, she tinkers with the truth.
   A. dishonest   B. lying   C. mendacious   D. honest

3. The traditional way of life has all but _____.
   A. vanished   B. faded away   C. missed   D. disappeared

4. Dinosaurs _____ millions of years ago.
   A. disappeared   B. became extinct C. vanished   D. discarded

5. A journalist should be a _____ reporter of fact.
   A. dispassionate B. passionate   C. right   D. justified

6. It is perfectly _____ that a prospective employer should want to know if you have a criminal record.
   A. reasonable   B. dispassionate   C. fair   D. legitimate

7. Parents should _____ their children from smoking.
   A. dishearten   B. discourage   C. dispirit   D. courage

8. My father was very _____ in me for choosing acting instead of a legal career.
   A. disillusioned B. discouraged   C. deflated   D. disappointed

9. With one movement, she _____ the man and pinned him against the wall.
   A. numbed   B. disarmed   C. disabled   D. cripple

10. A general strike _____ the coal industry.
    A. paralyzed   B. disarmed   C. immobilized   D. petrified

11. The slightest thing will _____ young children from getting on with their work.
    A. distract   B. disturb   C. bother   D. disrupt

12. He could not believe that one moment of foolishness could _____ his once happy marriage so drastically.
    A. distract   B. upset   C. bother   D. rock

13. These ideas have now been completely _____.
    A. disposed   B. scrapped   C. discarded   D. trashed

14. Please _____ these papers at once so that I can serve dinner.
    A. discard   B. remove   C. place   D. arrange

15. The motion is _____ from particle to particle, to a great distance.
    A. transmitted   B. borne   C. conveyed   D. carried

16. The city uses buses to _____ students to school.
    A. communicate   B. pass   C. transport   D. transmit

17. If you'll leave a message, I'll _____ it to him.
    A. convey   B. transport   C. transmit   D. carry
18. They were _____ to meet the great film star.
    A. enchanted   B. enraptured   C. transported   D. charmed
19. The train broke down so we _____ to a bus.
    A. transported   B. moved   C. transferred   D. switched
20. It was becoming increasingly _____ that he could no longer look after himself.
    A. opaque   B. apparent   C. lucid   D. transparent
21. The way the system works will be _____ to the user.
    A. transparent   B. translucent   C. airy   D. limpid
22. As she gazed down at the baby, her face was _____ with tenderness.
    A. metamorphosed   B. transmogrified   C. transformed   D. transfigured
23. He's _____ to Catholicism.
    A. changed   B. converted   C. transmuted   D. transfigured
24. Almost overnight, that sweet little child had _____ into an anti-social monster.
    A. transmogrified B. transfigured   C. transformed   D. converted
25. Strikes by prison officers _____ the need for reform in our goals.
    A. underlie   B. undermine   C. underline   D. underplay
26. The word "not" was heavily _____.
    A. emphasized   B. stressed   C. undergone   D. underlined
27. The ANC was forced to go _____ when its leaders were arrested.
    A. underlying   B. underground   C. underneath   D. surface
28. The sun's intense rays _____ the image on the horizon.
    A. transformed   B. varied   C. altered   D. distorted
29. He's 80 years old now and lives a very _____ life.
    A. secret   B. underground   C. secluded   D. intimate
30. I think you are _____ the importance to young people of a stable home life.
    A. understating   B. underestimating C. underage   D. underfeeding

Key to Words in Use

1. A	2. A	3. D	4. B	5. A
6. A	7. B	8. D	9. B	10. A
11. A	12. B	13. C	14. B	15. A
16. C	17. A	18. B	19. C	20. B
21. A	22. D	23. B	24. A	25. C
26. D	27. B	28. D	29. C	30. A

第2章 常用英语词汇后缀

第1单元 表示"人"的名词后缀

Words in Context

How to Learn English Vocabulary

Some **beginners** of English or even **graduates** from universities often complain that it is really hard to learn English vocabulary. Here are some vocabulary-learning strategies. You may find most of them extremely useful.

Contextualization: This means putting new vocabulary words into sentences to help you remember them and to test if you are using them correctly. You can use these sentences when talking to an English speaker to see if they understand, you can write these sentences in your learner portfolio for the **tutors** to see, or you can e-mail the tutors and ask them to check these words in your sentences.

Elaboration: This means relating new information to information you already know. For example, if you know the meaning of "information," it is easy to remember that the verb is "to inform," and that "**informative**" is an adjective, and that "an informant" is someone who gives information.

Inferencing: This means using available information to predict or guess the meanings of new vocabulary items. For example, if you know that you are reading about football, and you know that a field is often a large area covered in grass, then you can guess that a football field is a large, grassy, area for playing football.

Grouping: You can group words into different areas, such as words in the different courses you study. For example, business students could group vocabulary items into marketing vocabulary, accounting vocabulary and human resources vocabulary.

Word Building

More Words with the Suffixes Indicating Persona

后缀	释义	例词
-an, -er, -ese, -ean	某国或某地区的人	American, Chicagoan, Icelander, Chinese, European

（续表）

后缀	释义	例词
-er,-ian, -herd,-itor	具有某种职业的人	beautician, electrician, singer, worker, shepherd, competitor, servitor
-an, -arian, -ist	支持或信奉……的人，……主义者，……研究专家	republican, puritan, utilitarian, antiquarian, naturalist, materialist，biologist, zoologist
-ant,-ar, -ary, -ate, -ator, -eer, -ee, -ist,-or	行动者，做某事的人	informant, scholar, solitary, graduate, designator, dentist, cannoneer, translator, expellee
-ard, -art,-ie, -ster, -y	含有感情色彩的人	gamester, gangster, spinster, chorister，drunkard, coward, braggart, girlie, sweetie, missy, aunty
-enne, -ess, -ette, -ine, -ress, -rix , -trix	阴性名词	goddess, tragedienne, typette, heroine, tailoress, aviatrix, executrix
-nik	……人，……迷	citynik, computernik, filmnik, folknik
-ling	与某种食物或情况有关的人，具有某种性质的人	starveling, worldling, weakling
-ite	和……有关，属于……团体的人	cosmopolite, Tokyoite, Israelite
-ive	以形容词表示名词的后缀	captive, fugitive, native, relative

1.electrician: [iˌlekˈtriʃn] *n.* 电工；电器技师

　　分解记忆法： electric（电的）+ -ian（从事某种职业的人）= 电工

　　【例句】I think there is an electrical fault, and we have to find an electrician.

　　　　　我认为是电力出了故障，我们得请一位电工。

　　　　　After graduating from the high school, he became an electrician.

　　　　　毕业之后，他就当了一名电工技师。

　　常用派生词： electric → electrical → electricity → electrify

2.shepherd: [ˈʃepəd] *n.* 牧羊人，羊倌

　　分解记忆法： sheep（羊）+ -herd（管理家畜的人）= 牧羊者

　　【例句】There is a shepherd on the hill.

　　　　　山上有位牧羊人。

　　　　　There is a shepherd with a group of sheep.

　　　　　牧羊人赶着一群羊。

常用派生词：shepherd → shepherdess

3. beautician: [bjuːˈtiʃən] n. 美容师

分解记忆法：beauty(美丽)＋ -ian(从事某种职业的人)＝美容师

【例句】In order to give beauty treatment to your skin, you have to find a beautician.
为了使你的皮肤变得美丽，你得找一位美容师。

Nowadays to be a beautician is very popular.
当今从事美容师这一行业很流行。

常用派生词：beauty → beautiful → beautifully → beautify → beautician

4. puritan: [ˈpjuərɪtən] n. 清教徒

分解记忆法：pure(纯净的)＋ -an(支持或信奉……的人)＝清教徒

【例句】They have also been concerned to establish the existence of a puritan tradition.
他们还一直关心树立清教传统。

He is a devout puritan.
他是个虔诚的清教徒。

常用派生词：puritan → puritanical → puritanism

5. competitor: [kəmˈpetɪtə] n. 比赛者；竞争者；敌手

分解记忆法：compete(比赛，竞争)＋ -itor(从事某种职业的人)＝比赛者

【例句】The company's major competitor are all from Japan.
公司的主要竞争对手都是来自日本。

Two of the competitors became friends at the end of the competition.
比赛结束之后，其中的两个选手成了朋友。

常用派生词：compete→competition→competitive→competitiveness→competitor

6. servitor: [ˈsəːvɪtə(r)] n. 仆人；从仆

分解记忆法：service(服务)＋ -itor(从事某种职业的人)＝仆人

【例句】He was always her devoted servitor.
他无时不是她的虔诚的仆役。

Her father had been a servitor for all his life.
他的父亲一辈子都是个仆人。

常用派生词：serve → service → servitor

7. materialist: [məˈtɪərɪəlɪst] n. 物质主义者；实利主义者；唯物主义者

分解记忆法：material(材料；物质)＋ -ist(……主义者)＝物质主义者

【例句】He is a materialist.
他是个实利主义者。

As materialists, we do not put our faith in God but in the masses.
作为唯物主义者，我们不相信上帝，我们相信的是群众。

常用派生词：material → materialist → materialistic → materialize → materialism

8. naturalist: [ˈnætərəlist] *n.* 自然主义者；博物学者

　　分解记忆法：nature（自然）+ -ist（……主义者）= 自然主义者

　　【例句】The English naturalist W. H. Hudson was born in Argentina.

　　　　　英国博物学家W. H.哈得逊出生在阿根廷。

　　　　　Charles Darwin is a naturalist of evolution.

　　　　　查尔斯·达尔文是物种演化的博物学家。

　　常用派生词：nature → natural → naturalist

9. solitary: [ˈsɔlitəri] *n.* 隐居者，隐士

　　分解记忆法：solit-（单独）+-ary（行动者，做某事的人）= 隐居者

　　【例句】I'd like to be a solitary living in a place of social isolation.

　　　　　我想住在一个与世隔绝的地方，成为隐居者。

　　　　　He has been a solitary in the woodland for years.

　　　　　他住在林区，成为隐居者多年。

　　常用派生词：solitary →solitarily →solitariness

10. dentist: [ˈdentist] *n.* 牙医

　　分解记忆法：dent-（牙齿）+ -ist（……研究专家）= 牙医

　　【例句】I'm going to the dentist's tomorrow.

　　　　　我明天要去看牙医。

　　　　　It is money consuming to see a dentist.

　　　　　看牙医是件花钱的事儿。

　　常用派生词：dental →dentine →dentist →dentistry →dentures

11. cannoneer: [ˌkænəˈniə] *n.* 炮手

　　分解记忆法：cannon（大炮）+ -eer（表示做某事的人）= 炮手

　　【例句】The cannoneer had fired the blockhouse at once.

　　　　　炮兵一下子就射中了碉堡。

　　　　　To be a cannoneer is a dangerous thing.

　　　　　做炮手很危险。

　　常用派生词：cannon →cannoneer

12. gangster: [ˈɡæŋstə] *n.* 歹徒；盗匪

　　分解记忆法：gang（做坏事儿的一帮）+ -ster（含有感情色彩的人）= 歹徒

　　【例句】The gangsters ran into the bar and started shooting it up.

　　　　　歹徒们冲进酒吧胡乱扫射一通。

　　　　　Those gangsters commit all manners of crimes.

　　　　　那些歹徒们无恶不作。

13. spinster: [ˈspinstə] *n.* 未婚女性

　　分解记忆法：spin（纺线）+ -ster（含有感情色彩的人）= 未婚女性

　　【例句】Catherine is still a spinster.

凯瑟琳一直未婚，孑然一身。

The old spinster spent he days knitting and reading in her cozy cottage.

这位老姑娘在她舒适的小屋里编织读书，度过余生。

14. drunkard: [ˈdrʌŋkəd] *n.*

分解记忆法： drunk(喝醉了的) + -ard(含有感情色彩的人) = 酒鬼

【例句】The drunkard staggered along the street.

那醉汉趔趄着走在街上。

That drunkard died of alcohol intoxication.

那个醉汉死于酒精中毒。

常用派生词： drink → drunk → drunkard

15. tragedienne: [trəˌdʒiːdiˈen] *n.* 女悲剧演员

分解记忆法： tragedy(悲剧) + -enne(阴性名词) = 女悲剧演员

【例句】The tragedienne in that film got the best actress in Oscar.

那位女悲剧演员获得奥斯卡最佳女演员。

She successfully shaped a tragedienne image in that film.

她在那部电影中成功塑造了一个悲剧女演员的形象。

常用派生词： tragedy → tragedienne

16. aviatrix: [ˈeiviətriks] *n.* 女飞行员

分解记忆法： avi-(鸟) + -trix(阴性名词) = 女飞行员

【例句】To be an aviatrix is a matter of pride.

做一名女飞行员是件自豪的事。

She is the only aviatrix in her group.

她是团队中唯一的女飞行员。

17. filmnik: [ˈfilmnik] *n.* 影迷；电影爱好者

分解记忆法： film(电影) + -nik(……迷) = 影迷

【例句】He is a filmnik.

他是个影迷。

Many filmniks are waiting outside of the cinema to see this new film.

许多影迷正在影院外等着看这部新电影。

18. cosmopolite: [kɔzˈmɔpəlait] *n.* 世界公民

分解记忆法： cosmo-(宇宙) + -ite(和……有关的人) = 世界公民

【例句】We are all cosmopolites of the global village.

我们都是地球村的世界公民。

To be a cosmopolite means people should be polite to every country.

作为一名世界公民意味着要对每一个国家有礼。

19. captive: [ˈkæptiv] *n.* 俘虏

分解记忆法： cap-(拿，抓，握住) + -tive(以形容词表示名词的后缀) = 俘虏

【例句】The officers were held as captives for three months.

这些军官被当作俘虏关押达三个月之久。

Those captives passed the street in chains.

那些俘虏戴着锁链在街上走过。

常用派生词：captive →captivity →captor →capture

20. **fugitive:** [ˈfjuːdʒitiv] *n.* 逃亡者；亡命者

分解记忆法：fug-(逃走) + -ive (以形容词表示名词的后缀) = 逃亡者

【例句】The detective was killed together with the fugitive.

那个侦探和逃犯一起被杀死了。

He is a fugitive from justice.

他是个在逃的罪犯。

Words in Use

1. There is a break in the circuit. Please find a (n) _____.
   A. electrician　　　B. musician　　　C. beautician　　　D. magician

2. Whether Ingham is right or wrong, her supporters say _____ are trying unfairly to silence her.
   A. opponents　　　B. components　　　C. proponents　　　D. agents

3. The _____ expects the lenses to cost about a dollar a pair, about the same as conventional one-day disposable lenses.
   A. physic　　　B. physics　　　C. physicist　　　D. physician

4. Only in the past 20 years have _____ in language study realized that sign languages are unique—a speech of the hand.
   A. specialists　　　B. species　　　C. special　　　D. specialties

5. But college has never been able to work its _____ for everyone.
   A. magician　　　B. magnet　　　C. magic　　　D. magnetism

6. He was elected as a _____ to the annual conference.
   A. degenerate　　　B. advocate　　　C. apostate　　　D. delegate

7. Consumption has become a central _____ of life in industrial lands and is even embedded in social values.
   A. pillar　　　B. liar　　　C. solar　　　D. burglar

8. Is there enough oil beneath the Arctic National Wildlife _____ (ANWR) to help secure America's energy future?
   A. Refute　　　B. Refuge　　　C. Refugee　　　D. Refuse

9. Apple wants to stay in the high-price end of the personal computer market to finance research for even faster, more _____ computers.

A. sophisticated   B. philosophy   C. philosopher   D. sophomore
10. _____ is the land covered with grass and similar plants, suitable for grazing animals.
  A. Booster   B. Pasture   C. Paste   D. Poster
11. Only those who have the _____ to do simple things perfectly ever acquire the skill to do difficult things easily.
  A. patience   B. patient   C. impatient   D. compatible
12. A _____ is a person who has been forced to flee from danger.
  A. wanderer   B. refugee   C. resident   D. settler
13. She is the highest-paid _____ in Hollywood.
  A. hostess   B. princess   C. actress   D. witness
14. He wants to become a _____ , specializing in areas of treatment rather than surgery.
  A. dentist   B. surgeon   C. injector   D. physician
15. The police have called for more resources to help them fight against drug _____ .
  A. merchants   B. speculators   C. investors   D. deals
16. A brilliant _____, Palmer was probably the most accomplished pianist of her generation.
  A. engineer   B. chemist   C. mechanic   D. musician
17. She takes in _____ to make a bit of extra money.
  A. residents   B. migrants   C. inhabitants   D. lodgers
18. The _____ of various parties walked into the meeting room.
  A. managers   B. ambassadors   C. delegates   D. governors
19. A _____ is a fellow member of a profession, a staff, or an academic faculty.
  A. comrade   B. colleague   C. companion   D. partner
20. While being flown by a _____ amateur cyclist in 1963, the plane crashed on an airfield.
  A. champion   B. defender   C. protestor   D. conqueror
21. Now other _____ know how to design buildings to fit into the land.
  A. mechanics   B. carpenters   C. technicians   D. architects
22. The house _____ shook his head in disapproval of my proposal.
  A. performer   B. candidate   C. operator   D. agent
23. _____ is the general and most comprehensive term for one authorized to give legal advice to clients and to plead cases in a court of law.
  A. Attorney   B. Lawyer   C. Solicitor   D. Counselor
24. He was the _____ of the new law.
  A. politician   B. lawyer   C. attorney   D. architect
25. The impressionist movement was one of the _____ of abstract arts.
  A. ancestors   B. ambassadors   C. anchors   D. amateurs
26. The earliest _____ in the United States were not Europeans but the American Indians.
  A. residents   B. lodgers   C. customers   D. hostlers

27. Many television _____ seem to enjoy watching the program.
    A. spectators   B. audiences   C. viewers   D. lookers-on
28. During her illness she continued her school work with home _____ and returned in time for her exam.
    A. lecturers   B. professors   C. assistants   D. tutors
29. Lu Xun was one of the intellectual _____ in the 20th century.
    A. giants   B. monsters   C. dwarfs   D. masses
30. The good thing about her as a boss is that she treats us all as _____ .
    A. rivals   B. equals   C. opponents   D. inferiors

Key to *Words in Use*

1. A	2. A	3. C	4. A	5. C
6. D	7. A	8. B	9. A	10. B
11. A	12. B	13. C	14. D	15. D
16. D	17. D	18. C	19. B	20. A
21. D	22. D	23. B	24. D	25. A
26. A	27. C	28. D	29. A	30. B

第2单元　表示"缩小的名词"的后缀

Words in Context

Types of Pain Relief

Our Medical Center understands that unique circumstance of each patient and their complications. Our staff will work with you to find the most effective procedure or treatment for your relief. The following are the most common types of pain that our Medical Center treats.

Neck Pain

Often neck pain is caused by an auto accident, sports injury, or other traumatic injuries. Our Medical Center will work with our patients to understand the type of pain our patients are having. Treatment may include injections, selective nerve blocks, **facet** blocks and radio frequency.

Muscle Pain

Muscle pain is a normal experience for all of us; this could be blamed on a couple of reasons. **Muscle** pain can be due to overstretching the muscles or merely an advanced age. An effective muscle pain remedy may come from a number of methods. It is an effective way to have a hot shower or apply ice directly to the soreness.

Sciatica

Sciatica is the irritation of the sciatic nerve, a major nerve that passes down the back of each thigh. Sciatica typically causes pain that shoots down the back of one thigh or **buttock**. Treatment for sciatica focuses on relieving pressure and inflammation. Typical sciatica treatments include anti-inflammatory medication and injections. Our Medical Center can provide these therapies in an outpatient bases, through their office.

Word Building

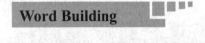

More Words with the Suffixes

后缀	释义	例词
-cle	小	pinnacle, particle, icicle, speckle, denticle
-en, -in		kitten, chicken, maiden, elfin

（续表）

后缀	释义	例词
-et,-ette	小	cigarette, kitchenette, cabinet, islet, arboret, facet, floweret
-ling		duckling, sapling, gosling, underling
-let		booklet, droplet, leaflet, streamlet, eaglet, outlet
-el		damsel, model, satchel
-kin		cannikin, lambkin, manikin
-(c)ule		animalcule, globule, granule, molecule, monticule
-ock		bullock, hillock, hummock
-ie(or –y)		birdie, doggie(doggy)
-aster		criticaster, medicaster, poetaster

1. particle: [ˈpɑːtikl] *n.* 小部分；极小量；粒子

　　分解记忆法：part（部分）+ -cle（缩小）= 小部分

　【例句】We can see the dust particles floating in the air clearly.

　　　　　我们可以很清楚地看到空气中的灰尘颗粒。

　　　　　There wasn't a particle of truth in what he said.

　　　　　他说的没有一点真话。

2. icicle: [ˈaisikəl] *n.* 冰柱，垂冰

　　分解记忆法：ice（冰）+-cle（缩小）=冰柱

　【例句】As water continues to drip, the icicle grows.

　　　　　随着水不断下滴，冰柱的体积也慢慢增大。

　　　　　This passionless girl was like an icicle in the sunshine.

　　　　　这个冷淡的姑娘就像是在阳光下的冰柱。

　常用派生词：icicle → icily

3.follicle: [ˈfɔlikl] *n.* 小囊；滤泡

　　分解记忆法：follis（口袋）+ -cle（缩小）= 小囊

　【例句】A follicle is one of the small holes in the skin that hairs grow from.

　　　　　毛囊就是皮肤上长出毛发的一个个小洞。

　　　　　Some kinds of trichomadesis are caused by follicle inflammation.

　　　　　一些脱发是由毛囊炎症引起的。

4.chicken: [ˈtʃikən] *n.* 小鸡；胆小；害怕

　　分解记忆法：chick（鸡）+ -en（缩小）= 小鸡

　【例句】This soup tastes of chicken.

　　　　　这汤里有鸡肉的味道。

　　　　　Don't be a chicken.

不要害怕。

常用派生词：chick →chicken

5. maiden: [ˈmeidən] *n.* 少女；处女；年轻未婚女子

分解记忆法：maid(侍女；女仆)＋-en(缩小)＝少女

【例句】She resumed her maiden name after the divorce.
她离婚后重新使用婚前的姓名。

Several maidens were invited to attend her wedding.
好几个少女被邀请去参加她的婚礼。

常用派生词：maid →maiden →maidenly

6. violin: [ˌvaiəˈlin] *n.* 小提琴

分解记忆法：viola(中提琴)＋-in(缩小)＝小提琴

【例句】He plays the violin for the fun of it.
他拉小提琴只是为了好玩。

The violin has a poor inflection.
这把小提琴的音调不准。

常用派生词：violin →violinist

7. cigarette: [ˌsigəˈret] *n.* 小雪茄；香烟

分解记忆法：cigar(雪茄)＋-ette(缩小)＝小雪茄

【例句】He asked me if I had a cigarette lighter with me.
他问我身上是否带着打火机。

My grandfather often coughs because of cigarette.
因为吸烟的缘故，我父亲经常咳嗽。

常用派生词：cigar →cigarette

8. kitchenette: [ˌkitʃiˈnet] *n.* 小厨房

分解记忆法：kitchen(厨房)＋-ette(缩小)＝小厨房

【例句】He rented a furnished apartment with a kitchenette and bathroom.
一种提供给客人小厨房和浴室的公寓。

My room had a refrigerator, an air conditioner and even a kitchenette.
我的房间有冰箱、空调甚至一个小厨房。

常用派生词：kitchen →kitchenette

9. duckling: [ˈdʌkliŋ] *n.* 小鸭子，幼鸭

分解记忆法：duck(鸭子)＋-ling(缩小)＝小鸭子

【例句】The duckling followed its mother everywhere.
小鸭子跟着鸭妈妈到处走。

That beauty once was an ugly duckling.
那美女以前是个丑小鸭。

常用派生词：duck → duckling → ducky

10. **underling:** [ˈʌndəlɪŋ] *n.* 部下，下僚，下属

   分解记忆法：under(处于……之下)+-ling(缩小)=职位低下的人

   【例句】The professor smiles sagely at the underling.

   教授狡黠地对着下属笑了笑。

   When you criticize a colleague or underling, you're spreading negative energy.

   当您指责同事或下属的时候，您也正在传播负面影响。

11. **booklet:** [ˈbuklɪt] *n.* 小册子

   分解记忆法：book(书)+-let(缩小)=小册子

   【例句】Recent changes in the tax law are clearly set out in the booklet.

   在那本小册子里清楚地描述了近来税务法的变更情况。

   This booklet is delicately made.

   这本小册子做得很精致。

   常用派生词：book →booklet

12. **droplet:** [ˈdrɒplɪt] *n.* 小滴

   分解记忆法：drop(滴)+-let(缩小)=小滴

   【例句】The average velocity of droplet swarm is much different from that of a single drop.

   测试表明液滴群的浮升速度同单液滴有显著不同。

   The scientists say the droplet itself becomes a little laboratory that can do things like pump, separate and mix.

   科学家说，滴液本身变成了小型实验室，可以抽吸、分离和混合。

   常用派生词：drop →droplet

13. **leaflet:** [ˈliːflɪt] *n.* 小叶；传单

   分解记忆法：leaf(叶子)+ -let(缩小)= 小叶

   【例句】It's better for you to scan the leaflet, and then make the decision.

   你最好先看看说明书，再作决定。

   He picked up a leaflet about care of the teeth.

   他拾起一张宣传保护牙齿的传单。

   常用派生词：leaf →leaflet

14. **streamlet:** [ˈstriːmlɪt] *n.* 小溪，细流

   分解记忆法：stream(流；水流)+ -let(缩小)= 小溪

   【例句】A streamlet spread out every here and there.

   到处可见小溪流淌。

   The car weaves through the villages, crosses the canyon, and then runs along a streamlet.

   小汽车迂回穿过村庄，翻越峡谷，沿着一条小溪行驶。

   常用派生词：stream →streamlet

15. cannikin: [ˈkænikin] *n.* 小罐，小杯

分解记忆法：can(金属罐) + -kin(缩小) = 小罐

【例句】Drinking one cannikin of vinegar can help you digest.
喝一小杯醋，就可以帮助你消化。
One cannikin once, twice a day.
每次一小杯，一日两次。

常用派生词：can → cannikin

16. lambkin: [ˈlæmkin] *n.* 小羊；好孩子，乖宝宝

分解记忆法：lamb(羊羔) + -kin(缩小) = 小羊

【例句】In my childhood, he is a lambkin boy who seldom brings trouble and worries to his parents.
在我童年记忆中，他一直是一个比较懂事的孩子，很少惹事也很少让父母担心。
He is as frisky as a lambkin.
他像羔羊一样活泼。

常用派生词：lamb → lambkin

17. model: [ˈmɔdl] *n.* 模特

分解记忆法：mode(方式，风格) + -el(缩小) = 模特

【例句】She is a world-famous model.
她是世界著名模特。
She has dreamt of being a model since she was a little girl.
她从儿时开始就梦想成为一名模特。

18. animalcule: [ˌænəˈmælkjul] *n.* 极微生物；微动物

分解记忆法：animal(动物) + -cule(缩小) = 极微生物

【例句】It kills the bacteria and other animalcule in the water by ultraviolet radiation.
它利用紫外线辐射消灭水中的细菌和其他微生物。
I hope for an opportunity to study in the area of animalcule more comprehensively.
我希望自己有机会在微生物领域进行更全面的学习。

常用派生词：animal → animalcule

19. globule: [ˈglɔbjul] *n.* 小球体（水珠；血珠；丸药）

分解记忆法：globe(球) + -ule(缩小) = 极小的球体

【例句】After the thermometer was broken, there were many globules of mercury on the floor.
体温计打碎后，许多细小的水银珠散落在地板上。
In the morning, there are many globules of water on the grassland.
早晨，草地上有许多水珠。

20.**molecule:** [ˈmɔlikjuːl] *n.* 分子；微粒

分解记忆法：mole(堆)+-cule(缩小)=分子

【例句】This system can turn the DNA molecule into an RNA molecule.
这种机制能将脱氧核糖核酸分子转变为核糖核酸分子。
Each molecule has its specific properties and functions.
每个分子都有其特定的性质和功能。

Words in Use

1. Some plants have neither root nor _____.
   A. leaflet   B. leafage   C. leaf   D. deaf
2. The _____ is not quite in tune with the piano.
   A. violet   B. violation   C. violin   D. violence
3. Every month he will go to the log _____ on the small island and stay there for 2 days.
   A. jail   B. cave   C. cabin   D. cell
4. Rain and heat are _____ in growing plants.
   A. components   B. particles   C. ingredients   D. factors
5. Over 200,000 Japanese people were killed or wounded when two _____ bombs were exploded.
   A. particle   B. molecule   C. atom   D. electron
6. We made these figures by pouring plaster into animal-shaped plastic _____.
   A. models   B. moulds   C. mules   D. moods
7. Much of her _____ as a writer was first published in magazines.
   A. output   B. outlet   C. outlook   D. outset
8. The _____ of New England make farming different.
   A. hillocks   B. hillsides   C. hilltops   D. hilts
9. I asked him to go skiing with me, but he is a _____. He's afraid he might get hurt.
   A. chickadee   B. chief   C. chicken   D. cherub
10. Mrs. Silver's _____ name was Rodriguez.
    A. maid   B. maiden   C. main   D. magpie
11. We keep dishes and canned food in the _____ over the kitchen sink.
    A. cables   B. caches   C. cachets   D. cabinets
12. A jeweler acts _____ in a rough diamond.
    A. fables   B. fabrics   C. facets   D. facades
13. The machine crushes salt into _____.
    A. grapes   B. globules   C. granules   D. granites

14. That _____ of government policy was put in jail.
    A. critter   B. criticaster   C. cricket   D. crockery
15. The _____ are swimming close to their mother.
    A. ducklings   B. ducts   C. duchesses   D. dubs
16. She lit a _____, without noticing the sign "No Smoking."
    A. cinder   B. cinch   C. cigarette   D. chute
17. I couldn't eat all of my meal, so I asked the waiter for a _____ bag.
    A. dogged   B. dog-eared   C. dodgy   D. doggie
18. Some hotel rooms have _____, but not big ones.
    A. kitchenettes   B. kitting   C. kingpins   D. kingfishes
19. Our cat just gave birth to four _____.
    A. kiwis   B. klutzes   C. kittens   D. knapsacks
20. From the _____ of the negotiations, it was clear that it would be hard for the two sides to reach an agreement.
    A. outbreak   B. outlook   C. outset   D. outlet
21. The grand old church had many small _____ and one large one.
    A. pinochle   B. pockets   C. parcels   D. pinnacles
22. _____ of sand cover the road.
    A. Participle   B. Particles   C. Partial   D. Partition
23. Why are those eggs that you bought yesterday _____?
    A. speckled   B. specialized   C. spectacular   D. speculated
24. His wife complains that her husband is an _____.
    A. iceberg   B. icepack   C. icicle   D. icon
25. The structure of _____ can be seen under an electron microscope.
    A. modules   B. models   C. molecules   D. miracles
26. _____ of water fell from the umbrella to the floor.
    A. Globes   B. Global   C. Globules   D. Globs
27. The hero in an old silent movie always saves the _____ in distress.
    A. damsel   B. damper   C. dandy   D. dander
28. I felt a few _____ of rain on my shoulder.
    A. dropouts   B. droplets   C. drop-offs   D. drudges
29. They had a picnic near a _____ that ran down the mountain.
    A. street   B. straw   C. strait   D. streamlet
30. A large central park called Stanley Park includes a zoo, gardens, _____ and aquarium!
    A. arboret   B. arboretum   C. arbiter   D. archery

Key to *Words in Use*

1. B	2. C	3. C	4. D	5. C
6. B	7. A	8. A	9. C	10. B
11. D	12. C	13. C	14. B	15. A
16. C	17. D	18. A	19. C	20. C
21. D	22. B	23. A	24. A	25. C
26. C	27. A	28. B	29. D	30. B

第3单元 表示抽象意义的名词后缀

Words in Context

Lantern Festival

The Lantern Festival falls on the 15th day of the 1st lunar month, usually in February or March in the Gregorian calendar. As early as the Western Han Dynasty, it had become a festival with great **significance**.

This day's important activity is watching lanterns. Throughout the Han Dynasty, Buddhism flourished in China. One emperor heard that Buddhist monks would watch sarira, or remains from the cremation of Buddha's body, and light lanterns to worship Buddha on the 15th day of the 1st lunar month, so he ordered to light lanterns in the imperial palace and temples to show respect to Buddha on this day. Later, the Buddhist rite developed into a grand festival among common people and its **influence** expanded from the Central Plains to the whole China.

Till today, the lantern festival is still held each year around the country. Lanterns of various shapes and sizes are hung in the streets. People eat yuanxiao, or rice dumplings, on this day, so it is also called the "Yuanxiao Festival." Yuanxiao also has another name, tangyuan. They are small dumpling balls made of glutinous rice flour with rose petals, sesame, bean paste, jujube paste, walnut meat, dried fruit, sugar and edible oil as filling. Tangyuan can be boiled, fried or steamed. It tastes sweet and delicious. What's more, tangyuan in Chinese has a similar pronunciation with "tuanyuan," meaning reunion. So people eat them to denote **union**, **harmony** and **happiness** for the family.

Word Building

More Words with the Suffixes

后缀	释义	例词
-age	表示性质、状态、情况	courage, passage, marriage
-ance, -ancy		appearance, attendance, vacancy, pregnancy
-ence, -ency		confidence, absence, decency, efficiency
-cy		accuracy
-ability, -ibility		capability, reliability, feasibility, compatibility

（续表）

后缀	释义	例词
-hood		falsehood, likelihood, livelihood
-ness		happiness, madness
-ice, -ise		cowardice, service, treatise
-al		approval, removal, refusal
-ion, -sion, -tion		coronation, submission
-ment, -mony（-ment 变化型）	表示行为、动作的结果	banishment, harmony
-ure		departure, exposure, pressure
-ship		scholarship, hardship
-t, -th	表示抽象的概念	restraint, thrift, growth, strength
-itude		altitude, aptitude, gratitude
-cracy	表示权力、统治、政府、政体	democracy, autocracy, theocracy
-ism, -asm	表示学说、主义、信条	Buddhism, optimism, hedonism, enthusiasm
-ship	表示关系、身份	friendship, fellowship
-ic(s)	表示学术	physic, electronics, optics
-ing	通常由动词转变而来	blessing, bearing, aging
-(i)um	多用于元素的名称	aluminum, barium, petroleum

1. **courage:** [ˈkʌrɪdʒ] *n.* 胆量；勇气

    分解记忆法：cor-(心脏)+-age(性质)=胆量

    【例句】She showed great courage throughout her illness.

    她在生病期间表现了极大的勇气。

    Driving again after his accident must have taken a lot of courage.

    他事故后再驾车一定需要很大的勇气。

    常用派生词：courage →courageous →encourage →discourage

2. **appearance:** [əˈpɪərəns] *n.* 出现；外表，外貌

    分解记忆法：appear(出现，表露)+-ance(状态)=出现

    【例句】He gives the appearance of being confident, but actually he isn't.

    他表面看起来很自信，但实际上并非如此。

    Don't judge people by their appearance.

    最好不要以貌取人。

    常用派生词：appear →appearance →disappear

3. vacancy: [ˈveikənsi] *n.* 空缺；空地

　　分解记忆法： vacant(空着的)+-ancy(性质、状态)=空缺

【例句】Do you have any vacancy right now?

　　　　你这儿现在有空缺的位置吗？

　　　　John is to fill the vacancy on the Education Bureau.

　　　　约翰要填补教育局的空缺。

　　常用派生词： vacate →vacant →vacancy

4. prudency: [ˈpru:dənsi] *n.* 谨慎

　　分解记忆法： prudent(谨慎的)+-ency(性质)=谨慎

【例句】Confucius thinks prudency must be exercised on three things, namely, abstinence, war and illness.

　　　　孔子认为必须谨慎处理三件事情，即斋戒、战争和疾病。

　　　　Prudency can be one of the traits of characters that you own.

　　　　谨慎是你应该具有的品格之一。

　　常用派生词： prude →prudent →prudential →prudence →prudery

5. absence: [ˈæbsəns] *n.* 缺乏；缺席；不存在

　　分解记忆法： absent(缺乏的)+-ence(情况)=缺乏

【例句】Absence makes the heart grow fonder.

　　　　久别情更深。

　　　　Miss Li will be in charge during my absence.

　　　　我不在的时候会由李小姐负责。

　　常用派生词： absent →absence →absently

6. accuracy: [ˈækjurəsi] *n.* 精确性，准确性

　　分解记忆法： accurate(精确的)+-cy(性质)=精确性

【例句】I wasn't convinced about the accuracy of the treatise.

　　　　我并不确信此篇论文的准确性。

　　　　He's a man of accuracy and strict method.

　　　　他是个精细而严谨的人.

　　常用派生词： accurate →accuracy →accurately

7. capability: [ˌkeipəˈbiliti] *n.* 能力；性能；才能

　　分解记忆法： capable(有能力的)+-ability(性质)=能力

【例句】Chomsky thinks that children are born with language capability.

　　　　乔姆斯基认为儿童生来就有语言能力。

　　　　Simultaneous translation is beyond my capability.

　　　　同声传译不是我力所能及的。

　　常用派生词： capable →capably →capability

8. feasibility: [ˌfiːzəˈbiliti] *n.* 可行性

分解记忆法： feasible（可行的）+-ibility（性质）=可行性

【例句】Before this, you must consider whether this is a feasibility study.
在此之前，你必须考虑这是否是一项可行性研究。

The simulation results of key modules show the feasibility of the system design.
对关键模块的仿真结果证明了系统设计的可行性。

常用派生词： feasible →feasibility

9. emptiness: [ˈemptinis] *n.* 空虚；无知

分解记忆法： empty（空着的）+-ness（通常将形容词变为名词）=空虚

【例句】She felt emptiness in her heart when he left.
他走后，她的心里感觉空荡荡的。

The silence and the emptiness of the desert make me feel lonely.
沙漠的寂静和空旷使我感到孤单。

常用派生词： empty → emptiness

10. treatise: [ˈtriːtis] *n.* 论文

分解记忆法： treat（对待）+-ise（性质）=论文

【例句】Recently, he has written a treatise on medical ethics.
最近他完成了一部论述医学伦理的专著。

Your feedback is helping me to improve this treatise.
你们的反馈帮助我改进这篇论文。

11. coronation: [ˌkɔrəˈneiʃn] *n.* 加冕；加冕礼

分解记忆法： corona-（王冠）+ -tion（状态）= 加冕

【例句】The ceremony at which someone is officially made king or queen is called coronation.
加冕典礼就是正式赋予某人国王或女王权力的仪式。

She is portrayed wearing her coronation robes.
给她画的是她穿着加冕礼服的像。

常用派生词： coronate →coronation

12. banishment: [ˈbæniʃmənt] *n.* 放逐，驱逐；充军

分解记忆法： banish（驱逐出境）+ -ment（状态）= 放逐

【例句】Qu Yuan suffered banishment as the victim of a court intrigue.
屈原成为朝廷中钩心斗角的牺牲品，因而遭到驱逐。

His banishment shocked us all.
他被驱逐使我们很震惊。

常用派生词： banish →banishment

13. **harmony:** [ˈhɑːməni] *n.* 协调，和谐；和睦

　　分解记忆法：harmonious(协调的)+ -mony(状态)= 协调

　　【例句】Your suggestion is not in harmony with the aims of this project.
　　　　　你的建议与本项目的目标不符。

　　　　　She always works in perfect harmony with her colleagues.
　　　　　她与同事共事总是十分融洽。

　　常用派生词：harmonize →harmony →harmonious

14. **pressure:** [ˈpreʃə] *n.* 压力；压迫

　　分解记忆法：press(压，压迫)+ -ure(状态)= 压力

　　【例句】Mary only agreed to go under great pressure from her parents.
　　　　　玛丽是在父母强大的压力下才答应去的。

　　　　　The water pressure may need adjusting.
　　　　　水压可能需要调整。

　　常用派生词：press →pressure →pressurize

15. **hardship:** [ˈhɑːdʃip] *n.* 艰难，困苦

　　分解记忆法：hard(艰难的)+-ship(抽象概念)=艰难

　　【例句】He had ever experienced a time of great economic hardship.
　　　　　他曾经历过经济极度困难的时期。

　　　　　People can endure amazing hardship if they receive support from others.
　　　　　当人们从他人那里得到支持时可以忍受惊人的困境。

16. **hedonism:** [ˈhiːdənizəm] *n.* 享乐主义

　　分解记忆法：hedonic(享乐的)+ism(信条，主义)=享乐主义

　　【例句】Hedonism has made the desire limitless.
　　　　　享乐主义使欲望变得没有边界。

　　　　　He is one of the advocators of hedonism.
　　　　　他是享乐主义的提倡者之一。

　　常用派生词：hedonist →hedonism →hedonistic

17. **enthusiasm:** [ɪnˈθjuːziæzəm] *n.* 热情；热心

　　分解记忆法：enthusiast(热衷者，渴慕者)+-asm(状态)=热情

　　【例句】Although he was a beginner, he played with great enthusiasm.
　　　　　虽然他是个新手，但演奏时却充满了激情。

　　　　　His advancement to the position of manager was greeted with enthusiasm.
　　　　　他被提拔为经理，大家都为之欢呼。

　　常用派生词：enthuse →enthusiasm → enthusiast →enthusiastic

18. **falsehood:** [ˈfɔːlshud] *n.* 错误；虚伪

　　分解记忆法：false(错误的，虚伪的)+ -hood(状态)= 错误

　　【例句】This is a bald falsehood.

这是赤裸裸的谎言。

Once you are clear-headed enough, you can tell truth and falsehood by yourself.

你一旦足够清醒，就能自己判断真理和谬误。

19. fellowship: [ˈfeləʃip] *n.* 伙伴关系

分解记忆法：fellow(家伙，会员)+-ship(关系，身份)=伙伴关系

【例句】A close fellowship is developed among them.

他们之间建立了密切的伙伴关系。

We are looking forward to having a good time of fellowship.

我们十分期待与你们有一个美好的时光！

20. aging: [ˈeidʒiŋ] *n.* 老化；成熟的过程

分解记忆法：age(变旧，成熟)+-ing(通常用于将动词转为名词)=老化

【例句】When will we prove that human aging can really be repaired?

我们什么时候能证明人类老化真的能被修复？

Many countries in the world have stepped into the aging society.

世界上许多国家已经步入老龄化社会。

常用派生词：age →aging→aged

21. petroleum: [piˈtrəuliəm] *n.* 石油

分解记忆法：petr-(岩石)+-oleum(油)=石油

【例句】This factory produces many petroleum-based products.

这个工厂生产许多石油产品。

Any new source of energy will be welcome, as there is a shortage of petroleum.

由于石油短缺，任何一种新能源都会受欢迎。

Words in Use

1. The research shows the ____ distance is about 20 meters.
   A. optimum   B. option   C. optimism   D. optimize

2. This _____ stuck in my mind because it confirmed my growing belief that children are changing.
   A. incidence   B. coincidence   C. accident   D. incident

3. The dictionary meaning of the term "associate" is "colleague";"friend;" ____."
   A. companion   B. accompany   C. company   D. corporation

4. Their _____ and analysis occupied scientists for years and led to a five-volume report, the last volume being published in 1895.
   A. classic   B. classical   C. classification D. classify

5. Believe it or not, optical ____ can cut highway crashes.
   A. allusion   B. illusion   C. delusion   D. elusion

6. C is for the ____ way you do your jobs.
   A. conscious   B. consciousness   C. conscience   D. conscientious
7. Fever is one of the characteristic ____ of the flu for all ages.
   A. feasts   B. defeat   C. feasible   D. features
8. Today, a perfectly good _____, capable of servicing hundreds of thousands of homes, sits rusting.
   A. fiber   B. facility   C. faculty   D. fabric
9. Specially, Conrad believes that many of the brain's capabilities stem from the pattern-recognition ____ of the individual molecules that make up each brain cell.
   A. efficiency   B. proficiency   C. sufficiency   D. deficiency
10. Yet it is an observation made so frequently that it deserves ____.
    A. commerce   B. commence   C. comment   D. commend
11. Our ____ with thinness is also fueled by health concerns.
    A. cession   B. confession   C. obsession   D. recession
12. One problem with the banned model is that the tubes connecting it to an external power source created a passage for ____.
    A. infection   B. affection   C. effect   D. defect
13. We all have ____ breath at one time or another.
    A. offence   B. offensive   C. defend   D. offend
14. As you get older your ____ towards death changes.
    A. altitude   B. aptitude   C. attitude   D. latitude
15. Her mother's ____ exacerbated the difficulties in their marriage.
    A. inference   B. interference   C. interface   D. intervene
16. You can teach your dog its subordinate role by teaching it to show ____ to you.
    A. demission   B. permission   C. submission   D. admission
17. The information revolution will touch every facet of _____, publication, distribution and reading.
    A. proposition   B. disposition   C. composition   D. imposition
18. On the positive side, emotional ____ may respond to a consumer's real concerns.
    A. removal   B. proposals   C. disposal   D. appeals
19. The computer extends this development to _____ and replace some aspects of the mind of human beings by electronic methods.
    A. instrument   B. equipment   C. appliance   D. supplement
20. California is the strictest, with a ____ driver prohibited from carrying any passenger under 20 for the first 6 months.
    A. invoice   B. advice   C. device   D. novice
21. Man's earliest ____ were carved from stone bone.

A. devices   B. implements   C. appliances   D. equipments

22. Nowadays, housework has been made easier and easier by electrical ____.

   A. mechanism   B. instruments   C. appliances   D. facilities

23. Modern medicine has great ____ to the health and welfare of mankind.

   A. distributions   B. attributions   C. contributions   D. substitutions

24. He couldn't overcome the ____ to take the money.

   A. suspicion   B. passion   C. emotion   D. temptation

25. The robin keeps other birds off——that's his ____.

   A. territory   B. circumstances   C. environment   D. surroundings

26. We apologize for the interruption to our _____ this afternoon, which was caused by an electrical fault.

   A. missions   B. commissions   C. permissions   D. transmissions

27. Evidence suggested that the AIDS _____ was spreading very quickly among the heterosexual community.

   A. germ   B. organism   C. virus   D. bacterium

28. The naughty boy richly deserves ____.

   A. whiling   B. whipping   C. whispering   D. whistling

29. In the face of danger, he showed great ____.

   A. courage   B. passage   C. average   D. luggage

30. The corporation offered to send us samples on ____.

   A. proposal   B. approval   C. removal   D. rival

Key to *Words in Use*

1. A	2. D	3. A	4. C	5. B
6. D	7. D	8. B	9. B	10. C
11. C	12. A	13. B	14. C	15. B
16. C	17. C	18. D	19. D	20. D
21. B	22. C	23. C	24. D	25. A
26. D	27. C	28. B	29. A	30. B

第4单元 表示集合名词的后缀

Words in Context

Your Laundry Can Make You Sick

A research has shown that your **laundry** can make you sick because of many illness-causing germs that lurk in your clothes.

Many people believe that a spin in a washing machine turns dirty clothes sparkly clean. But according to a study by Charles Gerba, household washers contain a shocking amount of bacteria. In his study, Gerba found that more than 60 percent of the machines contained bacteria associated with human or animal wastes. One type of the bacteria can even cause people to develop diarrhea. To prevent the bacteria from spreading from one laundry load to people, Gerba recommends separating underwear from the rest of the laundry and washing the load with germ-killing bleach.

Maybe you are shocked by the findings, but then you will face a dilemma: you don't have enough clothes to do separate loads of colored and white clothes, but to use strong chemical bleach in your mixed load of wash could ruin the colored clothes. Then how can you do the laundry? Don't worry, a teenage girl Aarthi from Colorado has the same dilemma as yours, however, she tries her best to think if there are natural antibacterial agents that could serve as alternatives to harsh bleach. That idea sparked a **science** project. Then she conducted the experiment several times. She did the same experiments in the **neighborhood**. Finally, she found that grapefruit seed extract and tea tree oil eliminated all seven types of bacteria found in the dirty underwear. Aarthi's germ-busting experiment earned her a spot as a national finalist of the Discovery Channel Young Scientist Challenge 2006.

Word Building

More Words with the Suffixes

后缀	释义	例词
-age	表示集合名词	baronage, foliage, peerage, plumage, baggage, tonnage, cottage, teenage, mileage, luggage, average

（续表）

后缀	释义	例词
-ary	表示集合名词	dictionary, vocabulary, missionary, glossary, commentary
-dom		newspaperdom, officialdom, gangsterdom
-hood		neighborhood, womanhood, spinsterhood
-ing		clothing, wearing
-ry		cavalry, gentry, machinery, poultry, scenery, ministry, shrubbery, peasantry, poetry, laundry, artistry

1. **baronage:** [ˈbærənɪdʒ] *n.* 男爵的总称；贵族的总称

    分解记忆法：baron（男爵）+ -age（表示集合）= 男爵的总称

    【例句】John had learned that Monarchy, as reconstructed by his father, and baronage were natural enemies.

    约翰已经看出由他父亲重建的君主统治跟贵族阶层是天然仇敌。

    His family is no more than a downfallen baronage.

    他的家庭只不过是一个没落的贵族。

    常用派生词：baron → baronage

2. **foliage:** [ˈfəuliidʒ] *n.* 叶子；树叶

    分解记忆法：folium（叶子）+ -age（表示集合）=（总称）叶子

    【例句】He crouched down among the tangled foliage.

    他蹲下藏在乱叶丛中。

    We carried armfuls of foliage to the bonfire.

    我们给篝火添了几抱枝叶。

3. **peerage:** [ˈpiərɪdʒ] *n.* 贵族阶级；贵族地位

    分解记忆法：peer（贵族）+ -age（表示集合）=（全体）贵族

    【例句】Sir Peter was raised to the peerage.

    彼得爵士被封为贵族。

    The king raised his general to the peerage for winning the war.

    由于赢得了这场战争，国王封他的将军为贵族。

    常用派生词：peer → peerage

4. **plumage:** [ˈpluːmɪdʒ] *n.* 鸟类羽毛；翅膀

    分解记忆法：plume（羽毛）+ -age（表示集合）= 鸟类羽毛

    【例句】Have you seen the brightly-colored plumage of tropical birds?

    你见过热带鸟类色彩斑斓的羽毛吗？

    Some plumage dropped from the bird.

    从鸟身上掉下来几根羽毛。

5. baggage: [ˈbægidʒ] *n.* 行李

分解记忆法：bag(包) + -age(表示集合) = 行李

【例句】Our baggage has cleared customs.
我们的行李已通过海关检查。

He deposited his baggage in my office and went out to lunch.
他把行李存放在我的办公室里然后出去吃午饭。

常用派生词：bag → baggage

6. tonnage: [ˈtʌnidʒ] *n.* 吨位；总吨数

分解记忆法：ton(吨) + -age(表示集合) = 吨位

【例句】The tonnage of the ship is 25.
这条船的登记吨位为25吨。

They want to double the tonnage of ships the port currently handles.
他们希望把这个港口目前的船只吞吐量吨位提高一倍。

常用派生词：ton → tonnage

7. cottage: [ˈkɔtidʒ] *n.* 小屋；村舍

分解记忆法：cot(小屋) + -age(表示集合) = 小屋

【例句】He built a cottage near the sea.
他在海边建了个小屋。

Love can turn a cottage into a golden palace.
爱情可以使小屋变成金碧辉煌的宫殿。

8. teenage: [ˈtiːneidʒ] *n.* 青少年；十几岁时期

分解记忆法：teen(少年) + -age(表示集合) = 青少年

【例句】The trouble with being parents of teenage children is that once you lose your grip, they can make life miserable for everyone.
做十几岁孩子的父母亲所碰到的麻烦是，一旦管教不当，他们可能使大家的生活都很痛苦。

He has a teenage boy who makes him feel frustrated.
他有个十几岁的儿子，这让他感到很苦恼。

常用派生词：teen → teenage → teenager

9. spinsterhood: [ˈspinstəhud] *n.* 独身，未婚

分解记忆法：spinster(未婚女人) + -hood(表示集合) = 独身

【例句】The world had made up its mind about her oddity in her spinsterhood.
对于她这种古怪的老姑娘，外面的世界早已经有了固定的成见。

He was her last chance: she was thirty, and spinsterhood was creeping toward her.
他是她最后的机会了。她已三十，孑然一身的命运正在逐渐向她逼近。

常用派生词：spinster → spinsterhood

10. neighborhood: ['neibəhud] *n.* 四邻，街坊

   分解记忆法：neighbor（邻居）+ -hood（表示集合）= 四邻

   【例句】You are going to wake up the whole neighborhood with that noise.

   你弄出那么大的声音，会把街坊四邻都吵醒的。

   I grew up in a quiet neighborhood of New Castle.

   我在纽卡斯尔的一个宁静的住宅区里长大。

   常用派生词：neighbor → neighborhood

11. womanhood: ['wumənhud] *n.* （总称）妇女

   分解记忆法：woman（女人）+ -hood（表示集合）=（总称）妇女

   【例句】She grew to womanhood, and gave her heart to one who could not know its worth.

   她渐渐长大成人，把她的心交给了一位不知道它的价值的人。

   I'm not sure exactly how old Tom is, but Mary has obviously grown and is blossoming into womanhood.

   我不确定汤姆到底有多大，但是玛丽很显然已经长大，并富有女人味。

12. dictionary: ['dikʃənəri] *n.* 字典，词典

   分解记忆法：diction（语法）+ -ary（表示集合）= 字典（语法的集合体）

   【例句】There is nothing but a dictionary on the desk.

   桌子上除了一本字典外什么也没有。

   Would you please lend your dictionary to me?

   把你的字典借我用一下可以吗？

   常用派生词：diction → dictionary

13. vocabulary: [vəuˈkæbjuləri] *n.* 词汇；词汇表

   分解记忆法：vocable（语，单词）+ -ary（表示集合）= 词汇

   【例句】How do you enearge your English vocabulary?

   你怎样增加你的英语词汇量？

   He has an extensive vocabulary.

   他的词汇量很丰富。

14. missionary: ['miʃənəri] *n.* 负有使命者；传教士；工作人员

   分解记忆法：mission（使命）+ -ary（表示名词）= 负有使命者

   【例句】He spent 30 years in Asia as a missionary.

   他在亚洲做了30年的传教士。

   She is an excellent missionary.

   她是一名优秀的传教士。

   常用派生词：mission → missionary

15. cavalry: ['kævəlri] *n.* 骑兵；骑兵队；装甲部队

   分解记忆法：caval-（马匹）+ -ry（表示集合）= 骑兵队

   【例句】His son is a soldier in a cavalry regiment.

他的儿子是骑兵团的一名战士。

He was an officer in the cavalry.

他曾是骑兵军官。

16. gentry: [ˈdʒentri] *n.* 上流社会人士，名流；贵族们

分解记忆法：gentle(文雅的) + -ry(表示集合) = 贵族们

【例句】The English gentry is next below the nobility.

英国绅士的地位仅次于贵族。

In old society, the gentry lived in luxury.

在旧社会，贵族们生活奢侈。

17. machinery: [məˈʃiːnəri] *n.* (总称)机器，机械

分解记忆法：machine(机器) + -ry(表示集合) = (总称)机器

【例句】John kept thinking about the problem with the machinery, but it was still out of work.

约翰一直在想机器到底出了什么问题，但是仍旧不管用。

The peasant wants to buy an expensive piece of agricultural machinery.

那个农民想要买一台昂贵的农业机械。

常用派生词：machine → machinery

18. poultry: [ˈpəʊltri] *n.* 家禽，家禽类；禽肉

分解记忆法：poult-(雏) + -ry(表示集合) = 家禽类

【例句】He owns a large-scale poultry farm.

他有一家大型家禽饲养场。

Infected poultry also excrete the virus in their faeces.

被感染的家禽还会通过粪便排出病毒。

19. scenery: [ˈsiːnəri] *n.* (集合用法)风景，景观

分解记忆法：scene(风景) + -ry(表示集合) = (集合用法)风景

【例句】The best part of the trip was the scenery. It was fantastic.

这次旅行最精彩的部分就是自然风光了，真是美极了。

The scenery is beautiful beyond description.

这儿的风景美得难以形容。

常用派生词：scene → scenery → scenic

20. shrubbery: [ˈʃrʌbəri] *n.* 灌木林，灌木丛

分解记忆法：shrub(灌木丛) + -ry(表示集合) = 灌木林

【例句】Who is there hiding in the shrubbery?

隐藏在灌木丛中的是谁？

There is a secluded mansion, islanded by shrubbery and fences.

那座幽深的大宅被灌木丛和篱笆隔开。

Words in Use

1. This almost doubled the number of _____ kept in the country all at once.
   A. poultry   B. puppy   C. peppy   D. pepper
2. Professor Smith recently persuaded 37 people, 25 of whom are women, to keep a _____ of all their absent-minded actions for a fortnight.
   A. daring   B. diary   C. dating   D. dazing
3. The market system is an imperfect _____ for achieving full employment.
   A. mechanism   B. machinery   C. mechanics   D. mechanic
4. The _____ used in the course book is printed at the back.
   A. curriculum   B. alphabet   C. philosophy   D. vocabulary
5. Some of the _____ members disagree with the president on the problem.
   A. cable   B. cabbage   C. captain   D. cabinet
6. All carry-on _____ must be stored under your seat or in the over head compartments.
   A. luggage   B. garbage   C. cabbage   D. sausage
7. Many students are interested in the subject which is not included in the _____.
   A. calendar   B. textbook   C. agenda   D. curriculum
8. There are _____ of great joys as the hostages were reunited with their families.
   A. scenery   B. landscapes   C. spots   D. scenes
9. When do you think I can get my _____ back?
   A. laundry   B. launch   C. luncheon   D. laughter
10. Our neighbor's cat uses our garden as a _____.
    A. cottage   B. closet   C. lavatory   D. bathroom
11. Food and _____ are basic necessities.
    A. clothing   B. cloth   C. clothes   D. closet
12. Christian _____ are sent all over the world to convert others to their faith.
    A. missions   B. missionaries   C. missiles   D. mistresses
13. Sibling _____ is the competition between brothers and sisters for the parents' attention.
    A. rival   B. rivalry   C. risky   D. ritzy
14. That family lives in _____, enjoying costly clothes, high-priced cars, and a beautiful house.
    A. luxury   B. luxurious   C. luxuriant   D. luxuriating
15. Why she left home without saying where she was going is still a _____.
    A. mystic   B. mysticism   C. mystique   D. mystery
16. There was a bank _____ this morning and four people were wounded.
    A. roar   B. robbery   C. rock   D. roaster

17. The _____ between San Francisco and L.A. is approx imately 640 km.
    A. milieu   B. mileage   C. mile   D. midst
18. Ships carry a huge _____ of wheat from the Great Lakes' ports.
    A. tonsil   B. torture   C. tonnage   D. toggle
19. Every year, we vacation in the mountains and enjoy the _____.
    A. scenery   B. scent   C. scenario   D. scatter
20. She put the dirty _____ into the washer.
    A. lavatory   B. laurel   C. laureate   D. laundry
21. A TV sports announcer gave the _____ on the football game, explaining what the players were doing, and how well they were doing it.
    A. commentator   B. comment   C. commentary   D. commencement
22. _____ in that textile mill is used to make fabric.
    A. Machinations   B. Macaroni   C. Machete   D. Machinery
23. Until _____ was ended in the United Stated, many African American people were not free.
    A. slave   B. slavery   C. slaughter   D. slavish
24. _____ are raised on farms for their eggs or meat.
    A. Poultry   B. Potter   C. Pottery   D. Poverty
25. The _____ of three and five is four.
    A. avenge   B. avenue   C. average   D. aversion
26. Many of the _____ from Newport, Rhode Island, live in very large, famous houses.
    A. genuine   B. gentile   C. genteel   D. gentry
27. She is taking _____ training to learn to be a hairdresser.
    A. vocational   B. vocabulary   C. vivacious   D. vociferous
28. We check our _____ in at the airport ticket counter.
    A. baggy   B. luggage   C. bagel   D. bakery
29. We are friends with many of the families who live in our _____.
    A. neighborly   B. negotiation   C. neighborhood   D. neighbor
30. Free medical treatment in this country covers sickness of mind as well as _____ sicknesses.
    A. normal   B. regular   C. average   D. ordinary

Key to *Words in Use*

1. A	2. B	3. A	4. D	5. D
6. A	7. D	8. C	9. A	10. C
11. A	12. B	13. B	14. A	15. D
16. B	17. B	18. C	19. A	20. D
21. C	22. D	23. B	24. A	25. C
26. D	27. A	28. B	29. C	30. D

第5单元 常用形容词后缀

Words in Context

Chinese Traditional Kite Craft

Kites were invented by the Chinese people over 2000 years ago. Around the 12th century, Chinese kite spread to the West and **Oriental** and Western kite culture was formed after years of development. In this process, the traditional culture integrated with the kite craft, and finally formed the kite culture with unique characteristics.

Uses of kites have been changed several times in history. According to historical record, the kite was first used in military. In the mid Tang Dynasty, in which the society was **stable** and **peaceful**, the use of kites was gradually changed from military to entertainment. With the innovation of papermaking, the raw material of kite changed from silk to paper. Kites became **popular** among civilians with a richer variety of forms and reached the peak point in the Song Dynasty. Participated by the literary, the making and the decoration of kites underwent great development. Kite making became a profession due to the large demand.

The Ming and Qing Dynasties were the peak period of the Chinese kite. The kites underwent great development in size, design, decoration and flying skills. Literators at that time made kites by themselves, and sent to relatives and friends as a gift, regarding it a **literary** pursuit. In recent years, kite flying has publicized as a sports activity as well as entertainment.

Word Building

More Words with the Suffixes

后缀	释义	例词
-able,-ible	可……的，能……的，易于……的	changeable, incredible
-ile		hostile, versatile, fertile, juvenile
-esque,-ique		arabesque, picturesque, antique,
-ish	如……的，似……的，……形状的	bookish, selfish, snobbish, sluggish
-like		dreamlike, manlike, businesslike
-y, -ly		silky, watery, cowardly, monthly

（续表）

后缀	释义	例词
-ed	有……的，多……的，充满……的	aged, bearded, talented, haired
-ful		grateful, harmful, successful
-ous		envious, industrious, spacious
-y		windy, snowy, bloody, greedy
-al	属于……的，与……有关的	personal, global, brutal, federal
-ial		aerial, cordial, racial, editorial
-an		republican, veteran, agrarian
-ar		polar, similar, vulgar, lunar
-ic		atomic, academic, exotic, domestic
-tic		antibiotic, fanatic, poetic, static
-ual		habitual, actual, spiritual, sexual
-iac		maniac, demoniac, insomniac
-acious, -ious	具有……性质的	fallacious, rebellious, glorious
-aneous		simultaneous, extraneous
-ant, -ent		indignant, defiant, ardent, fluent
-ary		customary, honorary, imaginary
-ate, -ete, -ite, -ute		accurate, complete, exquisite, solute
-ative, -itive, -ive		talkative, fugitive, exclusive, initiative
-atory, -ory		condemnatory, obligatory, explanatory
-ed		aged, skilled, advanced, ashamed
-fic		pacific, scientific, specific, horrific
-ful		sorrowful, forgetful, doubtful, truthful
-ical		periodical, typical, epidemical, historical
-id		vivid, splendid, radical surgical, tropical
-some		burdensome, meddlesome, tiresome
-ine		divine, feminine, genuine, masculine
-en	由……做成的	brazen, earthen, golden, wooden
-ern	方向	eastern, southern, modern
-an, -ese, -ian, -ish	某国的，某地的	American, Chinese, Mongolian, Spanish
-ing	通常接于动词之后	agonizing, promising, refreshing

（续表）

后缀	释义	例词
-ior	表示"比较级"	inferior, junior, superior, senior
-less	没有	aimless, helpless, priceless, reckless
-most	表示"最高级"	foremost, innermost, utmost
-proof	多加于名词之后，"防……的"	airproof, bulletproof, rainproof

1. **changeable:** [ˈtʃeindʒəbəl] *a.* 易变的，可变的

    分解记忆法：change(改变)+ -able(可……，易……)= 易变的

    【例句】The weather in London is changeable.

    伦敦的天气多变。

    His temper is changeable.

    他的脾气变化无常。

    常用派生词：change →changeable →unchangeable

2. **incredible:** [inˈkredəbəl] *a.* 不可信的；不可思议的；惊人的

    分解记忆法：in-(不)+ -cred(可信的)+ ible(可……)= 不可信的

    【例句】He told us his incredible story of his 84 hours in those ruins.

    他向我们讲述了他在废墟下84小时的惊人经历。

    It's incredible how much Mary has changed since she went to university.

    自从上了大学后，玛丽变化之大让人难以置信。

    常用派生词：credible →incredible →incredibly →incredibility

3. **juvenile:** [ˈdʒu:vənail] *a.* 少年特有的；幼稚的

    分解记忆法：juvenis(年轻的)+ -ile(易于……)= 少年特有的

    【例句】Last but not least, the shortcoming in education is the cause contributing to juvenile delinquency.

    最后，教育上的缺陷是助长青少年犯罪的原因。

    He has a very juvenile sense of humor.

    他有带稚气的幽默感。

4. **antique:** [ænˈti:k] *a.* 古代的，古时的

    分解记忆法：anti-(在……之前的；古代的)+ -ique(似……)= 古代的

    【例句】His dress was of the antique Dutch fashion.

    他的衣服是古代的荷兰装束。

    He has bought an antique rosewood desk.

    他买了一个古董红木书桌。

    常用派生词：antique →antiquated →antiquity

5. snobbish: ['snɔbiʃ] *a.* 势利的

分解记忆法：snob（势利小人）+-ish（如……）=势利的

【例句】It is strange that he has fallen in love with such a snobbish girl.
他爱上了这样一个势利的女孩，真是奇怪。

Jane feels she can never compete with these snobbish, elegant people.
简感到她永远无法同这些高雅却势利的人们竞争。

常用派生词：snob →snobbish →snobbery

6. manlike: ['mælaik] *a.* 男人似的，有男人气质的

分解记忆法：man（男人）+ -like（如……）= 男人似的

【例句】She has a manlike character.
她的性格像男人。

She has manlike physical strength.
她有着男人的体力。

7. inferior: [in'fiəriə] *a.* 劣等的；次的；下级的

分解记忆法：inferus（低的）+ -ior（用来表示"比较级"的后缀）= 次的

【例句】I felt very inferior among all those academics.
与那些大学教师相比，我自惭形秽。

The machine is technically inferior to those Western models.
这些机器在技术上不如西方国家的机器先进。

常用派生词：inferior →inferiority

8. monthly: ['mʌnθli] *a.* 每月的，每月一次的

分解记忆法：month（月）+ -ly（如……的）= 每月的

【例句】The mortgage is payable in monthly installments.
该抵押借款按月偿还。

What is your approximate monthly family income?
你家每月的家庭总收入大约是多少？

9. talented: ['tæləntid] *a.* 有才能的，有天资的

分解记忆法：talent（才能）+ -ed（有……的）= 有才能的

【例句】The students in this class are all highly talented young people.
这个班级的同学都是天赋极高的年轻人。

She is a highly talented actress.
她是一个很有天赋的演员。

10. harmful: ['hɑ:mful] *a.* 有伤害的，有损害的

分解记忆法：harm（伤害；损害）+- ful（有……的）= 有伤害的

【例句】Can a drug that helps hearts be harmful to the brain?
对心脏病治疗有用的药会对大脑产生损害吗？

Smoking is harmful to one's health.

吸烟对健康有害。

常用派生词：harm →harmful →harmfully → harmfulness →harmless →harmlessness →harmlessly

11. industrious: [inˈdʌstriəs] *a.* 勤勉的

分解记忆法：industry(勤勉)+ -ous(充满……)= 勤勉的

【例句】The Chinese are an industrious people.

中国人是个勤奋的民族。

His success is due to both his industrious character and help from friends.

他的成功是由于勤勉和朋友们的帮助。

常用派生词：industry → industrious →industriously →industriousness

12. greedy: [ˈɡriːdi] *a.* 贪心的；贪婪的

分解记忆法：greed(贪食；贪心)+ -y(多……的)= 贪婪的

【例句】The company has became too greedy for profit.

这个公司对于利益的要求过于贪婪。

Don't be too greedy and leave some for others.

不要过于贪婪，留一些给其他人。

常用派生词：greed →greedy

13. foremost: [ˈfɔːməust] *a.* 首要的；最佳的

分解记忆法：fore-(在……之前)+ -most(表示"最高级")= 首要的

【例句】One of the European foremost linguists will come to our university.

欧洲最杰出的语言学家要到我们学校。

First and foremost, a good teacher-student relationship is necessary for teaching.

首要的是，好的师生关系对于教学活动来说是必要的。

14. aerial: [ˈeəriəl] *a.* 空中的；飞机（航空）的

分解记忆法：aer-(空气)+ -ial(与……有关的)= 空中的

【例句】He showed me some aerial photographs.

他给我看了一些空中拍摄的照片。

This is a fierce aerial combat game.

这是一款紧张激烈的空战游戏。

常用派生词：aerate →aerial

15. veteran: [ˈvetərən] *a.* 老兵的；老练的，经验丰富的；资深的

分解记忆法：vetus(老的)+ -an(与……有关的)= 老兵的

【例句】He is a veteran traveler.

他是个富有经验的旅行家。

The veteran worker has two apprentices working with him.

这位老工人身边有两个徒弟一起工作。

16. lunar: [ˈluːnə] *a.* 月的，月球的

分解记忆法：luna-(月) + -ar(与……有关) = 月的

【例句】The Lantern Festival falls on the 15th day of the first lunar month.
农历正月十五是元宵节。

The astronaut piloted the craft down to the lunar surface.
宇航员驾驶宇宙飞船在月球表面降落。

常用派生词：lunar →lunatic

17. domestic: [dəˈmestik] *a.* 国内的；家(庭)的；家用的

分解记忆法：domus(房子) + -ic(与……有关) = 国内的；家(庭)的

【例句】I suspect that Jane's domestic life is not very happy.
我怀疑简的家庭生活不是很愉快。

GDP is the abbreviation of gross domestic product.
GDP 是国内生产总值的缩写。

常用派生词：domestic →domesticate →domesticated →domesticity →domestically

18. spiritual: [ˈspiritʃuəl] *a.* 精神上的；与宗教有关的

分解记忆法：spirit(精神) + -ual(与……有关的) = 精神上的

【例句】As a priest, I'm responsible for your spiritual welfare.
作为神父，我对你的精神上的幸福负责。

They seem to exist in different spiritual worlds.
他们似乎生活在不同的精神境界。

常用派生词：spirit →spiritual →spiritualism →spiritually

19. insomniac: [inˈsɔmniæk] *a.* 失眠的

分解记忆法：in-(不) + -somnus(睡觉) + -iac(与……有关的) = 失眠的

【例句】If you are insomniac, I advise you see an expert on sleeping.
如果你有失眠问题(难以入睡)，还应找个睡眠专家。

She's insomniac and she only sleeps for two or three hours a night.
她因失眠而每晚只睡两三个小时。

常用派生词：insomnia →insomniac

20. fallacious: [fəˈleiʃəs] *a.* 谬误的

分解记忆法：fallacy(谬论) + -acious(具有……性质的) = 谬误的

【例句】Such an argument is misleading, if not wholly fallacious.
这种观点即使不全是谬误，也是误导人的。

He showed them that the proof was fallacious.
他向他们指出证明是谬误的。

常用派生词：fallacy →fallacious →fallible

21. extraneous: [ikˈstreiniəs] *a.* 无关的

分解记忆法：extra-(额外的) +- aneous(具有……性质的) = 无关的

【例句】Such details are extraneous to the matter in hand.

这些细节与手头上的这事没有直接关系。

He was so cold-hearted that even his family had become extraneous to him.

他是如此的冷血，甚至家庭对他也无足轻重。

常用派生词：extraneous →extraneously

22. **indignant:** [inˈdignənt] *a.* 愤怒的，愤慨的，义愤的

分解记忆法：in-(不) + -dign(值得的) + -ant(具有……性质的) = 愤怒的

【例句】He felt indignant at those people's behavior.

他对那些人的行为感到气愤。

People are indignant by their shooting of innocent civilians.

对于他们枪杀无辜平民，人们感到义愤填膺。

常用派生词：indignant →indignation →indignantly

23. **ardent:** [ˈɑːdənt] *a.* 热心的，热情的，热烈的

分解记忆法：ardere(燃烧) + -ent(具有……性质的) = 热心的

【例句】He is an ardent supporter of free trade.

他是个自由贸易的热心支持者。

I cannot endure such ardent weather.

我不能忍受如此热的天气了。

常用派生词：ardent →ardently

24. **customary:** [ˈkʌstəməri] *a.* 习惯上的，惯常的；合乎习俗的

分解记忆法：custom(习惯) + -ary(具有……性质的) = 习惯上的

【例句】It is customary for the most important person to sit at the end of the table.

按惯例，最重要的人坐在首席。

He answered the question with his customary smile.

他用他惯有的微笑对此问题做了回答。

常用派生词：custom →customer →customize →customable →customary

25. **obsolete:** [ˈɔbsəliːt] *a.* 过时的

分解记忆法：ob-(反对的) + -sol(习惯的) + -ete(具有……性质) = 过时的

【例句】It is a kind of obsolete weapon.

它是一种老式的武器。

The typewriter is obsolete.

这架打字机老掉牙了。

26. **talkative:** [ˈtɔːkətiv] *a.* 健谈的，爱说话的

分解记忆法：talk(谈话；说话) + -ative(具有……性质的) = 健谈的

【例句】At times I am much more talkative or speak much faster than usual.

有时我的话比平常多得多，说话速度比平常快得多。

She is active, but a little bit talkative.

她很活泼，但是有点太爱说话了。

常用派生词：talk →talkative →talkativeness

27. **vivid:** ['vivid] *a.* 生动的；栩栩如生的；鲜活的

    分解记忆法：viv(生命)+- id(具有……性质的)= 生动的

    【例句】She is making a vivid account of her journey to the Europe.

    她正对她的欧洲之旅进行生动的叙述。

    This place conjures up vivid memories.

    这个地方使人回忆起许多生动的往事。

    常用派生词：vivid →vividness →vividly

28. **initiative:** [i'niʃiətiv] *a.* 创始的；初步的；自发的

    分解记忆法：initiare(开始)+ -ive(具有……性质的)= 创始的

    【例句】I put it all down to her hard work and initiative character.

    我把这一切归因于她工作又勤奋又主动。

    Being positive, diligent, creative and initiative can make a successful person.

    乐观积极、勤奋、富有创造力、具有主动精神能使一个人成功。

    常用派生词：initiate →initiation →initiative

29. **divine:** [di'vain] *a.* 神的；天赐的；极美好的

    分解记忆法：divinus(属于神的)+ -ine(具有……性质的)= 神的

    【例句】He contributes his success to divine help.

    他把成功归功于神的帮助。

    No one can challenge the authority of divine law.

    没有人能够挑战神律的权威。

Words in Use

1. Silver is used to make photographic films because it is _____ to light.
   A. sensible   B. sensitive   C. active   D. positive
2. This orange drink contains no _____ flavorings.
   A. artificial   B. superficial   C. surface   D. article
3. In the _____ universe, you are the only one.
   A. definite   B. infinite   C. refine   D. financial
4. Many people believe that the nuclear energy provides an inexhaustible and _____ source of power and that it is therefore essential for an industrially developing society.
   A. economic   B. economical   C. economics   D. economy
5. As far as oil energy is concerned, we cannot be too _____.
   A. fragrant   B. flagrant   C. frugal   D. fugitive
6. The opinion seems _____ because computers lack the drives and emotions of living

creatures.

　　A. ridicule　　B. meticulous　　C. ludicrous　　D. ridiculous

7. The appeal of advertising to buy motives can have both _____ and positive effects.

　　A. negative　　B. negligible　　C. negligent　　D. eligible

8. The results are of very high creative quality and provide plenty of substance for _____ discussions.

　　A. extensive　　B. intensive　　C. intense　　D. exclusive

9. Dispossessed peasants slash and burn down their way into the rain forests of Latin America, and hungry nomads turn their herds out onto _____ African grassland, reducing it to desert.

　　A. triple　　B. trivial　　C. futile　　D. fragile

10. He is too _____ for my taste.

　　A. respective　　B. respected　　C. respectable　　D. respectful

11. I feel _____ for you, on your account, as if I were you.

　　A. assured　　B. ashamed　　C. assumed　　D. assigned

12. The BBC English Dictionary contains background information on 1,000 people and places _____ in the news since 1988.

　　A. eminent　　B. imminent　　C. prominent　　D. super-eminent

13. Although the area is very poor just now, its _____ wealth is great.

　　A. potential　　B. substantial　　C. essential　　D. beneficial

14. There was _____ kindness and compassion in his eyes, which showed that he was a man with good nature.

　　A. apparent　　B. transparent　　C. magnificent　　D. evident

15. Babies are _____ about everything around them.

　　A. jealous　　B. zealous　　C. curious　　D. suspicious

16. In a good _____ position in his dealings with the opponent, he benefited a lot.

　　A. bargaining　　B. banging　　C. barking　　D. daring

17. Despite _____ differences in cultures, heroes around the world generally share a number of characteristics that instruct and inspire people.

　　A. immense　　B. immerse　　C. tremendous　　D. monstrous

18. You should make good use of every _____ minute to study.

　　A. precious　　B. previous　　C. pregnant　　D. obvious

19. I was told that these tickets were _____ only for three days.

　　A. fashionable　　B. available　　C. attainable　　D. reliable

20. Are there any relations between love and _____ life?

　　A. material　　B. marital　　C. martial　　D. marine

21. We humans have dominated every species we have come into _____ contact with.

　　A. frequent　　B. sequent　　C. consequent　　D. subsequent

22. Conversely, some European firms have half or more of their employees ____ in a second language.
    A. influent   B. affluent   C. fluent   D. frequent

23. I have a very ____ arrangement with my employer so I can work whatever hours suit me.
    A. advisable   B. changeable   C. comfortable   D. flexible

24. The ____ repairs to the motorway are causing serious traffic problem.
    A. tremendous   B. immense   C. extensive   D. enormous

25. Manufacturing companies spend millions of pounds trying to convince customers that their products are ____ to those of other companies.
    A. supreme   B. prior   C. inferior   D. superior

26. He believes that men who get young girls ____ should be severely punished.
    A. arrogant   B. ignorant   C. elegant   D. pregnant

27. He had a ____ fear of snakes.
    A. deathly   B. dead   C. deadly   D. death

28. We are sure a lot of this ____ work will be done by machines before long.
    A. mature   B. metal   C. manual   D. menu

29. In this area, the ____ snow, in spring often results in floods.
    A. melting   B. freezing   C. flying   D. falling

30. Though our weather forecast, generally speaking, is ____, it does not always make accurate prediction.
    A. durable   B. reliable   C. usable   D. sensible

Key to *Words in Use*

1. B	2. A	3. B	4. B	5. C
6. D	7. A	8. B	9. D	10. C
11. B	12. C	13. A	14. D	15. C
16. A	17. A	18. A	19. B	20. B
21. A	22. C	23. D	24. C	25. D
26. D	27. A	28. C	29. A	30. B

第6单元 常用副词后缀

Words in Context

Red Head Cover

When we speak of Chinese marriage, we mean the Chinese traditional marriage. In China, to get married was **traditionally** considered a must. Usually, at a traditional Chinese wedding, the bride is often seen with red veil on her head. It covers the bride's face. Chinese people call the veil, made of a laced silk square, red head cover.

This practice dates back to the Qi Period (479—502) of the Northern and Southern Dynasties. The head cover was used by women farmers to protect their heads against cold wind and hot sunshine while working in the fields. It could be a cloth of any color and was big enough to cover the head top. For its practical use and ornamental function, the head cover was widespread.

By the beginning of the Tang Dynasty, the cover had become a long veil down to the shoulder. The wife **readily** accepted the veil to show her loyalty to her husband. Veils are not unique in China. Even today veils can still be seen in some other places in the world.

This custom lasted over a thousand years. From Later Jin Dynasty, a veil became a must for a bride at the wedding. But the color of the bride's veil is **always** red as it is the symbolic color of happiness.

Word Building

More Words with the Suffixes

后缀	释义	例词
-ad	方向	sinistrad, dextrad, dorsad, ventrad
-ling, -long		darkling, sideling, flatling, headlong
-ward		forward, homeward, inwards, southward
-way(s)	方式	anyway, endways, sideways, straightway,
-wise		crosswise, clockwise, otherwise, sidewise
-ence	从……	hence, thence, whence

(续表)

后缀	释义	例词
-ily	大多数直接接于形容词后或是经过某种变化	happily, heartily, readily, steadily
-ly		absolutely, actually, barely, literally, roughly, shortly, violently
-ably, -ibly	状态	respectably, comfortably, possibly, sensibly

1. **sinistrad:** [ˈsinistræd] *adv.* 向左；向左方

   分解记忆法：sinistr-(左)+-ad(表方向)=向左

   【例句】He has form a habit of writing sinistrad.

   他养成了向左书写的习惯。

   I opened the door to the secret garden with an old key turning sinistrad.

   我左旋一把旧钥匙就打开了一扇通往神秘花园的大门。

2. **darkling:** [ˈdɑːklɪŋ] *adv.* 在黑暗中

   分解记忆法：dark(黑暗)+-ling(在……中)=在黑暗中

   【例句】Darkling I listened and for a long time, I even have fallen in love with easeful death.

   我默默地听着，很长一段时间我甚至爱上了平静的死亡。

   It was pitch-dark and we moved darkling, stumbled along, groping our way.

   天黑伸手不见五指，我们在黑暗中，深一脚，浅一脚，摸索前行。

3. **sideling:** [ˈsaɪdlɪŋ] *adv.* 倾斜地；横向地

   分解记忆法：side(旁边)+-ling(表方向)=倾斜地

   【例句】The day darkled little by little. And it was black. The light out of the window came in sideling.

   天渐渐地暗了，黑了，窗外灯光斜射了进来。

   The morning light sideling streamed into his room.

   清晨的阳光斜射进他的房间。

4. **headlong:** [ˈhedlɔŋ] *adv.* 头向前地；匆促而用力地

   分解记忆法：head(头部)+-long(表方向)=头向前地

   【例句】The child leaned towards his mother and fell headlong in front of her.

   孩子俯身凑向妈妈，头朝前面倒在妈妈的面前。

   Little Mary carried on for ten minutes after she fell headlong.

   小玛丽摔了个倒栽葱后，坚持了十分钟。

5. **forward:** [ˈfɔːwəd] *adv.* 向前地；提前地

   分解记忆法：fore-(早先；预先；之前)+-ward(表方向)=向前地

   【例句】The car stopped suddenly and he plunged forward.

   汽车突然停下，他的身子朝前一冲。

The soldiers crept forward under the cover of darkness.
士兵在黑夜的掩护下向前爬行。

6. homeward: [ˈhəumwəd] *adv.* 向家，向家乡

分解记忆法：home(家)+-ward(表方向)=向家，向家乡

【例句】He is driving homeward.
他开车回家。

Twilight was falling as he turned homeward.
他转身往家走时，已是黄昏时分。

7. inwards: [ˈinwədz] *adv.* 内部地；向内地

分解记忆法：in-(在……之内)+-wards(表方向)=内部地

【例句】The door opened inwards into the room.
门是朝房间里面开的。

Reform cannot turn inwards, because education modernization is an inevitable trend following the development of education reform.
改革不能闭关自守，教育现代化是教育发展与改革的必然趋势。

8. southward: [ˈsauθwəd] *adv.* 往南

分解记忆法：south(南方；南面)+-ward(表方向)=往南

【例句】Early in the morning, they set sail southward.
一清早，他们启航向南行驶。

The cornfields stretched southward as far as the eye could see.
麦田向南不断延绵，一眼望不到尽头。

9. anyway: [ˈeniwei] *adv.* 不管用什么方法都行，不管怎样

分解记忆法：any(任何)+-way(表方式)=不管用什么方法(或方式)都行

【例句】I never did believe you much anyway.
反正我从来没有怎么相信你。

Anyway, I want to see him, dead or alive.
无论如何，我想要看见他，不管他是死了还是活着。

10. endways: [ˈendweiz] *adv.* 末端朝前地；朝着末端地

分解记忆法：end(末尾)+-ways(表方式)= 末端朝前地

【例句】The box is quite narrow when you look at it endways on.
从两端看，这箱子就显得很窄。

The bed was pushed endways into the bedroom.
这张床已尾端朝前推入了卧室。

11. crosswise: [ˈkrɔswaiz] *adv.* 斜地；成十字状地；交叉地

分解记忆法：cross(横过；十字形；相反)+-wise(表方式)=斜地；成十字状地

【例句】The two chopsticks are placed crosswise.
那两根筷子交叉地放着。

Make a cut crosswise into the bag, where you want to introduce the sampler.

做一个十字状切口，进入袋内，取出你想要的样品。

12. clockwise: [ˈklɔkwaiz] *adv.* 顺时针方向地

　　分解记忆法：clock(时钟)+-ward(表方式)=顺时针方向地

　　【例句】Press down on the knob and turn clockwise one full turn to properly engage threads on stem boss.

　　　　　将旋钮压下，顺时针旋转一整圈，使其完全嵌入阀杆轮箍的螺纹里。

　　　　　Regulation is accomplished by rotating the hand wheel clockwise.

　　　　　规则要求按顺时针方向旋转手轮。

13. otherwise: [ˈʌðəwaiz] *adv.* 别的方式地；否则；要不然

　　分解记忆法：other(其他的)+-wise(表方式)=用别的方式地

　　【例句】Seize the chance, otherwise you'll regret it.

　　　　　抓住这个机会，否则你会后悔的。

　　　　　He seems to think otherwise.

　　　　　他似乎有另外的想法。

14. hence: [hens] *adv.* 从此时开始；今后

　　分解记忆法：here(这儿)+-ence(从……)=从此时开始

　　【例句】A year hence it will be forgotten.

　　　　　这事一年后将被遗忘。

　　　　　We have no chance to meet each other a week hence.

　　　　　我们今后一星期没有见面的机会了。

15. absolutely: [ˈæbsəlu:tli] *adv.* 完全地；绝对地

　　分解记忆法：absolute(纯粹的；绝对的)+-ly(常接于形容词后)=完全地

　　【例句】I absolutely agree with you.

　　　　　我完全同意你所说的。

　　　　　The thief took absolutely everything.

　　　　　小偷把一切都偷光了。

　　常用派生词：absolute →absolutely

16. roughly: [ˈrʌfli] *adv.* 粗糙地；毛糙地；概略地

　　分解记忆法：rough(粗野的)+-ly(常接于形容词后)=粗糙地

　　【例句】Roughly speaking, the market has the tendency to ascend.

　　　　　大致说来，市场行情有上升的趋势。

　　　　　He treated me roughly.

　　　　　他粗暴地对待我。

　　常用派生词：rough →roughen →roughly

17. heartily: [ˈhɑ:tili] *adv.* 衷心地；真心地

　　分解记忆法：hearty(热忱地)+-ily(形容词词尾-y变为-ily)=衷心地

【例句】We always heartily rejoice at the achievements of our friends.

对朋友们的成就，我们总是由衷地感到高兴。

We welcomed him heartily.

我们衷心地欢迎他的到来。

常用派生词：heart→ heartless →hearty →heartily →heartiness

18. **steadily:** [ˈstedili] *adv.* 坚定地；不断地；稳固地

分解记忆法：steady（稳的）+-ily（形容词词尾-y变为-ily）=坚定地

【例句】Prices have risen steadily during the past decade.

过去的十年间,物价一直在上涨。

The production of their factory goes steadily upward.

他们工厂的生产稳步上升。

常用派生词：stead →steady →steadiness →steadily

19. **sensibly:** [ˈsensəbli] *adv.* 合情合理地

分解记忆法：sensible（合理的）+-ly（接于-bile后表示相应副词）=合情合理地

【例句】She was sensibly dressed in tweeds.

她穿着实用的苏格兰粗花呢衣服。

At 6,000 feet the density of the air was sensibly thin.

在六千英尺高的地方，空气自然而然地稀薄了。

常用派生词：sense →senseless →sensible →sensitive →sensitiveness →sensitivity →sensation →sensational →sensationalize →sensationalism

20. **respectably:** [rɪˈspektəblɪ] *adv.* 高尚地；相当好地

分解记忆法：respectable（可敬的）+-ly（接于-able后表示相应副词）=高尚地

【例句】She is respectably dressed.

她穿得很高雅。

They live respectably from hand to mouth.

他们自食其力，过得相当不错。

常用派生词：respect →respected →respectful →respectable

Words in Use

1. You should deal _____ with them, without any discrimination.
   A. barely   B. rarely   C. hardly   D. fairly

2. Others _____ tried to put life boats down.
   A. desperately   B. hardly   C. impair   D. despair

3. We hope that every day a happy day to study well and every day _____.
   A. outward   B. onward   C. upward   D. award

4. Not _____, the process of choosing names varies widely from culture to culture.

    A. obviously   B. surprisingly   C. particularly   D. normally

5. The indecisive man was _____ persuaded into changing his mind.
    A. hardly   B. unwillingly   C. voluntarily   D. readily

6. Gill was _____ ill for a couple of months before she was finally taken off the danger list.
    A. anxiously   B. fatally   C. critically   D. mortally

7. Tumbling down the icy slope, he clutched _____ at the branch of a tree.
    A. ferociously   B. manually   C. desperately   D. vaguely

8. Keys should never be hidden around the house since thieves _____ know where to look for.
    A. virtually   B. variously   C. unavoidably   D. invariably

9. When we receive your instructions, we shall act _____.
    A. consequently   B. accordingly   C. beneficially   D. generally

10. I must go now, and _____ if you want that book, I'll bring it next time.
    A. incidentally   B. accidentally   C. occasionally   D. subsequently

11. In economic terms California is more _____ compared with nations than with states.
    A. tactfully   B. aptly   C. profitably   D. persistently

12. American steel production increased _____ right after 1900, from 10 to 25 million tons.
    A. unexpectedly   B. phenomenally   C. successfully   D. consistently

13. Reptiles avoid cold temperatures by finding shelter, _____ holes in the ground.
    A. occasionally   B. customarily   C. especially   D. rarely

14. Human facial expressions differ from those of animals in the degree to which they can be _____ controlled and modified.
    A. deliberately   B. noticeably   C. absolutely   D. inevitably

15. The Social Security Act must _____ be termed a major contribution of President Franklin D. Roosevelt.
    A. conventionally   B. assuredly   C. necessarily   D. universally

16. _____ colored flowers attract insects.
    A. Delicately   B. Sensibly   C. Harmoniously   D. Brilliantly

17. The windmill factor, the combination of low temperature and wind speed, _____ increase the degrees of cold felt by a person who is outdoors.
    A. effectively   B. strikingly   C. certainly   D. unquestionably

18. We walked along an _____ path and soon reached the temple.
    A. upward   B. upwards   C. upward(s) of   D. up

19. The reinforcements arrived at a (n) _____ critical moment.
    A. especially   B. specially   C. specifically   D. splendidly

20. _____ our women volleyball team will win the game.
    A. Certainly   B. Definitely   C. Seemingly   D. Naturally

21. I can _____ understand them.
    A. hardly   B. scarcely   C. barely   D. rarely

22. _____ on his beginning to speak, everyone was silent.
    A. Immediately   B. Constantly   C. Presently   D. Rightly
23. It was _____ not his fault but mine.
    A. continually   B. really   C. surely   D. truly
24. _____ sorry to trouble you, but could you help me for a moment?
    A. Frightfully   B. Awfully   C. Terribly   D. Dreadfully
25. I _____ didn't come yesterday, as I knew you would be out.
    A. purposely   B. casually   C. possibly   D. on purpose
26. Additionally, with the development of modern communication techniques, news of immoral practices can be carried to _____ every corner of the globe via newspapers, magazines, radio and television.
    A. virtually   B. hardly   C. popularly   D. entirely
27. She began walking slowly but _____ towards the bridge.
    A. purposefully   B. purposely   C. aimlessly   D. possibly
28. I'm on _____ familiar ground here because I've had a lot of experience with computers.
    A. quite   B. fairly   C. rather   D. pretty
29. The convict was _____ pursued.
    A. heatedly   B. extremely   C. extensively   D. hotly
30. The brass handles are _____ obscured by white paint.
    A. partially   B. practically   C. proficiently D. partly

Key to *Words in Use*

1. D	2. A	3. C	4. B	5. D
6. C	7. C	8. D	9. B	10. A
11. B	12. B	13. C	14. A	15. B
16. D	17. B	18. A	19. A	20. A
21. A	22. A	23. B	24. B	25. A
26. A	27. A	28. B	29. D	30. D

第7单元　常用动词后缀

Words in Context

In August, Li Yuchun won a **televised** American Idol-like singing contest produced by Hunan Province's Entertainment Channel.

The Li Yuchun phenomenon, however, goes far beyond her voice, which even the most ardent fans admit is pretty weak: Hei Nan, one of the event's judges, told *Guangzhou Daily* that Li was "the worst of the top six in terms of singing skills," but noted that she **garnered** the most audience votes.

What Li did possess was attitude, originality and a proud androgyny that defied Chinese norms. During the tryouts—in which 150,000 contestants were winnowed to 15—Li wore loose jeans and a black button-down shirt, with no make-up. In the main competition she sang some songs written for male performers and called herself "a tomboy." Her fans screamed openly and frantically when Li took the stage.

Li's victory was unusual in other ways: the program "Super Girl's Voice" is run democratically. Eight million SMS votes flooded in on the night of the finale. For a few weeks after, the press **debated** the relevance of this format. "Only something that **smashed** social norms could elicit such a response," a media expert commented. An editorial in *China Daily* wondered: "How come an imitation of a democratic system ends up selecting the singer who has the least ability to carry a tune?" But Li is more: She represents unabashed individuality, and that's why she's a national icon.

Word Building

More Words with the Suffixes

后缀	释义	例词
-ate	表示最常见的，名词后缀为 -ation	accommodate, fascinate, isolate, navigate, nominate
-en	做……，（使）成为……，（使）变成……	shorten, darken, fasten, worsen
-er, -le	"反复"的声音或动作	batter, chatter, flicker, glitter, chuckle, dazzle, scribble, startle

（续表）

后缀	释义	例词
-sh	拟声的动作	clash, crush, slash, crash
-esce	动作的开始或正在进行	acquiesce, coalesce, deliquesce
-fy	……化，（使）变成……，（使）成为……	classify, fortify, identify, justify
-ish	做……，致使……，造成……，成为……	banish, demolish, famish, publish
-ize,-ise	……化，使……，照……样子做	civilize, dramatize, generalize
-uce	做……	induce, introduce, seduce, deduce

1. **accommodate**: [əˈkɔmədeit] *v.* 给方便；容纳；使适应

    分解记忆法：accommodare（使适应）+-ate（动词后缀）＝给方便

    【例句】The hall can only accommodate 100 people.

    这个大厅只能容纳100人。

    We've made every effort to accommodate your point of view.

    我们已经尽力迁就你的观点。

    常用派生词：accommodate →accommodation

2. **fascinate**: [ˈfæsineit] *v.* 使迷惑；蛊惑

    分解记忆法：fascinum（符咒；魔力）+-ate（动词后缀）＝使迷惑

    【例句】The idea of traveling through time really fascinates me.

    穿越时间旅行的想法真的把我迷住了。

    This famous scenic spot fascinates many visitors.

    这个著名的景点吸引了许多游客。

    常用派生词：fascinate →fascinating →fascination

3. **navigate**: [ˈnævigeit] *v.* 驾驶；航行；领航

    分解记忆法：navis（船）+-ate（动词后缀）＝驾驶；航行

    【例句】Please you go first and navigate for me.

    请您走在前，为我指方向。

    People in the deserts are navigated by the sun.

    沙漠里的人们靠太阳来确定方向。

    常用派生词：navy →navigable→navigate → navigation →navigator

4. **shorten**: [ˈʃɔːtn] *v.* 缩短

    分解记忆法：short（短的）+-en（使变成……）＝缩短

    【例句】The days are shortening now.

现在白天变得越来越短了。

Those directors are thinking about shortening working time.

领导们正在考虑缩短工作时间。

常用派生词：short →shorten →shortage

5. worsen: [ˈwəːsən] *v.*（使）恶化；（使）变坏

分解记忆法：worse（更坏的；更差的）+-en（使变成……）=（使）恶化

【例句】Heavy storms worsened the food shortage.

暴风雨使食物的缺乏状况更加恶化。

The economic crisis worsened the world economic situation.

经济危机使世界经济状况更加恶化。

6. batter: [ˈbætə] *v.* 连续敲击

分解记忆法：bat（用棒击打）+-er（"反复"动作）=连续敲击

【例句】The waves battered against the shore.

波浪拍打着海岸。

She is often battered by her husband.

她常受丈夫毒打。

7. flicker: [ˈflikə] *v.* 摇曳；闪烁不定

分解记忆法：flick（轻快地移动）+-er（"反复"动作）=摇曳

【例句】The candle flickered in the wind.

烛光在风中摇曳着。

A smile flickered across her face as she heard the news.

听到消息后，她的脸上掠过一丝微笑。

8. dazzle: [ˈdæz(ə)l] *v.* 耀眼；使倾倒

分解记忆法：daze（使眩晕）+-le（"反复"声音）=耀眼

【例句】His eyes dazzled before the strong light.

他面对强光头晕目眩。

As a child, I was dazzled by my brother's good appearance and charm.

小时候，我为哥哥的英俊外貌和魅力而倾倒。

常用派生词：dazzle →dazzling

9. scribble: [ˈskribəl] *v.* 乱写；胡写；潦草书写

分解记忆法：scribere（写）+-le（"反复"动作）=乱写；胡写

【例句】The baby can't write but she likes to scribble with a pencil.

宝宝还不会写字，但她喜欢用铅笔乱涂。

Don't scribble on the desks.

不准在书桌上乱涂。

常用派生词：scribe →scribble →scribbler

10. startle: [ˈstɑːtl] *v.* 使吃惊；惊动

　　分解记忆法：start(惊起)+-le("反复"动作)=使吃惊

　　【例句】The girl will be startled by the least noise.

　　　　　一点儿声音都会把那个小女孩吓着。

　　　　　You really startled me, because I didn't notice you come in.

　　　　　你真的吓着我了，因为我没有注意到你进来了。

　　常用派生词：startle →startled →startling

11. twinkle: [ˈtwiŋkl] *v.* 闪烁；闪耀；闪闪发光

　　分解记忆法：twinken(眨眼)+-le("反复"动作)=闪烁；闪耀

　　【例句】The streets twinkled with lights all through the New Year.

　　　　　新年期间，街上灯火辉煌。

　　　　　There are many stars twinkling against the night sky.

　　　　　夜空中无数星星在闪烁。

　　常用派生词：twinkle →twinkling

12. acquiesce: [ˌækwiˈes] *v.* 默认；默许

　　分解记忆法：ac-(to)+-quiescere(保持安静)+-esce(动作正在进行)=默许

　　【例句】Her parents will never acquiesce in such an unsuitable marriage.

　　　　　她的父母决不会答应这门不相宜的婚事。

　　　　　They acquiesced in the decision.

　　　　　他们默许这个决定。

　　常用派生词：acquiescent →acquiesce →acquiescently

13. coalesce: [ˌkəʊəˈles] *v.* 合并；联合；携手合作

　　分解记忆法：co-(一起)+alescere(成长)+-esce(动作开始)=合并

　　【例句】These three themes coalesce at the end of the book.

　　　　　这三个主题在故事结尾合而为一。

　　　　　The views of all the party leaders coalesced to form a coherent policy.

　　　　　所有党的领导人的各种观点已统一为一致的政策。

　　常用派生词：coalesce →coalescence

14. classify: [ˈklæsifai] *v.* 分类；分成等级

　　分解记忆法：class(等级)+-fy(使变成……)=分类

　　【例句】How would you classify her literature works?

　　　　　你会对她的文学作品作怎样的划分？

　　　　　It will take much time to classify those books.

　　　　　对那些图书分类会花费很多的时间。

　　常用派生词：class →classify →classifiable →classification

15. fortify: [ˈfɔːtifai] *v.* 加强；设防

　　分解记忆法：fortis(强壮的；强大的)+-fy(使成为……)=加强

【例句】Recent high scores have fortified her vigor of study.
最近的高分鼓舞了她的学习劲头。
I had some coffee to fortify my study.
为了学习，我用咖啡来提提神。

常用派生词：fortify →fortification

16. justify: [ˈdʒʌstifai] v. 证明确有此事，证明……正当

分解记忆法：just（公平的）+-fy（使变成……）=证明确有此事

【例句】He tried to find some excuses to justify his mistake.
他试图找些理由来为他所犯的错误做辩解。
You must quote some famous sayings to justify your conclusion.
你必须要引用一些名言来证明你的结论。

常用派生词：just →justice →justifiable →justification →justify →justified

17. banish: [ˈbæniʃ] v. 放逐；驱逐

分解记忆法：ban（禁止）+-ish（致使；造成）=放逐

【例句】It is surprising to hear that he was banished.
他被驱逐出境的消息令人吃惊。
Qu Yuan was banished because of the court intrigues.
屈原因为朝廷阴谋而被驱逐。

常用派生词：banish →banishment

18. demolish: [diˈmɔliʃ] v. 毁坏；拆除；推翻

分解记忆法：demoliri（使推倒）+-ish（造成；成为）= 毁坏

【例句】He demolished the opinion immediately.
他立即就推翻了那个观点。
The government demolished all those houses.
政府将那些房子都拆除了。

常用派生词：demolish →demolition

19. civilize: [ˈsivilaiz] v. 使开化；教化；使文明化

分解记忆法：civi-（居民）+-ize（……化）=使开化；教化

【例句】There should not be rude behaviors in a civilized society.
在文明社会不应有粗鲁的行为。
They hope to civilize all primitive tribes on the island.
他们想把岛上所有原始部落变成文明社会。

常用派生词：civil →civilize →civilized →civilian →civility →civilization

20. utilize: [ˈjuːtilaiz] v. 利用；使用

分解记忆法：uti-（使用）+-ize（使……）=利用

【例句】They invented a heating system that utilized solar energy.
他们发明了一套利用太阳能的供暖系统。

One of the urgent problems that we are facing is how we can best utilize our limited resources.

我们现在面临的紧要问题之一就是如何最好地利用有限的资源。

常用派生词：utilize →utilizable →utilization →utility →utilitarian →utilitarianism

Words in Use

1. Most governments, perhaps all governments, justify public expenditure on scientific research in terms of the economic benefits the scientific _____ has brought in the past and will bring in the future.
   A. apprise   B. comprise   C. praise   D. enterprise

2. Life is a gift and privilege, one we should _____ every day of our lives.
   A. appreciate   B. applaud   C. applausive   D. plausible

3. This adaption is _____ by improving efficiency of the heart and certain systems within the muscle cells.
   A. accomplice   B. accomplish   C. accomplished   D. accomplishable

4. But in the executive _____, beauty can become a liability.
   A. circulate   B. circular   C. circle   D. circuit

5. Beyond the realm of information technology, the _____ pace of technological change in virtually every industry has created entirely new business.
   A. celebrated   B. accelerated   C. decelerated   D. isolated

6. Trying to do this will help _____ the problem and test the programmer's understanding of it.
   A. clarify   B. clarity   C. charity   D. classify

7. "Miss Baxter," he says, "could you please send in someone who can _____ right from wrong?"
   A. distinct   B. extinguish   C. distinguish   D. anguish

8. Faculty members who _____ themselves to teaching soon discover that they will not be granted tenure, promotion or substantial salary increases.
   A. dictate   B. dedicate   C. indicate   D. nominate

9. There are the hassles over bathrooms, telephones and privacy. Some families, however, manage the _____ balancing act.
   A. indicate   B. delicate   C. duplicate   D. dedicate

10. He didn't answer, but just continued to _____ at his food.
    A. grabble   B. gobble   C. nibble   D. bubble

11. Don't _____ in matters that don't concern you; mind your own business.
    A. huddle   B. meddle   C. paddle   D. peddle

12. Farmer has made the program publicly available, _____ much criticism.
    A. immediate   B. medium   C. intermediate   D. amid
13. It is important to _____ the furnace from any neighboring woodwork with brick and asbestos.
    A. obsolete   B. isolate   C. desolate   D. insulate
14. Death is normal. We are genetically programmed to _____ and perish, even under ideal condition.
    A. integrate   B. disintegrate C. integrity   D. integral
15. This struggle for existence does not _____ human war, but rather the competition of individuals for jobs, markets and materials.
    A. assemble   B. resemble   C. assimilate   D. scribble
16. But those studies can take a long time and often _____ more questions than they answer.
    A. rise   B. arise   C. raise   D. rouse
17. Sea levels shot up nearly 400 feet, flooding coastal settlements and forcing people to _____ inland.
    A. emigrate   B. immigrate   C. migrate   D. migrant
18. You will notice water rising in the tube, now what do you _____ from that?
    A. induce   B. deduce   C. reduce   D. seduce
19. The streets would be _____ with people lying here and there.
    A. glittered   B. flittered   C. littered   D. flickered
20. He _____ up in the morning and summons the rest of the world to its tasks.
    A. wakens   B. wakes   C. awakes   D. bewares
21. But what's really needed, critics say, is even tougher law and more resources aimed at _____ up border security.
    A. lightening   B. whitening   C. enlightening   D. tightening
22. Located on the shore of Sullivan's Island off the coast of South Carolina, the award-winning cube-shaped beach house was built to replace one _____ to pieces by Hurricane Hugo 10 years ago.
    A. clashed   B. smashed   C. flashed   D. crashed
23. Some huge American industries, such as consumer electronics, had shrunk or _____ in the face of foreign competition.
    A. varnished   B. rushed   C. vanished   D. brushed
24. I know I have seen that man before, but I can't _____ where.
    A. realize   B. remind   C. recognize   D. recall
25. Fresh air, nutritious food and enough exercise _____ to people's good health.
    A. attribute   B. promote   C. contribute   D. decorate
26. The plate glass must be capable of _____ very high temperatures.
    A. sustaining   B. maintaining   C. retaining   D. obtaining

27. If a little petrol is poured into the hand, it soon _____.
    A. liquefies   B. solidifies   C. vaporizes   D. modifies
28. In order to improve our living conditions, this new scheme must be _____.
    A. adopted   B. admired   C. adapted   D. advanced
29. To avoid an oil shortage we must develop machines to _____ solar energy.
    A. realize   B. revolutionize   C. utilize   D. modernize
30. He looked the word up in a dictionary to _____ its spelling.
    A. verify   B. simplify   C. purify   D. beautify

Key to *Words in Use*

1. D	2. A	3. C	4. C	5. B
6. A	7. C	8. B	9. B	10. C
11. B	12. D	13. D	14. B	15. B
16. C	17. C	18. B	19. C	20. B
21. D	22. B	23. C	24. D	25. C
26. A	27. C	28. A	29. C	30. A

第三篇　派生法：英语词根与构词

第1章　表示"看"的词根

Words in Context

Performance Management

This PM approach is used most often in the workplace but applies wherever people interact—schools, churches, community meetings, sports teams, health setting, governmental agencies, and even political settings. PM principles are needed wherever in the world people interact with their environments to produce desired effects. Cultures are different but the laws of behavior are the same worldwide, but how to make it more effective in the daily production process? According to the survey, we found that the relationship between **supervisors** and employees plays an important role. On the one hand, the supervisor should know the **conspectus** of every department, that is to say, he need have an overall view of the company and make the decisions **circumspectly**. On the other hand, the employees should share the same goals as the company and then make their efforts to the daily work and finally realize the settled goals. What's more, the communications between the supervisor and employees can't be ignored either. In other words, all staff, both the boss and employees should trust instead of **suspecting** each others. Only by this, when the company is in trouble, the financial crisis, for example, all the members can devote themselves to overcoming the problem. To sum up, the performance management is significant for the **prospect** of any company.

Word Building

More Words with the Word Roots

词根	释义	例词
vis	看	visible, invisible, visibility, vision, visual, revise, revision, envision, visa, visage, envisage, supervise, improvise
vid	看	evident, evidence, provident, improvidence, video
spect	看	spectacle, spectacular, spectator, speculate, speculation, circumspect, introspect
spic	看	specimen, suspect, perspicuous, suspicious

1. **visible:** [ˈvizəbəl] *a.* 看得见的

    分解记忆法：vis-(看) + ible(……的) = 看得见的

    【例句】The house is clearly visible from the beach.

    　　　　从海滩上可以清晰地看到那所房子。

    　　　　Most of the stars are not visible to the naked eye.

    　　　　大多数星星肉眼看不见。

    常用派生词：visible → visibility

2. **visual:** [ˈviʒjuəl] *a.* 视觉的

    分解记忆法：vis-(看) + ual(……的) = 视觉的

    【例句】The visual arts are painting or dancing, as opposed to music and literature.

    　　　　视觉艺术是指相对于音乐和文学而言的绘画、舞蹈等。

    　　　　The film brings the audience a strong visual impact.

    　　　　电影带给观众强烈的视觉冲击。

    常用派生词：visual → visualize

3. **revise:** [riˈvaiz] *v.* 修订，校订

    分解记忆法：re-(再次) + vis(看) + e = 修订，校订

    【例句】I revise my opinion on Tom — he is in fact quite clever.

    　　　　我改变了对汤姆的看法，事实上，他很聪明。

    　　　　He revised the manuscript of his book before sending it to the publisher.

    　　　　他把自己的手稿先校对了一遍，然后才交给出版社。

    常用派生词：revise → revision

4. **envision:** [enˈviʒən] *v.* 想象，预想

    分解记忆法：en-(使进入) + vision(画面，幻想) = 想象，预想

    【例句】They envision an equal society, free of poverty and disease.

    　　　　他们向往没有贫穷和疾病的平等的社会。

    　　　　They didn't envision any problems with the new building.

    　　　　他们没想到这栋新楼会有什么问题。

5. **visa:** [ˈvi:zə] *n.* 签证

    分解记忆法：vis(看) + a = 签证

    【例句】He has applied for an entry visa.

    　　　　他已申请入境签证。

    　　　　She was eventually granted an exit visa.

    　　　　她终于获得了出境签证。

6. **supervise:** [ˈsu:pəvaiz] *v.* 监督

    分解记忆法：super-(上面) + vise(看) = 监督

    【例句】The manager supervised the building work cautiously.

    　　　　经理谨慎地监督这个建筑工程。

She supervised the children playing near the pool.

她照料着在水池附近玩的几个孩子。

常用派生词：supervise → supervision → supervisor → supervisory

7. evident: [ˈevidənt] *a.* 明显的

分解记忆法：e-(出) + vid(看) + ent(……的) = 明显的

【例句】It has now become evident that our assembling line has problem.

很明显我们的生产线存在问题。

The growing interest in history is clearly evident in the number of people visiting museums and country houses.

从参观博物馆和乡村住宅的人数明显看出人们对历史越来越感兴趣。

常用派生词：evident → evidence

8. provident: [ˈprɔvidənt] *a.* 有远见的

分解记忆法：pro-(向前) + vid(看) + ent(……的) = 有远见的

【例句】She was born in a rich family but she was very provident.

她生在一个富裕的家庭，但她花钱很仔细。

He was quite provident and invested in stocks a few years ago.

他相当有远见，在几年前就买了股票。

常用派生词：provident → providence

9. improvise: [ˈimprəvaiz] *v.* 即兴发挥

分解记忆法：im-(不) + pro(预先) + vise(看) = 即兴发挥

【例句】There isn't much equipment, so we have to improvise.

设备不多，所以我们只能临时凑一些。

In order to calm down the strikers, the boss made an improvised speech.

为了安慰罢工者，老板做了一个即兴演讲。

10. vision: [ˈviʒən] *n.* 图像

分解记忆法：vis(看) + ion(名词后缀) = 图像

【例句】The girl moved outside her field of vision.

这个小女孩离开了她的视野范围。

He had a vision of a world in which there would be no wars.

他幻想一个没有战争的世界。

常用派生词：vision → visionary

11. spectacle: [ˈspektəkəl] *n.* 壮观的景象

分解记忆法：spect-(看) + acle(东西) = 壮观的景象

【例句】The carnival parade was a magnificent spectacle.

狂欢节游行场面热烈，蔚为壮观。

I can't forget the stunning spectacle of the sunset.

我无法忘记夕阳西斜的壮观景象。

常用派生词：spectacle → spectacular

12. spectacular: [spekˈtækjulə] *a.* 壮观的

分解记忆法：spect- (看) + aclar (……的) = 壮观的

【例句】She has a deep impression of the spectacular scenery in the desert.
壮丽的沙漠风光给她留下了深刻的印象。

It is a spectacular achievement on their part.
这是他们取得的一项了不起的成就。

13. speculate: [ˈspekjuleit] *v.* 思索

分解记忆法：spect- (看) + ulate (动词后缀) = 思索

【例句】We all speculated about the reasons for her resignation.
我们都推测过她辞职的原因。

It is useless to speculate why he did so.
推测他为什么这么做毫无用处。

常用派生词：speculate → speculation → speculative

14. circumspect: [ˈsə:kəmspekt] *a.* 谨慎的

分解记忆法：circum- (四周，圈) + spect (看) = 谨慎的

【例句】He is very circumspect about committing himself to anything.
他谨小慎微，从不轻易做出承诺。

The government has been circumspect in its response to the report.
政府对此报道的反应谨慎。

常用派生词：circumspect → circumspection

15. inspect: [inˈspekt] *v.* 检查

分解记忆法：in- (内，里) + spect (看) = 检查

【例句】The plants are regularly inspected for disease.
这些植物定期检查是否有病害。

Make sure you inspect the goods before signing for them.
要确保在签收货物前进行检验。

常用派生词：inspect → inspection → inspective → inspector

16. introspection: [ˌintrəˈspekʃən] *n.* 反省

分解记忆法：intro- (向内) + spect (看) + ion (名词后缀) = 反省

【例句】These situations are best resolved with the minimum of introspection or self-analysis.
这些情况只要稍加反省或自我分析就可以圆满解决。

If you want to make progress, you need to learn introspection first.
如果你想取得进步，首先要学会自我反省。

常用派生词：introspection → introspective

17. prospect: [prəsˈpekt] *n.* 展望

分解记忆法：pro- (向前) + spect (看) = 展望

【例句】There is no immediate prospect of peace in short period.
短期内没有和平的可能。

She is one of Britain's best prospects for the gold medal.
她是英国最有望夺得金牌者之一。

常用派生词：prospect → prospective

18. retrospect: [ˈretrəspekt] *n.* 回顾

分解记忆法：retro- (向后) + spect (看) = 回顾

【例句】In retrospect, I think I misunderstood her at that time.
回首往事，我觉得自己那时误解她了。

The decision seems extremely odd, in retrospect.
回想起来，这个决定显得极其荒谬。

常用派生词：retrospect → retrospective

19. suspect: [səˈspekt] *v.* 怀疑

分解记忆法：sus- (向下) + spect (看) = 怀疑

【例句】I began to suspect they were trying to get rid of me.
我开始怀疑他们试图摆脱我。

As I had suspected all along, he was not a real policeman.
他并不是警察，我一直就觉得不像。

常用派生词：suspect → suspicious → suspicion

20. conspicuous: [kənˈspikjuəs] *a.* 显著的

分解记忆法：con- (全部) + spic- (看) + uous (……的) = 显著的

【例句】Her red hair always made her conspicuous at the school.
她的红头发在学校里总是很显眼。

The advertisements were all posted in a conspicuous place.
广告都贴在了最显眼的地方。

Words in Use

1. The tower is clearly ____ from the beach.
   A. viscous   B. visible   C. vital   D. virulent

2. They <u>envision</u> a harmonious society, which is free of poverty and disease. Which of the following words is the synonym of the underlined word?
   A. pursue   B. search   C. image   D. imagine

3. The government has taken measures to control the spread of ____ infections.
   A. virus   B. vista   C. visa   D. virtue

4. You'll need to get your passport ____ if you want to go to America.
   A. virtual   B. visaed   C. virtuous   D. vista
5. An endless ____ of tedious days and nights stretched before us.
   A. visa   B. vista   C. visibility   D. vision
6. The author ____ the manuscript again and again.
   A. revived   B. reverted   C. revised   D. revitalized
7. She works there in a ____ capacity.
   A. supervisory   B. superlative   C. supple   D. supplicant
8. The report found no ____ of damage to crops by acid rain.
   A. eviction   B. exactitude   C. evidence   D. evolution
9. The company's profit is falling steadily, and his job is to ____ this trend.
   A. revoke   B. reverse   C. revitalize   D. revise
10. There has some ____ of interest in this composer's music.
    A. revetment   B. review   C. revision   D. revival
11. In order to calm down the workers, the manager made an ____ speech.
    A. improvised   B. improvident   C. imprecise   D. impractical
12. Gunpowder is now considered to be of Chinese ____.
    A. providence   B. provenance   C. evidence   D. confidence
13. We can ____ that the stone circles were used in some sort of pagan ceremony.
    A. introspect   B. specify   C. prospect   D. speculate
14. That book needs a lot of ____ before getting published.
    A. review   B. revolt   C. revive   D. revisions
15. The company has been circumspect in its response to the report. Which of the following words is the synonym of the underlined word?
    A. speculative   B. prospective   C. cautious   D. suspicious
16. From the top of the hill there's a beautiful ____ over the valley.
    A. speculate   B. prospect   C. inspect   D. auspice
17. I have tested my eyes and the optician says that my ____ is perfect.
    A. viscount   B. visualization   C. visitation   D. vision
18. Football is our most popular ____ sport.
    A. spectrum   B. spectator   C. spectacle   D. speck
19. The children seem to be ____ under their care.
    A. perspective   B. protective   C. prospective   D. prospering
20. His remarks have led to intense ____ about the possibility of tax cuts.
    A. speculation   B. suspicion   C. auspice   D. spectacle
21. We are very ____ that our design won the national prize.
    A. proverbial   B. provided   C. proud   D. provident

22. He has a deep impression of the spectacular scenery. Which of the following words is the synonym of the underlined word?

    A. cautious   B. despicable   C. suspicious   D. impressive

23. ____ there is no opposition, we shall hole the meeting here.

    A. Provided   B. Provident   C. Provide   D. Prove

24. He said his plan had the ____ of being the easiest to implement.

    A. virtuosity   B. visibility   C. visitation   D. virtue

25. Despite her ____ distress, she carried on working.

    A. affluent   B. existent   C. evident   D. confident

26. The president was so much under the influence of his wife that she was the ____ ruler of the company.

    A. virtual   B. visible   C. visionary   D. visual

27. The whole is in ____ against the tyrannical regime.

    A. reverie   B. reverse   C. revolt   D. revision

28. There is ____ water supply in case the main fails.

    A. supervisory   B. supplementary   C. supplicated   D. superior

29. She enjoys the pleasant ____ and forgets her miserable suffering right now.

    A. vista   B. visa   C. virus   D. vision

30. The ____ arts are painting, dancing, etc., which is opposed to music and literature.

    A. visible   B. visual   C. visionary   D. virtuous

Key to Words in Use

1. B	2. D	3. A	4. B	5. B
6. C	7. A	8. C	9. B	10. D
11. A	12. B	13. D	14. D	15. C
16. B	17. D	18. B	19. D	20. A
21. C	22. D	23. A	24. D	25. C
26. A	27. C	28. B	29. A	30. B

第2章　表示"听"的词根

Words in Context

Audit in a Company

The general definition of an **audit** is an evaluation of a person, organization, system, process, enterprise, project or product. Audits are performed to ascertain the validity and reliability of information; also to provide an assessment of a system's internal control. The goal of an **auditor** is to express an opinion on the person/ organization/system (etc) in question, under evaluation based on work done on a test basis. Due to practical constraints, an audit seeks to provide only reasonable assurance that the statements are free from material error. Hence, statistical sampling is often adopted in audits. Traditionally, audits were mainly associated with gaining information about financial systems and the financial records of a company or a business. However, recent **auditing** has begun to include other information about the system, such as information about security risks, information systems performance (beyond financial systems), and environmental performance. As a result, there are now professions conducting security audits, IS audits, and environmental audits.

Word Building

More Words with the Word Roots

词根	释义	例词
audi	听	audience, auditorium, audible, inaudible
audit		auditorium, audit, auditor, auditory, audition, audiphone, audio

1. **audience:** [ˈɔːdiəns] *n.* 听众，观众

   分解记忆法：audi-(听)＋ence(名词后缀)＝听众，观众

   【例句】The debate was televised in front of a live audience.

   　　　　这场辩论当着现场观众的面进行了电视转播。

   　　　　His book reached an even wider audience when it was made into a movie.

   　　　　他的书被搬上银幕后赢得了更多的观众。

2. **audible:** [ˈɔːdibəl] *a.* 听得见的

   分解记忆法：audi-(听)＋ble(……的)＝听得见的

【例句】Her voice was barely audible above the noise.
一片嘈杂中，她的声音只能勉强听得见。
The manager's voice was barely audible among the noise of the machinery.
在机器的轰响中，经理的声音几乎听不见。

常用派生词：audible→ inaudible

3. audit: [ˈɔːdit] *v. & n.* 查账

分解记忆法：audit 查账

【例句】The company has just had its accounts audited.
公司账目刚完成审计。
The yearly audit takes place each December.
年度审计在每年的12月份进行。

常用派生词：audit → auditor

4. audition: [ɔːˈdiʃən] *n.* 试听

分解记忆法：audit- (听) + ion（名词后缀）= 试听

【例句】They are holding auditions for the part next week.
他们下周为这个角色的演员试镜。
We auditioned over 200 children for the part.
我们为了这个角色面试了200多个孩子。

5. auditory: [ˈɔːditəri] *a.* 听觉的

分解记忆法：audit- (听) + ory（……的）= 听觉的

【例句】She needs an operation immediately because of auditory difficulties.
因为听觉障碍，她需要立刻手术。
The loud noise in the factory damages her auditory health.
工厂的噪声使她的听力下降了。

6. audio-visual: [ˌɔːdi-əuˈviʒjuəl] *n.* 视听的

分解记忆法：audit- (听) + visual (看) = 视听的

【例句】She works in a audio-visual publishing house.
她在一家音像出版社工作。
The theater has first class audio-visual facilities.
这家剧院拥有一流的视听设备。

Words in Use

1. The monks led an ____ life in the mountains.
   A. inaudible   B. austere   C. authentic   D. authoritative
2. I'm not really ____ to his way of thinking yet.
   A. attracted   B. attributed   C. audited   D. attuned

3. One of the difficulties ____ on shift work is lack of sleep.
   A. attribute	B. attorney	C. audience	D. attendant
4. The fall in the price usually ____ to a sharp reduction in demand.
   A. attributable	B. audible	C. attractive	D. attendant
5. The patient has ____ difficulties, so she needs an operation as soon as possible.
   A. autarchy	B. audacious	C. auditory	D. audit
6. He ____ for the role of Julius Caesar.
   A. automated	B. auditioned	C. averted	D. avoided
7. The school's ____ equipment includes videos and cassettes.
   A. audio-visual	B. auspicious	C. audible	D. august
8. She ____ her gaze from the terrible sight.
   A. audits	B. avails	C. averts	D. avoids
9. The government put a package of ____ measures into practice, aiming at restoring the country's economic health.
   A. austerity	B. audible	C. austere	D. audacious
10. Every ____ ambulance was rushed to the scene of the accident.
    A. automatic	B. available	C. audible	D. authentic
11. The little boy asked the footballer for his ____.
    A. authority	B. autograph	C. audition	D. autocrat
12. This conference has been arranged under the ____ of the UN.
    A. authenticity	B. audit	C. aurora	D. auspices
13. They ____ themselves on their enemy.
    A. avenge	B. audit	C. automat	D. avail
14. How you have the ____ to say such a thing, I don't know.
    A. audacity	B. augury	C. audience	D. autarchy
15. He was swept away in an ____.
    A. austerity	B. avalanche	C. audience	D. audition
16. She thinks that young people have no respect for ____.
    A. auditor	B. automat	C. autonomy	D. authority
17. More teachers use the ____ aids in class.
    A. averse	B. average	C. audible	D. audio-visual
18. She has an ____ to the housework.
    A. aversion	B. audition	C. aviation	D. avenue
19. Hong Kong enjoys a political system that allows a high degree of local ____.
    A. autocracy	B. audition	C. autonomy	D. avatar
20. Their ____ aim is to overthrow that.
    A. avowed	B. awaited	C. audited	D. axed

21. They explored every ____ but find no solution.
    A. authority	B. avenue	C. revenue	D. audit
22. The ability to speak Chinese was among his ____.
    A. attitude	B. attainments	C. audition	D. attempt
23. There is an ____ of decay in this empty village.
    A. austerity	B. augury	C. aura	D. audience
24. This rain ____ well for this year's harvest.
    A. augurs	B. auditions	C. audits	D. automates
25. The group practices religious ____, such as fasting.
    A. audit	B. audacity	C. audience	D. austerity
26. I can't spend this money without ____ from the Head Office.
    A. aura	B. authorization	C. augury	D. audition
27. The ____ at school is demanded by law.
    A. attainment	B. attendant	C. attendance	D. audience
28. The year began ____ with good trade figures for January.
    A. authentically	B. austerely	C. auspiciously	D. auditory
29. The castle is our biggest tourist ____.
    A. attraction	B. audition	C. attitude	D. attorney
30. The book reached more ____ when it was made into a movie.
    A. audition	B. audience	C. austerity	D. authority

Key to Words in Use

1. B	2. D	3. D	4. A	5. C
6. B	7. A	8. C	9. A	10. B
11. B	12. D	13. A	14. A	15. B
16. D	17. D	18. A	19. C	20. A
21. B	22. B	23. C	24. A	25. D
26. B	27. C	28. C	29. A	30. B

第3章　表示"说"的词根

Words in Context

The Movie *2012*

The movie *2012*, the latest arrival from the stable of Columbia Pictures and the brainchild of director Roland Emmerich, bears his signature everywhere. Watching the film, however, one can't help feeling that the ensemble cast of the finest actors is a waste because there is hardly much for them to do. All the **dialogues** are given to the special effects, the principal actor in the movie. Like any other film that is based on a dooms day **prediction**, *2012* is also loaded with graphic, detailed special effects. The film's editing leaves you gripping your seat as the characters go hurtling between crumbling towers and away from the heaving, volcanic earth. The scenes are nothing less than spectacular: they would leave one breathless if one had the time to appreciate them while being taken on a disastrous roller-coaster ride. Emmerich makes very nice use of the idea of the apocalypse. Instead of making a movie with a message that cautious humans of being responsible enough not to bring about the end of the world, he talks of the Mayan Calendar that **predict** the doom due to a cosmic occurrence. At the end of the film, when people from different countries solidify together, the director shows the **benediction** for all human beings.

Word Building

More Words with the Word Roots

词根	释义	例词
dict	说	contradict, contradiction, contradictory, dictation, dictate, predict, benediction
log(ue)		dialogue, monologue, eulogize, analogy
loqu		loquacious, eloquent circumlocution, eloquence
locu		elocution, obloquy, magniloquent

1. contradict: [ˌkɔntrəˈdikt] *v.* 反驳

　　分解记忆法：contra-（相反）+ dict（说）= 反驳

　　【例句】All the evening her husband contradicted everything she said.

153

整个晚上她说什么丈夫都跟她拌嘴。

If you contradict me once more, you are fired.

如果你再顶撞我，我就解雇你。

常用派生词：contradict → contradiction → contradictory

2. contradiction: [ˌkɔntrəˈdikʃən] *n.* 反驳

分解记忆法：contra- (相反) + dict (说) + ion (名词后缀) = 反驳

【例句】There is a contradiction between the two sets of figures.

两组数据互相矛盾。

His public speeches are in direct contradiction to his personal lifestyle.

他的公开言论与他本人的生活方式恰恰相反。

3. dictate: [dikˈteit] *v.* 听写；口述

分解记忆法：dict- (说) + ate (动词后缀) = 听写，口述

【例句】He can't type but can dictate.

他不会打字，但是可以口述。

She dictates a letter to her secretary.

她向秘书口述了一封信。

常用派生词：dictate → dictation → dictator

4. predict: [priˈdikt] *v.* 预先

分解记忆法：pre- (前，预先) + dict (说) = 预言

【例句】It is impossible to predict what will happen.

预知未来的事是不可能的。

It was predicted that inflation would continue to fall.

据预报，通货膨胀将持续下降。

常用派生词：predict → prediction → predictable

5. prediction: [priˈdikʃən] *n.* 预言

分解记忆法：pre- (前，预先) + dict (说) + ion (名词后缀) = 预言

【例句】Her prediction turned out to be correct.

她的预言证明是正确的。

A fortune-teller made a prediction that the child would be the king of the country.

算命的人预言这个孩子将会成为国王。

6. dictionary: [ˈdikʃənəri] *n.* 词典

分解记忆法：diction- (言辞) + ary (表示物) = 词典

【例句】You can look up in the dictionary if you don't know the word.

如果你不认识这个词的话，可以查词典。

This Chinese-English dictionary offers the new learners a lot of help.

这本汉英词典给初学者提供了很多帮助。

7. edict: [ˈiːdikt] *n.* 指示

分解记忆法：e- (出) + dict (说) = 指示

【例句】The king issued an edict forbidding the wearing of swords within the city.

国王颁布一项在城内不得佩剑的法令。

You must respect the edict seriously.

你必须严格遵守法令。

8. dialogue: [ˈdaiəlɔg] *n.* 对话

分解记忆法：dia- (在……之间) + logue(说话) = 对话

【例句】Finally there comes to be a reasonable dialogue between the two countries.

最后两个国家终于有了一个理智的对话。

He is not good at writing the dialogue.

他不擅长写对话。

9. indict: [inˈdikt] *v.* 起诉

分解记忆法：in- (进去) + dict (说) = 起诉

【例句】The senator was indicted for murder.

那位参议员被控谋杀。

The police indicted the man for the murder of a little girl.

警察起诉那个男人谋杀了一个小女孩。

常用派生词：indict → indictable → indictment

10. abdicate: [ˈæbdikeit] *v.* 放弃，退位

分解记忆法：ab- (离开) + dict (说) + ate (动词后缀) = 放弃，退位

【例句】According to some political reasons, the king abdicated.

因为一些政治原因，国王退位了。

He accused the government of abdicating its responsibility for the economy.

他指责政府在经济上失职。

常用派生词：abdicate → abdication

11. verdict: [ˈvəːdikt] *n.* 裁定，裁决

分解记忆法：ver- (真实) + dict (说) = 裁定，裁决

【例句】The jury reached a verdict of guilt.

陪审团做出了有罪的裁决。

The panel will give their verdict on the latest video releases.

专题小组将就最近发行的录像提出他们的意见。

12. monologue: [ˈmɔnəlɔg] *n.* 独白

分解记忆法：mono- (单一的) + logue (说话) = 独白

【例句】He went into a long monologue about life in America.

他开始滔滔不绝地谈起美国的生活。

The author is good at using the monologue to express the inner world.

作者擅长用独白来表达内心世界。

13. **eulogy:** [ˈjuːlədʒi] *n.* 颂歌，赞词

    分解记忆法： eu-（美好）+ log（说话）+ y（名词后缀）= 颂歌，赞词

    【例句】The pastor sent the couple a eulogy to marriage.

    牧师给这对夫妇做婚礼颂词。

    The eulogy expresses the appreciation of the people for their hero.

    这篇颂词表达了人们对他们的英雄的感激之情。

    常用派生词：eulogy → eulogize → eulogist

14. **analogy:** [əˈnælədʒi] *n.* 类似

    分解记忆法： ana-（一样）+ log（说话）+ y（名词后缀）= 类似

    【例句】The teacher drew an analogy between the human heart and a pump.

    老师打了个比喻，把人的心脏比作水泵。

    There are no analogies with any previous legal cases.

    以往的法律案件没有哪一宗可与此案类比。

15. **loquacious:** [ləuˈkweiʃəs] *a.* 多话的

    分解记忆法： loqu-（说）+ acious（多……的）= 多话的

    【例句】I can't bear such a loquacious woman.

    我受不了这个一直喋喋不休的女人。

    Don't be loquacious when you are at your working place.

    在工作的时候别说太多话。

16. **circumlocution:** [ˌsəːkəmləˈkjuːʃən] *n.* 累赘的说法

    分解记忆法： circum-（绕圈）+ locu（说话）+ tion（名词后缀）= 累赘的说法

    【例句】Tell me the truth. I don't want to hear the circumlocution.

    请告诉我实话，我不想听那些多余的言辞。

    Such circumlocution makes me crazy.

    这样繁复的表达让我很头痛。

17. **colloquial:** [kəˈləukwiəl] *adj.* 口语的

    分解记忆法： col-（共同）+ loqu（说）+ ial（……的）= 口语的

    【例句】"I am going nuts" — this sentence is a colloquial expression.

    "我要发疯了"这句话是俗语表达。

    In the business writing we should avoid the colloquial words.

    在商务信函中，我们应该避免使用俗语。

    常用派生词：colloquial → colloquialism

18. **eloquent:** [ˈeləkwənt] *a.* 雄辩的

    分解记忆法： e-（出）+ loqu（说）+ ent（……的）= 雄辩的

    【例句】The president of the party shows an eloquent appeal for support for the strike.

    该党主席有鼓动性地表达了对罢工的支持。

The ruins are an eloquent reminder of the horrors of war.
这些废墟形象地提醒人们不要忘记战争的恐怖。

常用派生词：eloquent → eloquence

19. **obloquy:** [ˈɔbləkwi] *n.* 谩骂

分解记忆法：ob- (反对) + loqu (语言) + y (名词后缀) = 谩骂

【例句】The new policy causes lots of obloquy.
新的政策招来一片骂声。

The film star bears much pressure because of the obloquy.
因为谩骂，这个电影明星承受了很多压力。

Words in Use

1. It is my _____ that the plan would never have been successful.
   A. contention   B. contradiction   C. contingency   D. contract
2. We can _____ how the money will be spent.
   A. verdict   B. predict   C. dictate   D. irritate
3. At last there can be a reasonable _____ between the two governments.
   A. dialect   B. diagram   C. dialogue   D. diary
4. In her speech she _____ the government's optimistic promise with its dismal achievements.
   A. contrasted   B. contracted   C. continued   D. contorted
5. The economists _____ an increase in the rate of inflation.
   A. predated   B. predestined   C. predicted   D. predicated
6. The government _____ its responsibility for the economy.
   A. interdicts   B. abbreviates   C. renounces   D. judges
7. Their offer was greeted with _____ distrust.
   A. predictable   B. predicative   C. predominant   D. preemptive
8. It is necessary for an actor to have a train in _____.
   A. interdiction   B. diction   C. dictation   D. prediction
9. The company's future is _____ on the outcome of the trial.
   A. contraceptive   B. continual   C. contingent   D. contradictory
10. The amount of money available will _____ the type of computer we buy.
    A. accomplish   B. determine   C. arrange   D. supervise
11. Don't be so _____! You should also follow others' advice.
    A. dialectic   B. didactic   C. dictionary   D. dictatorial
12. They were in a state of _____ after the baby was born.
    A. euphoria   B. eulogy   C. ethos   D. ethics
13. You could have a try to learn by _____.

A. eulogy B. analogy C. obloquy D. epilogue

14. If you don't deliver the goods by Friday, we will be breaking the _____.

    A. contrast B. contract C. contradiction D. contour

15. "Pass away" is a _____ term for "toilet."

    A. eulogistic B. euphemistic C. evasive D. eventual

16. He spoilt the poem by reading it in a _____ voice.

    A. monotonous B. loquacious C. colloquial D. magniloquent

17. Three people were killed in a dead-on _____ between a bus and a car.

    A. edict B. prediction C. collision D. colloquial

18. The council found that their traffic plans had been _____ by a government decision.

    A. predetermined B. preempted C. predicted D. prefaced

19. In the war many children were _____ from the cities to the countryside.

    A. eventuated B. evaded C. eulogized D. evacuated

20. The ruins are an _____ reminder of the history.

    A. elliptical B. eloquent C. elucidated D. elusive

21. I have been trying to get her on the phone, but she seems to be rather _____.

    A. elusive B. emaciated C. eloquent D. elucidated

22. The firm _____ to build the new railway within the year.

    A. contributes B. contracts C. contradicts D. contrasts

23. We are now in a position to _____ our own demands to the management.

    A. dictate B. edict C. verdict D. abdicate

24. The speech _____ the achievement of the dead king.

    A. evacuates B. evaporates C. evaluates D. eulogizes

25. It was as if we were _____ to meet.

    A. predestined B. predicted C. predisposed D. predicated

26. He made a _____ that the government would be defeated at the general election.

    A. malediction B. dictum C. prediction D. verdict

27. Her face was _____ with pain.

    A. contorted B. contracted C. contented D. contention

28. My ideas are _____ opposed to hers.

    A. didactically B. dialectically C. completely D. dictatorially

29. The book uses a simple _____ to explain the rules of chess.

    A. dictum B. diagram C. diction D. dialogue

30. It is obvious that their alibis _____ each other.

    A. contract B. contour C. contradict D. consistent

Key to Words in Use

1. A	2. B	3. C	4. A	5. C
6. C	7. A	8. B	9. C	10. B
11. D	12. A	13. B	14. B	15. B
16. A	17. C	18. B	19. D	20. B
21. A	22. B	23. A	24. D	25. A
26. C	27. A	28. C	29. B	30. C

第4章　表示"喊叫"的词根

Words in Context

Summary of Obama's Short Lecture about His Asian Visit

When US President Obama finished his visit in the Republic of Korea, he made a lecture to both American and Asian people. In the lecture, he **declaimed** the determination to recover American economy by strengthening the trade with Asian area. He said that there was nothing more important than to do everything they could to get American economy moving again and put Americans back to work, and he would go anywhere to pursue this goal. Meanwhile he **claimed** that Asia was a region where the USA now bought more goods and did more trades with than any other place in the world—commerce that supports millions of jobs back home. And since this region included some of the fastest-growing nations, there could be no solution to the challenge of climate change without the cooperation of the Asia Pacific. What's more, President Obama **advocated** that Iran and DPRK should live up to their international obligations and either forsake nuclear weapons or face the consequences. As for his visit in China, the president emphasized that he would speak with leaders to sustain the economic recovery and bring back jobs and prosperity for American people—a task he would continue to focus on relentlessly in the weeks and months ahead.

Word Building

More Words with the Word Roots

词根	释义	例词
claim	喊叫，声音	claim, acclaim, exclaim, proclaim, reclaim
clam		acclamation, exclamation, exclamatory, proclamation, reclamation, clamor, clamorous
vok		advocate, invoke, evoke, convoke,
voc		vocal, vocalist, equivocal, equivocate, invocatory, evocation, convocation

1. claim: [kleim] *v.* 声称，宣称

分解记忆法：claim = 声称，宣称

【例句】He claimed that he was not given a fair hearing.

他声称他未得到公正的申述机会。

Scientists are claiming a major breakthrough in the fight against cancer.

科学家宣称攻克癌症已有重大的突破。

常用派生词：claim→ claimant

2. acclaim: [əˈkleim] *v.* 欢呼

分解记忆法：ac= ad- (向、朝) + claim (喊) = 欢呼

【例句】The new drug has been acclaimed as the most important discovery for years.

这种新药很受欢迎，被认为是近年来最重要的发明。

They acclaimed him their leader.

他们拥戴他为领袖。

常用派生词：acclaim→ acclamation

3. declaim: [diˈkleim] *v.* 抨击；朗诵

分解记忆法：de-(加强)＋claim (喊) = 抨击，朗诵

【例句】She declaimed the famous opening speech of the play.

她慷慨激昂地朗读了戏中著名的开场白。

He declaimed against the evils of alcohol.

他猛烈地抨击了酗酒的罪恶。

常用派生词：declaim→ declamation

4. exclaim: [ikˈskleim] *v.* 惊叫

分解记忆法：ex- (出) + claim (喊) = 惊叫

【例句】She exclaimed in delight when she saw the presents.

她见到礼物高兴地叫了起来。

She opened her eyes and exclaimed in delight at the scene.

见到这情景，她瞪着眼睛，高兴得大叫。

常用派生词:exclaim → exclamation → exclamatory

5. proclaim: [prəˈkleim] *v.* 宣布，公布

分解记忆法：pro- (在前) + claim (喊) = 宣布，公布

【例句】The president proclaimed a state of emergency.

总统宣布了紧急状态。

The charter proclaimed that all states would have their own governments.

宪章规定，各州可建立各自的政府。

常用派生词：proclaim → proclamation

6. reclaim: [riˈkleim] *v.* 收回

分解记忆法：re- (回) + claim (喊) = 收回

【例句】You'll have to go to the police station to reclaim your wallet.

你得到警察局去领回你的钱包。

The team reclaimed the champion from their rivals.
这个队从对手手中夺回了冠军。

常用派生词：reclaim → reclamation

7. clamor: [ˈklæmə] *v.* 吵闹

分解记忆法：clam（喊）+ or（动词后缀）= 吵闹

【例句】Everyone was clamoring to know how much they would get.
大家都吵闹着想知道他们能得多少。
A crowd of reporters clamored around the car.
一群记者围着那辆车乱哄哄地提问。

常用派生词：clamor → clamorous

8. vocal: [ˈvəukəl] *a.* 声音的

分解记忆法：voc-（声音）+ al（……的）= 声音的

【例句】He has been very vocal in his criticism of the government's policy.
他对政府政策的批评向来直言不讳。
The protesters are a small but vocal minority.
抗议者人数不多但敢于直言。

常用派生词：vocal → vocalist

9. advocate: [ˈædvəkit] *v.* 提倡

分解记忆法：ad-（增强）+ voc（声音）+ ate（动词后缀）= 提倡

【例句】The group doesn't advocate the use of violence.
该团体不支持使用暴力。
Many experts advocate rewarding the child for good behavior.
很多专家主张要表扬孩子的良好表现。

常用派生词：advocate → advocacy

10. equivocal: [iˈkwivəkəl] *a.* 模棱两可的

分解记忆法：equi-（一样）+ voc（声音）+ al（……的）= 模棱两可的

【例句】I don't quite understand his equivocal words.
我没太明白他有些含糊其词的话。
You should avoid the equivocal words in the letter.
信件中应该避免模糊不清的语言。

常用派生词：equivocal → equivocate → equivocation

11. invoke: [inˈvəuk] *v.* 援用；引用

分解记忆法：in-（进入）+ vok（声音）+ e = 援用，引用

【例句】She invoked several eminent scholars to back up her argument.
她援引了几位赫赫有名的学者来支持她的论点。
His name was invoked as a symbol of the revolution.
他的名字被提出作为那次革命的象征。

常用派生词：invoke → invocatory

12. evoke: [iˈvəuk] *v.* 唤起

　　分解记忆法：e-（出）+ voke（喊叫）= 唤起

　　【例句】The music evoked memories of her youth.

　　　　　这乐曲勾起了她对青年时代的回忆。

　　　　　His case is unlikely to evoke public empathy.

　　　　　他的情况不大可能引起公众的同情。

　　常用派生词：evoke → evocation

13. convoke: [kənˈvəuk] *v.* 召集开会

　　分解记忆法：con-（一起）+ voke（喊叫）= 召集开会

　　【例句】The president convokes all the members to settle the emergency.

　　　　　主席召集所有的成员开会以解决紧急事件。

　　　　　The board convoked the meeting in order to get through the financial crisis.

　　　　　董事会开会商讨如何度过经济危机。

14. provoke: [prəˈvəuk] *v.* 煽动

　　分解记忆法：pro-（前面）+ voke（喊叫）= 煽动

　　【例句】The announcement provoked a storm of protest.

　　　　　这个声明激起了抗议的风潮。

　　　　　The lawyer claimed his client was provoked into acts of violence by the defendant.

　　　　　律师声称他的当事人是受到被告的挑衅才采取暴力行动的。

　　常用派生词：provoke → provocative → provocation

15. revoke: [riˈvəuk] *v.* 撤回；废除

　　分解记忆法：re-（回）+ voke（喊）= 撤回，废除

　　【例句】The unfair treaty has been revoked for years.

　　　　　不平等条约已经被废除多年了。

　　　　　It is necessary to revoke the trade barrier.

　　　　　有必要废除贸易壁垒。

　　常用派生词：revoke → revocation → revocable

Words in Use

1. ____ of unemployment benefit should fill in this form.
   　A. Servants　　　　B. Claimants　　　　C. Complaints　　　　D. Applicants
2. Make a written ____ of all the foods you bought abroad.
   　A. decision　　　　B. declension　　　　C. declamation　　　　D. declaration

3. It is their ____ intention to increase taxes.
   A. declined   B. declared   C. declarative   D. declaimed
4. "Good heavens!" is an ____ of surprise.
   A. excuse   B. explanation   C. exclamation   D. excursion
5. His accent ____ his American origins.
   A. proclaimed   B. procreated   C. procured   D. probed
6. They ____ to have discovered a cure for the disease, but this has not yet been proved.
   A. claim   B. prompt   C. indicate   D. revoke
7. This land was ____ from the sea.
   A. recharged   B. recited   C. recoiled   D. reclaimed
8. He ____ a reduction in military spending.
   A. advertises   B. advisers   C. advocates   D. advents
9. Please answer me clearly. Don't ____ your meaning.
   A. equivalent   B. equivocate   C. equalize   D. equate
10. He tends to ____ from making difficult decisions.
    A. recoil   B. recline   C. reclaim   D. rebel
11. The government says they have reduced income tax, but I would dispute this claim.
    A. renouncement   B. claim   C. clam   D. benediction
12. He ____ his intention of attending, despite their opposition.
    A. acclaimed   B. exclaimed   C. proclaimed   D. reclaimed
13. You may be my sister, but that doesn't mean that you have any ____ on me. Which of the following words is the synonym of the underlined word?
    A. consistency   B. formality   C. civility   D. demand
14. We have ____ you separately for these items a few days ago.
    A. invoked   B. invoiced   C. evoked   D. declaimed
15. The British political system has ____ over several centuries.
    A. evoked   B. evolved   C. revoked   D. provoked
16. The students tried to ____ the teacher into losing her temper.
    A. convoke   B. revoke   C. evoke   D. provoke
17. He can't ____ himself to the hot weather.
    A. acclaim   B. acclimatize   C. accolade   D. account
18. The government has ____ its permission for then to enter the country.
    A. revoked   B. revolted   C. revolved   D. revived
19. He thinks the whole world ____ around him.
    A. rewards   B. results   C. revokes   D. revolves
20. They attacked our border guards without the slightest ____.
    A. revolution   B. provocation   C. administration   D. determination

21. That old film ____ memories of my childhood.
    A. evolves   B. provides   C. evokes   D. responds
22. The medicine has been ____ as the most significant discovery for years.
    A. acclaimed   B. accommodated   C. acclimatized   D. accorded
23. The government _____ "reasons of national security" in order to justify arresting its opponents.
    A. involved   B. invoked   C. invoiced   D. invited
24. The lawyers have ____ against signing the contract.
    A. adventured   B. advanced   C. advised   D. advocated
25. Her mission was to ____ former criminals.
    A. ridicule   B. interdict   C. reclaim   D. consider
26. The customs officer asked me if I had anything to ____.
    A. proclaim   B. acclaim   C. declare   D. claim
27. You will be on ____ for the first two months.
    A. probity   B. procedure   C. proclamation   D. probation
28. His ____ from the negotiations infuriates the union.
    A. exclamation   B. exculpation   C. exclusion   D. excommunication
29. The election results were announced to the ____ of loud cheering.
    A. accompaniment   B. accommodation   C. acclamation   D. accomplishment
30. Old people are entitled to ____ a special heating allowance from the government.
    A. clamp   B. clamber   C. claim   D. clack

Key to *Words in Use*

1. B	2. D	3. B	4. C	5. A
6. A	7. D	8. C	9. B	10. A
11. B	12. C	13. D	14. B	15. B
16. D	17. B	18. A	19. D	20. B
21. C	22. A	23. B	24. C	25. C
26. C	27. D	28. C	29. A	30. C

第5章　表示"吃喝"的词根

Words in Context

Carnivores, Herbivores and Omnivores

Herbivores

Herbivores are animals which only eat plant material. This means leaves, flowers, fruits or even wood. Sheep, horses, rabbits and snails are well known examples of herbivores which eat grass and leaves. A parrot, however, which eats fruits and nuts can also be called a herbivore.

Omnivores

Omnivores eat both plants and meat. Chickens are omnivores. They eat seeds, but they can also eat worms. Human beings are also omnivores, although some people choose not to eat meat. These people are called vegetarians. The chimpanzee is **omnivorous**. It eats fruits, leaves, palm nuts, seeds and stems, as well as ants, birds' eggs, fish and termites. Chimpanzees will occasionally kill and eat baboons and wild pigs

Carnivores

Carnivores eat meat. A carnivore is a predator because it has to find and catch its prey. Some carnivores, such as wolves, hunt in a group called a pack. They move silently and slowly to form a circle around their prey before they attack. Other carnivores, such as the cheetah, usually hunt alone. The cheetah creeps towards its prey without being noticed, until it is 30 meters from it, then the cheetah starts to run. Some insects are carnivores. The dragonfly, which hovers so gracefully above a pond, is hunting for other insects. The eagle is a **carnivorous** bird. It flies high in the sky looking for animals, such as rabbits. When it finds one it quickly swoops to the ground. It uses its strong feet and pointed claws, called talons, to catch the rabbit. It has a very pointed beak to help it tear off the meat.

Word Building

More Words with the Word Roots

词根	释义	例词
ed	吃	edible, inedible
vor	吃	voracious, voracity, devour, omnivorous, herbivorous, carnivorous, carnivore
pot	喝	potable, potation, potion, compotator

1. edible: [ˈedəbl] *a.* 可食用的

　　分解记忆法：ed- (吃) + ible (……的) = 可食用的

　　【例句】The food at the hotel was barely edible.
　　　　　这家旅馆的食物简直不能入口。
　　　　　The nutrients in edible fruits are what we need.
　　　　　我们从可食用的水果中得到所需的营养。

　常用派生词：edible → inedible

2. voracious: [vəˈreiʃəs] *a.* 贪婪的

　　分解记忆法：vor- (吃) + acious (多……的) = 贪婪的

　　【例句】The little boy has a voracious appetite.
　　　　　这个小男孩胃口很大。
　　　　　She is a voracious reader.
　　　　　她是一个求知欲极强的读者。

　常用派生词：voracious → voracity

3. omnivorous: [ɔmˈnivərəs] *a.* 杂食的

　　分解记忆法：omni- (全) + vor (吃) + ous (……的) = 杂食的

　　【例句】The dinner is an omnivorous diet.
　　　　　晚餐有荤有素。
　　　　　She has always been an omnivorous reader.
　　　　　她一向阅读兴趣广泛。

4. herbivorous: [həːˈbivərəs] *a.* 食草的

　　分解记忆法：herbi- (草本植物) + vor (吃) + ous (……的) = 食草的

　　【例句】It is surprising that the parrot is a herbivorous animal.
　　　　　令人吃惊的是鹦鹉是食草动物。
　　　　　It is hard to imagine this kind of dinosaur is herbivorous.
　　　　　很难想象，这种恐龙是吃草的。

　常用派生词：herbivorous → herbivore

5. carnivorous: [kɑːˈnivərəs] *a.* 食肉的

　　分解记忆法：carni- (肉) + vor (吃) + ous (……的) = 食肉的

　　【例句】This nation is used to a carnivorous diet.
　　　　　这个民族习惯多肉的饮食。
　　　　　Such a carnivorous diet is not good for your health.
　　　　　这样多肉的饮食不利于你的健康。

　常用派生词：carnivorous → carnivore

6. potable: [ˈpəutəbl] *a.* 可喝的

　　分解记忆法：pot- (喝) + able (……的) = 可喝的

　　【例句】The water in the mountain is potable.

山上的水是能喝的。
The spring is potable.
泉水可以喝。

Words in Use

1. During the seventies, her acting career was in _____.
    A. edge   B. eclipse   C. edibility   D. edict
2. The dancer's movements were slow and _____.
    A. volatile   B. voluntary   C. voracious   D. voluptuous
3. They were in a(n) _____ position, with the enemy on the hill above them.
    A. potable   B. voracious   C. vulnerable   D. inedible
4. She's been a bit _____, waiting for the exam results.
    A. edgy   B. edible   C. ecstatic   D. eclectic
5. We need to work together to overcome the _____ task.
    A. hereabouts   B. hemline   C. herbaceous   D. herculean
6. These regulations are a _____ from restrictions that were imposed during wartime.
    A. carnivore   B. carry-over   C. carnival   D. carnation
7. The water from the river is _____.
    A. potential   B. drinkable   C. voracious   D. edible
8. She _____ the kids around with her wherever she goes.
    A. carnivores   B. carps   C. carts   D. carpets
9. Roman soldiers were often _____ of the Mars, the god of war.
    A. volley   B. voluntary   C. votary   D. voracity
10. I wish you don't _____ about the way I dress.
    A. carol   B. carp   C. carnivore   D. cart
11. She might be our _____ best tennis player, but she needs to practice much harder.
    A. potentially   B. potbelly   C. voraciously   D. clamorously
12. Newspaper often contains _____ of well-known politicians.
    A. carillon   B. caricatures   C. carnations   D. carnivore
13. Alcohol increases the drug's _____.
    A. potion   B. potency   C. potentate   D. potation
14. Professor Spinks is to talk about Mexican Pottery, for your _____.
    A. edifice   B. edibility   C. edition   D. edification
15. He was _____ by the boss for failing to win the contract.
    A. carpeted   B. carped   C. carnivorous   D. carnal

16. Come home with me and have supper, if you don't mind taking _____.
    A. pottery   B. potation   C. potential   D. potluck
17. The despotic rule of the _____ was overthrown.
    A. potation   B. potentate   C. potable   D. potential
18. The situation in the streets is highly _____, and the army is being called in.
    A. voracious   B. volatile   C. volcanic   D. votive
19. This new invention has enormous sales _____.
    A. potential   B. potation   C. potentate   D. potion
20. The children sang _____ during the week before Christmas.
    A. carnivore   B. carol   C. carp   D. carpenter
21. The bridegroom and best man wore white _____ in their buttonholes.
    A. carnivore   B. carpet   C. carnations   D. carport
22. These berries are _____ but those are poisonous.
    A. edict   B. eclipse   C. edgy   D. edible
23. There are some surprising _____ in the list of candidates.
    A. omen   B. omissions   C. omnibus   D. omnivorous
24. All the people in Rio de Janeiro are preparing for the _____ time.
    A. carnival   B. carnivore   C. voracity   D. potion
25. The house was full of expensive but very _____ furniture.
    A. vulnerable   B. voracious   C. votive   D. vulgar
26. She has the _____ on the other students because she spent a year in England.
    A. edibility   B. edge   C. edict   D. eclipse
27. We have a colorful _____ order round our garden.
    A. carnivorous   B. omnivorous   C. herbivorous   D. herbaceous
28. He is an _____ reader, who reads lots of books.
    A. omnibus   B. omnipotent   C. omnivorous   D. omniscient
29. She is a _____ reader of biographies.
    A. voracious   B. voluntary   C. voluminous   D. voluble
30. The king issued an _____ forbidding the wearing of swords within the city.
    A. echo   B. eclipse   C. edict   D. edible

Key to *Words in Use*

1. B	2. D	3. C	4. A	5. D
6. B	7. B	8. C	9. C	10. B
11. A	12. B	13. B	14. D	15. A
16. D	17. B	18. B	19. A	20. B
21. C	22. D	23. B	24. A	25. D
26. B	27. D	28. C	29. A	30. C

第6章 表示"推拉"的词根

Words in Context

Projectile Blood Collection Device

This is a blood-collecting apparatus for obtaining a blood sample from an **intruder** at a crime scene to be later analyzed for DNA. Many conventional technologies are routinely practiced by law enforcement agencies to identify a perpetrator, including fingerprinting, video surveillance, and foot printing.

Defenses against crimes of **intrusion** by potential victims routinely include handguns, mace, stunning devices and the like, which have in common the requirement that the victim must brandish the deterring weapon in close proximity to the criminal intruder. Besides being daunting and dangerous to the victim acting in self-defense, confronting seasoned criminals does not necessarily result in identification. Confronted by weapons, it is all too usual for the criminal to "get the drop" on the victim, or to withdraw from the crime scene. In either case the criminal is not likely to be identified.

This invention is a novel approach to deterring crimes of intrusion, by making it more likely that the perpetrator will be identified. Instead of attempting to deter a criminal with methodologies that can be circumvented or fairly readily overcome, such as in the case of guns or video surveillance, this invention is a mechanism for obtaining a blood sample from the intruder to be later analyzed for DNA.

The invention brings the elements of surprise and speed to the **extraction** of a blood sample; and thereafter, the invention effectively withdraws the sample from the point of contact by a random ejecting of the blood sample reservoir outside the cognizance of the criminal at the crime scene.

Word Building

More Words with the Word Roots

词根	释义	例词
pel	推	propel, expel, repel, dispel, compel, impel
trud, trus	推	extrude, intrude, protrude, intrusion, abstruse
tract	拉	abstract, contract, detract, extract, retract, tract

1. propel: [prəˈpel] *vt.* 推进

　　分解记忆法: pro-(向前) + pel(推) = 推进

　　【例句】A sailing boat is propelled by wind.
　　　　　　帆船是由风力推进的。
　　　　　　They invented a rocket-propelled grenade.
　　　　　　他们发明了一个用火箭发射的榴弹。

　　常用派生词: propel → propellant → propeller → propelling

2. expel: [ikˈspel] *v.* 驱逐；开除

　　分解记忆法: ex-(向外) + pel(推) = 驱逐

　　【例句】After the outbreak of the fighting, all foreign journalists were expelled.
　　　　　　战斗开始后，所有的外国记者都被驱逐出境。
　　　　　　If I catch you smoking in the school grounds again, you'll be expelled.
　　　　　　如果再让我发现你在学校操场上抽烟，就非开除你不可。

3. repel: [riˈpel] *v.* 击退；抵制

　　分解记忆法: re-(反) + pel(推) = 击退

　　【例句】The odor can repel mosquitoes.
　　　　　　这种香味可以驱蚊。
　　　　　　The crew repelled the attack.
　　　　　　船员击退了进攻。

　　常用派生词: repel → repellent

4. dispel: [diˈspel] *vt.* 消除（疑虑、错误观念等）

　　分解记忆法: dis-(分散) + pel(推) = 消除

　　【例句】The sun soon dispelled the mist.
　　　　　　阳光很快就驱散了薄雾。
　　　　　　Her reassuring words dispelled our doubts.
　　　　　　她令人放心的话消除了我们的疑虑。

5. compel: [kəmˈpel] *vt.* 强迫；迫使

　　分解记忆法: com-(共同) + pel(推) = 强迫

　　【例句】Employees are compelled to join the company's pension plan after a year's service.
　　　　　　雇员在服务一年之后，必须加入公司的退休金计划。
　　　　　　Lack of funds for the campaign compelled his withdrawal.
　　　　　　由于缺乏资金，他不得不退出竞选。

　　常用派生词: compel→compelling→compellingly

6. impel: [imˈpel] *vt.* 驱使；激励

　　分解记忆法: im-(内) + pel(推) = 驱使

　　【例句】I was so annoyed that I felt impelled to write a letter to the mayor.
　　　　　　我非常恼怒，以致觉得非给市长写信不可。

I felt impelled to go on speaking.
我想一直说下去。

7. extrude: [eks'tru:d] *v.* 挤压出

分解记忆法： ex-(向外) + trud(推) = 挤压出

【例句】Much pressure is required to extrude the toothpaste out of the tube.
需要很用力，才能将牙膏从管中挤出来。
Plastic material is extruded through very small holes to form fibres.
塑料从细孔中挤压出来形成纤维。

常用派生词：extrude→extrusion→extruding

8. intrude: [in'tru:d] *vi.* & *vt.* 闯入；侵入

分解记忆法： in-(进入) + trud(推) = 闯入

【例句】I don't want to intrude on you if you're busy.
如果您正忙的话，我就不打扰您了。
It would be very sensitive to intrude upon their private grief.
要是干涉人家不愿公开的伤心事儿，那就太不明白事理了。

常用派生词：intrude→intruder→intrusion→intrusive

9. protrude: [prə'tru:d] *v.* 突出；鼓出

分解记忆法： pro-(向前) + trud(推) = 突出

【例句】He glimpsed a gun protruding from the man's pocket.
他瞥见这人的口袋里露出了一支枪。
He has a protruding tooth.
他有颗龅牙。

常用派生词：protrude→protrusion→protrusive

10. abstruse: [əb'stru:s] *a.* 深奥的；晦涩难懂的

分解记忆法： abs-(离开) + trus(推) = 深奥的

【例句】He always talked about some abstruse theories.
他总是谈论一些深奥的理论。
That writer's ideas about the time and space are so abstruse that few people understand them.
这个作家有关时空的想法很抽象，很少有人明白。

常用派生词：abstruse→abstruseness

11. abstract: ['æbstrækt] *a.* 抽象的

分解记忆法： abs-(离开) + tract(抽) = 抽象的

【例句】Beauty is abstract but house is not.
美是抽象的，但是房屋不是抽象的。
"Beauty" and "truth" are abstract ideas.
"美"和"真理"都是抽象的概念。

常用派生词：abstract→abstracted→abstractedly

12. attract: [əˈtrækt] *v.* 吸引

    分解记忆法：at-=ad-(向) + tract(拉) = 吸引

    【例句】She is always attracted to foreign men.

            她总是喜欢外国男人。

            His new book has attracted a lot of attention.

            他的新书受到了许多的关注。

    常用派生词：attract→attraction→attractive→attractively→attractiveness

13. contract: [ˈkɔntrækt] *v.* 收缩；签订合同

    分解记忆法：con-(共同) + tract(拉) = 收缩

    【例句】Metal contracts as it becomes cool.

            金属冷却时收缩。

            In conversational English "is not" often contracts to "isn't."

            在英语口语里，"is not"常被缩写为"isn't"。

    常用派生词：contract→contraction

14. distract: [diˈstrækt] *v.* 分散注意力；使分心

    分解记忆法：dis-(分散) + tract(拉) = 分散注意力

    【例句】She was distracted from her work by the noise outside.

            外面的嘈杂声分散了她在工作中的注意力。

            The music distracted her from her work.

            音乐使她无法专心工作。

    常用派生词：distract→distracted→distraction

15. extract: [iksˈtrækt] *vt.* 拔出

    分解记忆法：ex-(出) + tract(拔) = 拔出

    【例句】She had a tooth extracted.

            她拔了一颗牙。

            They extracted a confession from the criminals.

            他们从罪犯那里逼取了口供。

    常用派生词：extract→extraction→extractor

16. protract: [prəˈtrækt] *v.* 延长

    分解记忆法：pro-(向前) + tract(拉) = 延长

    【例句】Let's not protract the debate any further.

            我们不要再继续争论下去了。

            The mandible is protracted and retracted in chewing.

            在咀嚼时大颌(骨)向前伸然后回缩。

    常用派生词：protract→protractor

17. retract: [riˈtrækt] *v.* 缩回，缩进；收回，撤销

   分解记忆法：re-（回）+ tract（拉）= 缩回

   【例句】At the trial, the prisoner retracted his confession.
   那个犯人在审讯的时候翻供。
   The turtle retracted its head into its shell.
   乌龟把脑袋缩进壳中。

   常用派生词：retract→retractable→retraction

18. subtract: [səbˈtrækt] *v.* 减去；减

   分解记忆法：sub-（下）+ tract（抽）= 减去

   【例句】Three subtracted from seven equals four.
   7减3得4。
   Subtracting the costs, the profit would be 1,000 pounds.
   扣除费用，其利润为1000镑。

   常用派生词：subtract→subtraction

19. detract: [diˈtrækt] *v.* 减损；贬低

   分解记忆法：de-（下）+ tract（拉）= 减损

   【例句】One mistake is not going to detract from your achievement.
   一次失误不会有损你所取得的成绩的。
   All the decoration detracts from the beauty of the building's shape.
   这一切装饰有损于大厦的外形美。

   常用派生词：detract→detraction→detractor

20. tractable: [ˈtræktəbəl] *a.* 易驾驭的；温顺的；易管教的

   分解记忆法：tract（拉）+ -able（可……的）= 易驾驭的，温顺的

   【例句】Gold and silver are tractable metals.
   金和银是容易加工的金属。
   Carrie seemed quite tractable, and he congratulated himself.
   嘉莉看上去很温顺，他暗自感到庆幸。

   常用派生词：tractable→tractability→traction→tractor

Words in Use

1. Does a student's desire to be admitted by a famous university ____ him to study hard?
   A. dispel   B. expel   C. repel   D. impel
2. The beggar wears shoes which are so worn out that his toes ____ from the shoes.
   A. extruded   B. intruded   C. abstruse   D. protruded
3. To him, hunger was a(n) ____ concept; he had never missed a meal.
   A. attract   B. abstract   C. contract   D. distract

4. He failed to drive the nail straight into the board and had to _____ it.
   A. extract   B. detract   C. subtract   D. protract
5. The eggs were in the bottom of the bag, but they did not break; they remained _____.
   A. intact   B. contact   C. retract   D. contract
6. The tiny rocket is attached to the spacecraft and is designed to _____ it toward the Mars.
   A. dispel   B. impel   C. propel   D. compel
7. The government tried to _____ the notion that smoking cigarettes can prevent SARS.
   A. impel   B. expel   C. repel   D. dispel
8. Conscience _____ him to admit his part in the affair.
   A. expelled   B. repelled   C. compelled   D. propelled
9. If you _____ 10 from 30 you get 20.
   A. subtract   B. contract   C. retract   D. detract
10. Don't _____ this phone conversation as I expect an important business call within the next few minutes.
    A. subtract   B. protract   C. abstract   D. detract
11. The oil is _____ from the seeds of certain plants.
    A. distracted   B. detracted   C. extracted   D. retracted
12. He is _____ by both guilt and the need to avenge his father.
    A. propelled   B. dispelled   C. expelled   D. compelled
13. There are too many _____ here to work properly.
    A. distributions   B. distractions   C. abstractions   D. extractions
14. Our shop _____ with a local clothing firm for 100 coats a week.
    A. retracted   B. distracted   C. attracted   D. contracted
15. Our main _____ on tonight's show is an interview with Clint Eastwood.
    A. attribution   B. attraction   C. abstraction   D. distribution
16. The principal _____ the trouble-making student from school.
    A. compelled   B. expelled   C. propelled   D. dispelled
17. Meanwhile meetings keep reverting to fruitless discussions about _____ resolutions.
    A. abhorrent   B. abstract   C. abstruse   D. aberrant
18. A huge round mass of smooth rock is _____ from the water.
    A. protecting   B. probing   C. proclaiming   D. protruding
19. She hesitated to _____ on their conversation.
    A. intend   B. intrude   C. invade   D. intact
20. It is the courage and competitiveness which _____ him to take risks.
    A. compels   B. dispels   C. impels   D. expels
21. In the 19th century people used steam to _____ ships.
    A. propel   B. protect   C. dispel   D. compel

22. The newspaper was forced to publish a _____ of all the allegations they had made against her.

   A. extraction   B. retraction   C. distraction   D. abstraction

23. Wet or muddy surfaces can cause a loss of ____.

   A. retraction   B. traction   C. distraction   D. attention

24. I don't want to _____ from their achievement in winning the cup, but the fact is that their opponents were very weak.

   A. contract   B. detract   C. extract   D. protract

25. More than five-thousand secondary school students have been ____ for cheating.

   A. impelled   B. expelled   C. repelled   D. compelled

26. An American diplomat was ____ from this country yesterday.

   A. expelled   B. repelled   C. dispelled   D. compelled

27. He read the ____ of the book before buying it.

   A. detract   B. contract   C. retract   D. abstract

28. His enormous belly ____ over his belt.

   A. abstruse   B. protrudes   C. intrudes   D. extrudes

29. There are a ____ group of pickets, and the director has to call the police.

   A. venerable   B. voluble   C. vociferous   D. vocational

30. To say that his work is strongly influenced by earlier film-makers is no ____.

   A. extraction   B. detraction   C. contraction   D. retraction

Key to *Words in Use*

1. D	2. D	3. B	4. A	5. A
6. C	7. D	8. C	9. A	10. B
11. C	12. A	13. B	14. D	15. B
16. B	17. C	18. D	19. B	20. C
21. A	22. B	23. B	24. B	25. B
26. A	27. D	28. B	29. C	30. B

第7章 表示"投掷"的词根

Words in Context

The General Rules of Basketball League

Objectives: The **objective** of Basketball League is to promote and conduct a positive leisure time activity, which encourages fitness, healthy competition and an atmosphere conducive for fun and fellowship.

League Schedules: The officials will make all league placements and schedules. Officials reserve the right to adjust league schedules. All possible notifications will be given to teams should it become necessary to change schedules.

Legal Waiver Form: All participants must read and sign the official waiver agreement form prior to start of the season. Failure to sign the waiver form may result in a **dejection** of the player from the league.

Awards: Awards are generally clothing items and trophies. Number of clothing issued will be the same as the number of players on the team roster, but only one trophy per team.

Fighting Penalty: If a member of a team engages in a fight with another player, the player (s) will be **ejected** from game or league, depending on the circumstances. The player in fault will be liable for any damages incurred, such as, but not limited to, losses to the event, damages to equipments and facility, medical recoveries, etc. In addition, the player will not be refunded the team fee.

Word Building

More Words with the Word Roots

词根	释义	例词
ject	投掷	project, inject, reject, interject, eject, abject, deject, object, conjecture, subject
jac		ejaculate, adjacent, subjacent

1. project: [ˈprɔdʒekt] *n.* 计划；方案；项目；工程；科研项目，课题

分解记忆法：pro-(向前) + ject(掷) = 计划

【例句】In their geography class, children are doing a special project on Native Americans.

在地理课上，孩子们正在做一个有关北美印第安人的项目。

The new dam is a major construction project, funded by the government.

新水坝是由政府出资建造的一个大工程项目。

2. **project:** [prəˈdʒekt] *v.* 投射；放映

　分解记忆法：pro-（向前）+ject（投）= 投射

　【例句】Try to project your mind into the future and imagine what life will be like then.

　　　　让你的思想飞向未来，想象那时的生活会是什么样子吧。

　　　　There is a signpost projecting from the wall.

　　　　有个广告柱突出在墙外。

　常用派生词：project→projection→projectionist→projector

3. **inject:** [inˈdʒekt] *v.* 注射；打针

　分解记忆法：in-（里，内）+ject（投）= 注射

　【例句】This drug can't be swallowed. It has to be injected.

　　　　这种药不能口服，必须注射。

　　　　The arrival of our friends with several crates of beers injected new life into the flagging party.

　　　　我们的朋友带着几瓶啤酒来到这里，给沉闷的聚会带来了生气。

　常用派生词：inject→injection

4. **reject:** [riˈdʒekt] *v.* 拒绝

　分解记忆法：re-（回，反）+ject（掷）= 拒绝

　【例句】She rejected my suggestion.

　　　　她拒绝了我的建议。

　　　　He was rejected for the army because of his bad eyesight.

　　　　由于视力差，他被拒绝入伍。

　常用派生词：reject→rejection

5. **interject:** [ˌintəˈdʒekt] *v.* 突然插嘴，打断（别人的谈话）

　分解记忆法：inter-（中间）+ject（掷）= 突然插嘴

　【例句】"I don't agree at all," he interjected.

　　　　"我根本就不同意。"他突然叫道。

　　　　I wonder if I may interject a few comments at this point.

　　　　不知道我是否可以在这里插上几句评语。

　常用派生词：interject→interjection

6. **eject:** [iˈdʒekt] *v.* 弹出；逐出；撵出；驱逐

　分解记忆法：e-（出）+ject（掷）= 弹出

　【例句】They were making such a noise in the restaurant that the police came and ejected them.

　　　　他们在饭店里大吵大闹，警察只好把他们给赶走了。

The noisy boys were ejected from the cinema.

那些大吵大闹的男孩们被赶出了电影院。

常用派生词：eject → ejection

7. abject: [ˈæbdʒekt] *a.* 可怜的；凄惨的

分解记忆法：ab-（离开）+ ject（抛）= 可怜的

【例句】In a slum, people live in abject poverty.

贫民窟里的人们都生活在赤贫之中。

He had to make an abject apology.

他不得不低声下气地道歉。

常用派生词：abject→abjection→abjectly

8. deject: [diˈdʒektid] *vt.* 使沮丧，使灰心

分解记忆法：de-（向下）+ ject（抛）= 使沮丧

【例句】Repeated failures have left them feeling very dejected.

三番五次的失败让他们感到很沮丧。

Everyone has days when they feel dejected or down.

每个人都会有感到沮丧的时候。

常用派生词：deject→dejected→dejectedly→dejection

9. object: [ˈɔbdʒikt] *n.* 物体；目标

分解记忆法：ob-（反，对立）+ ject（投）= 物体

【例句】What's the little black object?

那个黑色的小东西是什么？

The object of his visit was to open the new hospital.

他来访的目的是为这家新医院揭牌。

10. object: [əbˈdʒekt] *vi.* 反对

分解记忆法：ob-（反）+ ject（扔）= 反对，抗议

【例句】My colleagues objected strongly to further delays.

我的同事们强烈地反对继续延期。

I'd like to open the window, if no one objects.

如果没人反对的话，我想打开窗户。

常用派生词：object→objection→objectionable→objective

11. objectivity: [ˌɔbdʒekˈtivəti] *n.* 客观性

分解记忆法：ob-（反）+ ject（掷）+ ive（形容词）+ -ity（名词）= 客观性

【例句】Like this, the article lacks objectivity in the basic information.

这样一来，文章就缺乏对基本信息的客观态度。

The sample questions and answers demonstrated in the paper reveal the feasibility and objectivity of the approach.

通过对一些疑难问题的分析，展现了方法的易操作性和客观性。

12. objection: [əbˈdʒekʃən] *n.* 反对；异议

分解记忆法：ob-（反）+ ject（掷）+ -ion（名词）= 反对

【例句】If there is no objection, we'll hold the meeting here.

如果没有反对意见,我们就在这里开会。

Do you have any objection?

您有任何反对意见吗?

13. ejaculate: [iˈdʒækjuleit] *v.* 射出；突然喊出

分解记忆法：e=ex-（向外）+ jac（投）+ -ate（动词）= 射出

【例句】"What?" Catherine ejaculated.

"什么？"凯瑟琳突然喊道。

You may of course ejaculate to that thing if you like.

对那件事,你当然可以想说什么就说什么。

14. objective: [ɔbˈdʒektiv] *a. & n.* 客观的；目标

分解记忆法：ob-（反）+ ject（投）+ -ive（形容词）= 客观的

【例句】A journalist should be completely objective.

作为一名记者,应该保持客观的态度。

All our objectives were reached.

我们的目标均已拿下。

常用派生词：objective→objectively

15. subjacent: [sʌbˈdʒesnt] *a.* 低下的；下层的

分解记忆法：sub-（在……下）+ jac（投）+ -ent（形容词）= 低下的

【例句】The pavement, badly sustained by the subjacent sand, had given way and had produced a stoppage of the water.

铺路石的下面是沙子,没有坚实的支撑,所以铺路石弯曲,形成了雨水的积聚。

Have you noticed subjacent waters?

你注意到下方水域了吗?

16. conjecture: [kənˈdʒektʃə] *n.* 推测；臆测；推想

分解记忆法：con-（一起）+ ject（投）+ -ure（名词）= 推测

【例句】Origin of the universe will always be a matter of conjecture.

宇宙的起源将永远是个谜。

The general conjectured that the enemy only had five days' supply of food left.

将军推测敌人只剩下五天的粮食供给。

17. subject: [səbˈdʒekt] *v.* 使服从；使蒙受；使罹患

分解记忆法：sub-（在……之下）+ ject（投）= 使服从

【例句】He was subjected to torture.

他受到严刑拷打。

No one would willingly subject himself to such indignities.

没有人愿意让自己承受如此的侮辱。

18. **subjection:** [səbˈdʒekʃən] *n.* 隶属；从属；服从

    分解记忆法：sub-(在……之下)＋ject(投)＋-ion(名词)＝从属

    【例句】The country's subjection of its neighbor has been finished.

    该国对邻国的征服已经完成。

    This tribe was kept in subjection.

    这个部落已沦为附庸。

    常用派生词：subjection→subjective→subjectively→subjectivity

19. **trajectory:** [trəˈdʒektəri] *n.* 弹道；抛物线

    分解记忆法：tra-＝trans-(穿过)＋ject(掷)＋-ory(名词)＝弹道

    【例句】This is a trajectory of a bullet.

    这是子弹的弹道。

    The missile deflected from its trajectory.

    导弹已偏离轨道。

20. **adjacent:** [əˈdʒeisənt] *a.* 近邻的；毗连的

    分解记忆法：ad-(到……)＋jac(投)＋-ent(形容词)＝近邻的

    【例句】The Council offices are adjacent to the library.

    市政会各办公室在图书馆旁边。

    The schools were adjacent but there were separate doors.

    各学校是相邻的，但是有不同的门。

Words in Use

1. When I brought up the question of funding, he quickly ____ that it had been settled.

   A. rejected   B. projected   C. interjected   D. ejected

2. What ____ a surgeon most is his patient's death during an operation.

   A. injects   B. abject   C. objects   D. dejects

3. The professor is doing a ____ on the history of English literature.

   A. object   B. inject   C. project   D. deject

4. I strongly ____ to being treated like a child.

   A. inject   B. object   C. deject   D. eject

5. The doctor ____ the drug into my arm.

   A. ejected   B. injected   C. abject   D. objected

6. Those drugs are given by ____ as well as through the mouth.

   A. objection   B. subjection   C. interjection   D. injection

7. Cartridges are ____ from the gun after firing.
   A. ejected   B. objected   C. injected   D. dejected
8. There are books, pens, rulers and other ____ on the desk.
   A. dejects   B. ejaculates   C. objects   D. ejects
9. The ____ seems unable to be carried on for lack of capital.
   A. object   B. subject   C. interject   D. project
10. We should make a(n) ____ analysis of the political situation.
    A. subjective   B. projectile   C. objective   D. conjecture
11. Passengers queued ____ for the increasingly dirty toilets.
    A. objectively   B. dejectedly   C. subjectively   D. abjectly
12. Officials used guard dogs to ____ the protesters from the auditorium.
    A. deject   B. inject   C. object   D. eject
13. The tree ____ a shadow on the grass.
    A. objects   B. projects   C. subjects   D. injects
14. ____ is an object that is fired from a gun or other weapon.
    A. Subjection   B. Objection   C. Projectile   D. Injection
15. The Senator didn't know the facts; what he said was pure ____.
    A. adjacent   B. subjacent   C. conjecture   D. interjacent
16. Aztecs ____ the neighboring tribes to their rules.
    A. subjected   B. objected   C. injected   D. ejected
17. The ghostly presence was just a ____ sensation.
    A. objective   B. inject   C. conjecture   D. subjective
18. She was annoyed when a student ____ her lecture.
    A. interfaced   B. intervened   C. interfered   D. interjected
19. After the transplant his body ____ the new heart and he died.
    A. injected   B. dejected   C. rejected   D. ejected
20. The organization will need a massive ____ of government money.
    A. dejection   B. injection   C. objection   D. subjection
21. ____ speaking, he can't possibly succeed at all.
    A. Subjectively   B. Objectively   C. Intentionally   D. Conjecturally
22. She was feeling ____ and unhappy until the good news cheered her up.
    A. objected   B. dejected   C. ejected   D. injected
23. The pilot and bombardier sit in a forward capsule-shaped module, which can ____ and serve as an escape pod.
    A. inject   B. deject   C. object   D. eject

24. Witnessing the original flower-like daughter become so _____, her mother was more than heartbroken.
    A. object   B. subject   C. abject   D. inject
25. They accused her of flippancy and ____ in her reporting of events in their country.
    A. generally   B. abjectly   C. subjectively   D. objectively
26. How can you fully believe his ____ judgment? You should be more objective.
    A. subjective   B. conjecture   C. dejection   D. objective
27. His house is ____ to mine, and we can see each other almost every day.
    A. abject   B. adjacent   C. interjacent   D. subjacent
28. Who can ____ about tomorrow's weather conditions?
    A. conjunct   B. conjecture   C. connect   D. confect
29. When I brought up the question, he quickly ____ that it had been settled.
    A. interfacing   B. interceded   C. interdicted   D. interjected
30. The transplant was ____ by the surrounding tissue.
    A. dejected   B. rejected   C. objected   D. ejected

Key to Words in Use

1. C	2. D	3. C	4. B	5. B
6. C	7. A	8. C	9. D	10. C
11. B	12. D	13. B	14. C	15. C
16. A	17. D	18. D	19. C	20. B
21. B	22. B	23. D	24. C	25. C
26. A	27. B	28. B	29. D	30. B

第8章 表示"上升"的词根

Words in Context

Elevators

Elevators are driven by electric motors. The nature of these efficient motors is that when they start up they use minimum power and consequently, are at their weakest when the elevator cabin is empty. As the passenger load increases the motor draws more electric current to increase its power so that it can lift the cabin. The motor sparks increase proportionately to the greater electrical current being drawn. The sparks created are not needed for the motor to function.

There is a counterbalance that is usually equal to forty percent of the maximum cabin load. Therefore, if there is less than a forty percent load in the cabin the elevator **ascends** without the need of the motor power. However, the initial lift off after stopping at the floor is performed by motor power to overcome friction. The heavier the cabin is, the more power the motor uses for the initial lift off. The same is true in reverse when the cabin is heavier than the counterweight and the elevator is descending by gravity. The initial lift off to overcome friction is accomplished by the motor.

When **descending**, if the cabin is more than forty percent full, the cabin is then heavier than the counterweight and does not need the motor power to continue to bring it down after its initial lift off. The acceleration is stopped by the reverse electromagnetic force. The motor shaft is now being turned by the elevator cable and the combination of the turning motor shaft with its wiring in a weak magnetic field that exists within a non-functioning motor turns the motor into a generator.

Word Building

More Words with the Word Roots

词根	释义	例词
lev	举,升,轻的	elevate, lever, alleviate
scend, scal	攀,爬	ascend, descend, descent, transcend, condescend, scale

1. elevate: [ˈeliveit] *vt.* 抬起，举起；晋升，提升（职位）

　　分解记忆法：e-(出) + lev(举) + -ate(动词后缀) = 抬起，举起

　　【例句】Both were later elevated to positions of authority.

　　　　　　两个人后来都被提拔为领导。

　　　　　　These drugs may elevate acid levels in the blood.

　　　　　　这些药物可能增加血液酸度。

　　常用派生词：elevate→elevated→elevation

2. lever: [ˈli:və] *n.* 杠杆　*v.* 撬起

　　分解记忆法：lev(举) + -er(表示物) = 杠杆

　　【例句】A worker used an iron bar as a lever to lift a rock.

　　　　　　工人用一根铁棍作为杠杆撬起了一块石头。

　　　　　　They're trying to lever him out of his position.

　　　　　　他们正试图把他从现任岗位上赶走。

3. alleviate: [əˈli:vieit] *vt.* 减轻（痛苦）

　　分解记忆法：al=ad(加强意义) + lev(轻的) + -iate(动词后缀) = 减轻(痛苦)

　　【例句】The patient was able to go to sleep when the medicine alleviated the pain.

　　　　　　服了药物之后，痛苦减轻，病人就能睡着了。

　　　　　　Comfort can alleviate grief.

　　　　　　安慰能够减轻悲伤。

　　常用派生词：alleviate→alleviation

4. levity: [ˈleviti] *n.* 轻率；轻浮

　　分解记忆法：lev(轻的) + -ity(名词后缀) = 轻率

　　【例句】Levity would sure be tough for me. I'm not particularly funny, and I'm not particularly outgoing.

　　　　　　"轻佻"肯定对我而言很难做到。我不是特别幽默的人，我也不是很外向。

　　　　　　He felt certain that she is not a person of levity.

　　　　　　他确信不疑，她绝不是轻浮的人。

5. leverage: [ˈli:vəridʒ] *n.* 杠杆作用；手段；力量

　　分解记忆法：lev(举) + -er(表示物) + -age(抽象名词) = 杠杆作用

　　【例句】Diplomatic leverage by the US persuaded several governments to cooperate.

　　　　　　美国的外交手段说服了几个国家进行合作。

　　　　　　Do you have any leverage with the Senator?

　　　　　　你对那参议员有影响力吗？

6. levy: [ˈlevi] *n.* 赋税；征税；征收

　　分解记忆法：lev(举) + -y(名词) = 赋税

　　【例句】A new tax has just been levied on all goods.

　　　　　　对所有商品刚开始征收一种新税。

The court may have to levy on your estate to pay your debts.

法庭可能不得不扣押你的房地产，用来偿付你的债务。

7. levitate: [ˈleviteit] *v.* 轻浮；浮于空中

分解记忆法：lev(轻的) + -itate(动词后缀) = 轻浮

【例句】I want you to get swept away out there, and I want you to levitate.

我希望你神魂颠倒，我希望你欢心雀跃。

This instrument can levitate things and make them float when placed between its two ends.

当把它放在其两端时，这个设备能够让东西漂浮起来。

常用派生词：levitate→levitation

8. elevator: [ˈeliveitə] *n.* 升降运送机；电梯

分解记忆法：e-(出) + lev(举) + ate(动词后缀) + -or(名词后缀) = 电梯

【例句】I go up by the elevator.

我乘电梯上去。

You should never take the elevator. You should take the stairs.

你绝对不可以乘电梯，你应该爬楼梯。

9. relevant: [ˈreləvənt] *a.* 有关的；中肯的

分解记忆法：re-(又，再) + lev(举) + -ant(形容词后缀) = 有关的

【例句】For further information, see the relevant chapters in the users' manual.

详情请查阅使用说明中相关章节。

These issues are relevant to the needs of slow learners, although not directly.

这些问题均与接受慢的学习者的需要有关，尽管不是直接的。

常用派生词：relevant→relevance→relevantly

10. elevation: [ˌeliˈveiʃən] *n.* 高地；高度；海拔；上升

分解记忆法：e-(出) + lev(举) + -ation(名词后缀) = 高地

【例句】This drawing shows what the front elevation of the house will look like when it is built.

这张图显示这幢房子建成后正面的外观。

Mountaineers sometimes have to use oxygen at this elevation.

登山者在这个海拔有时会用到氧气。

11. ascend: [əˈsend] *v.* 攀登；上升

分解记忆法：a=ad-(向) + scend(爬) = 攀登，上升

【例句】I could feel a current of warm air ascending from the ground.

我能感受到一股热气从地面上升起。

The stairs ascended in a graceful curve.

楼梯呈优美的弧形向上盘旋。

常用派生词：ascend→ascendancy

12. descend: [diˈsend] *v.* 下降；下来

　　分解记忆法：de(向下) + scend(爬) = 下降

　　【例句】The elevator descended rapidly to the first floor.
　　　　　　电梯很快到了一楼。
　　　　　　The plane started to descend.
　　　　　　飞机开始降落。

　　常用派生词：descend→descendant

13. condescend: [ˌkɔndiˈsend] *v.* 屈尊俯就

　　分解记忆法：con-(全部) + descend(下降) = 屈尊俯就

　　【例句】The Queen condescended to speak to the peasant.
　　　　　　女王屈尊跟农民交谈。
　　　　　　The managing director condescended to have lunch with the workers in canteen.
　　　　　　总经理放下架子来到食堂和工人们一起吃午饭。

　　常用派生词：condescend→condescending→conscendingly

14. transcend: [trænˈsend] *v.* 超越；超过

　　分解记忆法：trans-(超过) + scend(爬) = 超越

　　【例句】They reached the agreement to stop this dispute when their desire for peace transcended political difference.
　　　　　　对和平的渴望超越政治的分歧，于是他们达成协议，停止纷争。
　　　　　　Her beauty transcends that of her younger sister.
　　　　　　她比妹妹更漂亮。

　　常用派生词：transcend→transcendent→transcendental→transcendentalism

15. scale: [skeil] *v.* 以梯登；爬越

　　分解记忆法：scal(登) + -e(动词) = 以梯登

　　【例句】Rescuers had to scale a 800m cliff to reach the injured climbers.
　　　　　　救援人员要登上800米的悬崖才能达到受伤登山者的旁边。
　　　　　　Both automobile companies announced plans to scale back production in 2010.
　　　　　　两家汽车公司均宣布在2010年缩减生产计划。

16. escalate: [ˈeskəleit] *v.* 用梯攀登；升级

　　分解记忆法：e-(向外) + scala(梯子) + -ate(动词后缀) = 用梯攀登，升级

　　【例句】They don't want the fighting to escalate into a full-scale war.
　　　　　　他们不想让这场战争升级为全面战争。
　　　　　　Even a limited confrontation can escalate into a major war.
　　　　　　即使是局部的对抗也可能扩大成一场大战。

17. escalator: [ˈeskəleitə] *n.* 自动梯

　　分解记忆法：e-(向外) + scala(梯子) + -tor(名词后缀) = 自动梯

【例句】Take that escalator over there and turn left.
搭那里的自动梯，然后向左转。
The new store has escalators to carry customer from one floor to another.
这家新商店有自动扶梯将顾客从一层楼运送到另一层楼。

18. **scan**: [skæn] *v.* 审视；按韵律吟诵（诗）；扫描；浏览

分解记忆法：scan（拉丁文中scandere表示爬）

【例句】The doctors gave him an ultrasonic brain scan.
医生给他做了脑部超声波扫描检查。
They first scanned the agenda at the beginning of the meeting.
他们在会议开始时先浏览了一下议程安排。

19. **descendant**: [diˈsendənt] *n.* 后裔

分解记忆法：de-（向下）+ scend（爬）+ -ant（名词后缀）= 后裔

【例句】He is a descendant of Queen Victoria.
他是维多利亚女王的后裔。
As a descendant of several men who fought in the War of Independence, I hesitate to criticize my forebears.
作为独立战争参战者的后代，我不愿意对前辈提出批评。

20. **descent**: [diˈsent] *n.* 降下；遗传

分解记忆法：de-（向下）+ scent（爬）= 降下

【例句】The spectators watched the descent of the balloon.
观看的人瞧着气球降落。
There was a descent of temperature after rain.
雨后气温下降了。

Words in Use

1. The President ____ to work with us in the workshop.
   A. condescended   B. ascended   C. descended   D. transcended
2. The Vice President was ____ to President.
   A. levered   B. alleviated   C. elevated   D. levity
3. This drug can ____ cold symptoms.
   A. allege   B. alliance   C. allocate   D. alleviate
4. Such ____ as telling jokes is not allowed in church.
   A. levity   B. lever   C. levee   D. level
5. The airplane took off and ____ into the sky.
   A. descended   B. ascended   C. condescended   D. transcended

6. His concern about his business ____ money; he puts his customers' benefit in the first place.
   A. transcends	B. descends	C. condescends	D. descends
7. She is a(n) ____ of our first president.
   A. ascendant	B. transcendent	C. condescend	D. descendant
8. She'd be a better teacher if she didn't ____ to her students.
   A. transcendent	B. ascendant	C. condescend	D. descendant
9. Though he is still a young man, his political career is already in the ____.
   A. ascendant	B. descendant	C. consent	D. transcendent
10. Those ideas ____ from those of the ancient philosophers.
    A. transcended	B. descended	C. ascendant	D. condescend
11. I felt so ____ that I haven't got to take the wretched examination.
    A. relied	B. relieved	C. reliable	D. related
12. Good books may ____ the mind, so we should read as many good books as possible.
    A. elevation	B. elevate	C. elevator	D. escalate
13. What good method can ____ hypoglycemia low blood pressure?
    A. allied	B. alleviate	C. allocate	D. allow
14. What you say has no ____ to the subject. It's nonsense.
    A. relevance	B. relation	C. relative	D. related
15. The company has begun to ____ down its operations in Asia.
    A. scald	B. scale	C. scalp	D. scan
16. The speed of rockets ____ that of airplanes.
    A. condescends	B. transcends	C. ascends	D. descends
17. The government ____ taxes on real estate and personal property.
    A. levers	B. levities	C. elevates	D. levies
18. His nationality isn't ____ to whether he's a good teacher.
    A. relevant	B. related	C. relative	D. relevance
19. ____ is a kind of simple machine that can be used to amplify physical force.
    A. Levity	B. Lever	C. Levy	D. Levite
20. We ____ the living standards blindly, but lower the quality of life.
    A. elevate	B. elevator	C. elevation	D. element
21. Human nature, as irrepressible as it is, will always manage to ____ somehow.
    A. transcend	B. ascend	C. descendant	D. condescend
22. When you use a ____, you work much less but you accomplish much more.
    A. lever	B. levity	C. levy	D. level
23. It is important that if we just get news and information from TV then our reading and writing ability will ____.
    A. descend	B. ascend	C. condescend	D. transcend

24. She is so proud that she will not ____ to speak to us.

    A. condescend   B. transcend   C. ascend   D. descend

25. You had better open your mouth to ____ the pressure on your eardrums.

    A. relief   B. believe   C. relieve   D. relative

26. He traces his ____ back to an old Norman family.

    A. descent   B. ascent   C. transcend   D. condescend

27. We should be exceedingly polite in life stages, and ____ polite to higher levels in later life.

    A. elevate   B. elevator   C. elevation   D. elective

28. Instead, spirit asks that each human focus inward and choose to evolve, choose to transcend and ____.

    A. ascend   B. descend   C. transcend   D. condescend

29. How do you ____ your mood when depressed?

    A. alleviate   B. allege   C. ally   D. allocate

30. They may be inherent rivals, but they also know that conflict would be a disaster and that their rivalry needs to be managed rather than being allowed to ____.

    A. escape   B. escalate   C. espouse   D. estate

Key to *Words in Use*

1. A	2. C	3. D	4. A	5. B
6. A	7. D	8. C	9. A	10. B
11. B	12. B	13. B	14. A	15. B
16. B	17. D	18. A	19. B	20. A
21. D	22. A	23. A	24. A	25. C
26. A	27. A	28. A	29. A	30. B

第9章 表示"写画"的词根

Words in Context

Scribbling of Children

Thoughtless and impulsive behavior is natural for a young child. Do not worry about "**pictures**" because much of **scribbling** is not art work for the child, they are only an action of children. Wise parents realize this and look for positive ways to motivate responsible and more "grown-up" types of behavior.

We encourage scribbling by providing a place and materials, by acknowledging the work, and by discussing the work in a nonjudgmental way. In the child's mind scribbling is not meant to be art work in the sense that we think of art work. Scribbling for a child is more about action than about creating a product. It is a process; it is an activity I never ask: "What is it?" I might say: "Wow, this looks like you are having fun. Your crayon is really going fast." As the child gets closer to the stage of image making, I might say. "This part looks neat; can you tell me about it?" As children become verbal and are able to **describe** their work, their minds are learning to think in an imaginary and abstract way. It is our ability to imagine that makes us human. It makes us care. It makes it possible for us to take responsibility.

Word Building

More Words with the Word Roots

词根	释义	例词
scrib, script	写	scribe, scribble, ascribe, conscript, describe
graph		graphic, biography, autograph, monograph
pict (pig)	画	picture, pictograph, depict, pigment, pictorial

1. ascribe: [əˈskraib] *vt.* 归因于,归咎于

分解记忆法:a-(在)+ scribe(写)= 归因于

【例句】He ascribes his success to luck.
他把他的成功归功于运气。
This song is often ascribed to Bach.
这首歌常被说成是巴赫的作品。

常用派生词：ascribe→ascribable

2. **conscript:** [kənˈskrɪpt] *vt.* 征募（服兵役）

分解记忆法：con-（共同，都）+ script（写）= 征募（服兵役）

【例句】My sons were conscripted into the navy in the last war.
我的几个儿子在上次战争中被征召入海军。
He was conscripted into the army shortly before the war broke out.
战争开始后不久他就被征召入伍。

常用派生词：conscript→conscription

3. **describe:** [diˈskraib] *v.* 描述，叙述

分解记忆法：de-（加强意义，着重）+ scribe（写）= 描述

【例句】The police asked me to describe the two men.
警察让我描述那两个男子的模样。
The falling star described a long curve in the sky.
流星在空中划出一道长长的弧线。

常用派生词：describe→description→descriptive→descriptively→descriptiveness

4. **inscribe:** [inˈskraib] *v.* 写；题；刻（作正式的或永久性的记录）

分解记忆法：in-（入）+ scribe（写）= 写

【例句】He inscribed his name in the book.
他在书上签上了自己的名字。
They have inscribed their names upon the pages of history.
他们已经留名青史。

常用派生词：inscribe→inscription

5. **manuscript:** [ˈmænjuskript] *n.* 手稿；原稿

分解记忆法：manu（手）+ script（写）= 手稿

【例句】I read his novel in manuscript.
我看过他小说的手稿。
Scientists found a valuable medieval manuscript.
科学家们发现了一本有价值的中世纪手抄本。

6. **prescribe:** [priˈskraib] *v.* 开（药方）

分解记忆法：pre-（先）+ scribe（写）= 开（药方）

【例句】What can you prescribe for the pain in my back?
您看我背疼需要开什么药？
What punishment does the law prescribe for this crime?
按照法律，这种罪该判什么刑？

常用派生词：prescribe→prescribed→prescription→prescriptive

7. **subscribe:** [səbˈskraib] *v.* 订阅；捐款

分解记忆法：sub-（在下面）+ scribe（写）= 订阅

【例句】We subscribe to an animal protection society.
我们定期给一个动物保护协会捐款。
Everyone in the office subscribed a couple of pounds toward his wedding present.
办公室里的每一个人都为给他买结婚礼物而拿出几英镑。

常用派生词：subscribe→subscriber→subscription

8. transcribe: [trænˈskraib] *v.* 誊写；转录

分解记忆法：trans-(横过，转换) + scribe(写) = 誊写

【例句】A secretary transcribed the witnesses' statements.
秘书记下了证人的口述。
His work is to transcribe the ancient manuscript.
他的工作就是抄写古代的手写本。

常用派生词：transcribe→transcription

9. graphic: [ˈɡræfik] *a.* 书写的；绘画的；生动的

分解记忆法：graph(写) + -ic(形容词) = 书写的

【例句】The newspaper article gave a graphic description of the earthquake.
报纸文章生动地描述了地震的情况。
The graphic arts include calligraphy and lithography.
平面造型艺术包括书法和平版印刷术。

常用派生词：graph→graphic→graphically

10. biography: [baiˈɔɡrəfi] *n.* 传记

分解记忆法：bio-(生命) + graph(写) = 传记

【例句】Boswell wrote a famous biography of Dr. Johnson.
博斯维尔为约翰逊博士写过一本著名传记。
After reading a biography of Lincoln I was able to tell many stories about the President.
读过林肯的传记之后，我能够讲述这位总统的许多故事。

常用派生词：biography→biographic→biographical→biographically

11. autograph: [ˈɔːtəɡrɑːf] *n.* 自传

分解记忆法：auto-(自己) + biography(传记) = 亲笔签名

【例句】The little boys asked the footballer for his autograph.
那些小男孩请求这位足球明星给他们签名。
He went backstage and asked for her autograph.
他走到后台管她要签名。

12. monograph: [ˈmɔnəɡrɑːf] *n.* 专著；专论

分解记忆法：mono-(一个) + graph(写) = 专题论文

【例句】The latter is characterized to a large extent by the monograph, which is a different publication format.

后者的作品以专著居多，是一种不同的出版形式。

What is our country's earliest traditional Chinese medical science monograph?

我国最早的中医学专著是什么？

13. photograph: [ˈfəutəɡrɑːf] *n.* 照片

　　分解记忆法：photo（光）+ graph（写）= 照片

　　【例句】He took a photograph of his son.

　　　　　他给儿子拍了一张照片。

　　　　　Did you see John's photograph in the local paper?

　　　　　你在本地报纸上看到约翰的照片了吗？

　　常用派生词：photograph→photography→photographer→photographic

14. lexicography: [ˌleksiˈkɔɡrəfi] *n.* 词典编纂

　　分解记忆法：lexicon（词典）+ graph（写）= 词典编纂

　　【例句】From the point of view of lexicography, polysemy is the core problem of sense division and arrangement.

　　　　　从词典学的角度上讲，多义性是义项划分和义项排列的核心问题。

　　　　　Phrase equivalence pair is very useful for bilingual lexicography, machine translation and crossing-language information retrieval.

　　　　　短语等价对在词典编纂、机器翻译和跨语言信息检索中有着广泛的应用。

　　常用派生词：lexicography→lexicographer

15. telegraph: [ˈteliɡrɑːf] *n.* 电报

　　分解记忆法：tele-（远）+ graph（写）= 电报

　　【例句】The news came by telegraph.

　　　　　这条新闻是通过电报传来的。

　　　　　The news was telegraphed across the Atlantic.

　　　　　这条消息通过电报从大西洋彼岸传来。

　　常用派生词：telegraph→telegrapher→telegraphese→telegraphy

16. demographic: [ˌdeməˈɡræfik] *a.* 人口统计学的；人口统计的

　　分解记忆法：demo-（人民）+ graph（写）+ -ic（形容词）= 人口统计学的

　　【例句】This graph reflects the changing demographic trends.

　　　　　这图表反映的是变化中的人口统计趋势。

　　　　　Demographic reports show that the world's population is rising.

　　　　　人口统计报告显示世界人口正在增加。

　　常用派生词：demography→demographic→demographer

17. picture: [ˈpiktʃə] *v.* 想象；描述

　　分解记忆法：pict（画）+ -ure（名词）= 图画

　　【例句】Just picture the scene. It must have been a terrible experience.

　　　　　只要想象一下这种情景，那一定是一次可怕的经历。

I can't quite picture myself as a mother.

我难以想象自己成为母亲。

18. pictorial: [pikˈtɔːriəl] *a. & n.* 图片的；画报

分解记忆法：pict（画）+ -orial（形容词）= 图片的

【例句】These are the pictorial records of the event.

这些是这一事件的图片记录。

Chinese garden-design is primarily a branch of pictorial art.

中国园林设计基本上是图像艺术的一个分支。

常用派生词：pictorial→pictorially

19. depict: [diˈpikt] *v.* 画，绘；描述，描写

分解记忆法：de-（向下）+ pict（画）= 画，绘

【例句】The painting depicts the birth of Venus.

这幅油画描绘的是维纳斯的诞生。

The book depicts him as a rather unpleasant character.

这本书把他刻画成一个相当令人讨厌的人物。

常用派生词：depict→depiction

20. pigment: [ˈpigmənt] *n. & v.* 颜料；给……着色；呈现颜色

分解记忆法：pig-（画）+ -ment（名词后缀）= 颜料

【例句】We added a yellow pigment to the blue paint to make it green.

我们在蓝色中加入了黄色就得到绿色。

A white lead pigment sometimes is used in cosmetics.

铅白是一种白色铅颜料，有时用于化妆品制造。

常用派生词：pigment→pigmentation→pigmented

Words in Use

1. The doctor _____ some pills to help me to sleep.

 A. circumscribed B. ascribed C. prescribed D. described

2. The author's book _____ was sent to the editor.

 A. manuscript B. script C. conscript D. postscript

3. The characters in Chinese writing have developed from _____.

 A. telegraphs B. autographs C. pictographs D. monographs

4. She added a _____ at the bottom of her letter.

 A. manuscript B. conscript C. postscript D. transcript

5. Can you read this _____? I was in a hurry when I wrote it.

 A. scribe B. scribble C. script D. scripture

6. Her doctor wrote her a(n) _____ for blood pressure medicine.
   A. subscription   B. description   C. prescription   D. inscription
7. He _____ a few words for his wife shortly before the plane crashed.
   A. scribbled   B. scribed   C. scrolled   D. scripted
8. After reading the book which is full of _____ passages about life in Tibet, I felt as if I had been there.
   A. prescriptive   B. descriptive   C. cognitive   D. assertive
9. A _____ in ancient Israel copied religious texts.
   A. scrub   B. scribble   C. scruffy   D. scribe
10. Although I do not wish to _____ your activities, I must insist that you complete this assignment before you start anything else.
    A. circumstance   B. circumference   C. circumscribe   D. circumspect
11. After the listening comprehension test, the students looked at the _____ to check their answers.
    A. script   B. scribe   C. scribble   D. scroll
12. Archeologists have been trying to find out the meanings of the _____ inscribed in the turtle shell.
    A. photographs   B. pictographs   C. picturesque   D. pictorial
13. The politician _____ the failing economy to high taxes.
    A. describe   B. ascribed   C. prescribe   D. subscribe
14. Peter was _____ like every other young man.
    A. conscripted   B. unscripted   C. postscripted   D. transcripted
15. The police have issued a detailed _____ of the missing woman.
    A. prescription   B. subscription   C. inscription   D. description
16. The Queen was presented with a specially _____ copy of the book.
    A. prescribed   B. inscribed   C. described   D. scribe
17. The engraver _____ the date of my college graduation on the ring.
    A. described   B. scribed   C. inscribed   D. prescribed
18. I am grateful to him for letting me read his early chapters in _____.
    A. transcript   B. conscript   C. script   D. manuscript
19. Someone who does such foolish things as you has no right to _____ how others should behave.
    A. prescribe   B. describe   C. subscribe   D. scribble
20. I've _____ for 10,000 yuan worth of shares.
    A. prescribed   B. subscribed   C. described   D. inscribed
21. Secretaries _____ tapes of a meeting into typed document.
    A. transcended   B. transcribed   C. transferred   D. transacted
22. Her _____ appeared on the front page of the *New York Times*.
    A. pictographs   B. photograph   C. autographs   D. graphs

23. After the football match, the boy rushed to the field to get the famous player's _____.
    A. autograph   B. graphs   C. biography   D. telegraph
24. Charles Dickens's _____ description of abused and neglected children shocked the English public of the 1800s.
    A. photographic   B. graphic   C. grateful   D. grasping
25. Please _____ a square by drawing a circle round it.
    A. circumscribe   B. circumstance   C. circumspect   D. circulate
26. I _____ to a monthly magazine about English learning.
    A. subscribed   B. describe   C. prescribe   D. transcribe
27. For his thesis, the student plans to write a _____ on the making of the country's constitution.
    A. photograph   B. autograph   C. monograph   D. telegraph
28. A _____ is a person whose job is to describe the language.
    A. lexicographer B. photographer   C. biographer   D. autobiographer
29. The story _____ the hero as a cynical opportunist.
    A. depletes   B. deplores   C. depicts   D. deports
30. This is a(n) _____ on her favorite author, John Masefield.
    A. monograph   B. photograph   C. autograph   D. telegraph

Key to *Words in Use*

1. C	2. A	3. C	4. C	5. B
6. C	7. A	8. B	9. D	10. C
11. A	12. B	13. B	14. A	15. D
16. B	17. C	18. D	19. A	20. B
21. B	22. B	23. A	24. B	25. A
26. A	27. C	28. A	29. C	30. A

第10章 表示"走"的词根

Words in Context

Torture and the Crime of <u>Aggressive</u> War

The U.S. government's torture of detainees in the "war on terror" can be traced directly to a Feb. 7, 2002 memo signed by President George W. Bush.

Torture, however, is only one of the crimes associated with the "war on terror." A few prominent examples of other crimes waiting to be "sourced" are: extraordinary rendition, illegal detention, abuse and murder of civilians in Iraq and elsewhere, and the creation of millions of impoverished refugees.

With these crimes, the need to find the origin is every bit as imperative as with torture. But we don't need to ask the Senate Armed Services Committee to **initiate** 18-month investigations for each of these as well.

The question of responsibility for these and all other war crimes, including torture, was answered over 60 years ago at Nuremberg when high-ranking Nazis were brought to account for their atrocities in World War II.

On Sept. 30, 1946, Sir Geoffrey Lawrence, president of the International Military Tribunal, read the judgment of the first Nuremberg trial, which included these memorable words:

"To initiate a war of **aggression**, therefore, is not only an international crime; it is the supreme international crime differing only from other war crimes in that it contains within itself the accumulated evil of the whole."

Word Building

More Words with the Word Roots

词根	释义	例词
gress	步伐，移动	aggression, congress
ambul	走	amble, preamble, ambulance
vad, vas	去	evade, invade, pervade
it		exit, initiate, transit, circuit
vag		vagary, vague, vagrant, divagate
ced, ceed, cess		cede, accede, concede, succeed, proceed, process

1. aggression: [əˈgreʃən] *n.* 侵略；攻击，进攻

　　分解记忆法：ag=ad-（向）+ gress（去）+ -ion（名词后缀）= 侵略

　　【例句】Television violence can encourage aggression in children.

　　　　　电视暴力会助长孩子们的攻击行为。

　　　　　This is an unprovoked act of aggression on a peaceful nation.

　　　　　这是对一个和平国家的无端侵犯。

　　常用派生词：aggression→aggressive→aggressor

2. congress: [ˈkɔŋgres] *n.* （代表）大会；国会

　　分解记忆法：con-（共同，一起）+ gress（走）=（代表）大会

　　【例句】Today is the annual congress of the miners' union.

　　　　　今天是矿工工会的年度代表大会。

　　　　　The President has lost the support of the Congress.

　　　　　总统失去了国会的支持。

　　常用派生词：congress→congression→congressional→congressman

3. digress: [daiˈgres] *v. & adj.* 离题，岔开话题；离题的

　　分解记忆法：di=dis-（离开）+ gress（走）= 离题

　　【例句】Do you mind if I digress for a moment?

　　　　　我说些题外话，你不介意吧？

　　　　　The speaker talked about modern art, and then digressed into a discussion of a mathematician from 500 years ago.

　　　　　演讲者谈了一些有关现代艺术的话题之后，就转到谈论500多年前的一位数学家。

　　常用派生词：digress→digression

4. progress: [ˈprəugres, prəˈgres] *n. & vi.* 前进；进步；进化；增长

　　分解记忆法：pro（向前）+ gress（走）= 前进

　　【例句】The hard-working student is showing rapid progress in his study.

　　　　　那位勤奋学习的学生在学习上取得了很大的进步。

　　　　　I'm afraid we're not making much progress.

　　　　　恐怕我们进步不大。

　　常用派生词：progress→progression→progressive→progressing

5. regress: [ˈri:gres] *v.* 倒退，退步；退化

　　分解记忆法：re-（回）+ gress（走）= 倒退

　　【例句】The patient has regressed to a state of childish dependency.

　　　　　病人退回到像个孩子一样依赖他人的状态。

　　　　　Many prisoners, on being freed, regress to a life of crime.

　　　　　许多囚犯，一旦获释，仍去犯罪。

　　常用派生词：regress→regression→regressive

6. evade: [iˈveid] *v.* 躲开；逃避（法律，职责）

分解记忆法：e-(出) + vad(走) = 躲开

【例句】Stop trying to evade the issue.

不要再试图回避这个问题了。

You can't go on evading your responsibilities forever.

你不能永远都逃避责任。

7. invade: [inˈveid] *vt.* 武装进入，入侵

分解记忆法：in-(入) + vad(走) = 武装进入

【例句】Every summer the town is invaded by tourists.

每年夏天，大量游客涌入该镇。

Does that give you an excuse to invade my privacy?

那就给你借口来干涉我的隐私吗？

常用派生词：invade→invader→invasion→invasive

8. pervade: [pəˈveid] *v.* 遍及；弥漫；普及

分解记忆法：per-(到处) + vad(走) = 遍及

【例句】After the war a spirit of hopelessness pervaded the country.

战争过后全国普遍存在着一种绝望的情绪。

Science and technology have come to pervade every aspect of our lives.

科学和技术已经开始渗透到我们生活的各个领域。

常用派生词：pervade→pervasive→pervasiveness→pervasively

9. amble: [ˈæmbəl] *vi.* 漫步，徐步

分解记忆法：ambul的变体，漫步

【例句】The old man came out and ambled over for a chat.

老人出来了，从容地走过去聊天。

Every evening, they amble along the bank.

每天晚上，他们都沿着江边悠闲地散步。

10. preamble: [priˈæmbl] *n.* 前言，序；开场白

分解记忆法：pre-(前) + amble(走) = 前言

【例句】"Murder," he said, without preamble. "No doubt about it."

"谋杀，"他开门见山地说，"毫无疑问是谋杀。"

He spoke without preamble.

他没有开场白地讲起来。

11. ambulance: [ˈæmbjuləns] *n.* 战时流动医院；救护车

分解记忆法：ambul(走) + -ance(名词后缀) = 战时流动医院

【例句】An ambulance came to the car accident in two minutes.

救护车两分钟内达到交通事故现场。

Do I need to call the ambulance?

我要不要打电话叫救护车？

12. exit: [ˈeksit] *n.* （公共建筑物的）出口；太平门

分解记忆法：ex-(出，外) + -it(走) = (公共建筑物的)出口

【例句】We made for the nearest exit.

我们走向最近的出口。

They made a swift exit when they saw the police approaching.

他们看见警察来时便迅速离开。

13. initiate: [iˈniʃieit] *vt.* 开始；发起

分解记忆法：in-(入) + -it(走) + -iate(动词后缀) = 开始

【例句】During that winter, she was initiated into knitting.

那年冬天，她初步学会了针织。

In August, Nick was initiated into that club in England.

八月，尼克被吸纳加入了英国的一个俱乐部。

常用派生词：initiate→initiation→initiative

14. transit: [ˈtrænzit, -sit] *n.* 搬运；运载；运输

分解记忆法：trans-(横过，越过) + -it(走) = 搬运

【例句】The goods are in transit from the warehouse to the customers.

这些货物要从仓库搬出卖给消费者。

These goods were damaged in transit.

这些货物在运输中受损。

常用派生词：transit→transition→transitional

15. sedition: [siˈdiʃən] *n.* 煽动叛乱的言论或行为

分解记忆法：sed=se-(分开) + -it(走) + -ion(名词后缀) = 煽动叛乱

【例句】Leading activists of their party were charged with sedition.

他们党的主要活动分子被指控犯有煽动反政府罪。

He was arrested for sedition of overthrowing the government.

他因为煽动推翻政府而被捕。

常用派生词：sedition→seditious→seditiously

16. circuit: [ˈsəːkit] *n.* 周线；圈；电路

分解记忆法：circu=circum-(环绕) + -it(走) = 周线

【例句】The circuit of the city walls is three miles.

这个城的城墙有三英里长。

We did a circuit of the old city.

我们绕着旧城墙走了一圈。

常用派生词：circuit→circuitous→circuitously

17. vagary: [ˈveigəri] *n.* 怪异多端；变幻莫测

分解记忆法：vag-(走) + -ary(名词后缀)(此词常以复数出现) = 怪异多端

【例句】She brought various kinds of clothes for the vagaries of the weather.

因为天气变化无常，所以她买了各式各样的衣服。

In his nine volumes he displayed the liveliest interest in human vagaries, together with the wide view that makes the work a classic.

他在这九卷巨著里，对于人类的异想天开显示了最浓厚的兴趣，加以涉及的幅度广阔，使这部巨作成了经典著作。

18. **vagabond:** [ˈvæɡəbɒnd] *n.* 无业游民，街头无赖，流浪者

    分解记忆法：vaga-(走，流浪) + bond(倾向于……的) = 无业游民

    【例句】He doesn't have a job and is a vagabond.

    他没有正式的职业，是个无业游民。

    Don't have any talk with vagabonds, because most of them act shamelessly.

    不要和那些街头的无业游民搭话，他们大多数都很无赖。

19. **accede:** [əkˈsiːd] *v.* 正式加入；答应；增加；开始任职

    分解记忆法：ac=ad-(向) + cede(走) = 同意

    【例句】The government would not accede to public pressure.

    政府不会屈从于公众的压力的。

    We are regretful for your loss and accede to compensate $500 to you.

    我们对你方遭受的损失深表歉意，同意向你们赔偿500美元。

20. **concede:** [kənˈsiːd] *vi.* （不情愿地）承认

    分解记忆法：con-(共同) + cede(走) = (不情愿地)承认

    【例句】"You should be right, I suppose," Catherine conceded.

    凯瑟琳承认道："我想你应该是对的。"

    The army conceded and the enemy claimed victory.

    军队承认战败，敌人宣称胜利。

Words in Use

1. We need a self-defense posture to deter the possible ____.
   A. aggression   B. interruption   C. incursion   D. excursion
2. After several long ____, he finally reached the interesting part of the story.
   A. intercessions   B. digressions   C. incursions   D. concessions
3. The ____ shape of a figure loomed through the mist.
   A. vagary   B. vague   C. vagrant   D. vegan
4. The ____ of farm life to city life is often very difficult.
   A. transmission   B. transfer   C. transaction   D. transition
5. The chess-player had to _____ that he lost the game when he saw that his position was

hopeless.

   A. proceed	B. concede	C. accede	D. succeed

6. Public pressures compelled the government to ____ to the demonstrators' demand.

   A. concede	B. precede	C. accede	D. cede

7. Mary was very ____ about her plans for the future and she felt really confused.

   A. vagrant	B. vagary	C. vegan	D. vague

8. If you try to ____ paying taxes, you risk going to prison.

   A. invade	B. evade	C. pervade	D. pervasive

9. His ____ speech incited the people to rebel against the government.

   A. seditious	B. seductive	C. seduce	D. reclusive

10. At the beginning of WWⅡ, Hitler ____ Poland without a declaration of war.

    A. persuaded	B. pervaded	C. evaded	D. invaded

11. He got out of the theatre in time when the fire started because he was sitting near the ____.

    A. exist	B. existence	C. excess	D. exit

12. The group was quiet until she ____ conversation by asking a question.

    A. incited	B. initiated	C. initial	D. initiative

13. Nick has made good ____ with his studies this year and he often got 100 in English.

    A. progress	B. process	C. procedure	D. pervade

14. His heart attack was ____ and he got well soon.

    A. transitional	B. transitory	C. transmission	D. transiency

15. When the fire started in the building, the people inside hurried to the ____ to get out of the building.

    A. degree	B. egress	C. depress	D. regress

16. The Republicans were deeply split between ____ and conservatives.

    A. aggressive	B. progressives	C. compressive	D. congestive

17. The dog always barks at strangers. It is very ____.

    A. invasive	B. pervasive	C. aggressive	D. regressive

18. He got a ticket for ____ the speed limit.

    A. preceding	B. acceding	C. conceding	D. exceeding

19. The referee had to ____ in the fight between the two basketball players.

    A. precede	B. intercession	C. intercede	D. proceed

20. The king agreed to ____ the city to Britain.

    A. accede	B. cede	C. concede	D. intercede

21. My good friend ____ on my behalf with my boss who would dismiss me for my lateness.

    A. receded	B. interceded	C. seceded	D. succeeded

22. The Chinese government will never allow Taiwan to ____ from China.

    A. exceed	B. proceed	C. secede	D. precede

23. Boyd's wife left him because of his ____ drinking.
    A. excessive   B. progressive   C. aggressive   D. regressive
24. We got refund for goods damaged in ____.
    A. transfer   B. transact   C. transmit   D. transit
25. Going to the moon was man's ____ victory.
    A. unprecedented   B. unpredictable   C. unprofitable   D. unprovoked
26. The conversation on politics at dinner _____ into an argument about which dessert tasted better.
    A. regressed   B. digressed   C. progressed   D. congressed
27. Coal was formed out of dead forests by a slow ____ of chemical change.
    A. process   B. success   C. recess   D. progress
28. More and more children in that country detest school because of ____ homework every day.
    A. pervasive   B. excessive   C. fugitive   D. persuasive
29. He put aside the papers after a(n) ____ study.
    A. ambulatory   B. vagary   C. cursory   D. transitory
30. I can't afford the mobile phone if the price ____ 500 yuan.
    A. exceeds   B. succeeds   C. proceeds   D. accedes

Key to *Words in Use*

1. A	2. B	3. B	4. D	5. B
6. C	7. D	8. B	9. A	10. D
11. D	12. B	13. A	14. B	15. B
16. B	17. C	18. D	19. C	20. B
21. B	22. C	23. A	24. D	25. A
26. B	27. A	28. B	29. C	30. A

第11章　表示"坐"的词根

Words in Context

In Praise of Positive Obsessions

The common wisdom of therapy has it that **obsessions** are always bad things. As a feature of its namesake disorder, obsessive-compulsive disorder, or as a feature of some other disorder, an obsession is a sign of trouble and a problem to be eliminated.

Defined this way, it is obviously always unwelcome. However, **dissidents** exist. Suppose a person is **possessed** thinking day and night about her current painting or about the direction she wants to take her art. Thoughts about painting "intrude" as she balances her checkbook or prepares her shopping list. She can hardly wait to get to her studio and her rhythms are more like Picasso's on painting jags than like the rhythms of a "normal" person. This artist is obsessed in an everyday sense of the word—and more than happy to be so!

Here we need to clarify two terms:

Negative obsessions (like fearing that your door isn't locked and checking it a hundred times a day, or fearing that your hands aren't clean and washing them over and over again) are a horror. No one would want them or no one needs them. Positive obsessions, by contrast, are the fruit of a creator's efforts to make meaning. Without positive obsessions, life is dull, dreary, and meaningless.

Most creators—and all would-be creators—simply aren't obsessed enough. For an artist, the absence of positive obsessions leads to long periods of blockage, repetitive work that bores the artist himself, and existential ailments of all sorts. As the German novelist Herman Hesse expressed it, positive obsessions will stay **assiduously** away.

Word Building

More Words with the Word Roots

词根	释义	例词
sid	坐 (to sit)	assiduous, dissident, insidious, preside, resident, residue, subside, subsidize
sed		sediment, sedate, sedentary, sedulous, supersede
sess		obsession, possess, dispossess

1. **assiduous:** [əˈsidjuəs] *a.* 专心致志的；勤勉的

   分解记忆法：as-(像) + sidu-(坐) + ous = 专心致志的

   【例句】He is one of the most assiduous members in his team.

   他是该队最勤恳努力的队员之一。

   The book was the result of ten years' assiduous research.

   那本书是十年苦心钻研的成果。

   常用派生词：assiduous → assiduously

2. **dissident:** [ˈdisidənt] *n. & adj.* 唱反调者，持不同政见者；持不同意见的

   分解记忆法：dis- (反) + si- (坐) + dent = 唱反调者

   【例句】They are left-wing dissidents.

   他们是左翼持不同政见者。

   There are dissident groups, writings and opinions.

   有持不同政见者的组织、著作和观点。

   常用派生词：dissident → dissidence

3. **insidious:** [inˈsidiəs] *a.* 潜在的；暗中为害的

   分解记忆法：in- (在里面) + sidi- (坐) + ous = 隐伏的

   【例句】He had insidiously wormed his way into her affections.

   他已神不知鬼不觉地逐渐赢得了她的爱情。

   They are of insidious approach of age.

   他们不知不觉就老了。

   常用派生词：insidious → insidiously → insidiousness

4. **preside:** [priˈzaid] *v.* 主持；负责；指挥

   分解记忆法：pre - (先于) + side (坐) = 主持

   【例句】Whoever presides will need patience and tact.

   无论谁做主席，都需要既有耐性，又机敏老练。

   They asked if I would preside over the meeting.

   他们问我是否主持会议。

   常用派生词：preside → president

5. **resident:** [ˈrezidənt] *n. & adj.* 住户，居民；定居的，常驻的

   分解记忆法：resi-(坐) + dent = 居民

   【例句】Restaurant opens to non-residents.

   餐厅对非住宿者开放。

   There were conflicts between local residents and the police.

   当地居民和警察之间有过冲突。

   常用派生词：resident → residential

6. **residue:** [ˈrezidjuː] *n.* 残渣；残余

   分解记忆法：resi-(坐) + due = 残渣

【例句】Always using the same shampoo means that a residue can build up on the hair.

总用同一种香波头发上会留有残余。

The residue of John's estate was divided equally among his children.

约翰的剩余财产被他的孩子们平分了。

常用派生词：residue → residual

7. subside: [səbˈsaid] *v.* 减弱；平息；洪水（退去）；（热度）消退

分解记忆法：sub- (在……以下) + side (坐) = 下沉

【例句】Gradually the flood waters subsided.

洪水逐渐退去。

The boiling water subsided when the pot was taken off the heat.

把锅从炉子上端开时，水就不再沸腾了。

常用派生词：subside → subsidence

8. subsidize: [ˈsʌbsidaiz] *v.* 资助；给……发津贴

分解记忆法：sub- (在……以下) + sid (坐) + -ize (动词后缀) = 资助

【例句】At the moment they are living on pensions that are subsidized by the government.

那时他们靠政府发放津贴过活。

She's not going to subsidize his gambling any longer.

她不愿拿钱供他去赌博了。

常用派生词：subsidize → subsidy

9. sediment: [ˈsedimənt] *n.* 沉淀物；沉渣

分解记忆法：sedi- (坐) + ment (物) = 沉淀物

【例句】He drank a wine with a gritty sediment.

他喝了有沙粒状沉淀物的葡萄酒。

The sediment is hard to define.

沉淀物很难辨别。

常用派生词：sediment → sedimentary

10. sedate: [siˈdeit] *a. & vt.* 泰然的，不慌不忙的，镇静的；使昏昏欲睡，使镇静

分解记忆法：sed- (坐) + ate = 泰然的

【例句】Tiger Woods had a sedate game of golf.

老虎伍兹打了一场平和的高尔夫比赛。

He chose to live in a sedate country town after retirement.

退休后他选择住在宁静的乡间小镇。

常用派生词：sedate → sedately → sedateness

11. sedentary: [ˈsedntri] *a.* 需要久坐的；惯于久坐不动的

分解记忆法：sed- (坐) + ent + -ary (形容词后缀) = 需要久坐的

【例句】She became increasingly sedentary after she retired.

她退休后变得越来越不爱动了。

He leads a sedentary life.

他过着久坐不动的生活。

12. sedulous: [ˈsedjuləs] *a.* 勤勉的；不懈的

分解记忆法：sedu-(坐)＋(l)ous(形容词后缀)＝勤勉的

【例句】Professor Brown is also a sedulous researcher.

布朗教授还是个勤奋的研究人员。

He pays sedulous attention to details when he works.

他工作时一丝不苟。

常用派生词：sedulous → sedulously

13. supersede: [ˌsuːpəˈsiːd] *v.* 取代；替代

分解记忆法：super-(上)＋sede(坐)＝取代

【例句】The theory was superseded by a new research.

这一理论被新近的研究取代了。

Will factory workers be entirely superseded by machines in the future?

工人将来能完全由机器取代吗？

14. obsession: [əbˈseʃən] *n.* 痴迷；着魔

分解记忆法：ob-＋ses(sed-坐)＋sion＝痴迷

【例句】95% of patients know their obsessions are irrational.

百分之九十五的病人知道他们的痴迷是不理智的。

Fitness has become an obsession with him.

他迷上了健身。

常用派生词：obsess → obsession → obsessional → obsessive

15. possess: [pəˈzes] *v.* 拥有；占有

分解记忆法：pos-＋sess(sed-坐)＝拥有

【例句】He possesses property all over the world.

他在世界各地均拥有财产。

She was possessed by jealousy.

她妒火中烧。

常用派生词：possess → possession → possessive

16. dispossess: [ˌdispəˈzes] *v.* 剥夺；夺去

分解记忆法：dis(非)＋pos-＋sess(sed-坐)＝剥夺

【例句】The nobles were dispossessed of their estates after the revolution.

革命后贵族们的地产被剥夺了。

Droves of dispossessed people emigrated to Canada.

大批被剥夺财产的人移民加拿大。

常用派生词：dispossess → dispossession

Words in Use

1. His spirit of ____ study is worthy of emulation.
   A. assiduous   B. insidious   C. insistent   D. listless

2. The nations you will ____ listen to those who practice sorcery or divination. But as for you, the Lord your God has not permitted you to do so.
   A. access   B. dispossess   C. stress   D. preside

3. He was exiled as a ____.
   A. consultant   B. sediment   C. dissident   D. resident

4. Long before children are capable of using and understanding verbal language, they ____ the ability to differentiate between objects with contrasting visual treatments.
   A. posit   B. endeavor   C. dispossess   D. possess

5. Our policy is known to be constructive and not to imply ____ dangers to their national life.
   A. cursive   B. dangerous   C. assiduous   D. insidious

6. Watergate had begun to turn into a national ____.
   A. decision   B. succession   C. obsession   D. possession

7. His experience enabled him to ____ over the business in an efficient way.
   A. take care   B. look   C. control   D. preside

8. We should ____ outdated regulations and customs.
   A. insist   B. preside   C. supersede   D. sedate

9. In a well-to-do house there is always a(n) ____ teacher.
   A. diligent   B. sedentary   C. assiduous   D. resident

10. She wondered what sort of herbs they were which the old man was so ____ to gather.
    A. lazy   B. sedulous   C. insidious   D. promoted

11. Pesticide persistence beyond the critical period for control leads to ____ problems.
    A. residue   B. sediment   C. chemical   D. physical

12. A(n) ____ person, no matter how busy he is, should take time out for exercise.
    A. sedentary   B. serious   C. somnolent   D. assiduous

13. The controversies surrounding population growth are unlikely to ____ soon.
    A. fade   B. rise   C. subside   D. exclude

14. In this government of my temper, I remained near a year, lived a very ____ retired life.
    A. gregarious   B. exclusive   C. sedate   D. sedentary

15. Provincial financial departments will also ____ those cities and counties in financial straits through transfer payments.
    A. authorize   B. subsidize   C. subside   D. subsidy

16. Channels generally contain coarser ____ than do the adjacent flood plains.
    A. basement   B. congregation   C. sediment   D. ailment
17. Whoever ____ will need patience and tact.
    A. sedates   B. supersedes   C. subside   D. presides
18. The authorities put the ____ author through the hoop by denouncing him as an enemy of the state and putting him under house arrest.
    A. insidious   B. sedentary   C. sedulous   D. dissident
19. The latest book was the result of twenty years' ____ research.
    A. assiduous   B. sedentary   C. insidious   D. marvelous
20. A lot of people are obsessed with the ____ pursuit of legal and moral principles.
    A. sedate   B. helpful   C. sedulous   D. sedentary
21. The hall was reserved exclusively for ____ or corresponding members.
    A. resident   B. dissident   C. student   D. sediment
22. Does he ____ the necessary patience and tact to do the job well?
    A. embrace   B. endow   C. possess   D. subside
23. The government has agreed to ____ the hotel industry.
    A. possess   B. subsidize   C. sedate   D. preside
24. If you are ____ of something that you own, especially land or buildings, it is taken away from you.
    A. dispossessed   B. capable   C. subsidized   D. sedated
25. Motorways have largely ____ ordinary roads for long-distance travel.
    A. displaced   B. superseded   C. subsidized   D. sedated
26. The cathedral looks prim and ____.
    A. assiduous   B. insidious   C. sedate   D. sedulous
27. The police asked me if I ____ a gun.
    A. possessed   B. obsessed   C. subsided   D. subsidized
28. The court ruled to ____ his political rights.
    A. obsess   B. dispossess   C. surpass   D. undergo
29. The old professor had ____ over a seminar for theoretical physicists.
    A. presided   B. subsidized   C. visualized   D. prepared
30. Tom was a(n) ____ worker who strove for perfection.
    A. insidious   B. cautious   C. dangerous   D. assiduous

Key to *Words in Use*

1. A	2. B	3. C	4. D	5. D
6. C	7. D	8. C	9. D	10. B
11. A	12. A	13. C	14. C	15. B
16. C	17. D	18. D	19. A	20. C
21. A	22. C	23. B	24. A	25. B
26. C	27. A	28. B	29. A	30. D

第12章 表示"伸展"的词根

Words in Context

Predicting the Future: Mirror Neurons <u>Reflect</u> the <u>Intentions</u> of Others

One of the more intriguing recent discoveries in brain science is the existence of "mirror neurons," a set of neurons in the premotor area of the brain that are activated not only when performing an action oneself, but also while observing someone else perform that action. It is believed mirror neurons increase an individual's ability to understand the behaviors of others, an important skill in social species such as humans. A critical aspect of understanding the behavior of another person is recognizing the <u>intention</u> of his actions—is he coming to praise me or to bury me? In this issue, Marco Iacoboni and colleagues use functional magnetic resonance imaging (MRI) to show that the mirror neuron system tracks not only the actions, but also the intentions, of others.

The researchers presented test <u>attendants</u> (subjects) with one of three types of movie clips, "context," "action," and "intention." The "context" clip came in two versions. In the first, a mug of tea, a teapot, a pitcher of cream, and a plate of cookies sit neatly on a nondescript surface. In the second, the mug is empty, the pitcher is on its side, and a napkin lies crumpled beside scattered cookie crumbs—the dregs of an apparently well-enjoyed snack. The "action" clip shows only an empty mug, being grasped either by the whole hand around the rim (called whole-hand prehension), or with the fingers on the handle (precision grip). The "intention" clip puts it all together, providing the context needed to understand the intent of the action.

Word Building

More Words with the Word Roots

词根	释义	例词
tend, tens, tent	伸展 (to stretch out)	extend, extensive, attend, attendant, attentive, contend, contention, tendency, intense, intensify, intensive, intention, distend, hypertension
flect, flex	弯曲 (to bend)	reflect, reflection, flexible

1. extend: [ikˈstend] *v.* 扩展；延长；扩大

分解记忆法：ex-（向外）+ tend (伸展) = 扩展

【例句】Alternatively, reefs may extend linearly across basins.
此外，礁可横穿盆地呈带状延伸。

My garden extends as far as the river.
我的花园一直伸展到河边。

常用派生词：extended → extensive → extension

2. extensive: [ikˈstensiv] *v.* 广阔的；广大的；大量的；广泛的

分解记忆法：ex-（向外）+ ten-（伸展）+ sive = 广阔的

【例句】Her knowledge of the subject is extensive.
她这方面的学识很渊博。

Extensive development can also cause conflicts.
粗放式发展还可能引起冲突。

常用派生词：extensive → extensively

3. attend: [əˈtend] *v.* 出席；参加

分解记忆法：at-（朝向）+ tend (伸展) = 出席

【例句】I shall be attending the meeting.
我会参加会议。

The school was attended almost entirely by local children.
上这个学校读书的几乎全是当地的孩子。

常用派生词：attend → attendance → attendant

4. attendant: [əˈtendənt] *n. & adj.* 服务者，侍者；伴随的，出席的

分解记忆法：at-（朝向）+ tend-（伸展）+ ant (者) = 服务者

【例句】If you need anything, just ring for the attendant.
如果您要什么，就按铃叫服务员。

I asked the attendant to conduct him to the door.
我让服务员领他们到门口。

5. attentive: [əˈtentiv] *a.* 注意的；专心的；留意的

分解记忆法：at- + tent-（伸展）+ -ive = 注意的

【例句】A good hostess is always attentive to the needs of her guests.
好客的女主人能随时留心客人的需要。

You should be attentive to what your parents have said.
你应该注意倾听父母所说的话。

常用派生词：attentive → attentively

6. contend: [kənˈtend] *v.* 竞争；斗争；声称；主张

分解记忆法：con-（共同）+ tend (伸展) = 竞争

【例句】Several teams are contending for the prize.

有几个队在争夺锦标。

There were too many problems to contend with.

要全力对付的问题真是太多太多了。

常用派生词：contend → contender

7. contention: [kənˈtenʃn] *n.* 争夺；争论；争辩

分解记忆法：con- (共同) + tent- (伸展) + -ion = 争夺

【例句】It is his contention that taxes are too low.

他的论点是课税太轻。

The border has always been a bone of contention between these two countries.

这两国之间的边界问题历来是争议的焦点。

常用派生词：contention → contentious

8. tendency: [ˈtendənsi] *n.* 趋向，倾向

分解记忆法：tend- (倾向) + -ency (名词后缀) = 趋向

【例句】There is a tendency towards regional cooperation.

有一种地区性合作的趋势。

He had a tendency to shrink up whenever attention was focused on him.

当别人注意他时，他就会退缩一旁。

常用派生词：tendency → tendentious

9. intense: [inˈtens] *a.* 强烈的，剧烈的，激烈的

分解记忆法：in- (不) + tense (拉) = 强烈的

【例句】The fracture caused him intense pain.

骨折给他造成了剧烈的疼痛。

Under his intense gaze she felt uncomfortable.

他目不转睛地看着她，使她觉得很不自在。

常用派生词：intense → intensity → intensely

10. intensify: [inˈtensifai] *v.* 加强，强化

分解记忆法：in- (向内) + tens (拉) + -fy (使) = 加强

【例句】My first failure only intensifies my desire to succeed.

我的初次失败只更加强了我成功的愿望。

His absence only intensified her longing.

他不在身边唯使她愈益渴念。

常用派生词：intense → intensify → intensification

11. intensive: [inˈtensiv] *a.* 集中的；密集的；精深的；强化的

分解记忆法：in- (向内) + tens- (拉) + -ive = 集中的

【例句】Intensive mechanized agriculture is typically regarded as being efficient.

机械化集约农业是高效率的典型。

Some books are for intensive study and some are for cursory reading.

有的书必须精读,有的只要稍加涉猎即可。

　　常用派生词: intensive → intensively

12. intention: [inˈtenʃn] *n.* 意图;打算

　　分解记忆法: in-(向内) + tent-(拉) + -ion = 意图

　　【例句】She's keeping her intentions to herself.
　　　　　她对自己的意图秘而不宣。

　　　　　I'm sorry I offended you; it wasn't my intention.
　　　　　对不起,我冒犯您了,但绝不是有意的。

　　常用派生词: intention → intentional

13. distend: [diˈstend] *v.* (使)膨胀;(使)扩张

　　分解记忆法: dis-(分散) + -tend(伸展) = (使)膨胀

　　【例句】The stomachs of starving people often distend.
　　　　　饥民的腹部常鼓得大大的。

　　　　　Distending pains are normal during treatment.
　　　　　治疗过程中会感到有一些胀痛。

　　常用派生词: distend → distended

14. hypertension: [ˌhaipəˈtenʃn] *n.* 高血压;过度紧张

　　分解记忆法: hyper-(在……之上) + tension(紧张) = 高血压

　　【例句】More and more people suffer from hypertension nowadays.
　　　　　现在越来越多的人患高血压。

　　　　　Hypertension is a common disease now.
　　　　　现在高血压是一种常见病。

　　常用派生词: distend → distended

15. reflect: [riˈflekt] *v.* 反射;反映

　　分解记忆法: re-(反) + -flect(弯曲) = 反射

　　【例句】He looked at his face reflected in the mirror.
　　　　　他照镜子看看脸。

　　　　　The literature of a period reflects its values and tastes.
　　　　　某一时期的文学可反映出该时期的价值观念和审美观念。

　　常用派生词: reflect → reflection

16. reflection: [riˈflekʃn] *n.* 反射;反映;反思

　　分解记忆法: re-(反) + -flect(弯曲) + -ion = 反射

　　【例句】Your clothes are a reflection of your personality.
　　　　　一个人的衣着可反映出其个性。

　　　　　A moment's reflection will show you are wrong.
　　　　　只要略加考虑就可看出你错了。

17. **flexible:** [ˈfleksəbl] *a.* 易弯曲的；灵活的

分解记忆法：flex- (弯曲) + -ible（能……的）= 易弯曲的

【例句】We need a foreign policy that is more flexible.
我们需要一个更为灵活的外交政策。
This tube is flexible but tough.
这管子柔软但很坚固。

常用派生词：flexible → flexibility

Words in Use

1. Careful maintenance can _____ the life of your car by several years.
   A. extend   B. contend   C. distend   D. attend
2. Besides taking medicine, does _____ still have new remedial method?
   A. hypothesis   B. hypertension   C. hypertensor   D. hyperthymia
3. English majors will have _____ reading course during their first two years in university.
   A. extension   B. intense   C. attentive   D. extensive
4. The gas _____ the animal's body.
   A. contended   B. intended   C. distended   D. distant
5. The meeting was well _____.
   A. attended   B. intended   C. resumed   D. made
6. I came with the _____ of staying, but now I've decided to leave.
   A. distend   B. intensity   C. intention   D. contend
7. If you need anything when you are staying in our hotel, please ring for the _____.
   A. attention   B. conductor   C. manager   D. attendant
8. The town was hit by _____ bombardment since the war began.
   A. sensitive   B. active   C. intensive   D. extensive
9. A good hostess is always _____ to the needs of her guests.
   A. extensive   B. intensive   C. active   D. attentive
10. My first failure only _____ my desire to succeed.
    A. intensify   B. satisfy   C. fury   D. enhance
11. I would _____ that unemployment is our most serious social evil.
    A. extend   B. contend   C. intend   D. content
12. The _____ heat has dried up the pond.
    A. intensive   B. extensive   C. intense   D. intensify
13. This is not a time for _____. We need to work together.
    A. extension   B. illusion   C. intention   D. contention

14. She had a _____ to avoid taking responsibility whenever there was something wrong.
    A. tenet   B. tenement   C. tendency   D. trend
15. One's dressing _____ his/her personality.
    A. reflects   B. represses   C. refits   D. relates
16. Adults are not _____; they do not transplant comfortably to another place.
    A. active   B. passive   C. attentive   D. flexible
17. The maid saw her _____ in a polished table-top.
    A. intention   B. infection   C. reflection   D. reflect
18. Professor, are you going to _____ the forum next Monday?
    A. attend   B. examine   C. preside   D. intend
19. Study of logic and rhetoric makes a man able to _____.
    A. imply   B. attend   C. intend   D. contend
20. As the election approaches, the war of words between the main political parties becomes increasingly _____.
    A. extensive   B. intense   C. intensive   D. heat
21. What enterprises in China should resolve as a matter of urgency is to further enhance their own human resources and to _____ corporation reforms.
    A. intend   B. intended   C. intensity   D. intensify
22. _____ funds will be needed in corporation reforms.
    A. Extensive   B. Intensive   C. Intense   D. Extended
23. I have no _____ of coming to this terrible place again!
    A. intention   B. contention   C. inclination   D. attention
24. He believes that pop music should _____ modern society, and he wants new challenges.
    A. inflame   B. reflect   C. defect   D. perfect
25. In any system, the most _____ person has the control.
    A. extensive   B. intensive   C. flexible   D. inflexible
26. People believe that society has an innate _____ toward improvement.
    A. consistency   B. attendance   C. flexibility   D. tendency
27. Could you _____ to this matter immediately?
    A. resort   B. attend   C. intend   D. extend
28. _____ economy is a sustainable economic growth pattern and regards quality and benefit as its center.
    A. Intensive   B. Extensive   C. Active   D. Passive
29. On further _____, I saw that she might be right, after all.
    A. thought   B. defection   C. reflection   D. impaction

30. _____ learning is the process whereby an individual aims to learn something and goes about achieving that objective.

A. Suitable   B. Deliberate   C. International   D. Intentional

Key to *Words in Use*

1. A	2. B	3. D	4. C	5. A
6. C	7. D	8. C	9. D	10. A
11. B	12. C	13. D	14. C	15. A
16. D	17. C	18. A	19. D	20. B
21. D	22. A	23. A	24. B	25. C
26. D	27. B	28. A	29. C	30. D

第13章　表示"引导，汇集"的词根

Words in Context

Cognitive Intervention Programs in Segregate Confinement

At the present time, most inmates **congregate** in one form or another for as much as twenty-four hours each day. This congregate environment facilitates considerable violence and disorder. Drug dealing, stabbings, and sexual assaults occur with distressing frequency.

Recent trends in inmate management have focused on the use of super maximum-security prisons, wherein recalcitrant inmates who fail to adjust to the routine of congregate imprisonment are transferred to **segregate** housing units where they live in solitary confinement up to twenty-three hours per day.

But inasmuch as **segregation** units assist prison officials in the management of violent inmates, isolated confinement has been criticized for inflicting psychological trauma on those confined to such idleness and deprivation. Therefore, cognitive intervention programs are **introduced** to restructure the offender's thinking patterns and facilitate more prosocial thinking. The movement began in Canada in the 1980s when the National Correctional Service chose cognitive restructuring as its principal treatment strategy.

Standard corrections policy mandates that convicted felons sentenced to prison be placed in **congregate** systems of confinement upon admission. The purpose of this research is to document how cognitive intervention programs affect conditions of confinement in segregation. If such strategies prove successful at **reducing** the harsh conditions of isolation while simultaneously transforming the attitudes and beliefs of offenders, then placing inmates in segregation at the onset of their sentences may prove to be the most humane and truly corrective method of incarcerating offenders.

Word Building

More Words with the Word Roots

词根	释义	例词
duct, duc	引导 (to lead)	aqueduct, conduct, conductor, semiconductor, abduct, viaduct, reduce, reduction, deduce, induce, induct, introduce, produce, seduce

（续表）

词根	释义	例词
greg	汇集（to collect）	gregarious, aggregate, congregate, congregation, egregious, segregate, segregation, segregationist

1. aqueduct: [ˈækwidʌkt] *n.* 水渠；导水管

　　分解记忆法：aque-(水) + duct(引导) = 导水管

　　【例句】There are some aqueducts here.

　　　　　这里有些导水管。

　　　　　The aqueducts are of high quality.

　　　　　这些导水管质量很好。

2. conduct: [kənˈdʌkt] *v.* 引导；指挥

　　分解记忆法：con-(一起) + -duct(引导) = 引导

　　【例句】He conducted the members of the audience to their seats.

　　　　　他将观众引到他们的座位上。

　　　　　Mr. Green will conduct the orchestra tonight.

　　　　　格林先生今晚将指挥这支管弦乐队。

常用派生词：conduct → conduction → conductor

3. conductor: [kənˈdʌktə] *n.* 指挥家；列车员；导体

　　分解记忆法：con-(一起) + duct(引导) + -or(人) = 指挥者

　　【例句】The young soprano was taken up by a famous conductor.

　　　　　那年轻的女高音歌手受到一著名指挥家的提携。

　　　　　The conductor is checking passengers' tickets.

　　　　　列车员正在查旅客的票。

常用派生词：conductor → conductress

4. semiconductor: [ˈsemikənˈdʌktə] *n.* 半导体；半导体装置

　　分解记忆法：semi-(半) + conductor(导体) = 半导体

　　【例句】Semiconductors are essential components in electronic devices such as smartphones and computers.

　　　　　半导体是智能手机和电脑等电子产品的基本元件。

　　　　　Where is the semiconductor made in?

　　　　　这台半导体是哪儿产的？

5. abduct: [æbˈdʌkt] *v.* 诱拐；绑架

　　分解记忆法：ab-(离开) + duct(引领) = 诱拐

　　【例句】Her mind reeled when she learned her son had been abducted.

　　　　　得知儿子被人拐走，她只觉得一阵眩晕。

The police caught the man who tried to abduct the boy for ransom.

警察抓住了那个企图拐走这男孩以便勒索赎金的家伙。

常用派生词：abduct → abduction → abductor

6. viaduct: [ˈvaiədʌkt] *v.* 高架桥；高架道路；高架铁路

分解记忆法：via- (经过) + duct (引导) = 高架桥

【例句】With their aid a vital viaduct on the main Athens railway line was destroyed.

在他们的帮助下，雅典铁路干线上的一座主要高架桥被破坏了。

A tragedy occurred on the viaduct early this morning, killing six people.

今晨高架路上发生了一起惨祸，致使6人死亡。

7. reduce: [riˈdjuːs] *v.* 减少；降低

分解记忆法：re- (回) + duce (引导) = 减少

【例句】The manager has worked out a suitable measure to reduce the domino effect.

经理想出了一个适当的举措来减少多米诺效应。

Poverty reduced him to begging.

贫穷迫使他行乞。

常用派生词：reduce → reduction → reducible

8. reduction: [riˈdʌkʃn] *n.* 减少；缩小；折扣

分解记忆法：re- (回) + duction (引导) = 减少

【例句】There has been some reduction in unemployment.

失业人数有所减少。

Cost reduction programs are often triggered by a drop in profits.

提出降低成本计划，往往是由利润下降引起的。

常用派生词：reduction → reductionism

9. deduce: [diˈdjuːs] *v.* 推理；演绎；推断

分解记忆法：de- (向下) + duce (引导) = 推理

【例句】From this fact we may deduce that he is sick.

从这个事实我们可推断他生病了。

On the basis of the evidence we deduced that he was guilty.

根据这些证据,我们推论他是有罪的。

常用派生词：deduce → deduction → deducible

10. induce: [inˈdjuːs] *v.* 劝诱；招致；引起

分解记忆法：in- (里面) + duce (引导) = 劝诱

【例句】Nothing in the world would induce me to do that.

什么也不能引诱我做那种事。

Too much food induces sleepiness.

吃得太饱会引起睡意。

常用派生词：induce → inducement

11. induct: [inˈdʌkt] *v.* 使正式就职；征召入伍

分解记忆法：in- (入) + duct (引) = 使正式就职

【例句】They were inducted into the skills of magic.
他们被传授了魔术。
Bamboo furniture can induct the moisture of certain amount.
竹制家具可以吸收一定水分。

常用派生词：induct → inductee → induction

12. introduce: [ˌintrəˈdju:s] *v.* 介绍；引进

分解记忆法：intro- (向里面) + duce (引导) = 介绍

【例句】She introduced me to her friend.
她把我介绍给她的朋友。
It was my younger brother who introduced me to pop music.
是我的弟弟介绍我听流行音乐的。

常用派生词：introduce → induction

13. produce: [prəˈdju:s] *v.* 生产；产生

分解记忆法：pro- (向前) + duce (引导) = 生产

【例句】He hopes to find the money to produce a film about China.
他希望筹集到资金以便拍一部关于中国的影片。
His announcement produced gasps of amazement.
他宣布的消息引起了一片惊叹声。

常用派生词：produce → production

14. seduce: [siˈdju:s] *v.* 勾引；引诱

分解记忆法：se- (离开) + duce (引导) = 勾引

【例句】Higher salaries are seducing many teachers into industry.
在高薪利诱之下，许多教师改行进入工业界。
Men are seduced by her beauty and wit.
她才貌双全倾倒众生。

常用派生词：seduce → seduction → seductive

15. gregarious: [griˈgeəriəs] *a.* 爱交际的；群居的；合群的

分解记忆法：greg- (群) + -arious (有倾向的) = 群居的

【例句】Man is a gregarious animal.
人是群居动物。
He is a gregarious man and enjoys the companionship of friends.
他是个喜爱社交的人，有一大群朋友。

常用派生词：gregarious → gregariousness

16. aggregate: [ˈægrigeit] *a.* 合计的；集合的；*n.* 合计；总计；集合体 *v.* 聚集；集合；合计

分解记忆法：ag- (向) + greg (群，聚) + -ate (形容词缀) = 聚合的

【例句】An increase in the budget deficit boosts aggregate demand.

预算赤字增加使总需求扩大。

The money collected will aggregate $10,000.

已收款合计将达一万美元。

常用派生词：aggregate → aggregation

17. congregate: [ˈkɔŋgrigeit] *v. & adj.* 聚集，集合；集合的，集体的

分解记忆法：con-（共同）+ greg（群）+ -ate（动词词缀）= 聚群到一起

【例句】A crowd quickly congregated round the speaker.

大群的人迅速地在演说者周围聚集起来。

The crowds congregated in the square to hear the president speak.

成群的人聚集在广场上听总统演讲。

常用派生词：congregate → congregation

18. congregation: [ˌkɔŋgriˈgeiʃən] *n.* 聚集，集合

分解记忆法：con-（共同）+ greg（群）+ -tion（名词词缀）= 集合

【例句】The congregation entered the church in procession.

教徒们排着队进入教堂。

The preacher blessed the congregation after his sermon.

牧师在讲道后祝福会众。

常用派生词：congregation → congregationism

19. egregious: [iˈgriːdʒəs] *a.* 异乎寻常的；过分的；糟糕透顶的

分解记忆法：e-（出）+ greg（群）+ -ious（形容词词缀）= 异乎寻常的

【例句】In this new book, he shows his egregious insight on drawing the character of American.

在这本新书里，他对美国人性格的描写表现出惊人的洞察力。

He is an egregious fool.

他是个大笨蛋。

20. segregate: [ˈsegrigeit] *v.* 隔离；分离；使分开

分解记忆法：se-（分开）+ greg（群）+ -ate（动词词缀）= 隔离

【例句】The two groups of fans must be segregated in the stadium.

必须把体育场中这两部分球迷隔开。

Why should the handicapped be segregated from the able-bodied?

为什么要把伤残人士和身体健康的人分开？

常用派生词：segregate → segregation

21. segregation: [ˌsegriˈgeiʃən] *n.* 隔离

分解记忆法：se-（分开）+ greg（群）+ -tion（名词词缀）= 隔离

【例句】An official policy of racial segregation was practiced in the country, involving political, legal, and economic discrimination against nonwhites.

那个国家实行一种官方的种族隔离政策，包括在政治、法律和经济诸方面对非白色人种的歧视。

There is still racial segregation in that country.

那个国家仍然存在种族隔离。

常用派生词：segregation → segregationist

22. **segregationist**：[ˌsegrɪˈgeɪʃənɪst] *n. & a.* 隔离主义者；隔离主义者的

分解记忆法：se- (分开) + greg (群) + -tion (名词词缀) + -ist (人) = 隔离主义者

【例句】They are really segregationists.

他们是真正的隔离主义者。

Segregationists tried to preserve the South's traditional color barriers.

种族隔离主义者试图维护南方传统的肤色壁垒。

Words in Use

1. There is an ____ underneath the new house.
   A. aqueduct   B. abduct   C. abruption   D. address

2. A(n) ____ is someone who thinks people of different races should be kept apart.
   A. dramatist   B. segregationist   C. protagonist   D. activist

3. I think he ____ himself admirably, considering the difficult circumstances.
   A. abrupt   B. abduct   C. conducted   D. aqueduct

4. Racial ____ is the separation of different racial groups in daily life, such as eating in a restaurant, drinking from a water fountain, using a rest room, attending school, going to the movies, or in the rental or purchase of a home.
   A. segregation   B. digression   C. succession   D. distinction

5. The bus ____ takes up the tickets strictly.
   A. conductor   B. visitor   C. insulator   D. insular

6. They ____ you from the rest of the community.
   A. introduce   B. segregate   C. reduce   D. abduct

7. Father bought him a ____ as birthday present.
   A. semicontinuity B. semivowel C. semiconductor D. conductor

8. People there suffer the most ____ abuses of human rights.
   A. ungracious   B. abusive   C. aggressive   D. egregious

9. She was charged with ____ a six-month-old child.
   A. inducing   B. reducing   C. abducting   D. conducting

10. He looked at every soul in the ____.
    A. integrity   B. reduction   C. integration   D. congregation

11. A /An ____ is a long, high bridge that carries a road or a railway across a valley.
    A. aqueduct   B. viaduct   C. abduct   D. conductor
12. The crowd ____ in front of the building on Christmas Eve.
    A. degraded   B. congregated   C. irrigated   D. separated
13. If you bargain with them, they might ____ the price.
    A. deduce   B. seduce   C. induce   D. reduce
14. England has beaten the Welsh three times in succession with a(n) ____ score of 80-12.
    A. gradate   B. irrigate   C. secrete   D. aggregate
15. When there is a(n) ____ in something, it is made smaller.
    A. conduct   B. abruption   C. reduction   D. seduction
16. She is such a(n) ____ and outgoing person.
    A. anxious   B. irritated   C. gregarious   D. grievous
17. From the presence of so many people at the fair, we can ____ that it is a welcomed one.
    A. introduce   B. induce   C. seduce   D. deduce
18. The warm weather ____ me away from my studies.
    A. excluded   B. induce   C. seduced   D. deduced
19. What ____ you to do such a stupid thing?
    A. included   B. induced   C. deduced   D. produced
20. Two new members have been ____ into the Cabinet.
    A. conducted   B. induced   C. inducted   D. delegated
21. The medicine ____ a violent reaction.
    A. benefitted   B. produced   C. introduced   D. increased
22. I was ____ to the president at the forum
    A. introduced   B. deduced   C. met   D. received
23. A guide ____ the visitors round the museum.
    A. abducted   B. conducted   C. inspired   D. moved
24. Detectives ____ from the clues who had committed the crime.
    A. seduced   B. conducted   C. deduced   D. induced
25. It was my brother who first ____ me to the pleasures of wine-tasting.
    A. released   B. deduced   C. introduced   D. conducted
26. Being ____ has its rewards. Your openness will lead you to new, fun people.
    A. incredulous   B. gregarious   C. avaricious   D. ingenious
27. Our team scored the most goals on ____.
    A. congregate   B. grade   C. rate   D. aggregate
28. A power firm, for example, might _____ its industrial customers from its residential customers.
    A. segregate   B. congregate   C. interrogate   D. update

29. Nothing in the world would ____ me to do that.
    A. provide   B. impute   C. deduce   D. induce
30. She cooperated with her ____ and both of them were sentenced to imprisonment.
    A. operator   B. visitor   C. abductor   D. suitor

Key to *Words in Use*

1. A	2. B	3. C	4. A	5. A
6. B	7. C	8. D	9. C	10. D
11. B	12. B	13. D	14. D	15. C
16. C	17. D	18. C	19. B	20. C
21. B	22. A	23. B	24. C	25. C
26. B	27. D	28. A	29. D	30. C

第14章 表示"信任"的词根

Words in Context

Tips for Staying Visible, <u>Credible</u>, Confident and Connected

For many women, re-entering the workforce after a long absence can be daunting. If you have been out of the workforce for more than a year and you plan to return at some point, use the following tips to help you start re-building your visibility, <u>credibility</u>, confidence and connections.

You should firstly remember your value. Prior to leaving the workforce you were valuable to your employer and made significant contributions to the organizations you worked for. Remembering your value is an important first step. So start by making a list of your top 10 most precious accomplishments, contributions and achievements.

Secondly you should expect <u>incredible</u> success. Many women on hiatus do not expect to reenter the workforce successfully. They lose their career confidence and discount their market-value. They are told by some re-entry experts to lower their expectations and be willing to accept less and eventually they get what they're told to settle for. Remember, if you expect defeat you are likely to be defeated. I recommend that you think BIG and Expect Success!

And finally you should pursue your passion. Of all the things you have done in your career thus far, what captured your interest and heart the most? What is most precious to you? Your greatest impact can be made when you are truly passionate about what you do.

Word Building

More Words with the Word Roots

词根	释义	例词
cred	相信 (to believe)	credible, incredible, credibility, incredibility, credulous, incredulous, credential, credit, accredit, discredit
fid	信任 (to trust)	confide, confidant, confidential, diffident, diffidence, fidelity, infidelity, infidel, perfidy, perfidious, affidavit

1. credible: [ˈkredəbl] *a.* 可信的；可靠的；可接受的

分解记忆法：cred- (相信) + -ible (可……的) = 可信的

【例句】It is hardly credible.
这是难以置信的。
Is there a credible alternative to the nuclear deterrent?
是否有可以取代核威慑力量的可靠办法？

常用派生词：credible → credibility

2. incredible: [inˈkredəbl] *a.* 难以置信的；惊人的

分解记忆法：in- (不) + cred- (相信) + -ible (可……的) = 难以置信的

【例句】That's the most incredible coincidence I've ever heard of!
那是我听说过的最难以置信的巧合！
For such a tiny woman she had an incredible appetite.
对这么一个小个子女人来说，她的胃口大得令人难以置信。

常用派生词：incredible → incredibility

3. credibility: [ˌkredəˈbiləti] *n.* 可靠性；可信性；确实性

分解记忆法：cred- (相信) + -blity (可……性) = 不可信

【例句】The silly ending robs the plot of any credibility.
这愚蠢的结尾使得整个情节变得一点都不可信。
The story strained our credibility.
这个故事超出我们信任程度。

4. incredibility: [inkredəˈbiliti] *n.* 不能相信；不可信

分解记忆法：in- (不) + cred- (相信) + -blity (可……性) = 不能相信

【例句】On this basis, the constructive countermeasure scheme to the incredibility was put forward according to the characteristics of SME of our country.
在此基础上，针对我国中小企业的特点和失信问题提出了具有建设性的对策方案。
The key points of solving the problems on their incredibility is to carry out the credibility education, establish the credibility file and adopt the practical and feasible measures.
开展诚信教育，建立诚信档案，采取切实可行的措施制止不诚信行为是解决当代大学生不诚信问题的关键。

5. credulous: [ˈkredjuləs] *a.* 轻信的；易受骗的

分解记忆法：credu- (相信) + -ous (可……的) = 轻信的

【例句】They are credulous people who believe in the advertisement.
他们是一些轻信广告的人。
We are less credulous than we used to be.
我们不再像以往那样轻易相信别人了。

常用派生词：credulous → credulously

6. incredulous: [inˈkredjuləs] *a.* 不轻信的；表示怀疑的

分解记忆法：in-(不)＋cred-(相信)＋ulous(……的)＝不轻信的

【例句】She looked incredulous.

她显出怀疑的样子。

They are incredulous of hearsay.

他们不轻信道听途说。

常用派生词：incredulous → incredulously

7. credential: [kriˈdenʃəl] *n.* 文凭；证明文件；外交使节所递的国书（常用复数）

分解记忆法：cred-(相信)＋-tial(后缀)＝证明文件

【例句】I examined his credentials.

我查验了他的证件。

That's where this credential can help.

这就是这个证书有用之处。

8. credit: [ˈkredit] *n.* 信用；赞扬；学分

分解记忆法：cred-(相信)＋-it(表名词)＝信用

【例句】It is greatly to your credit that you gave back the money you found.

你拾金不昧是非常难能可贵的。

She was given the credit for what I had done.

事情是我做的，她却受到称赞。

常用派生词：credit → creditable → creditably

9. accredit: [əˈkredit] *v.* 委任；委派；归因于

分解记忆法：ac(=ad朝向)＋credit(信任)＝委任

【例句】The president will accredit Jim as his assistant.

董事长将任命吉姆做他的助理。

He was accredited to Madrid.

他被委任为驻马德里的大使。

常用派生词：accredit → accredited → accreditation

10. discredit: [disˈkredit] *v.* 使不信；使丢脸

分解记忆法：dis-(不)＋credit(信任)＝使不信

【例句】There is no reason to discredit what she says.

没理由不信她说的话。

They made an effort to discredit the politician.

他们尽力败坏那政客的声誉。

常用派生词：discredit → discreditable

11. confide: [kənˈfaid] *v.* 吐露（秘密）；完全信任

分解记忆法：con-(共同，全部)＋fid(信任)＝吐露

【例句】He confided his troubles to his friend.
他向朋友倾诉烦恼事。
She confided to me the secret.
她向我吐露了那个秘密。

常用派生词：confide → confidence

12. confidant: [ˌkɔnfiˈdænt] *n.* 知己；密友

分解记忆法：con-(共同，全部)+fid(信任)+ent(人)=心腹朋友

【例句】He resigned himself to the role of confidant.
他退居到知心朋友的位置上。
Her cousin was a confidant.
他的表兄是一个可靠的人。

13. confidential: [ˌkɔnfiˈdenʃəl] *a.* 机密的；保密的

分解记忆法：con-(共同，全部)+fid(信任)+-tial(形容词后缀)=机密的

【例句】I must stress that what I say is confidential.
我要强调我说的话是保密的。
He told me confidentially that he's thinking of resigning next year.
他私下告诉我他打算明年辞职。

常用派生词：confidential → confidentially → confidentiality

14. diffident: [ˈdifidənt] *a.* 缺乏自信的；自卑的

分解记忆法：dif-(不)+fid(信任)+-ent(形容词后缀)=缺乏自信的

【例句】Don't be so diffident about your talents.
别对自己的才能如此缺乏信心。
He is diffident about expressing his opinions.
他对于表达自己的意见感到胆怯。

常用派生词：diffident → diffidence → diffidently

15. diffidence: [ˈdifidəns] *n.* 缺乏自信；自卑

分解记忆法：dif-(不)+fid(信任)+-ence(名词后缀)=自卑

【例句】It is with diffidence and hesitation that I approach this work.
我是带着怯懦和犹豫接近这部作品的。
The director looked at her as if with contempt for ner diffidence.
主任打量着她，似乎对她的怯懦有些瞧不起。

16. fidelity: [fiˈdeləti] *n.* 忠贞；忠实；忠诚；保真

分解记忆法：fid(信任)+-ity(名词后缀)=忠贞

【例句】History is more full of examples of the fidelity of dogs than of friends.
历史上狗儿忠诚的事例较之朋友忠诚的事例多得多。
His fidelity and industry brought him speedy promotion.
他的忠于职守和勤于工作使他得到迅速晋级。

17. infidelity: [ˌinfiˈdeliti] *n.* 不忠贞；失真

分解记忆法：in-(不)+ fid(信任)+ -ity (名词后缀)= 不忠贞

【例句】His wife has winked at his infidelity for years.
他多年来对妻子不忠，妻子也只装作不知情。
I can take the pain of your infidelity.
我能接受你背叛我。

18. infidel: [ˈinfidəl] *n.* 异教徒 *a.* 无宗教信仰的；不信教的；异端的

分解记忆法：in-(不)+ fid(信任)+ el (后缀)= 不信教的

【例句】He promised to continue the fight against infidel forces.
他承诺继续与异端势力斗争。

常用派生词：infidel → infidelity

19. perfidy: [ˈpəːfədi] *n.* 不忠诚

分解记忆法：per-(假)+ fid(信任)+ y (形容词后缀)= 不忠诚

【例句】As devotion unites lovers so perfidy estranges friends.
忠诚是爱情的桥梁，欺诈是友谊的敌人。
Perfidy crime is originally a notion in German and Japanese criminal laws.
背信犯罪原是德日刑法中的一个概念。

常用派生词：perfidy → perfidious → perfidiously → perfidiousness

20. perfidious: [pəˈfidiəs] *a.* 不忠诚的；背信弃义的

分解记忆法：per-(假)+ fid(信任)+ -ious (形容词后缀)= 不忠诚的

【例句】This is a perfidious crime of aggression against the freedom and independence of all nations.
此种背信弃义的侵略罪行，是反对一切民族的自由和独立的。
The benefits of technology have a perfidious habit of flowing to the users, not the inventors.
技术带来的好处总是惠及技术的使用者而不是投资者。

常用派生词：perfidious → perfidiously → perfidiousness

21. affidavit: [ˌæfiˈdeivit] *n.* 宣誓书；书面证词

分解记忆法：af-(一再)+ fid(信任)+ -avit(后缀) = 宣誓书

【例句】Please fill out this lost passbook affidavit and list the code word you used when you opened your account.
请您填写一下这张丢失存折声明书，并写出您开立账户时所用的密码。
Fairford ran over the affidavit.
费尔福特把宣誓书匆匆看了一遍。

Words in Use

1. He talked ____ before the committee.
   A. credibly   B. credibility   C. infidelity   D. confidentially
2. A(n) ____ is a written statement which you swear is true and which may be used as evidence in a court of law.
   A. credit   B. affidavit   C. bid   D. accredit
3. ____, no one had ever thought of such a simple idea before.
   A. Perfidiously   B. Credibly   C. Incredibly   D. Generally
4. The ____ Judas was despised by people.
   A. anxious   B. ambitious   C. dangerous   D. perfidious
5. Incidents like these began to undermine Angleton's ____.
   A. fidelity   B. infidelity   C. credibility   D. incredibility
6. Therefore we can have a glimpse of Nelly's ____ as a simple servant and her conscious involvement in the crucial moments of the plots.
   A. obesity   B. necessity   C. comprehensiveness   D. incredibility
7. ____ is the action of betraying someone or behaving very badly towards someone.
   A. Purify   B. Perfidy   C. Prudery   D. Prodigy
8. All fighters for Communism are ____.
   A. candidates   B. pagan   C. confidants   D. infidels
9. ____ attitude will only make you take anything for granted.
   A. Credulous   B. Incredible   C. Infidel   D. Fidelity
10. "I cannot take the pain of your ____," cried the wife.
    A. credibility   B. incredibility   C. infidelity   D. fidelity
11. I might have been ____ had I not been accustomed to such responses.
    A. uncountable   B. unable   C. incredulous   D. incredible
12. I had to promise ____ to the Queen.
    A. infidelity   B. fidelity   C. ability   D. credibility
13. The graduate has the perfect ____ for the job.
    A. inability   B. rituals   C. initials   D. credentials
14. The outer crust of her life, all of her natural ____ and reserve, was torn away.
    A. diffidence   B. confidant   C. decadence   D. accidents
15. I can't take any ____; the others did all the work.
    A. creed   B. credit   C. addict   D. credibility
16. Jim was always ____ when it came to staff matters, and not been able to summon up the

gumption to bang the table.

    A. confident   B. confidant   C. diffident   D. different

17. He is ____ with having first introduced this word into the language.

    A. submitted   B. accredited   C. added   D. called

18. She accused them of leaking ____ information about her private life.

    A. diffident   B. initial   C. confident   D. confidential

19. His corrupt activities were a ____ to the Senate.

    A. deface   B. credit   C. discredit   D. dogface

20. Can I ____ my children to your care?

    A. confide   B. confine   C. conjecture   D. conduce

21. I had no resource, no friend, no ____ but my old governess.

    A. confinement   B. diffident   C. confident   D. confidant

22. He is ____ of rumors.

    A. indifferent   B. credulous   C. credible   D. confidant

23. The _____ military attack on our fatherland, begun on 22 June by Hitler's Germany, is continuing.

    A. assiduous   B. credulous   C. perfidious   D. industrious

24. Emil looked ____, but he did not dispute the point.

    A. marvelous   B. ambitious   C. incredulous   D. credulous

25. That's the most ____ coincidence I've ever heard of!

    A. uncountable   B. incredible   C. sociable   D. sustainable

26. I knew she had some fundamental problems in her marriage because she had ____ in me a year earlier.

    A. confided   B. prided   C. departed   D. concluded

27. You can ask a dealer for a discount whether you pay cash or buy on ____.

    A. credulity   B. aqueduct   C. subsidence   D. credit

28. However, too much fictional, idiosyncratic biography is a distraction and makes your personas less ____.

    A. incredible   B. credible   C. bubble   D. grabble

29. He had never thought of his sweetheart as of so superior a being, and he was instantly taken with a feeling of ____.

    A. assonance   B. confidence   C. diffidence   D. indifference

30. Please translate this passage into Chinese with the greatest ____.

    A. ability   B. fact   C. truth   D. fidelity

Key to *Words in Use*

1. A	2. B	3. C	4. D	5. C
6. D	7. B	8. D	9. A	10. C
11. C	12. B	13. D	14. A	15. B
16. C	17. B	18. D	19. C	20. A
21. D	22. B	23. C	24. C	25. B
26. A	27. D	28. B	29. C	30. D

第15章　表示"心智"的词根

Words in Context

The Human-Animal Bond

The human-animal bond is a relationship between a human and an animal that involves love, admiration, and trust. Many pet owners in the United States consider their animals to be "part of the family" and treat them as such, training them to be appropriately socialized and obedient, and accepting responsibility for their welfare.

Animals such as those described, which are normal, healthy, and happy, can benefit humans in many ways. Use of companion animals as a team with staff, and therapists, can help improve cognition, socialization, reminiscence, as well as trust, **memory**, sequencing, self-esteem, problem-solving, attention, and concentration. Petting or grooming an animal can assist in the physical and emotional recovery of the patient. Humans of all ages and needs are able to work toward these goals and others, through the therapeutic use of companion animals.

To help understand how this interaction works, let's look at the following case. An 80-year-old woman is working with a voluntary physical therapist and speech therapist toward her rehabilitative goals which are attention and concentration, memory, improving right and left neglect, walking, enunciation and ability to use correct words. She is unable to do any of these very well, basically due to her inability for concentration. A HABIC team **volunteers** to assist in the therapeutic sessions, and meet the patient along with a physical therapist. Immediate responses are very positive, enabling the patient to relax and focus on the dog. The patient's speech and selection of words are still confused, but improve with subsequent visits. Memory was helped by the patient trying to **remember** a sequence of commands for the dog while it retrieved an object thrown by the patient.

Word Building

More Words with the Word Roots

词根	释义	例词
psych(o)	心理，精神 (mind, spirit)	psyche, psychic, psychedelic, psychosis, psychotic, psychopath, psychoanalysis, psychoanalyst, psychology, psychologist, psychosomatic, psychotherapy

（续表）

词根	释义	例词
memor, mem	记忆（memory）	commemorate, memorial, immemorial, memento, memo, memorandum, memoir, memorable, memorabilia, memorize, memory, remember
vol	意志（will）	volition, benevolent, benevolence, malevolent, malevolence, volunteer, voluntary, voluntarily
anim	心灵（soul）	animate, inanimate, magnanimous, unanimous, equanimity, animadvert

1. **psychic:** [ˈsaikik] *a. & n.* 精神的；心灵的；通灵的；巫师

    分解记忆法：psych- (精神) +ic (……的) =精神的

    【例句】She claims to be psychic and to be able to foretell the future.

    她自称有特异功能，能预知未来。

    Jim helped police by using his psychic powers.

    吉姆用他的超能力帮助了警察。

    常用派生词：psychic→ psychical→ psychically

2. **psychedelic:** [ˌsaikəˈdelik] *a. & n.* 引起幻觉的；迷幻的；迷幻剂

    分解记忆法：psyche- (精神) +del- (看) +ic (……的) =引起幻觉的

    【例句】Some music is psychedelic.

    有些音乐能引起幻觉。

    Mescalin and LSD are psychedelic drugs.

    仙人球毒和麦角酸二乙基胺都是迷幻药。

    常用派生词：psychedelic→ psychedelically

3. **psychosis:** [saiˈkəusis] *n.* 精神病；变态心理

    分解记忆法：psycho- (精神) +sis (病症) =精神病

    【例句】Since World War II, psychologists have focused on fixing what is broken—repairing psychosis and neurosis.

    第二次世界大战以来，心理学的研究重点是如何弥合创伤，即治疗精神症和神经症。

    The drug is used to treat psychosis.

    这种药是用来治疗精神疾病的。

4. **psychopath:** [ˈsaikəpæθ] *n.* 精神病患者

    分解记忆法：psycho- (精神) +path (疾病) =精神病患者

    【例句】She was abducted by a dangerous psychopath.

    她被一个危险的精神病患者劫持。

The newspapers say there's a psychopath going around the college.
报纸上说，有个精神病患者在这所大学里转来转去。

常用派生词：psychopath→psychopathic

5. psychoanalysis: [ˌsaikəuəˈnæləsis] *n.* 心理分析；精神分析

分解记忆法：psycho- (精神) +analysis (分析)＝心理分析

【例句】The student finally became a licensed practitioner of psychoanalysis.
这个学生最终成为有开业许可证的心理分析医生。

He is so obsessed with the desire of being an expert of psychoanalysis.
他一心想成为心理分析的专家。

常用派生词：psychoanalysis→psychoanalyst

6. psychoanalyst: [ˌpsaikəuˈænəlist] *n.* 心理分析学者；精神分析学家

分解记忆法：psycho- (精神) +analyst (分析者)＝心理分析学者

【例句】Sigmund Freud is an Austrian psychoanalyst.
西格蒙德·弗洛伊德是位奥地利心理分析学家。

Bayard is a 52-year-old professor of literature and a psychoanalyst.
伯亚德是一位52岁的文学教授兼心理分析学者。

7. psychology: [saiˈkɔlədʒi] *n.* 心理学

分解记忆法：psycho- (心理) +logy (学)＝心理学

【例句】We need some male subjects for a psychology experiment.
我们需要几个男子作心理学实验对象。

I can't understand that man's psychology.
我无法理解那个人的心理。

常用派生词：psychology→psychological

8. psychologist: [saiˈkɔlədʒist] *n.* 心理学家

分解记忆法：psycho- (心理) +logist (学家)＝心理学家

【例句】The psychologist always assigns work to each researcher.
这个心理学家总是将工作分派给每个研究人员。

He fancies himself a bit of a psychologist.
他自以为有一点心理学家的天分。

常用派生词：psychologist→psychology→psychological

9. psychosomatic: [ˌsaikəusəˈmætik] *a.* 由心理负担引起的；精神身体相关的

分解记忆法：psycho- (心理) +somatic (身体的)＝由心理负担引起的

【例句】Doctors refused to treat her, claiming that her problems were all psychosomatic.
医生拒绝医治她，声称她的问题都是由心理负担引起的。

Psychosomatic disorders may include hypertension, respiratory ailments, etc.
心身性疾病可能有高血压、呼吸系统的病症等。

常用派生词：psychosomatic→psychosomatically

10. psychotherapy: [ˈsaikəuˈθerəpi] *n.* 心理疗法；精神疗法

分解记忆法：psycho- (心理) +therapy (治疗)=心理疗法

【例句】The psychotherapy is carried out in small interactive groups.

这种心理治疗是在互动小组中进行的。

Psychotherapy may help you with your illness.

心理治疗或许能对你的病有所帮助。

常用派生词：psychotherapy→ psychotherapist

11. commemorate: [kəˈmeməreit] *v.* 纪念，庆祝；成为……的纪念

分解记忆法：com- (共同) +memor (记忆) +ate=纪念

【例句】This memorial commemorates those who died in the war.

这座纪念碑是纪念战争中牺牲者的。

Christmas commemorates the birth of Christ.

圣诞节是为了纪念耶稣的诞生。

常用派生词：commemorate→ commemorative→commemoration

12. memorial: [miˈmɔːriəl] *n. & a.* 纪念碑；纪念堂；纪念的

分解记忆法：memor- (记忆) +ial (表示物；……的)=纪念碑

【例句】The Lincoln Memorial is an importaut historical landmark in the United states.

林肯纪念堂是美国重要的历史地标。

The site of the memorial is granted in perpetuity to Canada.

纪念馆址已选定在加拿大作为永久的纪念。

常用派生词：memorial→ memorialize

13. immemorial: [ˈimiˈmɔːriəl] *a.* 太古的；远古的；无法追忆的

分解记忆法：im (不) +memor- (记忆) +ial (……的)=太古的

【例句】Exotic, mysterious, fascinating China from time immemorial has tantalized the imagination of Westerners.

自远古以来，奇特、神秘、迷人的中国就激起了西方人的幻想。

There have been ponies on Dartmoor from time immemorial.

自远古以来，达特穆尔高原就一直有小型马。

14. memento: [məˈmentəu] *n.* 纪念品

分解记忆法：mem- (记忆) +ento (表示物)=纪念品

【例句】My friend gave me his picture as a memento before going away.

我的朋友在离别前给我一张照片留作纪念品。

We bought a cup as a memento of our trip to Italy.

我们买了个杯子当作此次意大利之旅的纪念品。

15. memorandum: [ˌmeməˈrændəm] *n.* 备忘录

分解记忆法：memor- (记忆) +andum (表示物)=备忘录

【例句】He sent us a memorandum about the meeting.

他给我们寄来了会议备忘录。

Let's give this memorandum the once-over.

让我们大略地看一下备忘录。

常用派生词：memorandum→ memo

16. memoir: ['memwɑː] *n.* 回忆录

分解记忆法：mem-（记忆）+oir（表示物）=回忆录

【例句】She wrote a memoir of her stay in France.

她写了一篇旅法记事录。

Yesterday we attended a lecture about the memoirs of a retired politician.

昨天我们参加了一个退休政治家的回忆录的讲座。

17. memorable: ['memərəbl] *a.* 值得纪念的；难忘的

分解记忆法：memor-（记忆）+able（可……的）=值得纪念的

【例句】This was indeed the most memorable day of my life.

这的确是我一生中最难忘的日子。

Nicole Kidman's performance as Virginia Woolf in *The Hours* was truly memorable.

妮可·基德曼在《时时刻刻》中对弗尼吉亚·伍尔芙一角的饰演着实令人难忘。

常用派生词：memorable→ memorably

18. memorize: ['meməraiz] *v.* 记住

分解记忆法：memor-（记忆）+ize（动词后缀）=记住

【例句】She can memorize facts very quickly.

她能很快记住许多资料。

An actor must be able to memorize his lines.

演员须善于熟记台词。

常用派生词：memorize→ memorable

19. memory: ['meməri] *n.* 记忆

分解记忆法：memor-（记忆）+y（名词后缀）=记忆

【例句】These frightful experiences are branded on his memory.

这些可怕的经历深深印入他的记忆。

He has a good visual memory.

他有良好的视觉记忆力。

常用派生词：memory → memo

20. remember: [ri'membə] *v.* 记住

分解记忆法：re-（再）+member（记忆）=记住

【例句】I remember seeing him once.

我记得见过他一次。

I'm sorry I can't remember your name.

对不起,我想不起你的名字了。

常用派生词:remember → rememberable→ rememberablity

21. volition: [vəˈliʃn] *n.* 选择;决定

分解记忆法:vol- (意志) +ition(名词后缀)=选择

【例句】She offered to help us of her own volition.

她自愿提出要帮助我们。

Is a person's true volition with so great power?

人的意志真的有那么大的力量吗?

常用派生词:volition →volitional

22. benevolent: [bəˈnevələnt] *a.* 慈善的;仁爱的

分解记忆法:bene- (好) +vol(意愿)+ent(形容词后缀)=慈善的

【例句】The old woman had a benevolent feeling towards all cats.

那个老太太对所有的猫都怀有仁慈之心。

The club received a benevolent donation.

该俱乐部接受了一笔慈善捐款。

常用派生词:benevolent →benevolently

23. benevolence: [biˈnevələns] *n.* 慈善;仁爱

分解记忆法:bene- (好) +vol(意愿)+ence(名词后缀)=慈善

【例句】He is a man with benevolence.

他是一个有善心的人。

For a moment his mask of benevolence fell and the real man was revealed.

一刹那间,他慈善的假面扔掉,露出了他的真面目。

常用派生词:benevolence →benevolent

24. malevolent: [məˈlevələnt] *a.* 有恶意的;坏心肠的

分解记忆法:male- (好) +vol(意愿)+ent(形容词后缀)=有恶意的

【例句】Her stare was malevolent.

她凝视的目光含有恶意。

Jamie's malevolent face twists in surprise.

杰米那张狰狞的脸孔惊讶地瘪了起来。

常用派生词:malevolent →malevolently

25. volunteer: [ˌvɒlənˈtiə] *a., v. & n.* 志愿者;志愿

分解记忆法:volunt- (意愿) +eer(人)=志愿者

【例句】The volunteers for community service are doing a good job.

社区服务的志愿者做得很出色。

They volunteered to repair the house for the old lady.

他们主动提出替老太太修缮房子。

常用派生词：volunteer →volentary

26. animate: ['ænimeit] *v. & a.* 给予活力；使有生气；生机勃勃的；活的

分解记忆法：anim- (精神) +ate(使……的)=给予活力

【例句】A smile animated her face.

一丝笑容使她脸上平添了生气。

The dog lay so still it scarcely seemed animate.

那条狗卧着一动也不动，简直不像活的。

常用派生词：animate →inanimate

27. magnanimous: [mæɡ'nænɪməs] *a.* 有活力的，有生气的；生机勃勃的

分解记忆法：anim- (精神) +ate(使……的)=给予活力

【例句】He is a leader who was magnanimous in victory.

他是位在胜利时宽宏大度的领袖。

I hope you will be magnanimous enough to excuse any incorrect behavior of me.

对不住的地方，望您海量包涵。

常用派生词：magnanimous →magnamously

28. unanimous: [ju(:)'næniməs] *a.* 一致同意的；意见一致的

分解记忆法：un- (一个) +anim(心灵)+ ous(……的)= 一致同意的

【例句】The Chinese are unanimous in their condemnation.

全中国人民一致提出谴责。

Politicians from all parties were completely unanimous in condemning his action.

所有党派的政治家们都一致谴责他的行为。

常用派生词：unanimous →unanimously

29. equanimity: [ˌiːkwə'nɪmɪtɪ] *n.* 心情平静；情绪镇静

分解记忆法：equ- (平等) +anim(心灵)+ ity(名词后缀)= 心情平静

【例句】He received the bad news with surprising equanimity.

听到这个坏消息时，他镇定得令人吃惊。

30. animadvert: [ˌænimæd'vəːt] *v.* 批判；责难

分解记忆法：anim(心灵)+ ad(向)+ vert(转)= 批判

【例句】Although they animadvert on the traditional culture, their purpose is to protect it.

虽然也批判传统文化，但这种批判是以维护为其前提的。

Doubt and animadvert are inner motive force of innovation of science and culture.

怀疑和批判是促进科学与文化不断创新的内推力。

常用派生词：animadvert →animadversion

Words in Use

1. Winning is central to the American _____.

  A. psyche   B. psychosis   C. psychopath   D. memory

2. _____ is the use of psychological methods in treating people who are mentally ill.

  A. Psychotherapy   B. Psychology   C. Psychoanalysis   D. Psychopath

3. Jane helped the police by using her _____ powers.

  A. psychotic   B. memorial   C. psychedelic   D. psychic

4. The taste of marijuana gave him his first real, full-blown _____ experience.

  A. psychedelic   B. psychotic   C. psychic   D. psychosomatic

5. If someone has a _____ illness, their symptoms are caused by worry or unhappiness rather than by a physical problem.

  A. psychic   B. psychedelic   C. psychosomatic   D. psychotic

6. The _____ explained my problem in homely terms.

  A. psychologist   B. psychosis   C. psychopath   D. psychoanalysis

7. _____ is mental illness of a severe kind which can make people lose contact with reality.

  A. Psychoanalysis   B. Psychosis   C. Psychopath   D. Psychology

8. A ferocious religious _____ in Washington has killed five people.

  A. psychotic   B. psychedelic   C. psychosomatic   D. psychosis

9. Parents should pay attention to the _____ of the adolescent

  A. psychotherapy   B. psychosis   C. psychoanalysis   D. psychology

10. Sigmund Freud is a precursor in the field of _____.

  A. psychosis   B. psychotherapy   C. psychology   D. psychoanalysis

11. We _____ the founding of our nation with a public holiday.

  A. memorize   B. animate   C. commemorate   D. remember

12. Bill, _____ yourself! Don't swear in front of the children.

  A. take care of   B. remember   C. memorize   D. mind

13. He has a poor _____ for dates.

  A. memo   B. memorandum   C. memory   D. commemoration

14. The Dr. Sun Yat-sen _____, as the name suggests, is a _____ built in memory of Dr. Sun Yat-sen.

  A. Immemorial   B. Memento   C. Memorabilia   D. Memorial

15. If you _____ a poem, you can say it without looking at a book.

  A. memorize   B. memorial   C. memorization   D. commemorate

16. _____ are things that you collect because they are connected with a person or organization in which you are interested.

  A. Memorabilia   B. Memorials   C. Immemorial   D. Memos

17. Members of my family have lived in this house since time _____.

  A. long ago   B. ancient   C. memorial   D. immemorial

18. Dr. King gave me his autobiography as a _____ before going away.
    A. memorandum   B. memento   C. memo   D. memorial
19. Do you look forward to distributing this _____ to the department?
    A. memorial   B. memento   C. memorabilia   D. memo
20. Former President Herbert Hoover's _____ included details of figures for dried fruit exports.
    A. immoral   B. moral   C. memoir   D. memorial
21. We like to think that everything we do and everything we think is a product of our _____.
    A. volition   B. violation   C. volunteer   D. benevolence
22. Try not to _____ on one's shortcomings unless it is necessary.
    A. malevolent   B. animadvert   C. ambivalent   D. ambiguity
23. Nothing disturbs his _____.
    A. equanimity   B. equality   C. ambiguity   D. congruity
24. His heroic act of saving the drowning boy is the manifestation of his _____.
    A. benevolence   B. equivalence   C. malevolence   D. volunteer
25. The cat stared at him from its corners, _____ and unblinking.
    A. transparent   B. animadvert   C. ambivalent   D. malevolent
26. Today its executive committee voted _____ to reject the proposals.
    A. authentically   B. posthumously   C. anonymously   D. unanimously
27. "You were right, and we were wrong," he said _____.
    A. enormously   B. magnetically   C. magnanimously   D. unanimously
28. We could see how excited he was by the _____ in his face.
    A. ammonization   B. animation   C. inanimation   D. excitation
29. Rejoicing over the decision, the peasants rushed to _____ for the work.
    A. help   B. volute   C. volunteer   D. voile
30. Charities rely on _____ donations.
    A. voluntarily   B. voluntary   C. compulsory   D. illusory

Key to *Words in Use*

1. A	2. A	3. D	4. A	5. C
6. A	7. B	8. A	9. A	10. D
11. C	12. D	13. C	14. D	15. A
16. A	17. D	18. B	19. D	20. C
21. A	22. B	23. A	24. A	25. D
26. D	27. C	28. B	29. C	30. B

第16章　表示"人"的词根

Words in Context

Can Philanthropy Strengthen Democracy?

September 11 is significant for many reasons. One of them is that the war on terrorism, like all wars, challenges democracy. Crises put enormous pressure on representative government to make sound decisions and carry them out effectively. They test the values of a **democratic** system, as seen in the tension between security and the protection of civil liberties. And they can divert resources from domestic to international problems. Discussing the connection between philanthropy and democracy is, to say the least, appropriate at times like these.

The relationship between philanthropy and democracy goes deeper, however, than September 11. Our **philanthropic** institutions are a product of a particular brand of democracy that has prized benevolence, which is not charity but rather a self-interest in the well-being of others. It is no coincidence that the period in our history when self-rule was quite strong — the first half of the nineteenth century — was also an era of benevolent reforms that led to better treatment of the mentally ill, a more humane penal system, and a host of collective actions that roots out the ills of society. These same concerns are now on the agendas of many of our grant makers.

Surely foundations have an obligation to the democracy that nourishes them. Our laws make it clear that we expect them and other nongovernmental organizations (NGOs) to act on that obligation; legislative bodies have chartered small groups of citizens to act in the larger public interest throughout history.

Word Building

More Words with the Word Roots

词根	释义	例词
anthrop(o)	人，人类 (mankind)	anthropology, anthropologist, philanthropy, philanthropist, philanthropic, misanthropist, misanthropic, misanthropy, anthropocentric
dem(o)	人民 (people)	democracy, democrat, democratic, democratize, demography, demographic, epidemic, epidemiology, epidemiologist, pandemic

1. anthropology: [ænθrəˈpɔlədʒi] *n.* 人类学

　　分解记忆法：anthropo-(人类)＋-logy (学)＝人类学

【例句】Anthropology is the scientific study of people, society, and culture.
人类学科学地研究人、社会和文化。
I believe he has started reading up anthropology.
我相信他已开始攻读人类学。

　常用派生词：anthropology → anthropologist

2. anthropologist: [ænθrəˈpɔlədʒist] *n.* 人类学家；人类学者

　　分解记忆法：anthropo-(人类)＋-logist(学者)＝人类学家

【例句】Anthropologist is still trying to decipher the rune found in the grave.
人类学家仍然在尽力破译在这个坟墓里发现的神秘记号。
The anthropologist maintained that customs and beliefs have specific social functions.
那个人类学家坚持认为习俗和信仰具有特定的社会功能。

3. philanthropy: [fiˈlænθrəpi] *n.* 慈善事业；慈善活动；博爱

　　分解记忆法：phil-(爱)＋anthrop-(人类)＋-y(名词后缀)＝慈善

【例句】Philanthropy is the refuge of people who wish to annoy their fellow creature.
博爱主义，是那些存心和自己的同类过不去的人的避难所。
She committed herself to philanthropy.
她专心从事慈善事业。

　常用派生词：philanthropy → philanthropic → philanthropist

4. philanthropist: [fiˈlænθrəpist] *n.* 慈善家

　　分解记忆法：phil-(爱)＋anthrop-(人类)＋ist(名词后缀)＝慈善家

【例句】He is the only philanthropist I can think of who gave away his fortune with absolutely no strings binding its use.
他是我能想起来的唯一一位把自己的钱财送人而绝不附带任何条件的慈善家。
An American philanthropist donated millions of dollars for the benefit of the public.
一位美国慈善家捐助公益事业数百万美元。

5. philanthropic: [filənˈθrɔpik] *a.* 博爱的；慈善的

　　分解记忆法：phil-(爱)＋anthrop-(人类)＋-ic(形容词后缀)＝博爱的

【例句】He is philanthropic in assistance to the poor.
他在救助穷人方面是博爱的。
U.S. District court judge Woodrow Seal was active in a philanthropic organization known as the Society of St. Stephen.
美国联邦地方法院的法官伍德罗·希尔活跃在一个叫圣·斯蒂芬协会的慈善机构。

　常用派生词：philanthropic → philanthropist

6. misanthropist: [miˈzænθrəpist] *n.* 厌恶人类者；厌世者

　　分解记忆法：mis-(恨)＋anthrop-(人类)＋-ist(名词后缀)＝厌恶人类者

　　【例句】A situation so completely removed from the stir of society is a perfect misanthropist's heaven.

　　这样一个与尘世喧嚣完全隔绝的地方，正是厌世者理想的天堂。

　　We wonder how he became a misanthropist at the peak of his career.

　　我们很奇怪他为什么会在事业巅峰变成了个厌世者。

　常用派生词：misanthropist→misanthropic

7. misanthropic: [ˌmizənˈθrɔpik] *a.* 厌恶人类的；愤世嫉俗的

　　分解记忆法：mis-(恨)＋anthrop-(人类)＋-ic(形容词后缀)＝厌恶人类的

　　【例句】Jane is filled with sympathy for the misanthropic Rochester. Nevertheless, she realizes she must now depart.

　　简对愤世嫉俗的罗切斯特满怀同情，但意识到此时她必须离开。

　　I was misanthropic and sullen; I brooded and worked along, and had no friends, at least, only one.

　　我郁郁寡欢，愤世嫉俗；我深居简出，奋力攻读；我鲜朋少友，只有唯一的一个朋友。

　常用派生词：misanthropic → misanthropist

8. misanthropy: [miˈzænθrəpi] *n.* 厌恶人类；不愿与人来往

　　分解记忆法：mis-(恨)＋anthrop-(人类)＋-y(名词后缀)＝厌恶人类

　　【例句】His eyes were full of melancholy, and from their depths occasionally sparkled gloomy fires of misanthropy and hatred.

　　他的眼睛里充满了抑郁的神色，从中不时地闪现出愤世嫉俗的仇和恨的神情。

　　From misanthropy or fatigue, Dan had received his jailer in bed.

　　为了避免麻烦或是因为疲倦，丹曾这样躺在床上等狱卒来。

　常用派生词：misanthropy→misanthropic →misanthropist

9. anthropocentric: [ˌænθrəpəuˈsentrik] *a.* 以人类为中心的

　　分解记忆法：anthropo-(人类)＋centr-(中心)＋-ic(形容词后缀)＝以人类为中心的

　　【例句】How anthropocentric of us!

　　我们多么人类中心主义呀！

　　The point of ethics includes anthropocentric, non-anthropocentric and sustainable development environmental ethics study.

　　从伦理学的角度看，有人类中心主义、非人类中心主义、可持续发展环境伦理说。

10. democracy: [diˈmɔkrəsi] *n.* 民主；民主政治；民主国家；民主主义

　　分解记忆法：demo-(人民)＋-cracy(统治)＝民主

　　【例句】Democracy is a bulwark of freedom.

民主是自由的保障。

The election demonstrates democracy in action.

这次选举是以实际行动体现了民主。

常用派生词：democracy→democratic

11. democrat: [ˈdeməkræt] *n.* 民主党人

分解记忆法：demo-（人民）+ -crat（政体）= 民主党人

【例句】The presiding officer recognized the young Democrat and responded: "The gentleman from New York."

主席认出那位年轻的民主党人并回答说："来自纽约州的先生。"

The man is neither fish nor fowl; he votes Democrat or Republican according to which will do him the most good.

这个人在左右摇摆，他投民主党的票还是共和党的票得看哪个党对他更有益处。

常用派生词：democrat → democratic → democracy

12. democratic: [ˌdeməˈkrætik] *a.* 民主的

分解记忆法：demo-（人民）+ crat-（政体）+ -ic（形容词词缀）= 民主的

【例句】If we want to live a peaceful and democratic life, we cannot help object to war.

如果我们要过和平与民主的生活，一定要反对战争。

It's a democratic government.

它是个民主的政府。

13. democratize: [dimˈɔkrətaiz] *v.* （使）民主化

分解记忆法：demo-（人民）+ crat-（政体）+ -ize（使）=（使）民主化

【例句】It is necessary to democratize and scientialize the administration decision-making for constructing the harmonious society, and that is the only way.

决策民主化、科学化是构建和谐社会的必然要求，也是构建和谐社会的必由之路。

We hope this study will further our understanding of women's life in organizations and eventually help democratize the work culture in a new era.

我们希望可增进读者对女性上班族现况的了解，并间接促进职场文化朝向平等。

常用派生词：democratize → democratic → democracy

14. demography: [diˈmɔɡrəfi] *n.* 人口统计学

分解记忆法：demo-（人民）+ graph-（写）+ -y（名词词缀）= 人口统计学

【例句】Demography is a very intimate deal.

人口统计涉及十分个人化的问题。

He finally became an expert at demography.

他最终成为人口统计学的专家。

常用派生词：demography → demographer → demographic

15. demographic: [deməˈɡræfik] n. 人口统计学的；人口统计的

分解记忆法：demo-（人民）+ graph-（写）+ -ic（形容词词缀）=人口统计学的

【例句】Market segments play a role in persona development. They can help determine the demographic range within which to frame the persona hypothesis.

市场划分在人物角色创建过程中起着作用，它们能帮助确定人群统计数据的范围，在这种范围内形成人物角色假设的框架。

Given the difficulty in accurately anticipating behavioral variables before user data is gathered, another helpful approach in building a persona hypothesis is making use of demographic variables.

考虑到收集用户数据之前精确预测行为变量十分困难，另外一个建立人物角色假设时的有用方法是使用人口统计学变量。

常用派生词：demography → demographer → demographic

16. epidemic: [ˌepiˈdemik] a. & n. 流行的，传染的；流行病，迅速的传播

分解记忆法：epi-（在……中间）+ dem-（人民）+ -ic（形容词词缀）=流行的

【例句】A flu epidemic raged through the school for weeks.

流感在这所学校里蔓延了几个星期。

The village is suffering from a cholera epidemic.

这个村庄正流行霍乱。

17. epidemiology: [ˌepiˌdiːmiˈɔlədʒi] n. 流行病学

分解记忆法：epi-（在……中间）+dem-（人民）+ -logy（学）=流行病学

【例句】He studied epidemiology at a medical university.

他在医学院学流行病学。

Epidemiology studies the spread of control of diseases.

流行病学研究疾病的传播与控制。

常用派生词：epidemiology → epidemiological → epidemiologist

18. epidemiologist: [ˈepiˌdiːmiˈɔlədʒist] n. 流行病学家

分解记忆法：epi-（在……中间）+dem-（人民）+ -logist（学家）=流行病学家

【例句】"There seems to be something in the air that can harm developing fetuses," Beate Ritz, an epidemiologist who headed the study, said in a statement.

领导这项研究的流行病学家贝亚特·里兹在一次声明中说："空气中似乎有某种东西会伤害正在发育的胎儿。"

"This is going to be a landmark study," said Harold Kohl, an epidemiologist who helped perform some of the best-known studies demonstrating the benefits of exercise.

曾就锻炼的益处作过一些重要研究的流行病学家哈罗德·科尔说："这是一项划时代的研究。"

19. **pandemic:** [pænˈdemik] *a. & n.* 广泛流行的；流行疾病

分解记忆法：pan-（泛）+ dem-（人民）+ -ic（形容词词缀）= 广泛流行的

【例句】The vaccine might be of little use if a different virus causes the next pandemic.
如果不同的病毒导致新的流感，这种疫苗可能就不太有用了。

To draw lessons from history, make an analysis of current situation and discuss the relationship between prevention flu pandemic and creating an harmonious society.
通过总结历史教训，分析目前可能引起流感大流行的原因，展开预防流感大流行与共建和谐社会关系的讨论。

Words in Use

1. If research institute shows ____, the mankind has glorious the past and brighter future, but walk with difficulty at all times.
   A. anthropology   B. epidemiology   C. misanthropy   D. philanthropy

2. The university was founded by a millionaire ____.
   A. dentist   B. playwright   C. philanthropist   D. dramatist

3. Some of the best services for the ageing are sponsored by ____ organizations.
   A. consultant   B. philanthropic   C. dissident   D. resident

4. ____ is a system of government in which people choose their rulers by voting for them in elections.
   A. Posit   B. Endeavor   C. Democracy   D. Possess

5. A ____ is a person who believes in the ideals of democracy, personal freedom and equality.
   A. Republic   B. Democrat   C. Pandemic   D. Philanthropist

6. That year, he became the country's first ____ elected president.
   A. republically   B. legally   C. publically   D. democratically

7. There is a further need to ____ the life of society as a whole.
   A. criticize   B. dramatize   C. democratize   D. publicize

8. ____ is the study of the changes in numbers of births, deaths, marriages, and cases of disease in a community over a period of time.
   A. Demography   B. Pornography   C. Philosophy   D. Epidemiology

9. The ____ of a place or society are the statistics relating to the people who live there.
   A. demographics   B. geographies   C. ideologies   D. logics

10. Football hooliganism is now reaching ____ proportions.
    A. demographic   B. democratic   C. epidemic   D. academic

11. There is a ____ outbreak of A/H1N1.
    A. demotic   B. pandemic   C. chemical   D. physical

12. A(n) ____ is someone who freely gives money and help to people who need it.
    A. physicist   B. philanthropist   C. misanthropist   D. industrialist
13. If you describe a person or their feelings as _____, you mean that they do not like other people.
    A. philanthropic   B. epic   C. ethnocentric   D. misanthropic
14. There is a(n) ____ fear of nuclear war.
    A. pandemic   B. exclusive   C. inclusive   D. sedentary
15. The principal's ____ made him popular among teachers and students.
    A. anarchy   B. democracy   C. autocracy   D. illiteracy
16. ____ is a general dislike, distrust, or hatred of the human species.
    A. Misanthropy   B. Photography   C. Biography   D. Philanthropy
17. A flu ____ raged through the southern part of the country for months.
    A. mimic   B. epidemic   C. tropic   D. epic
18. This is the time for ____ and not dictators.
    A. statesmen   B. diplomats   C. democrats   D. dissidents
19. ____ is still trying to decipher the rune find in the grave.
    A. Anthropologist   B. Pianist   C. Architect   D. Musician
20. Some of the best services for the ageing are sponsored by ____ organizations.
    A. sedate   B. diplomatic   C. philanthropic   D. sedentary
21. The newest _____ in the U.S. Senate, former Republican Arlen Specter, is urging the president to add to the diversity of the court.
    A. Democrat   B. Dissident   C. Democratic   D. Sediment
22. A flu ____ which originated in China in 1918 went on to kill more than 20 million people worldwide.
    A. academic   B. pandemic   C. influenza   D. panaceas
23. ____ is a bulwark of freedom.
    A. Democracy   B. Dictatorship   C. Anarchy   D. Autocracy
24. Bolivia returned to ____ rule in 1982, after a series of military governments.
    A. tyrannical   B. titanic   C. demographic   D. democratic
25. A flu ____ is sweeping through Moscow.
    A. displaced   B. epidemic   C. medic   D. deictic
26. Every one of us has to keep this still untreatable disease from becoming ____.
    A. pandemic   B. empiric   C. realistic   D. idyllic
27. A naive idealist supports ____ or humanitarian reforms.
    A. possessed   B. philanthropic   C. subsided   D. subsidized
28. There comes a(n) ____ of crime in our major cities
    A. epidemic   B. genetic   C. sarcastic   D. attic

29. This committee will enable decisions to be made ____.
   A. tyrannically   B. chronically   C. democratically   D. quickly
30. Buying goods on the installment plan has become ____ in recent years.
   A. insidious   B. cautious   C. dangerous   D. epidemic

Key to *Words in Use*

1. A	2. C	3. B	4. C	5. B
6. D	7. C	8. A	9. A	10. C
11. B	12. B	13. D	14. A	15. B
16. A	17. B	18. C	19. A	20. C
21. A	22. B	23. A	24. D	25. B
26. A	27. B	28. A	29. C	30. D

第17章　表示"父母"的词根

Words in Context

Family in Britain

"Family" is of course an elastic word. But when British people say that their society is based on family life, they are thinking of "family" in its narrow, peculiarly European sense of mother, father and children living together alone in their own house as an economic and social unit. Thus, every British marriage indicates the beginning of a new and independent family — hence the tremendous importance of marriage in British life. For both the man and the woman, marriage means leaving one's parents and starting one's own life. The man's first duty will then be to his wife, and the wife's to her husband. He will be entirely responsible for her financial support, and she for the running of the new home. Their children will be their common responsibility and theirs alone. Neither the **maternal** grandparents or the **paternal** grandparents, nor their brothers or sisters, aunts or uncles, have any right to interfere with them — they are their own masters.

Readers of novels like Jane Austin's *Pride and Prejudice* will know that in former times marriage among wealthy families was arranged by the girl's parents, that is, it was the parents' duty to find a suitable husband for their daughter, preferably a rich one, and by skillful encouragement to lead him eventually to ask their permission to marry her. Until that time, the girl was protected and maintained in the parents' home, and the financial relief of getting rid of her could be seen in their giving the newly married pair a sum of money called a dowry. It is very different today. Most girls of today get a job when they leave school and become financially independent before their marriage. This has had two results. A girl chooses her own husband, and she gets no dowry.

Word Building

More Words with the Word Roots

词根	释义	例词
part, patri, pater,	父 (father; man; family; native country)	patriarch, patriarchy, patriarchal, patrimony, patriot, compatriot, expatriate, repatriate, patron, patronage, paternal, paternalism, paternalist
matr, matri, mater	母 (mother; woman; marriage)	matriarch, matriarchy, matrimony, maternal, matron

1. **patriarch:** [ˌpeitrɑːk] *n.* 家长；族长；元老；（特指）犹太民族的祖先

   分解记忆法：patri-（父）+ -arch（统治）=家长

   【例句】A biblical patriarch is said to have lived 969 years.

   基督教圣经中有个元老，据传享年969岁。

   In the Old Testament, the patriarch was chosen by God to build an ark, in which he, his family, and a pair of every animal were saved from the flood.

   在旧约圣经中，这位元老被上帝选去建造方舟，借此方舟，元老及其家人以及每种动物的一对，在大洪水中保全了性命。

   常用派生词：patriarch → patriarchal → patriarchate → patriarchy

2. **patriarchy:** [ˈpeitriɑːki] *n.* 父权制；家长制；家长统治

   分解记忆法：patri-（父）+ arch-（统治）+ -y（名词后缀）=父权制

   【例句】Wookiees have a primitive patriarchy with a complicated lineage structure.

   武技族有原始的宗族社会和复杂的家族结构。

   Female's independence is still in its first step, and traditional patriarchy remains to be the main gender ideology in culture and society.

   女性的自主仍在起步阶段，而传统的父权意识仍是社会文化主流的性别意识形态。

   常用派生词：patriarchy → patriarchal → patriarchate

3. **patriarchal:** [ˌpeitriˈɑːkəl] *a.* 家长的，族长的

   分解记忆法：patri-（父）+ arch-（统治）+-al（形容词）=家长

   【例句】In this parciarchal clan society, there has been monogamous family.

   在这个父系氏族社会，已经出现了一夫一妻制家庭。

   Today we will discuss the status of female in the patriarchal system.

   今天我们将讨论在西方父权制下女性的地位问题。

   常用派生词：patriarchal → patriarchate

4. **patrimony:** [ˈpætriməni] *n.* 祖传的财物；继承物；遗产

   分解记忆法：patri-（祖）+ -mony（名词后缀）=祖传的财物

   【例句】His grandfather left the patrimony to him.

   他的祖父留下大量财产给他。

   Much of the patrimony is mauaged by a fowndation.

   大部分祖产由一个基金会管理。

   常用派生词：patrimony → patrimonial

5. **patriot:** [ˈpeitriət] *n.* 爱国者

   分解记忆法：patri-（祖国）+ -ot（者）=爱国者

   【例句】An Irish patriot who fought for the rights of Irish Catholics and was executed for his part in a bungled uprising against the British.

   一个爱尔兰爱国者为爱尔兰天主教的权利而战，在反对英国的事件中，因失败而被处决。

He was anxious to show himself as a patriot.

他急于表现自己是个爱国者。

常用派生词：patriot → patriotic → patriotically → patriotism

6. compatriot: [kəmˈpætriət] *n.* 同胞；同国人

分解记忆法：com-(共同)+ patri(国)+-ot(者)=同胞

【例句】He believes that he and his compatriot students are the future leaders.

他相信他和同国的学生是未来的领导人。

We learned that he was a compatriot from overseas.

听说他是海外侨胞。

7. expatriate: [eksˈpætrieit] *n. & v.* 居于国外的人；侨民；逐出国外

分解记忆法：ex-(出)+patri-(祖国)+ -ate(名词或动词词缀)=侨民，逐出国

【例句】He was expatriated on suspicion of spying for the enemy.

他涉嫌里通敌国而被驱逐出境。

He has taught ESL to grades five and six Chinese-students, and English Liberal Arts to expatriate students from grades one to three.

他曾经给中国五六年级学生上过英语课程，同时还给国外的一年级到三年级学生上过文科课程。

8. repatriate: [riːˈpætrieit] *v. & n.* 遣返回国；被遣返回国者

分解记忆法：re-(回)+ patri-(祖国)+ -ate(动词后缀)= 遣返回国

【例句】Our country repatriated refugees, prisoners-of-war, immigrants, etc. to their homeland.

我们国家把难民、战俘、外来移民等遣送回国。

Some Asian countries hit hard by recession in the late 1990s tried to repatriate migrant workers.

一些亚洲国家在20世纪90年代末期受到经济衰退的严重冲击，因此想将外劳遣送回母国。

常用派生词：repatriate → repatriation

9. patron: [ˈpeitrən] *n.* 保护人

分解记忆法：patr-(父)+ -on(名词后缀)=保护人

【例句】St. Christopher is the patron saint of travelers.

圣·克里斯托弗是旅行者的守护神。

Modern artists have difficulty in finding patrons.

现代艺术家们很难找到赞助人。

常用派生词：patron → patronage

10. patronage: [ˈpætrənidʒ] *n.* 保护人的身份

分解记忆法：patron-(保护人)+ -age(名词后缀)=保护人的身份

【例句】This orchestra has been established under the patronage of the government.

这个交响乐团是在政府资助下成立的。

The theatre is under the patronage of the Arts Council.

那家剧院得到了艺术委员会的赞助。

11. **paternal:** [pəˈtɜːnl] *a.* 父亲的，像父亲的

分解记忆法：patern-（父）+ -al（形容词后缀）=父亲的

【例句】The woman in the photo is my paternal grandmother.

照片上的这个妇人是我祖母。

He has a paternal concern for your welfare.

他像慈父般关怀你。

常用派生词：paternal → paternalism → paternalist → paternalistic

12. **paternalism:** [pəˈtɜːnəlɪzəm] *n.* 家长式作风

分解记忆法：paternal-（父的）+ -ism（主义）=家长式作风

【例句】In the Confucian tradition, paternalism has been a pillar for the management of enterprises.

儒家传统中的家长制已成为该企业管理的支柱。

The coming quake may reverberate politically, too, particularly affecting the public paternalism that prevails in the city's approach to disaster management as in so much else.

地震会反过来影响政治，尤其是影响那些在该城市灾难管理和其他方面占主导地位的家长式统治。

常用派生词：paternalism→ paternalist→ paternalistic

13. **paternalist:** [pəˈtɜːnəlist] *a.* 实行家长制统治的人

分解记忆法：paternal-（父的）+ -ist（人，主义者）=实行家长制统治的人

【例句】My boss is a paternalist employer.

我的老板是个专断的雇主。

It used to be a paternalist state.

那曾是个专制国家。

常用派生词：paternalist→ paternalistic

14. **matriarch:** [ˈmeɪtriɑːk] *a.* 女家长，女族长；高雅的女妇人

分解记忆法：matri-（母）+ -arch（家长）=女家长

【例句】Jia Baoyu's grandmother is the matriarch of Jia family.

贾宝玉的祖母是贾府的家长。

The most severe punishment a matriarch can dispense is exile from the house.

女族长所能判处的最重刑罚是流放。

常用派生词：matriarch→matriarchal→matriarchy

15. **matriarchy:** [ˈmeɪtriɑːki] *n.* 母系社会，母权制

分解记忆法：matri-（母）+ -arch（家长）+ -y（名词后缀）=母系社会

【例句】The reverence on females is originated in the history of nomadic tribes traced from matriarchy times when women are thought to create the society of human being.

由母系氏族社会发展而来的游牧民族部落，仍然对女性充满崇敬心理，认为是女性创造了人类社会。

As a sign invented by the ancient matriarchy to guard against an act of blood marriage, the tattoo of the Li ethnic group holds more profound ethical reasons than assumed to be.

黎族文身有着深刻的伦理原因，是古代黎族母系氏族为抑制血缘婚所创造的氏族标志。

常用派生词：matriarchy→ matriarchal

16. matrimony: [ˈmætriməni] n. 婚姻生活，婚姻

分解记忆法：matri-(母)＋-mony(名词后缀)＝婚姻生活

【例句】The priest unites a couple in holy matrimony.

牧师使双方正式结婚。

Dearly beloved, we are gathered here today to join this man and this woman in holy matrimony.

尊敬的来宾，今天我们欢聚一堂，参加这位先生和这位女士的神圣婚礼。

常用派生词：matrimony→ matrimonial

17. maternal: [məˈtɜːnl] a. 母亲的，母性的

分解记忆法：mater-(母)＋-al(形容词后缀)＝母亲的

【例句】She feels very maternal towards him.

她对他充满母爱。

Your maternal instincts go deeper than you think.

你的母性本能远比你想象的强。

常用派生词：maternal→ maternally

18. matron: [ˈmeitrən] n. 受人尊敬的已婚老妇人

分解记忆法：matr-(母)＋-on(表示"人")＝受人尊敬的已婚老妇人

【例句】The matron looked a comfortable, motherly soul but she soon showed her teeth if any of the inmates gave signs of having minds of their own.

那个女看守看上去内心平静，待人像慈母一般，但是只要被收容者有迹象自作主张，她可就不那么客气了。

The matron told me not to worry about the operation.

护士长告诉我不要为手术担心。

常用派生词：matron→ matronly

Words in Use

1. The _____ of the house, Mr Jawad, rules it with a ferocity renowned throughout the neighborhood.
   A. patriarch   B. maniac   C. hierarchy   D. monarchy

2. Primo de Rivera was a benevolent and sincere ____.
   A. pesticide   B. paternalist   C. patent   D. partner

3. A ____ is a woman who rules in a society in which power passes from mother to daughter.
   A. matriarchy   B. bishop   C. matriarch   D. patriarch

4. They were staunch British ____ and had portraits of the Queen in their flat.
   A. dissidents   B. rioters   C. parrots   D. patriots

5. ____ smoking can damage the unborn child.
   A. Mammal   B. Mother   C. Maternal   D. Ambiguous

6. Catherine the Great was a ____ of the arts and sciences.
   A. patron   B. patronage   C. matriarch   D. patria

7. I left my parents' house, relinquished my estate and my ____.
   A. patrimony   B. matrimony   C. ambiguity   D. bigamy

8. A(n) ____ is a system in which power or property is passed from mother to daughter.
   A. monarchy   B. matriarchy   C. anarchy   D. autocracy

9. He is notorious for his ____ behavior.
   A. matriarchal   B. hierarchal   C. chronically   D. patriarchal

10. Your ____ are people from your own country.
    A. compatriots   B. companions   C. partners   D. colleagues

11. ____ means taking all the decisions for the people you govern, employ, or are responsible for, so that they cannot or do not have to make their own decisions.
    A. Egoism   B. Paternalism   C. Existentialism D. Surrealism

12. The research centers on the state of ____ of the early married couple in China.
    A. matrimony   B. mammal   C. monetary   D. industry

13. The poet inscribed those poems to his ____.
    A. patron   B. patronage   C. patriarch   D. matrimony

14. She showed her daughter's picture with ____ pride.
    A. paternal   B. maternal   C. material   D. mammal

15. In the past, the woman in charge of the nurses in a hospital was also called a ____.
    A. patron   B. matron   C. mistress   D. doctor

16. He has a(n) ____ concern for your welfare, i.e. like that of a father for his child.
    A. paternal   B. maternal   C. aerial   D. internal

17. A(n) ____ society, family, or system is one in which the men have all or most of the power and importance.
    A. architectural   B. archetypal   C. contractual   D. patriarchal
18. An elephant family is ruled by a ____ (older female), and generally consist of her female offspring and their young.
    A. matriarch   B. matrimony   C. leader   D. governess
19. The scandal destroys the company's reputation for ____.
    A. materialism   B. nihilism   C. paternalism   D. realism
20. Someone who is a ____ loves their country and feels very loyal towards it.
    A. patriot   B. compatriot   C. lealer   D. patron
21. He put his hand under her chin in an almost ____ gesture.
    A. notorious   B. maternal   C. weird   D. paternal
22. Ma Lin beat his ____ Wang Liqin in the final.
    A. compatriot   B. patriot   C. partner   D. conductor
23. Ezra Pound is a(n) ____ poet in the beginning 20th century.
    A. material   B. repatriate   C. expatiate   D. expatriate
24. The Government decided to ____ refugees, prisoners-of-war, immigrants, etc. to their homeland.
    A. expatriate   B. repatriate   C. flee   D. elapse
25. Miss Leigh takes a ____ attitude toward the Chinese girl.
    A. maternal   B. paternal   C. maternity   D. momentary
26. This paper analyzes Hardy's feminism under the influence of ____ society from Tess's rebellion consciousness.
    A. matriarch   B. patriarch   C. patriarchal   D. constitutional
27. The woman on the photo is my ____ grandmother.
    A. paternal   B. patriarchal   C. patrimony   D. patron
28. ____ leave, now often called parental or family leave, is the time a mother takes off from work for the birth a child.
    A. Monetary   B. Momentary   C. Maternity   D. Modality
29. Without the ____ of several large firms, the festival could not take place.
    A. patronage   B. patron   C. patriot   D. compact
30. The crowd sang "Land of Hope and Glory" and other ____ songs.
    A. picric   B. patriotic   C. expatriate   D. compatriot

Key to *Words in Use*

1. A	2. B	3. C	4. D	5. C
6. A	7. A	8. B	9. D	10. A
11. B	12. A	13. A	14. B	15. B
16. A	17. D	18. A	19. C	20. A
21. D	22. A	23. D	24. B	25. A
26. C	27. A	28. C	29. A	30. B

第18章　表示"身体"的词根

Words in Context

Marxian Political Economy

Capitalism is an economic and social system in which capital, the non-labor factors of production, is privately controlled. Karl Marx considered capitalism to be a historically specific mode of production in which capitalism has become the dominant mode of production. For Marx, the use of labor power had itself become a commodity under capitalism; the exchange value of labor power, as reflected in the wage, is less than the value it produces for the capitalist. This difference in values, he argues, constitutes surplus value, which the capitalists extract and accumulate. In his book *Capital*, Marx argues that the **capitalist** mode of production is distinguished by how the owners of capital extract this surplus from workers. He argues that a core requirement of a capitalist society is that a large portion of the population must not possess sources of self-sustenance that would allow them to be independent, and must instead be compelled, in order to survive, to sell their labor for a living wage. In conjunction with his criticism of capitalism was Marx's belief that exploited labor would be the driving force behind a revolution to a socialist-style economy. For Marx, this cycle of the extraction of the surplus value by the owners of capital or the bourgeoisie becomes the basis of class struggle. This argument is **incorporated** with Marx's version of the labor theory of value asserting that labor is the source of all value, and thus of profit.

Word Building

More Words with the Word Roots

词根	释义	例词
corp(or)	身体（body, group）	corporal, corporate, corporation, incorporate, incorporation, corps, corpse, corpulent, corpulence
capit	头（primary, first）	captain, capitation, decapitate, decapitator, capital, Capitol, capitalism, capitalist, capitulate

1. corporal: [ˈkɔːpərəl] *a.* 身体的

分解记忆法：corpor-(身体) + -al (……的) =身体的

【例句】What is your stance on corporal punishment?
你对体罚持什么态度？
A teacher should not give students corporal punishment.
老师不应该体罚学生。

2. corporate: [ˈkɔːpərit] *a.* 团体的；社团的；公司的

分解记忆法：corpor-(体) + -ate (形容词后缀) =团体的

【例句】This university is a corporate body formed from several colleges.
这所大学是由几个不同学院组成的。
Plenty of Web sites still exist out there, in the form of personal sites, corporate marketing and support sites, and information-centric intranets.
现在互联网上存在大量的网站，有各种形式的个人网站、公司的销售和支持网站，以及提供大量信息的企业内部网站。

常用派生词：corporate → corporation

3. corporation: [ˌkɔːpəˈreiʃən] *n.* 团体；社团；公司

分解记忆法：corpor-(体) + -ation (名词后缀) =团体

【例句】This establishment opened under the sponsorship of a large corporation.
这一机构是在一家大企业倡导下开办的。
Several new members have come into this corporation.
这个公司又有新人员加入。

4. incorporate: [inˈkɔːpəreit] *v.* 合并；包含；组成公司

分解记忆法：in(进入) + corpor-(团体) + -ate (动词后缀) =合并

【例句】Many of your suggestions have been incorporated in the new plan.
你的很多建议已经被纳入新计划中。
We had to incorporate for a company for tax reasons.
鉴于税务原因，我们得组成公司。

常用派生词：incorporate→incorporated→incorporation

5. incorporation: [inˌkɔːpəˈreiʃən] *n.* 合并；包含；吸收；社团

分解记忆法：in(进入) + corpor-(团体) + -ation (名词后缀) =合并

【例句】Incorporation is a university practice which is popular among students.
社团是深受学生欢迎的大学活动。
Incorporation is the forming of a new corporation.
合并是新公司的组成过程。

6. corps: [kɔː] *n.* 军团；兵队；团队

【例句】The Marine Corps began to slim down under budget restrictions.
由于预算的限制，海军陆战队开始裁员。

Now her teachers' corps, called *Teach for America*, is off and running.

现在她的教师工作团，名为教师报国团，已迅速展开工作。

7. **corpse:** [kɔ:ps] *n.* 尸体

    【例句】There is a decomposing corpse of a deer.

    那儿有一具鹿的腐尸。

    When the police exhumed the corpse, they discovered traces of poison in it.

    警方掘出尸体，发现有中毒的痕迹。

8. **corpulent:** [ˈkɔ:pjulənt] *a.* 肥胖的

    分解记忆法：corp-(肉体)＋-ulent(多……的)=肥胖的

    【例句】Her father is too corpulent to play handball.

    她父亲太胖以至不能玩手球。

    I had expected that Mr. Gatsby would be a florid and corpulent person in his middle years.

    我本来以为盖茨比先生是个红光满面，肥头大耳的中年人。

    常用派生词：corpulent → corpulence

9. **corpulence:** [ˈkɔ:pjuləns] *n.* 肥胖

    分解记忆法：corp-(肉体)＋-ulence(名词后缀)=肥胖

    【例句】In any case, her corpulence was an indication of the restaurant's wholesome food.

    她那样肥硕，表示这店里的饭菜也营养丰富。

10. **captain:** [ˈkæptin] *n.* 船长；机长

    分解记忆法：capt-(头)＋-ain(人)=船长

    【例句】The sailors are asked to take their positions by their captain.

    船长要求水手们各就各位。

    The captain is absolved from all blame and responsibility for the shipwreck.

    那位船长被免除了因船只失事而招致的非难和罪责。

11. **capitation:** [kæpˈteiʃən] *n.* 人头税；按人收费

    分解记忆法：capit-(头)＋-ation(名词后缀)=人头税

    【例句】The vast majority of secondary schools receive allowances and capitation funds from the state.

    绝大部分中学都接受国家津贴和人头补助。

    The capitation fee for each pupil is not appropriate.

    摊派到每个小学生头上的收费是不合理的。

12. **decapitate:** [diˈkæpiteit] *a.* 斩首

    分解记忆法：de-(除去)＋capit(头)＋-ate(动词后缀)=斩首

    【例句】Park officials say the 17-year-old climbed two fences to retrieve his hat and was decapitated by the roller coaster.

游乐园负责人说这个17岁的少年为了取回自己的帽子爬过两道栅栏后被云霄飞车轧过头部。

They say they have broken up a plot to assassinate the leader and shoot or decapitate 50 people in a murder spree.

他们称他们阻止了一个暗杀那位领导人及杀掉50人的计划。

常用派生词：decapitate→ decapitation→ decapitator

13. **decapitator:** [diˈkæpiteitə] *n.* 斩首者；刽子手

    分解记忆法：de-（除去）+ capit（头）+ -ator（人）=斩首者

    【例句】The fierce decapitator had a tender heart in his bosom.

    那个凶狠的刽子手有颗温柔的心。

    If Renée could see me, I hope she would be satisfied, and would no longer call me a decapitator.

    假如蕾妮看到我这个样子，我希望她会满意，也不再叫我刽子手了。

14. **capital:** [ˈkɔːpjulənt] *a.* & *n.* 首都的；首都；大写；资本

    分解记忆法：capit-（头）+ -al（形容词，名词后缀）=首都的

    【例句】Cairo is the capital of Egypt.

    开罗是埃及的首都。

    Write your name in block capitals, please.

    姓名请用大写。

    常用派生词：capital→ capitalism→ capitalization

15. **Capitol:** [ˈkæpitəl] *n.* 美国国会大厦

    分解记忆法：capit-（头）+ ol（名词后缀）=美国国会大厦

    【例句】Reagan sent Secretary of State Shultz to Capitol Hill in an effort to shore up wavering Republicans.

    里根派国务卿舒尔茨到国会山去给意志动摇的共和党议员打气。

    The conference will be held in the Capitol in Washington.

    会议将在华盛顿的国会大厦举行。

16. **capitulate:** [kəˈpitjuleit] *v.* 有条件投降

    分解记忆法：capitu-（头）+ -late（动词后缀）=有条件投降

    【例句】They capitulated on agreed conditions.

    他们按照事先谈妥的条件投降了。

    Smith capitulated to John's demand.

    史密斯屈从于约翰的要求。

    常用派生词：capitulate→ capitulation

Words in Use

1. ____ punishment is the punishment of people by hitting them.

   A. Coral   B. Corporal   C. Portal   D. Body

2. His hands held onto the upper part of the platform, his legs huddled up and his ____ body tipped slightly towards the left, obviously making an enormous exertion.

   A. corpulent   B. corpulence   C. corpus   D. corral

3. ____ executives usually have high salaries.

   A. Captain   B. Corey   C. Corporate   D. Cooperate

4. A ____ is a dead body, especially the body of a human being.

   A. corpse   B. corps   C. core   D. cop

5. Large multinational ____ survived in the economic crisis; however, small ones weren't that lucky.

   A. compatriots B. corporates   C. corporations D. cooperation

6. The press ____ arrived right before the opening ceremony of the summit.

   A. choir   B. corpse   C. core   D. corps

7. The new cars will ____ a number of major improvements.

   A. incomplete   B. incorporate   C. incompliant   D. incompact

8. ____ is the union of different ingredients in one mass.

   A. Incorporation B. Cooperation   C. Inaction   D. Incompletion

9. He was the ____ of the football team for five years.

   A. patriarch   B. captain   C. capital   D. capitol

10. If you ____, you stop resisting and do what someone else wants you to do.

    A. compete   B. compile   C. capsulate   D. capitulate

11. ____ tax is a tax levied on the basis of a fixed amount per person.

    A. Capitation B. Capitan   C. Captain   D. Capital

12. Economic crisis is the inevitable outcome of the ____ system.

    A. monetary   B. capitalist   C. capital   D. industrial

13. A worker was ____ when a lift plummeted down the shaft on top of him.

    A. capsulated B. captured   C. decapitated   D. capitalized

14. The teacher was fired for giving students ____ punishment.

    A. corporal   B. corpus   C. proper   D. physical

15. The ____ of a ship is the sailor in charge of it.

    A. patron   B. captain   C. mistress   D. doctor

16. London, Beijing, Paris and Rome are ____ cities.

    A. capital   B. captain   C. continental   D. provincial

17. The ___ building in Washington is the place where the United States Congress meets.
    A. Capitol   B. Capital   C. Captain   D. Parliament
18. He was a large and ___ individual, surfeited with good clothes and good eating.
    A. ambulant   B. corpulent   C. reluctant   D. callous
19. This Game was sponsored by an international ___.
    A. corpulent   B. incorporation   C. proportion   D. corporation
20. ___ conscience is a term used to represent this development in managerial behavior.
    A. Corporate   B. Compatriot   C. Comrade   D. Responsibility
21. The agreement would allow the rebels to be ___ into a new national police force.
    A. identified   B. excluded   C. incorporated   D. cooperated
22. In this sentence, the word SMALL is in ___.
    A. italics   B. captains   C. capitals   D. bold
23. ___ punishment has been abolished in many countries.
    A. Capital   B. Capitol   C. Corporal   D. Candid
24. A large amount of ___ is invested in all these branches.
    A. caption   B. currency   C. capital   D. cash
25. Colmar has long been considered the ___ of the wine trade.
    A. industry   B. provincial   C. capital   D. place
26. He learned to read between the lines of ___ annual reports and found several fiscal weaknesses.
    A. incorporate   B. corporate   C. corporal   D. coppery
27. They didn't move the ___ before they sent for the police.
    A. corpse   B. corps   C. carcass   D. lych
28. Periodic crises wrack the ___ system, and they grow in size and duration.
    A. material   B. capital   C. capitalism   D. capitalist
29. As the most alienated social class in ___ society, the proletariat exist on the basis of private property, itself the source of alienated labor.
    A. agricultural   B. capitalist   C. communist   D. socialist
30. When they discovered the ___, they found some poison in it.
    A. corpse   B. man   C. woman   D. corps

Key to *Words in Use*

1. B	2. A	3. C	4. A	5. C
6. D	7. B	8. A	9. B	10. D
11. A	12. B	13. C	14. A	15. B
16. A	17. A	18. B	19. D	20. A
21. C	22. C	23. A	24. C	25. C
26. B	27. A	28. D	29. B	30. A

第19章 表示"手足"的词根

Words in Context

Laws and Regulations That <u>Impede</u> E-Commerce

The rapid growth of the Internet and its increasing use throughout the world for electronic commerce holds great promise for American consumers and for the Nation. Consumers will have significantly greater choice and convenience and will benefit from enhanced competition for their businesses.

It is essential for consumers and the health of the economy that government facilitate not only retail activity, which has increased substantially, but also the movement to the online environment of other categories of transactions. We must update laws and regulations developed before the advent of the Internet that may have the unintended effect of the **<u>impediments</u>** for business-to-business and business-to-consumer online transactions.

Within 60 days of the date of this memorandum, the Working Group shall invite the public to identify laws or regulations that may obstruct or hinder electronic commerce, including those laws and regulations that should be modified on a priority basis because they are currently inhibiting electronic commerce that is otherwise ready to take place. The Working Group also shall invite the public to recommend how governments should adapt public interest regulations to the electronic environment. These recommendations should discuss ways to ensure that public interest protections for online transactions will be equivalent to that now provided for offline transactions; **<u>maintain</u>** technology neutrality; minimize legal and regulatory barriers to electronic commerce; and take into account cross-border transactions that are now likely to occur electronically.

Word Building

More Words with the Word Roots

词根	释义	例词
manu, main	手（hand）	manuscript, manufacture, manufacturer, manual, manage, manager, management, manner, manacle, maintain, maintenance, manipulate, manicure, manicurist, maneuver
ped	足（foot）	pedal, peddle, pedestal, pedicure, expedite, expeditious, expedient, impede, impediment, pedestrian, centipede

1. manuscript: [ˈmænjuskript] *n.* 手稿；原稿

分解记忆法：manu-(手) + script(写) = 手稿

【例句】The manuscript requires an expert to understand it.
这份手稿只有专家才看得懂。

He revised the manuscript of his book before sending it to the publisher.
他对自己那本书的手稿先进行校订，然后才把它交给出版社。

2. manufacture: [ˌmænjuˈfæktʃə] *v. & n.* 制造；加工；制造业

分解记忆法：manu-(手)+fact-(做) + -ure(动词、名词后缀) = 制造

【例句】In design and quality of manufacture they were outclassed by the Italians.
在产品设计和质量上，意大利人远远超过了他们。

Ammonia, coal tar and coke are all by-products obtained in the manufacture of coal gas.
氨气、煤焦油、焦煤都是煤气生产过程中的副产品。

常用派生词：manufacture→ manufacturing→ manufacturer

3. manufacturer: [ˌmænjuˈfæktʃərə] *n.* 制造者；厂商

分解记忆法：manu-(手)+fact-(做) + -ure (名词后缀) + -er(名词后缀) = 制造者

【例句】She wants to buy directly from the manufacturer and cut out the middleman.
她想避开分销商直接自厂家买进货物。

They bought the machine directly from the manufacturer.
他们直接从厂商那里购买了这台机器。

常用派生词：manufacturer→ manufacturing

4. manual: [ˈmænjuəl] *n. & a.* 手的；体力的；手册；指南

分解记忆法：manu-(手) + -al (表示形容词或名词) = 手的

【例句】Work done by machines has replaced manual labor.
机器生产已经代替了手工劳作。

This manual is full of useful tips.
这本小册子里有很多实用的小建议。

常用派生词：manual→ manually

5. manage: [ˈmænidʒ] *v.* 管理；处理；设法

分解记忆法：man-(手) + -age = 管理

【例句】In spite of these insults, she managed not to get angry.
她尽管受到这些侮辱，还是忍着没发火。

He managed the company when his father was away ill.
在他的父亲生病不在的时候，他管理公司。

常用派生词：manage→ manager→management

6. manager: [ˈmænidʒə] *n.* 管理者；经理

分解记忆法：manage-(管理) + -er(人) = 管理者

【例句】A manager has to learn some economics if he wants to improve his management.
一个管理人员要想改善管理的话，就必须学点经济学。
Our manager has an invincible will.
我们的经理有着坚强的意志。

常用派生词：manager→ management

7. management: [ˈmænidʒmənt] *n.* 管理

分解记忆法：manage-(管理)+ -ment(名词后缀)=管理

【例句】If labor and management don't reach an accommodation, there will be a strike.
如果劳资双方达不成妥协，就会发生罢工。
The farm prospered through good management.
由于管理有方，农场兴旺发达。

8. manner: [ˈmænə] *n.* 举止；风度；行为

分解记忆法：mann-(手)+ -er(名词词缀)=举止

【例句】I don't like to talk with him; he has a very rude manner.
我不喜欢和他说话，他态度粗鲁。
It is a bad manner to interrupt.
打断别人是不礼貌的。

常用派生词：manner→ mannered

9. manacle: [ˈmænəkl] *n. & v.* 手铐；铐

分解记忆法：mana-(手)+ -cle(小)=手铐

【例句】The policeman usually binds the criminal with manacles.
警察通常用手铐铐住犯人。
He was manacled by the police.
他被警察铐住了。

10. maintain: [meinˈtein] *v.* 维持；保持；继续

分解记忆法：main-(手)+ -tain(持，握)=维持

【例句】Mankind has been trying every means to maintain the balance of nature.
人类采用一切手段保持生态平衡。
The government has taken a measure to maintain the stability of prices.
政府已经采取了措施以确保物价稳定。

常用派生词：maintain→ maintenance

11. maintenance: [ˈmeintinəns] *n.* 维持；保持

分解记忆法：maintain-(维持)+ -ance(名词)=维持

【例句】System is currently under maintenance.
系统正在维护中。
Maintenance of PC is in my element.
我对电脑的维修保养很在行。

12. **manipulate:** [məˈnipjuleit] *v.* 巧妙处理；操作

　　分解记忆法：mani-(手)＋pul(捆)＋-ate(动词后缀)＝巧妙处理

　【例句】A clever politician knows how to manipulate public opinions.

　　　　　聪明的政客知道如何操纵公众舆论。

　　　　　In other words, it must be visible to manipulate it.

　　　　　换句话说，必须是可见的，人们才能操作。

　常用派生词：manipulate→ manipulation→ manipulative

13. **manicure:** [ˈmænikjuə] *v. & n.* 修指甲；美甲

　　分解记忆法：mani-(手)＋-cure(治疗)＝修指甲

　【例句】I have beautifully manicured nails.

　　　　　我有修剪得很漂亮的指甲。

　　　　　I have a manicure once a week.

　　　　　我一星期修剪一次指甲。

　常用派生词：manicure→ manicurist

14. **manicurist:** [ˈmænikjuərist] *n.* 美甲师

　　分解记忆法：mani-(手)＋cur(治疗)＋-ist(人)＝美甲师

　【例句】The manicurist will be right here.

　　　　　美甲师马上就过来。

　　　　　He grows restless, seducing a manicurist.

　　　　　他开始变得不安分,去引诱美甲师。

15. **maneuver:** [məˈnu:və] *v. & n.* 巧妙地操纵；花招；策略

　　分解记忆法：man-(手)＋-euver(劳动)＝巧妙地操纵

　【例句】These shameful maneuvers were aimed at securing his election.

　　　　　这种可耻的伎俩都是为了能让他当选。

　　　　　The matching problem of terminal maneuver and terminal guidance trajectory of anti-ship missile is analyzed.

　　　　　对反舰导弹的末端机动与末端制导弹道之间的配合问题进行了分析。

　常用派生词：maneuver→maneuverable

16. **pedal:** [ˈpedl] *v. & n.* 踏板；踩……的踏板

　　分解记忆法：ped-(脚)＋-al(名词后缀)＝踏板

　【例句】She climbed on her bike with a feeling of pride and pedalled the five miles home.

　　　　　她怀着一种自豪感跨上自行车，蹬了5英里回到家。

　　　　　He pushed hard on the brake pedal to avoid a collision.

　　　　　他使劲踩下刹车踏板以避免撞车。

17. **peddle:** [ˈpedl] *v.* 沿街叫卖

　　分解记忆法：pedd-(脚)＋-le(后缀)＝沿街叫卖

　【例句】He peddled small household articles around the town.

他在城里挨家挨户兜售日用百货。

Go peddle your papers. I'm certainly not going to pay for the damage that wasn't my fault.

你走开吧！损失不是由于我的过错造成的，我一分钱也不会付给你。

常用派生词：peddle→ peddler

18. **pedestal:** ['pedistl] *n.* 基座

    分解记忆法：ped-(脚)＋ estal =基座

    【例句】Before it could be transported to the United States, a site had to be found for it and a pedestal had to be built.

    在雕像可以运往美国之前，必须给它选个场地，还要建造一个雕像底座。

    The statue reposes on a pedestal.

    塑像安放在台座上。

19. **pedicure:** ['pedikjuə] *n. & v.* 修趾甲医师；修脚；足部治疗

    分解记忆法：pedi-(脚)＋ -cure(治疗)=修趾甲医师

    【例句】Don't you want me to varnish your toe-nails since you've had a pedicure?

    既然修了脚趾甲，是否要涂亮趾甲呢？

    Would you like a manicure or pedicure today?

    你今天要不要修一修手指甲或脚趾甲呢？

20. **expedite:** ['ekspədait] *v.* 派出；加速

    分解记忆法：ex-(出)+ped(脚)+ -ite(动词词缀) =派出

    【例句】Please do what you can to expedite the building work.

    请尽量加快建筑工作。

    We will try to help you expedite your plans.

    我们尽量帮忙加速完成你的计划。

21. **expeditious:** [ekspi'diʃəs] *a.* 迅速的；敏捷的

    分解记忆法：expedit-(加速)＋ -ious(形容词词缀) =迅速的

    【例句】Please send the package by the most expeditious means.

    请以最快速有效的方式送包裹。

    We will carry out the enquiry as expeditiously as possible.

    我们将尽快进行调查。

    常用派生词：expeditious→ expeditiously

22. **expedient:** [iks'pi:diənt] *a.* 有助益的；应急有效的；有利的

    分解记忆法：expedi-(跨出脚)＋ -ent(形容词词缀) =有助益的

    【例句】As he had forgot his keys, he got into the house by the simple expedient of climbing through the window.

    他由于忘了带钥匙，便以简单的应急办法从窗户爬进屋里。

    He thought it expedient not to tell his wife where he had been.

他认为最好不告诉妻子他去过哪里。

常用派生词：expedient→ expedience→ expediently

23. impede: [imˈpiːd] *v.* 阻止；妨碍

分解记忆法：im-（进入）+ -pede（脚）=阻止

【例句】The development of the project was seriously impeded by a reduction in funds.

由于基金削减，工程进度严重受阻。

He impedes me to do the job well.

他妨碍我把工作做好。

常用派生词：impede → impediment

24. impediment: [imˈpedimənt] *n.* 阻止

分解记忆法：im-（进入）+ pedi（脚）+ -ment（名词词缀）=阻止

【例句】The main impediment to growth is a lack of capital.

影响发展的主要障碍是缺乏资金。

The main impediment to development is the country's large population.

发展的主要障碍是这个国家人口太多。

25. pedestrian: [peˈdestriən] *n. & a.* 步行者；徒步的

分解记忆法：ped-（脚）+ -estrian（……的人）=步行者

【例句】The driver was slanging a pedestrian who had got in his way.

那司机破口大骂挡他路的行人。

Being a good pedestrian is just as important as being a good driver.

做一个好的行人就像做一个好的司机一样重要。

26. centipede: [ˈsentipiːd] *n. & a.* 蜈蚣

分解记忆法：centi-（百）+ -pede（脚）=蜈蚣

【例句】Instinctively, he pushed off the centipede.

本能地，他拂去那一只蜈蚣。

A huge, hairy, scary centipede was crawling up Master Lianchi's sleeve.

一只硕大多毛的可怕的蜈蚣正在莲池大师的袖子上爬。

Words in Use

1. On receipt of the ____ the compositors started casting it off.

  A. descript   B. manuscript   C. prescript   D. transcript

2. The prime minister thwarted the opposition's ____ to gain control of the government.

  A. menu   B. manner   C. manual   D. maneuver

3. The plant changed over to the ____ of storage batteries last year.

  A. infrastructure   B. maneuver   C. manufacture   D. manufacturer

4. A ____ is a person whose job is manicuring people's hands and nails.

  A. manicurist B. pedicurist C. prescript D. cosmetician

5. A ____ is a business or company which makes goods in large quantities to sell.

  A. facture B. manufacturer C. manicure D. pedicure

6. A ____ is necessary if you'd like to try nailing enamel.

  A. pedicure B. manure C. manicure D. manual

7. Making small models requires ____ skill.

  A. maneuver B. manual C. mane D. annual

8. He is a clever politician who knows how to ____ public opinion.

  A. update B. maneuver C. manipulate D. inflame

9. He's good at ____ his money, i.e. at controlling how much he spends.

  A. managing B. spending C. expending D. expanding

10. She's not a very good ____ she always spends more money than she earns.

  A. manager B. shopper C. expender D. expander

11. The ____ of good relations between countries is of great importance.

  A. menace B. maintenance C. maintaining D. sustenance

12. The business is under new ____.

  A. manager B. management C. encouragement D. movement

13. One needs enough food to ____ his strength.

  A. sustain B. maintain C. contain D. remain

14. I don't object to what she says, but I strongly disapprove of her ____ of saying it.

  A. ideology B. methodology C. manicure D. manner

15. ____ are metal devices attached to a prisoner's wrists or legs in order to prevent him or her from moving or escaping.

  A. Vehicles B. Manacles C. Obstacles D. Credible

16. The ____ on a bicycle are the two parts that you push with your feet in order to make the bicycle move.

  A. paddle B. pedals C. peddles D. piddle

17. A(n) ____ is a long, thin creature with a lot of legs.

  A. impede B. omnipede C. centipede D. millionpede

18. He was arrested for ____ malicious gossip.

  A. peddling B. pedaling C. paddling D. padding

19. Two ____ and a cyclist were injured when the car skidded.

  A. pedestrians B. passengers C. bootleggers D. peddlers

20. Since childhood, I put my own parents on a ____. I felt they could do no wrong.

  A. confidential B. pedal C. pedestal D. papal

21. He was satisfied there was no legal ____ to the marriage.

  A. impediment B. diffident C. occident D. confidant

22. If you have a ____, you have your toenails cut and the skin on your feet softened.
    A. medi-care   B. pedicure   C. manicure   D. therapy
23. Fallen rock is ____ the progress of rescue workers.
    A. backing   B. peaking   C. impeding   D. impoverishing
24. Governments frequently ignore human rights abuses in other countries if it is politically ____ to do so.
    A. marvelous   B. necessity   C. credulous   D. expedient
25. If you ____ something, you cause it to be done more quickly.
    A. speed   B. expedite   C. associate   D. sustain
26. We will carry out the enquiry as ____ as possible.
    A. impromptu   B. prompt   C. expeditiously   D. hurriedly
27. His wife knows how to ____ him when he is angry.
    A. manipulate   B. manage   C. subside   D. credit.
28. Her prose is far too ____ and self-conscious.
    A. hindered   B. bubbled   C. mannered   D. grabbled
29. All photocopying machines need careful usage, and regular cleaning and ____.
    A. assonance   B. maintenance   C. diffidence   D. indifference
30. The main ____ to development is the country's huge foreign debt.
    A. impediment   B. improvement   C. assortment   D. segment

Key to *Words in Use*

1. B	2. D	3. C	4. A	5. B
6. C	7. B	8. C	9. A	10. A
11. B	12. B	13. B	14. D	15. B
16. B	17. C	18. A	19. A	20. C
21. A	22. B	23. C	24. D	25. B
26. C	27. B	28. C	29. B	30. A

第20章 表示"生死"的词根

Words in Context

Generation Gap

The generation gap is a popular term used to describe differences between people of a younger generation and their elders, especially between a child and his or her parents' generation. The term first became **generated** and popularized in Western countries during the 1960s and described the cultural differences between the young and their parents.

Although some generational differences have been **engendered** since early time, because of more rapid cultural change during the modern era differences between the two generations increased in comparison to previous times, particularly with respect to such matters as musical tastes, fashion, culture and politics. This may have been magnified by the unprecedented size of the young generation during the 1960s, which gave it unprecedented power, and willingness to rebel against societal norms.

In the 1990s and 2000s, cultural differences concerning what should be the sexual norm, as well as new technology, political differences, workplace behavior, age of consent, age of responsibility, the education system, and many other political, cultural, and generational issues, has produced a generation gap between Generation X and Y and their Baby Boomer parents. However, many Baby Boomers grew up during the late 1960s, and can relate to their young **progeny** better than their parents related to them. Nevertheless, the portrayal of teenagers in popular reality television channels, like MTV, has caused concern for parents and a sense of alienation amongst teens and young adults of today.

Word Building

More Words with the Word Roots

词根	释义	例词
nat	出生,诞生(born, birth)	cognate, innate, nascent, natal, prenatal, postnatal, native
gen	出生,起源,种族(birth, born, produce, origin, race)	genital, congenital, gene, genetics, eugenic, eugenics, progeny, genesis, genealogy, engender, generate, generator, generation, degenerate, regenerate, antigen, congenial, ingenuous, ingenious, genius, genocide, heterogeneous, homogeneous

（续表）

词根	释义	例词
mort	死（death）	mortal, immortal, immortalize, mortality, mortician, mortuary, moribund, mortify, mortification, mortgage, morbid, postmortem

1. **cognate:** [ˈkɔgneit] *a. & n.* 同源的；有许多共同点的；相关的

    分解记忆法： cog-(同)+nat(出生)+e=同源的

    【例句】Physics and astronomy are cognate sciences.

    物理学和天文学是相关联的科学。

    German and Dutch are cognate languages.

    德语和荷兰语为同源语言。

2. **innate:** [ˈineit] *a.* 天生的；生来的

    分解记忆法： in-(进)+nat(出生)+e=天生的

    【例句】Correct ideas are not innate in the mind, but come from social practice.

    正确的思想不是头脑中固有的，而是来源于社会实践。

    People have an innate knowledge of right and wrong.

    人们有一种内在的对正确和错误的判断。

    常用派生词：innate → innately

3. **nascent:** [ˈnæsnt] *a.* 初生的；新生的；尚未成熟的

    分解记忆法： na-(出生) + -escent(逐渐变成……的)=初生的

    【例句】This idea of property was slowly formed in the human mind, remaining nascent and feeble through immense periods of time.

    财产观念在人类的心灵中是慢慢形成的，它在漫长的岁月中一直处于初萌的薄弱状态。

    Economists worry a burst could sap the pucehasing power of the nascent consumer class and reverberate through global commodity and stock markets.

    经济学家们担心股票市场爆破会影响新生的消费阶层的购买能力，并且通过全球商品市场和股票市场进一步恶化。

4. **natal:** [ˈneitəl] *a.* 出生的；出生时的

    分解记忆法： nat-(出生) + -al(……的)=出生的

    【例句】One unique characteristic of salmon is they will come back to the same natal stream or area where they were born and raised.

    鲑鱼有一个独一无二的特征就是它们会回到原来它们出生和成长的地方，比如某条小溪或者某个地区。

    Some researchers or drug companies might see this as an opportunity to develop a pre-natal treatment.

一些研究者或医药企业可能会把这看作开发出生前治疗手段的机会。

常用派生词：natal→ natality

5. prenatal: [ˈpriːˈneitl] *a.* 出生以前的；产前的

分解记忆法：pre-(在……之前)+nat-(出生) + -al(……的)=出生以前的

【例句】Husbands had better learn some prenatal medical care.

丈夫最好学些产前的医学护理。

Prenatal anxiety of the mother had a direct impact on the fetus.

孕妇产前焦虑会对母亲及胎儿造成直接的影响。

6. postnatal: [ˈpəustˈneitl] *a.* 出生以前的；产后的

分解记忆法：post-(在……之后)+nat-(出生) + -al(……的)=出生以后的

【例句】The stem cells of lymphocytes are in the liver in fetal development and in the bone marrow in postnatal life.

淋巴细胞的干细胞，在胎生期来自肝脏，出生后则由骨髓产生。

It is necessary for women to have postnatal check-up.

妇女做产后检查是必要的。

7. native: [ˈneitiv] *a. & n.* 出生地的；当地人

分解记忆法：nat- (出生) + -ive (……的,名词后缀)=出生地的

【例句】He's emigrated to the USA and gone completely native.

他已移居美国，完全成了美国人。

The kangaroo is a native of Australia.

袋鼠是产于澳大利亚的动物。

常用派生词：native→ nativity

8. genital: [ˈdʒenitl] *a. & n.* 生殖的；生殖器（多用于指男性的外生殖器）

分解记忆法：gen- (生) + it+ -al(……的,名词后缀)=生殖的

【例句】The genital infections rarely produce symptoms early on.

性器官的感染在初期很少表现出症状。

A severe and gangrenous inflammation of the mouth or genitals occurs usually after an infectious disease.

口部或生殖器部分严重的发炎多为坏疽性的发炎，通常在感染了传染病后发生。

常用派生词：genital→ genitalia

9. congenital: [kɔnˈdʒenitl] *a. & n.* 天生的；先天的

分解记忆法：con-(一起)+ gen- (生) +it+ -al(……的,名词后缀)=天生的

【例句】He was born with a congenital condition characterized by the incomplete expansion of the lungs at birth.

他生来就有一种先天性疾病，特征为出生时肺部不完全膨胀。

What should be noticed after operation of congenital heart disease?

先天性心脏病手术后应注意什么？

常用派生词：congenital→ congenitally

10. gene: [dʒi:n] *n.* 遗传因子；基因

【例句】In addition to gene, intelligence also depends on an adequate diet, a good education and a decent home environment.

除了遗传基因外，智力的高低还取决于良好的营养、良好的教育和良好的家庭环境。

A single gene may have many effects.

一个基因可能产生多种效应。

常用派生词：gene→ genetic→genetically

11. genetics: [dʒi'netiks] *n.* 遗传学

分解记忆法：genet - (遗传因子) + -ics（学）=遗传学

【例句】He specializes in genetics.

他专门从事遗传学研究。

Genetics is beyond my scope.

遗传学我是外行。

常用派生词：genetics→ geneticist

12. eugenic: [ju:'dʒenik] *a.* 优生的

分解记忆法：eu- (好，优) +gen-(生)+ -ic (……的)=优生的

【例句】Others, recalling Germany's eugenic practices, have an equally strong abhorrence of genetic-based reproductive decisions.

其他人则会联想到德国当年实施的优生政策，从而对这一做法怀有同样强烈的厌恶。

常用派生词：eugenic→eugenitics

13. eugenics: [ju:'dʒeniks] *n.* 优生学

分解记忆法：eu- (好，优) +gen (生)+ -ics（学）=优生学

【例句】Politicians take no interest in eugenics because the unborn have not vote.

政治家对优生学不感兴趣，因为未出生者并无选举权。

A lot of scholars have defined eugenics as a pseudoscience.

不少学者认为优生学是伪科学。

常用派生词：eugenics→ eugeniticist

14. progeny: ['prɔdʒini] *n.* 子孙；后代；后裔

分解记忆法：pro- (向前) +gen (生)+ -y (表名词)=子孙

【例句】Her numerous progeny were all asleep.

她的小辈们都睡着了。

He appeared, surrounded by his numerous progeny.

他出现时，子女前呼后拥不计其数。

15. genesis: [ˈdʒenisis] *n.* 起源；创始；《圣经》中的《创世记》

分解记忆法：gene- (起源) + -sis (名词后缀) = 起源

【例句】 In Genesis it says that it is not good for a man to be alone, but sometimes it is a great relief.

《创世记》里面有一段话说："男人鳏居是不好的，但有时那是一种大大的欣慰。"

We cannot yet satisfactorily explain the genesis of the universe.

我们仍不能令人满意地解释宇宙的起源。

16. genealogy: [ˌdʒiːniˈælədʒi] *n.* 家谱学；总谱学；家谱；宗谱

分解记忆法：gene- (起源) + -logy (学) = 家谱学

【例句】 I intend that my ancestors research my genealogy for new healthy DNA to replace sick DNA anywhere in my biology.

我意愿我的祖先研究我的遗传宗谱，在我生物体的任何地方将新的健康DNA替换疾病的DNA。

All of this was created from innate wisdom that was carried in the genealogy of each human tribe.

所有这些都创建自每一个人类部落宗谱内所携带的内在智慧。

17. engender: [inˈdʒendə] *v.* 造成

分解记忆法：en- (使) + gender (产生) = 造成

【例句】 Crime is sometimes engendered by poverty.

犯罪有时是由贫困引起的。

Sympathy often engenders love.

同情经常引发爱情。

18. generate: [ˈdʒenəreit] *v.* 产生；发电

分解记忆法：gen- (产生) +er +ate (动词后缀) = 产生

【例句】 A dynamo is used to generate electricity.

发电机用于发电。

Investment generates higher incomes.

投资带来更高的收入。

常用派生词：generate → generation

19. degenerate: [diˈdʒenəreit] *v.* 退化；退化的

分解记忆法：de- (降) + generate (产生) = 退化

【例句】 His health is degenerating rapidly.

他的健康状况迅速恶化。

Her commitment to a great cause degenerated from a crusade into an obsession.

她致力于一项伟大事业，但其崇高的奋斗精神已变质成为偏执的狂热。

常用派生词：degenerate → degeneration

20. **regenerate:** [riˈdʒenərit] *v.* 使再生

　　分解记忆法：re-（再次）+generate（产生）=使再生

　　【例句】After his holiday he felt regenerated.

　　　　　　他休假之后觉得又有了精神。

　　　　　　Their aim is to regenerate British industry.

　　　　　　他们的目的是复兴英国的工业。

　　常用派生词：regenerate→ regeneration

21. **genius:** [ˈdʒi:njəs] *n.* 天才

　　分解记忆法：gen-（出生）+ -ius（名词后缀）=天才

　　【例句】He makes much account of her musical genius.

　　　　　　他重视她的音乐天才。

　　　　　　He is not so much a genius as a hard worker.

　　　　　　他的努力胜于天分。

　　常用派生词：genius→ geniuses

22. **mortal:** [ˈmɔ:tl] *a.* 终有一死的

　　分解记忆法：mort-（死）+ -al（……的）=终有一死的

　　【例句】It's beyond mortal power to bring a dead man back to life.

　　　　　　要死人复活非凡人所能为。

　　　　　　All things that live are mortal.

　　　　　　所有生物都会死的。

　　常用派生词：mortal→mortality

23. **immortal:** [iˈmɔ:tl] *a.* 不死的；不朽的

　　分解记忆法：im-（不）+mort-（死）+ -al（……的）=不死的

　　【例句】He left behind an immortal example to all posterity.

　　　　　　他给后世留下了不朽的典范。

　　　　　　The little girl is very interested in the old legend of immortal creatures.

　　　　　　小女孩对有关永生的精灵的古老传奇非常感兴趣。

　　常用派生词：mortal→ immortal→ immortality

24. **mortality:** [mɔ:ˈtæliti] *n.* 不免一死；死亡率

　　分解记忆法：mort-（死）+ -ality（名词）=不免一死

　　【例句】The mortality from lung cancer is increasing.

　　　　　　肺癌死亡人数在增多。

　　　　　　Infant mortality was 20 deaths per thousand live births in 1986.

　　　　　　1986年的婴儿死亡率为生育成活率的千分之二十。

　　常用派生词：mortality→ immortality

25. **moribund:** [ˈmɔribʌnd] *a.* 垂死的；即将灭亡的

　　分解记忆法：mori-（死）+ bund（边界）=垂死的

【例句】The way of life is moribund.

这种生活方式过时了。

Many economists point to America's moribund housing market as a major contributor to the economic downturn.

许多经济学家指出美国没落的房地产市场是导致经济衰退的主要原因。

26. **mortify**: [ˈmɔːtifai] *v.* 使受辱；克制

分解记忆法：mort-（死）+ -ify（使）=羞辱（别人）

【例句】The knowledge of future evils mortified the present felicities.

对未来苦难的了解压抑了目前的喜悦。

He felt mortified for his mistake.

他对他的错误深感羞愧。

常用派生词：mortify→ mortifying

27. **mortification**: [ˈmɔːtifiˈkeiʃən] *n.* 羞辱

分解记忆法：morti-（死）+fi + -cation（名词）=羞辱

【例句】To his mortification, he was criticized by the manager.

他被经理批评，感到很难堪。

It is our nation's mortification.

这是我们国家的耻辱。

28. **mortgage**: [ˈmɔːgidʒ] *n. & v.* 抵押品；抵押

分解记忆法：mort-（死）+ gage（抵押品）=抵押品

【例句】We're having difficulty keeping up our mortgage payments.

我们难以继续支付分期偿还的抵押贷款。

Paying my mortgage was an enormous weight off my mind!

我还了抵押借款，如释重负！

29. **morbid**: [ˈmɔːbid] *a.* 病态的；忧郁的

分解记忆法：morb-（死）+ -id（……的）=病态的

【例句】Don't be so morbid!

别尽往坏处想！

She always has a morbid imagination.

她总在做病态的想象。

常用派生词：morbid→ morbidity

30. **postmortem**: [ˈpəustˈmɔːtəm] *a., n. & v.* 死后的；尸体检查；验尸；对……尸检

分解记忆法：post-（后）+mort（死）+ -em =死后的；尸体检查；对……验尸

【例句】Definite diagnosis requires postmortem identification of amyloid plaques and neuro-fibrillary tangles linked to the disease.

最终确诊需要尸检发现与本病相关的淀粉样蛋白斑及神经纤维缠结。

The bereaved requests himself to invite the expert to participate in the postmortem examination.

死者家属要求自己邀请专家参与尸检。

Words in Use

1. Mathematics and astronomy are _____ sciences.
   A. cognac   B. cosmos   C. cognate   D. cosmetic
2. The white people here don't mix socially with the _____.
   A. relations   B. relatives   C. natives   D. nations
3. Americans have an _____ sense of fairness.
   A. native   B. innate   C. outdate   D. intimate
4. It is necessary to strengthen the family planning work in rural areas and among the floating population, stabilize the low fertility level, and promote good _____ and _____ care.
   A. prenatal, postnatal   B. psychotic, psychedelic
   C. psychic psychosomatic   D. paternal, maternal
5. _____ things or processes are just beginning, and are expected to become stronger or to grow bigger.
   A. Crescent   B. Natal   C. Scent   D. Nascent
6. When John was 17, he died of _____ heart disease.
   A. congenital   B. genital   C. instrumental D. crystal
7. _____ is the deliberate murder of a whole community or race.
   A. Secede   B. Genocide   C. Suicide   D. Pesticide
8. A _____ is the part of a cell in a living thing which controls its physical characteristics, growth, and development.
   A. garnet   B. gene   C. genet   D. genetic
9. Racial prejudice often _____ hatred.
   A. generates   B. migrates   C. immigrates   D. genetics
10. Einstein was a mathematical _____.
    A. psychosis   B. physics   C. marvelous   D. genius
11. _____ is the study of heredity and how qualities and characteristics are passed on from one generation to another by means of genes.
    A. Gymnasiums   B. Genetics   C. Mathematics   D. Logics
12. The roof has been _____ designed to provide solar heating.
    A. genially   B. ingeniously   C. assiduously   D. willingly
13. _____ is the study of methods to improve the human race by carefully selecting parents who will produce the strongest children.
    A. Genetics   B. Eugenics   C. Euphemism   D. Eugene

14. Old Jim was never loquacious on the subject of his _____.
    A. genetics   B. momentum   C. progeny   D. gene
15. Only the most _____ person would believe such a weak excuse!
    A. melodious   B. ingenuous   C. genius   D. marvelous
16. She and he were _____ companion in youth.
    A. congenital   B. congenial   C. immemorial   D. memorial
17. Some people believe poverty _____ crime.
    A. endangers   B. engenders   C. pops   D. inflame
18. The government will continue to try to _____ inner city areas.
    A. degenerate   B. generate   C. regenerate   D. degrade
19. The Employment Minister said the reforms would _____ new jobs.
    A. generalize   B. moderate   C. generate   D. degenerate
20. My _____ behaves differently from my father's and grandfather's.
    A. generation   B. relation   C. motivation   D. degradation
21. A man is deliberately designed to be _____. He grows, he ages, and he dies.
    A. motivate   B. mobile   C. mortal   D. immortal
22. Some people have a _____ fascination with death.
    A. morbid   B. malevolent   C. ambivalent   D. mortal
23. Beethoven is regarded as one of the _____ of classical music.
    A. mortals   B. equalities   C. immortals   D. congruities
24. They had to _____ their home to pay the bills.
    A. garage   B. mortgage   C. moralize   D. mobilize
25. The nation's infant _____ rate has reached a record low.
    A. morality   B. mortality   C. immortality   D. reality
26. To his _____, he was criticized by the managing director in front of all his junior colleagues.
    A. mortgage   B. moralization   C. immortalization D. mortification
27. A _____ is a person whose job is to deal with the bodies of people who have died and to arrange funerals.
    A. mortician   B. cosmetician   C. nuisance   D. unction
28. If you describe something as _____, you mean that it is in a very bad condition.
    A. mortuary   B. moribund   C. modified   D. mortified
29. _____ is the study of the history of families, especially through studying historical documents to discover the relationships between particular people and their families.
    A. Geography   B. Genealogy   C. Archaeology   D. Biology
30. It is _____ of you to believe what he says.
    A. ingenuous   B. benevolent   C. industrious   D. assiduous

Key to *Words in Use*

1. C	2. C	3. B	4. A	5. D
6. A	7. B	8. B	9. A	10. D
11. B	12. B	13. B	14. C	15. B
16. B	17. B	18. C	19. C	20. A
21. C	22. A	23. C	24. B	25. B
26. D	27. A	28. B	29. B	30. A

第21章　表示"光热"的词根

Words in Context

How to Be a Good Teacher

To be a good teacher, you need some of the gifts of a good actor: you must be able to use your passion and **fervor** to hold the attention and interest of your students; you must be a clear speaker, with a good, strong, pleasing voice which is fully under your control; and you must be able to act what you are teaching, in order to **elucidate** the knowledge clearly. The fact that a good teacher has some of the gifts of a good actor doesn't mean that he will be able to act well on the stage, for there are very important differences between the teacher's work and the actor's. The actor has to speak words which he has learnt by heart; he has to repeat exactly the same words every time; even his movements and the ways in which he uses his voice are usually fixed beforehand. What he has to do is to make all these actions seem natural on the stage. A good teacher works in quite a different way. His students take an active part in his every class: they ask and answer questions and obey orders which are set by the teacher. While the teacher has to change his class properly in order to meet every student's needs. The teaching process couldn't be the repetitious reciting but a teaching process which wakens the students' **fervent** desire to gain the knowledge. At the same time, this process is not the mere teaching process but the **illuminating** process that can help widen the students' sights.

Word Building

More Words with the Word Roots

词根	释义	例词
luc	光	lucid, elucidate, translucent, illuminate, illuminating, illumination, luminary, luminous
lumen		
therm(o)	热	thermal, thermos, thermometer, thermostat, fervent, fervid, fervor
ferv		

1. lucid: [ˈluːsid] *adj.* 明白易懂的；清醒的

分解记忆法：luc- (光) + -id (形容词后缀) = 明白易懂的，清醒的

【例句】The company gives a lucid explanation about the reason of the redundancies.
公司对裁员的原因做了简单的解释。
The old man is confused most of the time but he does have lucid moments.
这位老人大部分时间都是迷迷糊糊的，但他也有清醒的时候。

常用派生词：lucid → lucidity

2. elucidate: [iˈluːsideit] *vt.* 解释

分解记忆法：e-(外面) + lucid-(光) + -ate(动词后缀) = 解释

【例句】He elucidated the purpose of the task.
他解释了这项任务的目的。
I will try to elucidate where I think the problems are.
我将尽力阐明我认为的问题所在。

常用派生词：elucidate → elucidation

3. translucent: [trænszˈluːsənt] *a.* 半透明的

分解记忆法：trans- (穿过的) + luc-(光) + -ent (形容词后缀) = 半透明的

【例句】The sky was a pale translucent blue.
天空当时是隐隐约约的淡蓝色。
Her skin was translucent with the young age.
由于年轻，她的皮肤透亮。

4. illuminate: [iˈljuːmineit] *vt.* 照明；说明

分解记忆法：il-(在……之上) + lumin-(光) + -ate (动词后缀) = 照明，说明

【例句】The earth is illuminated by the sun.
太阳照亮了地球。
This text illuminates the philosopher's early thinking.
这篇课文解释了这位哲学家的早期思想。

常用派生词：illuminate → illuminating → illumination

5. illumination: [iˌljuːmiˈneiʃən] *n.* 照明；启迪

分解记忆法：il-(在……之上) + lumina-(光) + -tion (名词后缀) = 照明，启迪

【例句】The only illumination in the room came from the fire.
屋里唯一的光亮来自火炉。
The teacher's words gave him the spiritual illumination.
老师的话给了他精神上的启发。

6. illuminating: [iˈluːmineitiŋ] *a.* 启发的

分解记忆法：in(在)+lumin- (光) + ate + -ing (形容词后缀) = (把光投在某物上)

【例句】We didn't find the examples he used particularly illuminating.
我们认为他的例证启发性不是很强。
He used an illuminating example to explain the theory.
他用了一个启发性的例子来解释这个理论。

7. luminary: [ˈluːminəri] *n.* 名人

分解记忆法：lumin-(光) + -ary (……的人) =(照亮别人的人) 名人

【例句】Liu Xiang is the leading luminary among China's athletes.
刘翔是中国运动员的杰出代表。
She is the luminary of the top actresses.
她是中国顶级女演员的代表。

8. luminous: [ˈluːminəs] *a.* 发亮的；光明的

分解记忆法：lumin-(光) + -ous (形容词后缀) = 发亮的，光明的

【例句】The child is staring at the blackboard with luminous eyes.
这个孩子用亮晶晶的眼睛盯着黑板。
They painted the door a luminous green.
他们把门漆成了翠绿色。

9. thermal: [ˈθəːməl] *a.* 热的；保暖的

分解记忆法：therm- (热的) +-al (形容词后缀) = 热的，保暖的

【例句】You'd better wear the thermal underwear.
你最好穿上保暖内衣。
It is very healthy to bathe in the thermal spring.
泡温泉很健康。

10. thermometer: [θəˈmɔmitə] *n.* 体温计；温度计

分解记忆法：thermo- (热的) + meter(计)= 体温计，温度计

【例句】The thermometer shows that it is now 38℃ here.
温度计显示现在这里有38摄氏度。
A thermometer is used to test whether you have a fever.
体温计用来测人们是否发烧。

11. thermostat: [ˈθəːməstæt] *n.* 恒温计；温控计

分解记忆法：thermo- (热的) +stat(站)= 恒温计，温控计

【例句】Turn up the thermostat of the air conditioner when it's cold in your room.
屋子里冷的时候就调高空调的温控计。
Don't touch the thermostat of the machine.
别碰机器上的温控计。

12. fervent: [ˈfəːvənt] *a.* 热情的；热烈的

分解记忆法：ferv- (热) + -ent(……的)= 热情的，热烈的

【例句】His mother is a fervent Buddhism believer.
他妈妈是位虔诚的佛教信徒。
The fans showed their fervent swppot for the team.
球迷们狂热地支持这支球队。

13. **fervid:** [ˈfə:vid] *a.* 热情的；热烈的

   分解记忆法：ferv- (热) + -id(……的) = 热情的，热烈的

   【例句】The new manager gave the workers a fervid lecture.

   新经理给员工做了一次激情澎湃的演讲。

   His fervid desire is to establish his own company some day.

   他很希望有天能组建自己的公司。

14. **fervor:** [ˈfə:və] *n.* 热情；激情

   分解记忆法：ferv- (热) + -or(名词后缀) = 热情，激情

   【例句】He hugs his friend with fervor.

   他热情地拥抱自己的朋友。

   Patriotic fervor spreads quickly around the country.

   爱国热情很快席卷全国。

Words in Use

1. The boss gives a ____ explanation about the redundancy.
   A. translucent　　B. transparent　　C. lucid　　D. luminous
2. The manager ____ the target of the task in the second half of the year.
   A. elucidates　　B. emancipates　　C. anticipates　　D. expects
3. After the rain, the sky is a pale ____ blue.
   A. translucent　　B. transparent　　C beautiful　　D luminous
4. He was in a ____ of impatience waiting for her to come.
   A. ferry　　B. fetter　　C. fever　　D. feud
5. You are a little ____ so you should go to bed for a rest.
   A. fervid　　B. fetish　　C. feudal　　D. feverish
6. He, who has revolutionary ____, devotes himself to his country.
   A. fervor　　B. fester　　C. fetish　　D. fever
7. He ____ begged us not to go.
   A. festival　　B. fetidlytive　　C. feverishly　　D. fervently
8. Football ____ gripped the town when the local team reached the cup final.
   A. fever　　B. heat　　C. thermos　　D. thermostat
9. Before his retirement, the boss gave the employees a ____ farewell speech.
   A. fervent　　B. fervor　　C happy　　D. last
10. Patriotic ____ spreads quickly around the country.
    A. grief　　B. fervent　　C. vent　　D. fervor
11. Having ____ spring regularly is good for your health.
    A. fervent　　B. thermal　　C. fetish　　D. feverish

12. David Beckham is a famous football player from Britain, who has many ____ fans.
    A. fervor   B. fervent   C. hot   D. cold
13. The ____ paint, shining in the dark, can be applied to road sign.
    A. luminous   B. translucent   C. transparent   D. light
14. Is the room dark when it is ____?
    A. illuminating   B. hot   C. fervent   D. illuminated
15. It is a fervid speech full of ____ and enthusiasm.
    A. grief   B. happiness   C. encouragement   D. braveness
16. I don't understand it; could you please ____? Which is the synonym of the underlined?
    A. clarify   B. allude   C. mention   D. remind
17. The proposed reform has been ____ by changes made to it by the parliament.
    A. emancipated   B. elucidated   C. emasculated   D. emanated
18. Strange-smelling gases ____ from the holes in the ground.
    A. emancipate   B. eliminate   C. elucidate   D. emanate
19. The ____ is too weak to show the detail of the painting.
    A. illusion   B. illumination   C. illustration   D. illusory
20. Can anyone ____ the reasons for this strange decision?
    A. eliminate   B. elucidate   C. elude   D. allude
21. He is an ____ writer of the 19th century.
    A. illustrious   B. illustrative   C. illusory   D. illuminating
22. His story about her ____ her true generosity very clearly.
    A. alludes   B. illustrates   C. illuminates   D. eludes
23. The problem had been ____ to briefly earlier discussions.
    A. confirmed   B. eluded   C. elucidated   D. alluded
24. He cherished the ____ that she loved him, but he was wrong.
    A. illegibility   B. illumination   C. illusion   D. delusion
25. A cure for this disease has so far ____ the scientists.
    A. verified   B. clarified   C. eluded   D. elucidated
26. Can you see what this note says? His writing is ____.
    A. illegible   B. illusory   C. illustrative   D. illustrious
27. The new machine will ____ us from all the hard work we once had to do.
    A. elucidate   B. emerge   C. emancipate   D. emasculate
28. You're just ____ yourself if you think she still loves you.
    A. illuminating   B. elucidating   C. deluding   D. deluging
29. He is under the ____ that he is Napoleon.
    A. confusion   B. delusion   C. illusion   D. lucidity

30. The fox succeeded in ____ the hunters by running in the opposite direction.
   A. eluding   B. eliminating   C. falsifying   D. cheating

Key to *Words in Use*

1. C	2. A	3. A	4. C	5. D
6. A	7. D	8. A	9. A	10. D
11. B	12. B	13. A	14. D	15. C
16. A	17. C	18. D	19. B	20. B
21. A	22. B	23. D	24. C	25. C
26. A	27. C	28. C	29. B	30. A

第22章　表示"水"的词根

Words in Context

Dalian

Located on the southern tip of the Eastern Liaoning Peninsula, Dalian has a superb geographical location, with the Yellow Sea on its east and the Bohai Sea on its west. The ideal location, agreeable climate and beautiful scenery enable Dalian to develop fast in a short period of time. It is a famous summer resort and one of the tourist terminals of China with its beautiful scenery and pleasant environment. It is also an outstanding tourist city in China, which includes the Southern Coast, the Forest Zoo, Lüshun Port, Golden Pebble Beach and the Bingyu Valley are important and famous provincial or national tourist spots. We could see that all those sceneries are connected with the sea more or less. In local people's eyes, the sea in Dalian is different from that in any other place, because it is much cleaner and more **aquamarine**. And the most famous specialties of Dalian are undoubtedly the various kinds of seafood. So the **aquiculture** develops fast in Dalian. By the aid of the local government's technical support, the seafood production companies could make use of the latest **dehydration** method to preserve the seafood, which could be exported to the other countries much easier and thus brings huge economical benefits to the locals. Besides the things we mention above, Dalian, which will accelerate her developing pace, is regarded as an important center of international shipping, finance, business, tourism and information in North China. In a word, Dalian is a young city which is worthy of paying a visit to.

Word Building

More Words with the Word Roots

词根	释义	例词
aqua	水	aquamarine, aquaplane, aquarium, aquatic
aque		aqueduct
aqui		aquiculture
hydro		hydrocarbon, hydroelectric, hydrophobia
hydr		hydrant, dehydrate
mar	海	marine, mariner, submarine

1. **aquarium:** [əˈkweəriəm] *n.* 水族馆；鱼缸

    分解记忆法：acqu-(水) + -rium(地点) = 水族馆；鱼缸

    【例句】It's a good idea to go to the aquarium at weekend.
    周末去水族馆，这是个好主意。

    I bought a beautiful glass aquarium yesterday.
    昨天我买了一个好看的玻璃鱼缸。

2. **aquatic:** [əˈkwætik] *a. & n.* 水生的，水上的；水生动植物；水上运动

    分解记忆法：aqua-(水) + -tic(……的) = 水生的，水上的

    【例句】This flower belongs to the aquatic plant.
    这种花属于水生植物。

    Swimming and windsurfing are both aquatic sports.
    游泳和帆板都是水上运动。

3. **aquiculture:** [ækwɪkʌltʃər] *n.* 水产养殖

    分解记忆法：aqui-(水) + culture(养殖) = 水产养殖

    【例句】The government helps the locals develop the technology of the aquiculture.
    政府帮助当地居民发展水产养殖技术。

    Many fishermen get rich by the aquiculture of the seafood.
    很多渔民通过水产养殖致富了。

4. **Aquarius:** [əˈkweəriəs] *n.* 水瓶座

    分解记忆法：aqua-(水) + ius(地点) = 水瓶座

    【例句】People who are born between 21 January and 19 February belong to Aquarius.
    在1月21号和2月19号之间出生的人是水瓶座的。

5. **hydrogen:** [ˈhaidrədʒən] *n.* 氢

    分解记忆法：hydro-(水) + -gen(产生，源于) = 氢

    【例句】The hydrogen bomb has huge destructive power.
    氢弹具有极大的杀伤力。

    Hydrogen is a colorless gas that is the lightest of all the elements.
    氢是所有元素中最轻的无色气体。

6. **hydroelectric:** [ˌhaɪdrəʊɪˈlektrɪk] *n.* 水电的

    分解记忆法：hydro-(水) + electric(电) = 水电的

    【例句】The city is developing the construction of the hydroelectric station.
    这座城市正在大力发展水电站建设。

    The hydroelectric station is much less polluting than the traditional power station.
    水力发电站比传统的火力发电站的污染小得多。

7. **hydrant:** [ˈhaidrənt] *n.* 消防栓

    分解记忆法：hydr-(水) + -ant(名词后缀) = 消防栓

【例句】The hydrants are set on every floor in case of the emergency.
为了防止突发事件，每个楼层都配备了消防栓。
Almost all the hydrants are paint red.
基本上所有的消防栓都被漆上了红色。

8. **dehydrate:** [ˌdiːˈhaidreit] *v.* 使脱水

   分解记忆法：de- (除掉，去掉) + hydr- (水) + -ate (动词后缀) = 使脱水

   【例句】The runners can dehydrate very quickly in this heat.
   天这么热，赛跑运动员很快就会脱水的。
   It is the dehydrating effects of alcohol.
   这是酒精引起的脱水。

9. **hydrotherapy:** [haidrˈθerəpi] *n.* 水疗法

   分解记忆法：hydro- (水) + therapy (疗法) = 水疗法

   【例句】The hydrotherapy is more popular in the recovery exercises.
   在复健练习中，水疗法越来越受欢迎。
   The hydrotherapy is introduced from the west.
   水疗法是从西方引进的。

10. **hydrophobia:** [haidrəʊˈfəʊbiə] *n.* 狂犬病

    分解记忆法：hydro- (水) + -phobia (对……的恐惧症) = 狂犬病

    【例句】After snapped by a dog, one needs the injection in case of hydrophobia.
    被狗咬了以后人们需要注射疫苗以防止狂犬病。
    The hydrophobia can be prevented.
    狂犬病是可以预防的。

11. **marine:** [məˈriːn] *a.* 海的

    分解记忆法：mar- (海) + -ine (形容词后缀) = 海的

    【例句】He is a famous marine biologist.
    他是著名的海洋生物学家。
    The national economy mainly depends on the marine trade.
    这个国家的经济主要依靠海上贸易。

12. **mariner:** [ˈmærinə] *n.* 海员

    分解记忆法：marin- (海) + -er (名词后缀) = 海员

    【例句】Mariners' life is so hard and boring.
    海员的生活辛苦又单调。
    He dreams to be a mariner.
    他梦想成为一名海员。

Words in Use

1. Huge amounts of ____ power will come from the Great Three Gorges Dam.
   A. destructive   B. hydroelectric   C. dynamic   D. huge
2. After snapped by a dog, man needed the injection in case of the ____.
   A. therapy   B. hydrotherapy   C. hydrophobia   D. hydrophobia
3. ____ is sill the major problem to be solved by the Chinese Government.
   A. Aquiculture   B. Agriculture   C. Architecture   D. Archetype
4. After snapped by a dog, the boy was sent to have an injection in case of the ____.
   A. nephritis   B. acrophobia   C. phobia   D. hydrophobia
5. Which is the synonym of the mariner?
   A. Navigator.   B. Negotiator.   C. Astronaut.   D. Fisherman.
6. ____ is the final method to cure the cancer.
   A. Hydrotherapy   B. Chemotherapy   C. Radiation   D. Therapy
7. You'd better have a holiday in the ____ to improve your health.
   A. sanatorium   B. aquarium   C. auditorium   D. gymnasium
8. The athlete could ____ very easily in such hot weather.
   A. faint   B. hydrant   C. dehydrate   D. hydrate
9. Swimming and windsurfing are both ____ sports with lots of skills.
   A. hydraulic   B. aquatic   C. marine   D. athletic
10. Many fishermen get rich by the development of the seafood ____.
    A. aquiculture   B. agriculture   C. architecture   D. architect
11. It is very important that the hydrants need be set on every floor in case of emergent fire.
    A. hydrant   B. hybrid   C. water-tap   D. firemen
12. The _____ solves the shortage of water of this area, which is the good news for people living here.
    A. subway   B. flyover   C. overpass   D. aqueduct
13. After the war, the extremists of fascism were sent to the ____ court.
    A. governmental   B. local   C. marine   D. military
14. Every time when I have the food which is cooked with ____, I always recall my hometown.
    A. marina   B. marine   C. marinade   D. margin
15. The ____ waved flags to warn the drivers of the danger ahead.
    A. martyr   B. marine   C. marshal   D. marvel
16. ____ are set along the streets, which one may take the water from the public supply.
    A. Hydrants   B. Hybrids   C. Hydrates   D. Hydrofoils

17. The _____ will display the latest scientific discovery.
    A. museum   B. aquarium   C. auditorium   D. gymnasium
18. Judo and Karate are both _____ arts which can build our body.
    A. maritime   B. marine   C. martial   D. martyr
19. _____ is a science which studies the use of water to produce the power.
    A. Hydrotherapy   B. Hydraulics   C. Hypothermia   D. Hydrology
20. This food is processed in a very _____ condition.
    A. hydrophobia   B. hygienic   C. safe   D. hydroponics
21. He serves in _____ Corps, which is also his dream when he is young.
    A. Navy   B. marvel   C. Marine   D. marsh
22. The country once had a great _____ power.
    A. maritime   B. navy   C. marina   D. marginal
23. The accident happened because the car _____ in such a rainy day.
    A. accelerates   B. slips   C. collapses   D. aquaplanes
24. Millions of people believe in _____ and Aquarius is a term of this field.
    A. astronaut   B. astrology   C. asteroid   D. astronomy
25. You can't bring the _____ plant out of the water. It will die.
    A. aquamarine   B. marine   C. terrestrial   D. aquatic
26. The doctors finally decide to use the _____ to cure the patient.
    A. hysteria   B. hyperbole   C. hypothermia   D. hydrotherapy
27. If we accept this _____, it may provide the explanation for the change of weather.
    A. hypothesis   B. hydrotherapy   C. hymn   D. hypochondria
28. You can _____ the meat for one hour before you cook.
    A. marshal   B. marsh   C. margin   D. marinate
29. The newly-built _____ will solve the city's heavy traffic effectively.
    A. aqueduct   B. overpass   C. zebra   D. subway
30. The quick development of the _____ provinces stimulates the economy of the inner-land at the same time.
    A. maritime   B. marine   C. marinating   D. marginal

Key to *Words in Use*

1. B	2. C	3. B	4. D	5. A
6. B	7. A	8. D	9. B	10. A
11. A	12. D	13. D	14. C	15. C
16. A	17. A	18. C	19. B	20. B
21. C	22. A	23. D	24. B	25. D
26. D	27. A	28. D	29. B	30. A

第23章 表示"土地"的词根

Words in Context

Mediterranean Sea

The **Mediterranean** Sea connects to the Atlantic Ocean, which is surrounded by the Mediterranean region and almost completely enclosed by land: on the north by Anatolia and Europe, on the south by Africa, and on the east by the Levant. **Geographically**, it is the **territory** of the Atlantic Ocean, although it is usually identified as a completely separate body of water. The name Mediterranean is derived from the Latin Mediterranean, meaning "inland"). It covers an approximate area of 2.5 million km² (965,000 sq mi), but its connection to the Atlantic (the Strait of Gibraltar) is only 14 km (9 mi) wide. In **oceanography**, it is sometimes called the European Mediterranean Sea to distinguish it from mediterranean seas elsewhere. The Mediterranean Sea has an average depth of 1,500 meters (4,920 ft) and the deepest recorded point is 5,267 meters (about 3.27 miles) in the Calypso Deep in the Ionian Sea. It was an important route for merchants and travelers of ancient times that allowed for trade and cultural exchange between emergent peoples of the region — the Mesopotamian, Egyptian, Phoenician, Carthaginian, Greek, Illyrian, Levantine, Roman, Moorish, Slavic and Turkish cultures. The history of the Mediterranean region is crucial to understanding the origins and development of many modern societies. For the three quarters of the globe, the Mediterranean Sea is similarly the uniting element and the centre of World History. What's more, the Mediterranean climate is also very famous for its **humidity** in winter. All the things above make Mediterranean region a popular place for travelers all over the world.

Word Building

More Words with the Word Roots

词根	释义	例词
terr	土地	territory, Mediterranean, terrace, terrain, extraterritorial, terrestrial
geo		geography, geology
hum	人类；土地；湿；卑微	humble, humility, humiliate, posthumous

1. territory: [ˈteritəri] *n.* 领土；领域

分解记忆法：terr- (地) + -itory (名词后缀) = 领土；领域

【例句】They refuse to allow the UN troops to be stationed in their territory.
他们拒绝联合国的部队驻扎在他们的国土上。
This type of work is uncharted territory for us.
我们从未涉足过这类工作。

2. Mediterranean: [ˌmeditəˈreiniən] *a.* 地中海的

分解记忆法：medi- (中间) + terra- (地) + -nean (……的) = 地中海的

【例句】Rome shows the typical Mediterranean climate.
罗马是典型的地中海气候。
It often rains in winter because of the Mediterranean climate.
由于地中海气候的影响，这里冬季多雨。

3. terrace: [ˈterəs] *n.* 梯田；露天平台

分解记忆法：terr- (地) + -ace (名词后缀) = 梯田，露天平台

【例句】The house has a huge terrace.
这所房子有个大露台。
There are many terraces in Sichuan Province.
四川有很多梯田。

4. terrain: [ˈterein] *n.* 地势；地貌

分解记忆法：terr- (地) + -ain (名词后缀) = 地势；地貌

【例句】The area has very complicated terrain.
这片地区地势复杂。
We can collect samples to do further research about the rocky terrain.
我们可以采集样本来做关于岩石地貌的进一步研究。

5. terrestrial: [tiˈrestriəl] *a.* 地球的；陆地的

分解记忆法：terr- (地) + -estrial (……的) = 地球的；陆地的

【例句】The geography teacher uses a terrestrial globe to show the students the location of every country.
地理老师用一个地球仪来告诉学生每个国家的位置。
Birds belong to the terrestrial animal.
鸟类是陆栖动物。

6. extraterritorial: [ˌekstrəˌteriˈtɔːriəl] *a.* 治外法权的

分解记忆法：extra- (外) + terr- (地) + -itorial (……的) = 治外法权的

【例句】The ambassador enjoys the extraterritorial rights and privileges.
大使享有治外法权及其特权。
The ordinary people don't have the extraterritorial rights.
普通人并不享有治外法权。

7. geography: [dʒiˈɔgrəfi] *n.* 地理

分解记忆法：geo- (地) + graph- (写) + -y (名词后缀) = 地理

【例句】He teaches geography in a middle school.
他在中学教地理。
Tom is familiar with the geography of New York City.
汤姆很熟悉纽约的地形。

8. humble: [ˈhʌmbəl] *a.* 谦逊的；卑微的

分解记忆法：hum- (地) + -ble (……的) = 谦逊的；卑微的

【例句】Be humble enough to learn from the mistakes.
虚心地从错误中学习。
She is the daughter of a humble shopkeeper.
她是一个小店主的女儿。

9. humiliate: [hjuːˈmilieit] *v.* 丢脸

分解记忆法：humi- (地) + -ate (使) = 丢脸

【例句】I never felt so humiliated.
我从未感到如此丢脸。
I don't want to humiliate her in front of her colleagues.
我不想当着她同事的面让她难堪。

10. posthumous: [ˈpɔstjuməs] *a.* 死后的；遗腹的

分解记忆法：post- (后) + hum- (地) + -ous (……的) = 死后的；遗腹的

【例句】He is a posthumous child.
他是个遗腹子。
This novel is the posthumous work by this author.
这部小说是这位作家的遗作。

Words in Use

1. You can't bring the ____ plant of the water. It will die.
   A. aquamarine   B. marine   C. terrestrial   D. aquatic
2. After such a rough voyage we were glad to reach the ____ again.
   A. coast   B. country   C. island   D. terra firma
3. I'm tired of ____ all this luggage around.
   A. humble   B. humbug   C. humiliating   D. humping
4. She drove at a ____ speed, which is very dangerous.
   A. humble   B. terrible   C. terrific   D. terrified
5. The two countries have a ____ dispute over which one owned the island.
   A. territorial   B. terrain   C. terrace   D. terra firma

6. I don't like such a ____ life. I want to change it.
   A. humdrum   B. humble   C. humorous   D. humid
7. The explorers ____ the cave carefully in order to find some clue but they failed finally.
   A. disinterred   B. dug   C. entered   D. looked
8. He is ____ at the thought of parachuting.
   A. terrestrial   B. terrific   C. territorial   D. terrified
9. The resistance movement started a ____ campaign against the colonial rulers.
   A. terror-stricken B. terror   C. terrorism   D. terrorizing
10. Your contract with the company has been ____.
    A. terrible   B. terminal   C. terminated   D. terrestrial
11. The satellite is ____ with the earth that is the way we see it at the same position every day.
    A. geosynchronous B. accompanied C. accomplished   D. geographic
12. We were ____ that the bridge would collapse.
    A. terrified   B. terrace   C. tertiary   D. texture
13. It is not easy to find the way out until you know the ____ of the building.
    A. position   B. geography   C. location   D. direction
14. The accident was caused by a ____ error, not by a fault of the machine.
    A. humiliated   B. humble   C. humane   D. human
15. I am not used to the ____ weather in the south.
    A. dry   B. cold   C. humid   D. cool
16. It is not the heat but the humidity ____ makes it so uncomfortable today.
    A. that   B. what   C. how   D. which
17. Our winning ____ the enemy greatly.
    A. humbles   B. overcomes   C. defends   D. humiliates
18. I want to change the ____ life.
    A. human   B. ordinary   C. daily   D. boring
19. The poor guy was finally ____ by some kind persons.
    A. entombed   B. entered   C. managed   D. arranged
20. The police arrested him because he had clear ____ tendency.
    A. alcoholic   B. suicide   C. homicidal   D. homicide
21. The newspaper ____ an old scandal of the former president.
    A. disinherits   B. disillusions   C. disinfects   D. disinters
22. The ambassador enjoys the ____ rights and privileges in a foreign country.
    A. territory   B. extraterritorial C. territorial D. terrestrial
23. He rises from the ____ origin to prime minister.
    A. humid   B. humble   C. humiliated   D. humane
24. The newspaper is always talking about the decline of moral standards, but that's

sheer ____ because it is full of pornographic pictures.
   A. lie   B. fault   C. fallacy   D. wrong
25. Be____ enough to learn from the mistakes.
   A. humble   B. anxious   C. eager   D. hard
26. There are significant ____ differences between the two editions of this book.
   A. tercentennial   B. territorial   C. tepid   D. textual
27. The body was ____ on the order of the judge.
   A. hidden   B. exhumed   C. interred   D. kept
28. One of the conditions of ____ is that you must keep the land under cultivation.
   A. terrain   B. terminal   C. tenure   D. territory
29. They stood in silent ____ around the grave.
   A. moment   B. gesture   C. position   D. homage
30. The connection between the film and the book is supposed to be fairly ____.
   A. tenuous   B. territorial   C. terrified   D. tepid

Key to *Words in Use*

1. D	2. D	3. D	4. C	5. A
6. A	7. A	8. D	9. B	10. C
11. A	12. A	13. B	14. D	15. C
16. A	17. A	18. B	19. A	20. C
21. D	22. B	23. B	24. A	25. A
26. D	27. B	28. C	29. D	30. A

第24章　表示"动植物"的词根

Words in Context

The Urgent Problems We Are Facing Now

Admittedly, it is certain that some urgent problems need to be solved as soon as possible, since these problems are afflicting the normal living of today. For most people, they are more concerned about the immediate problems that they are confronted. As we all know, pollution and resource exhaustion are our two main environmental problems. Many others, such as species extinctions, possible global warming, and urban noise and **vegetation** destruction, etc., can be regarded as aspects of the two main problems. Due to those problems, it is hard to see some **flowers** and animals in the forest or countryside. Instead, these species could only be preserved in the **zoo** or in the **botanic** garden. These problems have a detrimental effect on our daily life. Therefore they need to be solved as soon as possible. Besides, if unemployment rate is higher than normal, more civilians lose jobs and cannot be able to afford their livings. If this problem cannot be solved for a long time, it will cause lots of other social problems, such as starvation, poverty, stealing even crime and so on. With respect of these negative effects of the urgent problems, we should pay a lot of attention to them and try our best to solve them.

Word Building

More Words with the Word Roots

词根	释义	例词
zoo	动物	zoo, zoology, zootomy
botan-	植物	botany, botanist, botanic
veget-		vegetable, vegetate, vegetation
flor-	花	flora, floral, florid, florist, defloration, flourish
flour		
radic-	根	radical, eradicate, eradicable
foli-	叶	foliage, foliate, defoliate, defoliant, folio, portfolio

1. zoo: [zuː] *n.* 动物园

　　分解记忆法： zoo 动物园

　　【例句】There are many animals in the zoo.

　　　　　　动物园里有很多动物。

　　　　　　We can take the children to the zoo.

　　　　　　我们可以带孩子到动物园去玩。

2. botany: [ˈbɔtəni] *n.* 植物学

　　分解记忆法： botan- (植物) + -y (学) 植物学

　　【例句】He studies botany in the university.

　　　　　　他在大学里学习植物学。

　　　　　　We can explain the puzzle from the aspect of botany.

　　　　　　我们可以从植物学的角度来解释这个疑惑。

3. botanic: [bəˈtænik] *a.* 植物的

　　分解记忆法： botan- (植物) + -ic (……的) = 植物的

　　【例句】We will visit the National Botanic Garden this afternoon.

　　　　　　今天下午我们将参观国家植物园。

　　　　　　This medicine belongs to the botanic drugs.

　　　　　　这类药品属于植物性药品。

4. vegetable: [ˈvedʒitəbl] *n. & a.* 蔬菜；植物性的

　　分解记忆法： veget- (植物) + -able (……的) = 蔬菜；植物性的

　　【例句】Vegetable oil is good for health.

　　　　　　植物油对身体有好处。

　　　　　　She has a vegetable diet for a long time.

　　　　　　她吃素食有段时间了。

5. vegetate: [ˈvedʒiteit] *v.* 无所事事

　　分解记忆法： veget- (植物) + -ate (动词后缀) = 无所事事

　　【例句】It's a pity that you are vegetating every day.

　　　　　　你每天都无所事事，真可悲。

　　　　　　You can't vegetate every day.

　　　　　　你不能每天都无所事事。

6. vegetation: [ˌvedʒiˈteiʃən] *n.* 植被

　　分解记忆法： veget- (植物) + -ation (名词后缀) = 植被

　　【例句】This is the typical tropical forest vegetation.

　　　　　　这是典型的热带雨林植被。

　　　　　　We should protect the vegetation from damage.

　　　　　　我们应该保护植被免受破坏。

7. **floral:** [ˈflɔːrəl] *a.* 花的

   分解记忆法：flor- (花) + -al (……的) = 花的

   【例句】That floral dress is very expensive.
   那件有花卉图案的连衣裙很贵。

   The floral arrangement is an art.
   插花是种艺术。

8. **florid:** [ˈflɔrid] *a.* 花哨的；华丽的；红润的

   分解记忆法：flor- (花) + -id (……的) = 花哨的；华丽的

   【例句】The article has much florid language.
   这篇文章有太多华丽的词语。

   She is a florid writer.
   她是位辞藻华丽的作家。

9. **flourish:** [ˈflʌriʃ] *v.* 繁荣

   分解记忆法：flour- (花) + -ish (动词后缀) = 繁荣

   【例句】Few businesses are flourishing in the present UK economic climate.
   英国目前的经济形势下，很少有企业兴旺发达。

   These plants flourish in a humid climate.
   这些植物在湿热的气候中长势旺盛。

10. **radical:** [ˈrædikəl] *a.* 根本的；激进的

    分解记忆法：radic- (根) + -al (……的) = 根本的；激进的

    【例句】There exists the radical faults in the design.
    设计中存在根本性的错误。

    He is a radical politician.
    他是个激进的政治家。

11. **eradicate:** [iˈrædikeit] *v.* 根除

    分解记忆法：e- (出) + radic- (根) + -ate (动词后缀) = 根除

    【例句】We are determined to eradicate racism from the sports.
    我们决心杜绝体育竞技中的种族歧视现象。

    We should eradicate the cheat in the examination.
    我们要杜绝考试中的作弊现象。

    常用派生词：eradicate → eradication

12. **foliage:** [ˈfəuliidʒ] *n.* 叶子的总称

    分解记忆法：foli- (叶) + -age (名词后缀) = 叶子的总称

    【例句】The tree has dense green foliage.
    这棵树有茂密的绿叶。

    This is a foliage plant.
    这是一株观叶植物。

13. **defoliate:** [diːˈfəulieit] *v.* 除叶；使落叶

    分解记忆法：de-（去除）+ foli-（叶）+ -ate（动词后缀）= 除叶；使落叶

    【例句】The plant is defoliated by the scientist.
    科学家给这株植物除叶了。
    The trees begin to defoliate in the fall.
    秋天，树木开始落叶了。

14. **portfolio:** [pɔːtˈfəuliəu] *n.* 文件夹；证明资历的作品；公文包

    分解记忆法：port-（拿）+ folio（对开本）= 文件夹；证明资历的作品

    【例句】She spent most of last year getting her portfolio together.
    她去年花大部分时间整理自己的代表作品集。
    The paper is in the lecture portfolio.
    文件在讲义夹里。

Words in Use

1. In order to find a good job, she spent most of last year getting her ____ together.
   A. defoliant   B. foliage   C. portfolio   D. folio
2. This medicine belongs to the ____ drugs
   A. bouffant   B. botches   C. botanic   D. bossy
3. This is the typical tropical forest ____, which is very common to see in this area.
   A. vegetarian   B. vehement   C. vehemence   D. vegetation
4. It's a pity that you are ____ every day. You should go out to do some work.
   A. vegetating   B. vegetarian   C. vegetation   D. vegetated
5. The tree has dense green ____.
   A. flora   B. defloration   C. foliage   D. defoliant
6. The ____ sells the flowers at very low prices.
   A. vegetarian   B. florist   C. flora   D. botanist
7. A system of roads ____ from the downtown, which helps to resolve the traffic problem in the rash hours.
   A. erases   B. rages   C. eradicates   D. radiates
8. That ____ skirt is very expensive, but I like it very much.
   A. floral   B. flourishing   C. florid   D. flora
9. The data shows that few businesses are ____ in the present economic climate.
   A. flower   B. flourishing   C. floral   D. florid
10. She follows the doctor's suggestion and has a ____ diet for a long time.
    A. vegetation   B. vegetable   C. vegetating   D. vegetarian
11. These plants hardly ____ in such a humid climate.

    A. flourish   B. flush   C. defoliate   D. foliate
12. He ____ self-confidence and optimism.
    A. eradicates   B. radiates   C. racks   D. radicalizes
13. People who ____ authority will receive penalty.
    A. flow   B. flout   C. floury   D. flub
14. No societies can ____ the crime, but we can make efforts to reduce its quantities.
    A. eradicate   B. commit   C. continue   D. insist
15. ____ is a kind of chemical materials.
    A. Botany   B. Pedestrian   C. Radiant   D. Defoliant
16. I'm glad to hear you're all ____.
    A. fresh   B. healthy   C. flourishing   D. blessing
17. His abrupt change of subject left her ____ helplessly.
    A. floundering   B. flourishing   C. flouncing   D. flouting
18. ____ does study about the plants.
    A. Vegetarian   B. Zoologist   C. Botanist   D. Scientist
19. There exist the ____ faults in the design.
    A. radical   B. radiant   C. raffish   D. racial
20. We are determined to ____ racism from the sports.
    A. delete   B. go away   C. eradicate   D. resolve
21. Recent events have ____ opinion on educational matters.
    A. developed   B. radicalized   C. eradicated   D. improved
22. ____ is the final method to cure the cancer.
    A. Radish   B. Radiotherapy   C. Radiation   D. Therapy
23. The city has a ____ pattern of public transport facilities.
    A. radical   B. radial   C. radiant   D. eradicable
24. We should ____ cheating in the examination.
    A. eradicate   B. go with   C. delete   D. resolve
25. The society demands for ____ reform of the law.
    A. racial   B. radical   C. partial   D. radiant
26. The florid is very ____.
    A. radiant   B. radical   C. radish   D. racial
27. In fact the old man was ____ with health.
    A. radiant   B. radical   C. racial   D. racket
28. All doubts were suddenly ____ from his mind.
    A. motivated   B. moved   C. eradicated   D. erased
29. Stores spend more and more on crime ____ every year.
    A. persuasion   B. commitment   C. prevention   D. eradication

30. She tried to ____ the memory of that evening.

A. move	B. decrease	C. eradicate	D. erase

Key to *Words in Use*

1. C	2. C	3. D	4. A	5. C
6. B	7. D	8. A	9. B	10. B
11. A	12. B	13. B	14. A	15. D
16. D	17. A	18. C	19. A	20. C
21. B	22. B	23. B	24. A	25. B
26. B	27. A	28. D	29. C	30. D

第25章　表示"流动"的词根

Words in Context

Water Pollution

One of the world's most critical environmental problems is water pollution; millions of people lack access to clean drinking water; a large number of lakes and rivers are polluted; and major pollution incidents happen almost every day. Water pollution not only strains the environment, but also severely **influences** the public health. Water becomes dirty in many ways: industrial pollution is one of them. With the development of industry, plants and factories pour tons of industrial **effluent** into rivers every day. The rivers have become seriously polluted, and the water is becoming unfit for drinking or irrigation. The same thing has also happened to our seas and oceans. Over the past few years, there has been a noticeable shift in behavior by governments as they pertain to environmental issues, particularly water pollution. People believe that improvements will only be successful and sustainable if local, regional and national environmental groups cooperate together to deal with the water pollution problem.

Word Building

More Words with the Word Roots

词根	释义	例词
flu	流动	fluent, influence, confluent, circumfluent, effluvial, superfluous, flush, affluent, influx
fus	泻；流动	refuse, refute, confusion, effuse, diffuse, infuse, profuse, suffuse, transfusion

1. **fluent:** ['flu:ənt] *a.* 流利的

    分解记忆法：flu-(流动) + -ent(……的) = 流利的

    【例句】She is fluent in Polish.
    她的波兰语很流利。
    He speaks fluent Italian.
    他说一口流利的意大利语。

2. influence: [ˈinfluəns] *n. & v.* 影响力；影响

分解记忆法：in- (向内) + flu- (流动) + -ence(名词后缀) = 影响力；影响

【例句】What is the influence of television on the children?
电视对儿童有什么影响？
His writings have influenced the lives of millions.
他的作品影响了千百万人的一生。

3. confluent: [ˈkɔnfluənt] *a.* 汇合的；汇流的

分解记忆法：con- (一起) + flu- (流动) + -ent(……的) = 汇合的；汇流的

【例句】The two rivers are confluent here.
两条河在这里汇流了。
The troops finally are confluent in this city.
军队最后在这座城市汇合了。

4. effluent: [ˈefluənt] *n.* 污水

分解记忆法：ef- (出) + flu- (流动) + -ent(名词后缀) = 污水

【例句】The production process produces an amount of effluent.
生产过程会产生大量污水。
The effluent shouldn't be put into the lake directly.
废水不该直接排入湖中。

5. effluvial: [ˈefluːviəl] *a.* 恶臭的

分解记忆法：ef- (出) + fluv- (流动) + -ial(……的) = 恶臭的

【例句】The polluting lake is effluvial, especially in summer.
被污染的湖水散发出臭味，尤其是在夏天。
The hot weather makes the decayed food effluvial.
炎热的天气使得烂掉的食品发出阵阵恶臭。

6. superfluous: [suːˈpəːfluəs] *a.* 多余的

分解记忆法：super- (超过) + flu- (流动) + -ous(……的) = 多余的

【例句】She gave him a look that made words superfluous.
她看了他一眼，这已表明一切，无须多言了。
The last comment was a little superfluous.
最后的评论有些多余。

7. mellifluous: [miˈlifluəs] *a.* 声音甜美的

分解记忆法：melli- (超过) + flu- (流动) + -ous(……的) = 声音甜美的

【例句】His song is very mellifluous.
他歌声甜美。
He fell in love with the girl who has a mellifluous sound.
他爱上了那个声音甜美的女孩。

8. **flush:** [flʌʃ] *n. & v.* 脸红；冲走

   分解记忆法：flu- (流动) + -sh (动词后缀) = 脸红；冲走

   【例句】A pink flush spread over his cheeks.
   他满脸通红。
   The sick boy had an unhealthy flush and breathed with difficulty.
   生病的孩子满脸通红，显出病态，呼吸困难。

9. **flux:** [flʌks] *n.* 变迁

   分解记忆法：flu- (流动) + -x = 变迁

   【例句】Our future plans are very unsettled, so everything is in a state of flux.
   我们未来的计划根本没定下来，所以一切都处于不断变化中。
   The social flux is on and on and we must adapt ourselves to it as soon as possible.
   社会变迁持续进行，因此我们必须尽快适应它。

10. **affluent:** [ˈæfluənt] *a.* 富裕的

    分解记忆法：af- (向) + flu- (流动) + -ent (……的) = 富裕的

    【例句】America is an affluent Western country.
    美国是个富裕的西方国家。
    We are endeavoring to establish an affluent society.
    我们努力建设小康社会。

    常用派生词：affluent → affluence

11. **influx:** [ˈinflʌks] *n.* 流入，涌入

    分解记忆法：in- (入) + flux (流动) = 流入，涌入

    【例句】The remote town suddenly has a massive influx of visitors.
    这座偏远的城市突然有大量的游人涌入。
    The coastal area develops fast because of the influx of the foreign investment.
    由于外商投资的涌入，沿海地区发展很快。

12. **refuse:** [riˈfju:z] *v.* 拒绝

    分解记忆法：re- (回) + -fuse (流) = 拒绝

    【例句】He refused to accept that there was a problem.
    她拒不承认有问题存在。
    I politely refuse their invitation.
    我礼貌地拒绝了他们的邀请。

    常用派生词：refuse → refusal

13. **refute:** [riˈfju:t] *v.* 反驳

    分解记忆法：re- (回) + fute - (流) = 反驳

    【例句】The scholar uses the evidence to refute the theory.
    这个学者用事实来反驳这个理论。
    I don't have enough evidence to refute his argument.

我没有足够的证据来反驳他的论点。

常用派生词：refute → refutation

14. confuse: [kənˈfjuːz] *v.* 混淆；糊涂

分解记忆法：con- (共同) + fuse (流) = 混淆；糊涂

【例句】They confused me with conflicting accounts of what happened.

他们对所发生的事情给出矛盾的解释，这让我困惑不已。

People often confuse me with my twin sister.

人们常常把我和我的孪生妹妹搞错。

常用派生词：confuse → confusion → confused

15. effusive: [iˈfjuːsiv] *a.* 溢于言表的

分解记忆法：ef- (出) + fus- (流) + -ive (形容词后缀) = 溢于言表的

【例句】The government offers an effusive welcome.

政府给予热烈的欢迎。

Her effusive welcome made us feel uncomfortable.

她过分殷勤的欢迎使我们很不舒服。

16. diffuse: [diˈfjuːs] *v. & a.* 散布；冗长的

分解记忆法：dif- (分散) + -fuse (流) = 散布；冗长的

【例句】Clouds cause the diffusion of light from the sun.

云层引起阳光的漫射。

The diffuse article doesn't illustrate its meaning clearly.

这篇冗长的文章没有说清它的主旨。

17. infuse: [inˈfjuːz] *v.* 注入

分解记忆法：in- (入) + -fuse (流) = 注入

【例句】His lecture infused people with a desire to win.

他的演说使人们充满获胜的欲望。

Politics infuses all aspects of our lives.

政治影响我们生活的各个方面。

常用派生词：infuse → infusion

18. profuse: [prəˈfjuːs] *a.* 大量的；丰富的

分解记忆法：pro- (向前) + -fuse (流) = 大量的；丰富的

【例句】The flowers are profuse in spring.

春天繁花似锦。

She was profuse in thanks.

她一再表示感谢。

常用派生词：profuse → profusion

19. profusion: [prəˈfjuːʒən] *n.* 大量；众多

分解记忆法：pro- (向前) + fuse- (流) + -ion (名词后缀) = 大量；众多

【例句】The garden has a profusion of flowers.

花园里繁花似锦。

The room was spoilt by a profusion of little ornaments.

这间房被过多的小装饰品糟蹋了。

20. **suffuse:** [səˈfjuːz] *v.* 弥漫

分解记忆法：suf-(到处) + -fuse(流) = 弥漫

【例句】The whole area is suffused with grief.

整个地区弥漫着悲伤的情绪。

The light of the wetting sun suffused the clouds.

落日的余晖染遍云层。

常用派生词：suffuse → suffusion

Words in Use

1. He is ____ in five languages.
   A. flushed   B. fluent   C. flowing   D. fluid

2. We've only just begin to plan the work and our ideas on the subject are still ____. Which is the synonym of the underlined word?
   A. unknown   B. unsettled   C. unable   D. unadvised

3. He promised to use his ____ with the chairman to get me the job.
   A. reference   B. difference   C. affluence   D. influence

4. Let the tea ____ for a few minutes.
   A. inflate   B. infringe   C. infuse   D. infuriate

5. The price of the vegetable ____ according to the weather.
   A. flushes   B. influences   C. flows   D. fluctuates

6. He's still very weak and must be fed ____ only.
   A. fluff   B. fluid   C. flue   D. fluctuation

7. I wish she wouldn't go around with him because he is such a bad ____.
   A. influence   B. inflection   C. infraction   D. infusion

8. The room was spoilt by a ____ of little ornaments.
   A. profile   B. progenitor   C. profusion   D. profundity

9. The light of the wetting sun ____ the clouds, which is a beautiful scene.
   A. infused   B. suffused   C. defused   D. refused

10. His feelings ____ between excitement and fear.
    A. influence   B. fluctuate   C. flow   D. flush

11. Her ____ of gratitude was clearly insincere.
    A. refusion   B. profusion   C. diffusion   D. effusion

12. The boy's heart ____ with excitement.
    A. fluttered	B. fluted	C. flushed	D. flurried
13. There is ____ food for everyone here. Which is the synonym of the underlined word?
    A. confluent	B. effluent	C. affluent	D. influx
14. It is a common phenomenon that clouds cause the ____ of light from the sun.
    A. suffusion	B. profusion	C. diffusion	D. diffidence
15. She ____ to have any contact with that plan.
    A. regards	B. refuses	C. refunds	D. regains
16. The coastal area develops fast because of the ____ of the foreign investment.
    A. attention	B. promotion	C. influx	D. flood
17. The party is in ____ after its election defeat.
    A. confirmation	B. confusion	C. allusion	D. condition
18. The argument is completely irrelevant. You are ____ the issue.
    A. confronting	B. confusing	C. confirming	D. conflicting
19. His hometown is the ____ of the Rhine and the Mosel.
    A. congregation	B. confirmation	C. conflict	D. confluence
20. We have ____ with several other societies in the town.
    A. affirmation	B. affliction	C. affiliations	D. affluence
21. Her ____ welcome made us feel uncomfortable.
    A. effusive	B. influential	C. controversial	D. effective
22. He passed his examination by a ____; he knew little about his subject.
    A. fluency	B. flu	C. fluke	D. flush
23. The sick boy who had an unhealthy flush and breathed with difficulty was sent to hospital in time.
    A. flush	B. fluster	C. flurry	D. flunk
24. The government is determined to bring down ____ to below 5%.
    A. fluency	B. flux	C. inflation	D. infusion
25. The chairman's lecture ____ the men with a desire to win.
    A. infused	B. refuted	C. refused	D. informed
26. The shouts of the crowd ____ the speaker and he forgot what to say.
    A. flummoxed	B. fluttered	C. flustered	D. flushed
27. The remote town suddenly has a massive ____ of visitors.
    A. infraction	B. influx	C. influence	D. inform
28. He considers that the school ____ his rights as a parent by punishing his son in that way.
    A. influenced	B. infringed	C. infuriated	D. infused
29. We've just begun to plan the work and our ideas on the subject are still ____.
    A. flourished	B. fluent	C. fluffy	D. fluid

30. He is famous for his ____ of English to communicate with the foreigners.
    A. influence   B. affluence   C. fluency   D. effluent

Key to *Words in Use*

1. B	2. B	3. D	4. C	5. D
6. B	7. A	8. C	9. B	10. B
11. D	12. A	13. C	14. C	15. B
16. C	17. B	18. C	19. D	20. C
21. A	22. C	23. A	24. C	25. A
26. C	27. B	28. B	29. D	30. C

第26章 表示"声音"的词根

Words in Context

Wolfgang Amadeus Mozart

Wolfgang Amadeus Mozart was a prolific and influential composer of the Classical era. He composed over six hundred works, many acknowledged as pinnacles of **symphonic**, piano, operatic, and choral music. He is among the most enduringly popular of classical composers. His music, like Haydn's, stands as an archetypal example of the Classical style. At the time he began composition, European music was dominated by the style galant: a reaction against the highly evolved intricacy of the Baroque. But progressively, and in large part at the hands of Mozart himself, the contrapuntal complexities of the late Baroque emerged once more, moderated and disciplined by new forms, and adapted to a new aesthetic and social milieu. Mozart was a versatile composer, and wrote in every major genre, including **symphony**, opera, the solo concerto, chamber music including string quartet and string quintet, and the piano **sonata**. These forms were not new; but Mozart advanced the technical **sophistication** and emotional reach of them all. He almost single-handedly developed and popularized the Classical piano concerto. He wrote a great deal of religious music, including large-scale masses: but also many dances, divertimenti, serenades, and other forms of light entertainment. The central traits of the Classical style are all present in Mozart's music. Clarity, balance, and transparency are the hallmarks of his work, but any simplistic notion of its delicacy masks the exceptional power of his finest masterpieces. The audiences can easily find **resonance** from his compositions. And there is no doubt that Mozart is still an import ant and influential musician even today.

Word Building

More Words with the Word Roots

词根	释义	例词
ton	声音	ton, tonal, atonal, monotone, monotonous, baritone, intonation
son		sonic, supersonic, subsonic, unison, consonant, dissonant, dissonance, resonant, resonance, sonata
phon		telephone, symphony, microphone, phonetics, euphony, cacophony

1. tone: [təun] *n.* 语气；口气

  分解记忆法：ton- (声音) + -e = 语气；口气

  【例句】He tells the story in a light tone.

  　　　　他用轻松的口吻讲这个故事。

  　　　　Her friendly opening speech set the tone for the whole conference.

  　　　　她友好的开幕词奠定了整个大会的基调。

  常用派生词：tone → tonal

2. atonal: [eiˈtəunl] *a.* (音) 无调的

  分解记忆法：a- (无) + ton- (声音) + -al(……的) = (没在声音上的)无调的

  【例句】The song is totally atonal.

  　　　　这曲子一点儿调也没有。

  　　　　Her song is atonal.

  　　　　她唱歌跑调。

  常用派生词：atonal → atonality

3. monotone: [ˈmɔnətəun] *n., a. & v.* 单调；单调的

  分解记忆法：mono- (一) + ton- (声音) + -e = 单调；单调的

  【例句】His class is very boring because he speaks in a monotone all the time.

  　　　　他的课很无聊，因为他一直用单调的声音讲课。

  　　　　I don't like this monotone engraving.

  　　　　我不喜欢这幅单调的版画。

  常用派生词：monotone → monotonous

4. monotonous: [məˈnɔtənəs] *a.* (一般指声音或话语) 单调乏味的

  分解记忆法：mono- (一) + tone- (声音) + -ous(……的) = 单调乏味的

  【例句】I want to quit the monotonous work.

  　　　　我想辞掉这份单调乏味的工作。

  　　　　You should find the interest from the monotonous work.

  　　　　你应该从单调的工作中找到乐趣。

5. intonation: [inˈtəuneiʃən] *n.* 语调

  分解记忆法：in- (内) + ton- (声音) + -ation(名词后缀) = 语调

  【例句】In English, some questions have a rising intonation.

  　　　　英语中有些疑问句用升调。

  　　　　The violin's intonation was poor.

  　　　　这把小提琴音不准。

6. unison: [ˈjuːnisən] *n.* 齐唱

  分解记忆法：uni- (一) + -son(声音) = 齐唱

  【例句】The performance of unison is perfect.

  　　　　这个合唱节目很成功。

All people are working in unison to overcome the difficulty.
所有人都齐心工作来渡过这个难关。

7. consonant: [ˈkɔnsənənt] *a.* 一致的

分解记忆法：con-（一起）+ -son（声音）+ -ant（……的）= 一致的

【例句】The policy is popular because it is consonant with people's needs.
因与人们的需求一致，这个政策很受欢迎。
The new task is consonant with the market development.
新的政策和市场发展一致。

常用派生词：consonant → consonance

8. dissonant: [ˈdisənənt] *a.* 不和谐的

分解记忆法：dis-（分开）+ -son（声音）+ -ant（……的）= 不和谐的

【例句】I cannot bear the dissonant voices upstairs.
我再不能忍受楼上刺耳的噪声了。
The dissonant sound makes the whole performance a failure.
这个不和谐的声音导致演出失败了。

常用派生词：dissonant → dissonance

9. resonant: [ˈrezənənt] *a.* 共鸣的；回荡的

分解记忆法：re-（回）+ -son（声音）+ -ant（……的）= 共鸣的；回荡的

【例句】He read the article in a deep resonant voice.
他用低沉洪亮的声音朗读了这篇文章。
The poem is filled with resonant imagery.
这首诗歌充满了能引起共鸣的意象。

10. resonance: [ˈrezənəns] *n.* 共鸣；反响

分解记忆法：re-（回）+ son-（声音）+ -ance（名词后缀）= 共鸣；反响

【例句】The poem created the resonance of the readers.
这首诗引起了读者的共鸣。
Her voice had a strange and thrilling resonance.
她的声音洪亮，有种奇特的震撼人心的效果。

11. sonorous: [ˈsɔnərəs] *a.*（声音）浑厚的

分解记忆法：son-（声音）+ -rous（多的，大的）=（声音）浑厚的

【例句】He has a sonorous voice.
他嗓音浑厚。
His sonorous voice is so charming.
他浑厚的嗓音让人着迷。

12. sonata: [səˈnɑːtə] *n.* 奏鸣曲

分解记忆法：son-（声音）+ -ata（曲）= 奏鸣曲

【例句】The sonata is the masterpiece of the composer.

这首奏鸣曲是作曲者的代表作。
I can't play the sonata well.
我演奏不好这首奏鸣曲。

13. **phone:** [fəun] *n. & v.* 电话；打电话

    分解记忆法：phon- (声音) + -e = 电话；打电话

    【例句】I have to make a phone call.

    我得打个电话。

    He phoned to invite me out for dinner.

    他打电话请我出去吃饭。

14. **symphony:** [ˈsimfəni] *n.* 交响曲

    分解记忆法：sym- (共同) + phon- (声音) + -y = 交响曲

    【例句】She is playing Beethoven's Fifth Symphony.

    她正在演奏贝多芬的《第五交响曲》。

    He works in a symphony orchestra.

    他在一个交响乐团工作。

15. **phonetic:** [fəˈnetik] *a.* 语音的；语音学的；音形一致的

    分解记忆法：phon- (声音) + -etic(……的) = 语音的

    【例句】The children are learning the international phonetic alphabet.

    孩子们在学习国际音标。

    Spanish spelling is phonetic, unlike English spelling.

    与英语不同，西班牙语的拼写与发音相同。

16. **euphony:** [ˈjuːfəni] *n.* 悦耳的声音

    分解记忆法：eu- (好) + phon- (声音) + -y = 悦耳的声音

    【例句】It is an amazing feeling when I hear the euphony at night.

    夜晚听见这么动听的声音是种奇妙的感觉。

    The music is a kind of euphony.

    音乐很动听。

17. **cacophony:** [kəˈkɔfəni] *n.* 噪音；刺耳的声音；不和谐的声音

    分解记忆法：caco- (坏) + phon- (声音) + -y = 噪音

    【例句】The cacophony makes me crazy.

    噪音让我焦躁不安。

    It is bad for health to live in such cacophony.

    在噪音下生活有害健康。

Words in Use

1. That orange paint's rather garish for the bedroom; I'd ____ it down a bit.
   A. change   B. mix   C. tone   D. reverse
2. He tried to ____ for his rudeness by sending her some flowers.
   A. attack   B. atone   C. tone   D. recover
3. My job is rather ____, so I want to quit to find another one.
   A. monochrome   B. monomaniac   C. monolithic   D. monotonous
4. Her friendly opening lecture set the ____ for the party.
   A. unison   B. sound   C. voice   D. tone
5. The policy is ____ with the government's declared aims.
   A. conservative   B. consonant   C. consolatory   D. consistent
6. Sea air has a ____ quality, which is good for your recovery.
   A. torpid   B. torn   C. tonic   D. torrid
7. The ____ between husband and wife makes their love story a legend.
   A. constituency   B. consonance   C. conspiracy   D. constancy
8. I can't really remember him at such ____ of time.
   A. distance   B. dissonance   C. distaste   D. dissenter
9. These dreadful people bring down the ____ of the neighborhood.
   A. monotone   B. tone   C. air   D. characteristic
10. She reads the article in a ____ voice, which wins long-lasting applause.
    A. sonic   B. dissonant   C. resourceful   D. resonant
11. We can hear the ____ resonant of his sound. But the problem is where he is.
    A. resistance   B. resonance   C. resort   D. resource
12. Swimming is the best way to ____ up your body.
    A. tone   B. establish   C. build   D. match
13. Playing the piano set up ____ in those note ornaments.
    A. resonance   B. tonality   C. intonation   D. unison
14. Her paintings are well ____ abroad, which is very surprising.
    A. constant   B. considered   C. consonant   D. conspicuous
15. She has inner ____ of courage to confront the difficulty.
    A. resource   B. resonance   C. consonance   D. unison
16. Brighton is one of the most popular ____ on the south coast of England.
    A. resources   B. resolutions   C. resonances   D. resorts
17. It is not ____ to be drunk in the street.
    A. responsible   B. resonant   C. respectable   D. respective

18. Although the advertising plan is ____ with the main goal of the company, it is far beyond our budget.
    A. conscientious   B. constant   C. consonant   D. conscious
19. I don't accept the offer because it is a rather ____ job.
    A. distasteful   B. dissonant   C. dissimilar   D. dissident
20. In the last ____, we could borrow more money from the bank.
    A. respecter   B. resound   C. resonance   D. resort
21. The air was ____ with the shouts of children after school.
    A. resonant   B. resolute   C. resistant   D. resolvable
22. In its public statement he ____ down the criticisms he had made in private.
    A. exchanged   B. reversed   C. moderated   D. turned
23. There are too many ____ opinions so that up till now we don't find a solution.
    A. distant   B. dissonant   C. dissolved   D. dissociated
24. The ____ between my grandparents makes their love story a legend.
    A. constraint   B. belief   C. consonance   D. loyalty
25. I think the black shoes would ____ in better with your coat than the red ones.
    A. match   B. decorate   C. go   D. absorb
26. The machinery requires ____ maintenance, which will cost us a lot.
    A. consummate   B. constant   C. consonant   D. consolatory
27. The heat and humidity made me feel ____.
    A. tonal   B. tonic   C. torpid   D. tortuous
28. We should abandon the ____ attitude to the primary education of the child.
    A. consolatory   B. consequent   C. conservative   D. consonant
29. He spoilt the poem by reading it in a ____ voice.
    A. monotonous   B. sonic   C. phonetic   D. synchronous
30. The optimistic ____ of the report shows that the finial plan got the goal.
    A. unison   B. intonation   C. tone   D. tonality

Key to *Words in Use*

1. C	2. B	3. D	4. D	5. B
6. D	7. D	8. A	9. B	10. D
11. B	12. A	13. A	14. B	15. A
16. D	17. C	18. C	19. A	20. D
21. A	22. C	23. B	24. D	25. A
26. B	27. C	28. C	29. A	30. C

第27章 表示"重量"的词根

Words in Context

How a Eulogy Speech Can Help to Alleviate Grief

One of the hardest things is the passing of a loved one. For many the thought of the upcoming funeral or memorial service is very hard. They are afraid that they will not be able to get through the service with any kind of dignity or grace. They are afraid that the **grievous** feelings they have will be intensified. However, if a loved one could deliver a strong eulogy speech at the funeral, this will often help those who are still so overwhelmed with the passing of the loved one and the **grief** by which they are currently feeling consumed. As you are delivering the eulogy speech, you are, in fact, helping to heal the hearts of all those who are grief stricken. You are helping to redirect their thoughts and emotions to the powerfully wonderful things about the deceased. You are helping to take their attention and pain away from the loss of it all. That is why the eulogy is such an important speech to **alleviate** the grief. You open up the door to heal as you speak. Try to prepare yourself mentally to write the eulogy speech. You should have enough time, a quiet space, and privacy to write the eulogy speech. Do not be surprised or upset if your attempts to write the eulogy speech result in your own emotions coming up. It is to be expected.

Word Building

More Words with the Word Roots

词根	释义	例词
lev	轻	levity, alleviate, levitate
grav	重	grave, aggravate, aggravation, engrave, gravity, grief, gravity,
griev		grief, grieve, grievous, gravitate

1. **levity:** [ˈleviti] *n.* 轻浮;浮躁

   分解记忆法:lev-(轻)＋-ity(名词后缀)=轻浮;浮躁

   【例句】This is no time for levity. We have important matters to discuss.

   现在可不是开玩笑的时候,我们有很重要的事情要讨论。

   He gives others an impression of levity.

他给别人留下举止轻浮的印象。

2. alleviate: [əˈliːvieit] *v.* 减轻（痛苦）；减少（困难）

分解记忆法：al- (加强意义) + lev- (轻) + -iate (使) = 减轻(痛苦)；减少(困难)

【例句】The government takes a number of measures to alleviate the problem.

政府采取一系列措施缓解这个问题。

She eats lots of anodyne to alleviate the pain.

她吃了很多止痛药来减轻疼痛。

常用派生词：alleviate→ alleviation

3. levitate: [ˈleviteit] *v.* （使）轻轻浮起，（使）漂浮空中

分解记忆法：lev- (轻) + it (去) + -ate (使) = (藉魔力)升空

【例句】The witch levitated to the sky by his big broom.

巫师坐着他的大扫把飞上了天。

Don't dream to levitate to the sky by witchcraft.

别做梦可以用魔法飞上天了。

4. grave: [greiv] *n. & a.* 坟墓；严重的

分解记忆法：grave (重的) = 坟墓；严重的

【例句】We visit Grandma's grave annually.

我们每年都来给祖母扫墓。

The police have expressed grave concern about the missing child's safety.

警方对失踪孩子的安全深表关注。

5. gravitate: [ˈgræviˌteit] *v.* 由于引力而下降或向某处移动；被吸引而移向

分解记忆法：gravit- (重) + -ate (动词后缀) = (因为重而跟着走)

【例句】In the 19th century, industry gravitated towards the north of England.

19世纪时，工业逐渐转移到英格兰北部地区发展。

However often you mix it up in the water, the mud will gravitate to the bottom again.

不管你怎么搅拌，水里的泥土还是会沉到底部。

常用派生词：gravitate→ gravitation

6. aggravate: [ˈægrəveit] *v.* 加重；恶化

分解记忆法：ag- (加) + grav- (重) + -ate (动词后缀) = 加重；恶化

【例句】The lack of rain aggravated the already serious shortage of food.

干旱少雨使本来就很严重的粮食短缺问题更严重了。

Their debt problem was further aggravated by the rise in interest rates.

他们的债务问题因利率的提高而进一步恶化了。

常用派生词：aggravate→ aggravation

7. **engrave:** [inˈgreiv] *v.* 雕刻；铭记

   分解记忆法：en-(里)+ grave(重)=(往里用重力)雕刻；铭记

   【例句】His memorial was engraved on the stone.

   　　　　石碑上刻有他的纪念碑文。

   　　　　The terrible scene was engraved on his memory.

   　　　　那可怕的情景铭记在他的记忆里。

   常用派生词：engrave→ engraving

8. **aggrieve:** [əˈgriːv] *v.* 苦恼

   分解记忆法：ag-(加)+ grieve(重)=(使心情沉重)苦恼

   【例句】He aggrieved so much because of the unfair treatment in the company.

   　　　　因为在公司里的不公正对待，他非常苦恼。

   　　　　The young man aggrieved for losing the chance of the interview.

   　　　　失去了面试机会，这个年轻人很苦恼。

   常用派生词：aggrieve→ aggrieved

9. **grieve:** [griːv] *v.* 悲伤；悲痛

   分解记忆法：griev-(重)+ -e =(使内心负重)悲伤；悲痛

   【例句】She is still grieving for her dead husband.

   　　　　她仍然为死去的丈夫伤心。

   　　　　It grieves me to see him wasting his youth.

   　　　　看他浪费青春让真伤心。

   常用派生词：grieve→ grievance→ grief → grievous

10. **grief:** [griːf] *n.* 悲痛；忧伤

    分解记忆法：grie-(重)+ -f =(心情沉重)悲痛；忧伤

    【例句】She went nearly mad with grief after the child died.

    　　　　孩子死后，她悲伤得快要疯了。

    　　　　The plans come to grief when the bank refused to lend them more money.

    　　　　银行拒绝给他们提供更多贷款，他们的计划因而失败了。

11. **grievance:** [ˈgriːvəns] *n.* 委屈；抱怨

    分解记忆法：griev-(重)+ -ance(名词后缀)=(心情沉重)委屈；抱怨

    【例句】She has a very strong grievance against the hospital because of the operation which ruined her health.

    　　　　由于医院的手术毁了她的健康，她对医院很不满。

    　　　　A committee was set up to look into the workers' grievance.

    　　　　成立了一个委员会来调查工人的不满。

12. **grievous:** [ˈgriːvəs] *a.* 严重的；令人伤心或痛苦的

    分解记忆法：griev-(重)+ -ous(……的)= 严重的；严重受伤的

    【例句】In the accident, the poor guy had a grievous wound.

在事故中，这个可怜的人受到严重的创伤。

You have made a grievous mistake which could affect the rest of your life.
你犯了会危害你终身的错误。

Words in Use

1. This is no time for ____, because we have important matters to discuss.
   A. levity   B. levy   C. lever   D. leverage
2. The president has expressed ____ concern about the missing child's safety.
   A. greasy   B. grave   C. grassy   D. grateful
3. The government ____ over $100 million to the job creation program.
   A. allocates   B. alleviates   C. arranges   D. allays
4. The government takes a number of measures to ____ the problem.
   A. allege   B. allocate   C. alleviate   D. allot
5. The way you behave now would make my grandfather turn in his ____.
   A. sepulcher   B. tumulus   C. tomb   D. grave
6. In the 18th century, industry ____ towards the north of the country.
   A. grazed   B. gravitated   C. changed   D. removed
7. From amateur tennis he was finally ____ to the professional team.
   A. admitted   B. entered   C. committed   D. resigned
8. She eats lots of anodyne to ____ the pain.
   A. allot   B. alleviate   C. allocate   D. allege
9. I had a strange dream that I can ____ the sky freely. It is so amazing.
   A. levy   B. liaise   C. lever   D. levitate
10. His face is ____ as he tells them about the accident.
    A. solemn   B. grateful   C. furious   D. anxious
11. The scores were ____ with the first round totals to decide the winner.
    A. aggregated   B. aggravated   C. engraved   D. grieved
12. The lack of rain ____ the already serious shortage of food.
    A. agonized   B. aggravated   C. aggregated   D. agitated
13. The terrible scene was ____ on his memory.
    A. enhanced   B. engrossed   C. engraved   D. engaged
14. I bought an old ____ of London Bridge.
    A. engine   B. engraving   C. engaging   D. enlarging
15. He devotes himself to the ____ of the conflicts within the country all his life.
    A. allocation   B. alleviation   C. alliteration   D. allegation

16. They won 4 vs. 2 on ____.
    A. grief   B. aggravate   C. aggregate   D. aggravation
17. The military exercise was condemned as an act of ____.
    A. aggression   B. aggravation   C. aggregation   D. agglutination
18. The young mother went nearly mad with ____ after the child died.
    A. gripe   B. grill   C. grief   D. grimace
19. The allegations of fraud were proved and the court awarded the _____ parties substantial damages.
    A. aggravated   B. aggrieved   C. aggressive   D. ailed
20. There's more ____ news from the war zone; more of our men were killed today.
    A. greedy   B. gossip   C. grievous   D. grim
21. A committee was set up to look into the workers' ____.
    A. dissatisfaction B. complain   C. nagging   D. grief
22. A loophole in the law ____ them to escape prosecution.
    A. alludes   B. alleges   C. allows   D. alleviates
23. Their debt problem was further ____ by the rise in interest rates.
    A. agonized   B. aggravated   C. aggregated   D. agitated
24. You have made a ____ mistake which could impact you seriously.
    A. graceful   B. grateful   C. grief   D. grievous
25. The government takes a number of measures to ____ the problem. What is the synonym of the underlined word?
    A. reduce   B. increase   C. decrease   D. decline
26. She has a strong ____ against the hospital because the operation which ruined her health.
    A. appraisal   B. grievance   C. grief   D. resent
27. I was so ____ in my work that I completely forgot the time.
    A. enhanced   B. engrossed   C. engraved   D. engaged
28. The plans come to ____ when the bank refused to lend them more money.
    A. grind   B. grief   C. grievance   D. grasp
29. She didn't mention Mr. Smith by name, but it was clear she ____ to him.
    A. allayed   B. alleged   C. alleviated   D. alluded
30. No matter how often you mix it up in the water, the mud will ____ to the bottom.
    A. gravitate   B. levitate   C. alleviate   D. allege

Key to *Words in Use*

1. A	2. B	3. A	4. C	5. D
6. B	7. A	8. B	9. D	10. A
11. A	12. B	13. C	14. B	15. B
16. C	17. A	18. C	19. B	20. D
21. D	22. C	23. B	24. D	25. A
26. B	27. B	28. B	29. D	30. A

第28章 表示"真假"的词根

Words in Context

Crimes

Of many problems in the world today, none is as widespread, or as old, as crime. It is **verifiable** that crime has many forms, including crimes against property, person, and government. Crime, in all its forms, penetrates every layer of society and touches every human being. You may never have been robbed, but you suffer the increased cost of store-bought items because of other's shoplifting and you pay higher taxes because of other's tax evasion. Perhaps your house is not worth as much today as it was a few years ago because of the increased crime rate in your neighborhood, or maybe your business is not doing as well as it used to because tourism is down due to increased terrorism in your part of the world. Whatever you do, wherever you go, you are a victim of crime whether you like it or not, whether you know it or not.

Expert argues whether the number of crimes committed is actually on the rise. This issue is particularly **verified** in cases of family violence, the abuse of husbands, wives or children. Throughout much of history, cases of family violence and neglect often went unreported because of the attitude of society, which considered family matters to be private.

Word Building

More Words with the Word Roots

词根	释义	例词
ver	真实的	veracious, veracity
veri		verify, verification, verisimilitude, veritable, variability
fall	伪的，假的	fallacy, fallacious, fallible
fals		false

1. veracious: [vəˈreiʃəs] *a.* 诚实的

分解记忆法：ver-（真实）+ -acious（……的）= 诚实的

【例句】You must give the veracious testimony in the court.

在法庭上你必须给出诚实的证词。

Although he is quite rude, he is a veracious witness.

虽然他举止粗鲁，但他是一个诚实的证人。

常用派生词：veracious→ veracity

2. veracity: [vəˈræsəti] *n.* 诚实；真实

分解记忆法：ver- (真实) + -acity (名词后缀) = 诚实

【例句】Some people questioned the veracity of her report.

有些人质疑她报告的真实性。

3. verify: [ˈverifai] *v.* 核实；证实

分解记忆法：veri- (真实) + -fy (动词后缀) = 核实；证实

【例句】The prisoner's statement was verified by several witnesses.

犯人的供词得到几个证人的证实。

Before the bank was willing to lend him money, it had to verify that he was the true owner of the house.

银行必须证实他是这房子真正的主人，才愿借钱给他。

常用派生词：verify→ verification → veritable

4. veritable: [ˈveritəbəl] *a.* 真实的

分解记忆法：veri- (真实) + -table (……的) = 真实的

【例句】Thank you for that meal; it was a veritable feast!

谢谢你的晚餐，它真是一个名副其实的盛宴。

I believe all his veritable emotion is in this song.

我相信他所有真实的感情都包含在这首歌里。

5. fallacy: [ˈfæləsi] *n.* 谬论

分解记忆法：fall- (错的) + -acy (名词后缀) = 谬论

【例句】It is a fallacy that success always brings happiness.

成功总会带来幸福，这是一种谬论。

I was able to show the fallacy of his argument.

我能指出他论据中的推理错误。

常用派生词：fallacy → fallacious

6. fallacious: [fəˈleiʃəs] *a.* 谬误的

分解记忆法：fall- (错的) + -acious (……的) = 谬误的

【例句】There is an obvious fallacious argument in his article.

在他的文章里有一处明显的谬误论点。

I don't agree on the fallacious opinion that success always brings happiness.

成功总会带来幸福，我不赞同这种谬解。

7. fallible: [ˈfæləbəl] *a.* 易错的；可能犯错的

分解记忆法：fall- (错的) + -ible (……的) = 易错的；可能犯错的

【例句】All human beings are fallible.

人人都难免犯错。

Memory is selective and fallible.

记忆有选择性而且会出错。

常用派生词：fallible → fallibility → infallible → infallibility

8. **infallible:** [inˈfæləbəl] *a. & n.* 不会错的；可靠的；一贯正确的人；可靠的事物

分解记忆法：in- (没有) + fall- (错的) + -ible (……的) = 不会错的；可靠的

【例句】It is infallible to make enough preparation before the interview.

面试前做好充足的准备，这是不会错的。

Although he is rude, he is an infallible friend.

虽然他举止粗鲁，但他是一个可靠的朋友。

9. **false:** [fɔːls] *a.* 错的；假的

分解记忆法：false 错的；假的

【例句】Prediction of an early improvement in the housing market proved false.

认为房屋市场很早就好转的预测结果证实是错误的。

It is only a false dawn for the economy.

这只是经济复苏的假象。

10. **falsify:** [ˈfɔːlsifai] *v.* 篡改；伪造

分解记忆法：fals- (错的) + -ify (动词后缀) = 篡改；伪造

【例句】They suspected that he had been falsifying the accounts.

他们怀疑他一直在做假账。

The company falsifies the accounts to evade tax.

这家公司做假账逃税。

常用派生词：falsify → falsity

Words in Use

1. They didn't say the ____ of the crime that they committed.
   A. importance   B. truthfulness   C. core   D. essence
2. The criminal's statement was ____ by several witnesses.
   A. verified   B. confessed   C. defended   D. ventured
3. Before the bank was willing to lend him money, it had to ____ that he could pay it back.
   A. venture   B. verge   C. vest   D. verify
4. To add ____, the stage is covered with sand for the desert scenes. Which of the following is the synonym of the underlined word?
   A. authenticity   B. altitude   C. attitude   D. latitude
5. It is a ____ that beauty always brings happiness.
   A. fain   B. fairy   C. fallacy   D. fake

6. You must give the ____ testimony in the court.
   A. verbose   B. veracious   C. venturesome   D. venial
7. There is an obvious ____ argument in his article.
   A. conscious   B. ambitious   C. fallible   D. fallacious
8. The ____ of the event described in this letter is beyond doubt.
   A. latitude   B. veracity   C. altitude   D. attitude
9. It is natural that all human beings are ____.
   A. fagged   B. falsified   C. famed   D. fallible
10. Although he is quiet rude, he is a ____ witness.
    A. veracious   B. venturesome   C. vengeful   D. verbose
11. I was vaguely ____ that I was being watched.
    A. creative   B. fallacious   C. conscious   D. emotional
12. It is ____ to make enough preparation before the interview.
    A. impossible   B. infallible   C. invariable   D. irritable
13. They suspected that he had been ____ the accounts.
    A. falsifying   B. fallacy   C. faltering   D. flaunting
14. In order to build a harmonious society we should comply with the behavior ____ all the time.
    A. verity   B. venture   C. verification   D. version
15. Prediction of an early improvement in the housing market proved ____.
    A. infallible   B. fallacious   C. fallible   D. false
16. When the sick man ____, the nurse took his arm.
    A. fell   B. faltered   C. falsified   D. faded
17. Some people questioned the ____ of her performance.
    A. veracity   B. venture   C. verdict   D. verge
18. Her testimony of the crime was ____ by neighbors.
    A. carried out   B. confirmed   C. indicated   D. operated
19. We ____ in the closing music as the hero rides off the sunset.
    A. fall   B. falter   C. falsify   D. fade
20. I don't like the ____ criticism in his voice.
    A. testified   B. confirmed   C. verified   D. implied
21. The machine has a big ____.
    A. fame   B. failure   C. failing   D. fallacy
22. They didn't say the ____ of the crime that they committed.
    A vengeance   B. veracity   C. verdict   D. venture
23. She made a ____ attempt at a smile.
    A. faint   B. false   C. fair   D. facial

24. He became actually ____ of having failed his parents.
    A. ambitious　　　B. veracious　　　C. conscious　　　D. conscientious
25. Thank you for that meal; it was a ____ feast!
    A. inevitable　　　B. invaluable　　　C. invariable　　　D. veritable
26. Please ____ that there is sufficient memory available before loading the program.
    A. check　　　B. make sure　　　C. ensure　　　D. test
27. After a day's hard work, he is tired and ____.
    A. veritable　　　B. changeable　　　C. infallible　　　D. irritable
28. The prisoner's statement was ____ by several witnesses.
    A. confirmed　　　B. venerated　　　C. ventilated　　　D. confessed
29. I believe all his ____ emotion is in this article.
    A. veritable　　　B. inevitable　　　C. vertical　　　D. vertiginous
30. Many readers questioned the ____ of the report.
    A. verification　　　B. verisimilitude　　　C. essence　　　D. veracity

Key to *Words in Use*

1. B	2. A	3. D	4. A	5. C
6. B	7. D	8. B	9. D	10. A
11. C	12. B	13. A	14. A	15. D
16. B	17. A	18. B	19. D	20. D
21. C	22. B	23. A	24. C	25. D
26. A	27. D	28. A	29. A	30. D

第29章　表示"相同"的词根

Words in Context

Metaphor

Writers use many styles or techniques, for instance *metaphor* or *simile*, to connect with their readers so that the readers will be able to become invested in their work. Metaphor is figure of speech that implies comparison between two unlike entities, as distinguished from simile, an explicit comparison signaled by the words *like* or *as*. The distinction is not simple. A metaphor makes a qualitative leap from a reasonable, perhaps prosaic, comparison to an identification or fusion of two objects, the intention being to create one new entity that partakes of the characteristics of both.

Metaphor is a figure of speech that actually transfers the meaning of one thing directly on another unit. It is actually an implicit comparison that inventively points something with another thing. This is actually being used in stories or poems by authors to put a twist to the meaning of certain word. A simile is a figure of speech that utilizes "like" or "as" to compare two **similar** things in a very interesting way. Similes are an important tool that makes language more creative, descriptive, and entertaining. The mind thinks in images and associations, so similes are used to make stronger and more effective descriptions than if only adjectives or literal descriptions were used; they can stir up associated emotions, create new connections in the mind, and add **verisimilitude**. Similes are almost essential to creative expression from everyday speech to poetry. Similes are very abundant in the literary world and even in other industries like in the music industry.

Word Building

More Words with the Word Roots

词根	释义	例词
simil	一样	similar, similarity, dissimilar, verisimilar, verisimilitude, simile, assimilate, dissimilate, facsimile
simul		simulate, simultaneous, dissimulate
semble		semblance, dissemble, resemble

1. **similar:** [ˈsimələ] *n.* 相似的；类似的

    分解记忆法：simil- (相似) + -ar (……的) = 相似的；类似的

    【例句】The two houses are similar in size.

两座房子大小差不多。

My teaching style is similar to that of most other teachers.

我的教学风格和多数老师相似。

常用派生词：similar → similarity

2. similarity: [ˌsiməˈlærəti] *n.* 类似；相似

分解记忆法：similar(相似的)+ -ity(名词后缀)= 类似；相似

【例句】The report highlights the similarity between the two groups.

这份报告强调两组之间的相似性。

The karate bout has many similarities to a boxing match.

空手道比赛和拳击比赛有很多类似的地方。

3. dissimilar: [diˈsimilə] *a.* 不同的；相异的

分解记忆法：dis-(不) + simil-(相似) + -ar(……的)= 不同的；相异的

【例句】The two writers are not dissimilar in style.

两位作家的文风没什么不同。

These wines are not dissimilar.

这些葡萄酒都差不多。

常用派生词：dissimilar → dissimilarity

4. simile: [ˈsiməli] *n.* 明喻

分解记忆法：simil-(相似) + -e = 明喻

【例句】You should know the difference between simile and metaphor.

你应该知道明喻和暗喻的区别。

The teacher let the student make a sentence with simile.

老师让学生造个明喻的句子。

5. dissimulate: [diˈsimjuleit] *v.* 掩饰；假装

分解记忆法：dis-(不) + simul-(相似) + -ate(动词后缀)= 掩饰；假装

【例句】The young man dissimulates the sadness and continues to work.

这个年轻人掩饰好悲伤继续工作。

He dissimulates his deep love for her.

他掩藏了对她深深的爱恋。

常用派生词：dissimulate → dissimulation

6. verisimilar: [ˌveriˈsimilə] *a.* 逼真的

分解记忆法：veri-(真实) + similar(相似的)=(类似真实的)逼真的

【例句】The description of the life in that period in the novel is quite verisimilar.

这篇小说中对那个时代的描写相当逼真。

The verisimilar character in the story makes him into deep thought.

故事中逼真的人物刻画使他陷入沉思。

7. verisimilitude: [ˌverisiˈmilitjuːd] *n.* 逼真

分解记忆法：veri-(真实) + simil-(相似的) + -itude(名词后缀)= 逼真

【例句】To add verisimilitude, the stage is covered with sand for the desert scenes.
为了更加逼真，舞台上铺满了沙子作为沙漠的场景。
The verisimilitude of the description of the character makes the novel successful.
对人物逼真的描写使得这本书取得巨大的成功。

8. **assimilate:** [əˈsimileit] *v.* 同化；理解；掌握

   分解记忆法：as-(向) + simil-(相似的) + -ate(动词后缀) =(使与别人相同)

   【例句】America has assimilated many people from Europe.
   美国同化了很多来自欧洲的人。
   You have to assimilate the facts not just remember them.
   你必须掌握这些事实而不是仅仅记住它们。

   常用派生词：assimilate → assimilation

9. **facsimile:** [ˌfækˈsimili] *n.* 临摹

   分解记忆法：fac-(做) + -simile(相似的) =(做得相同) 临摹

   【例句】The canvas we bought yesterday is a facsimile version.
   我们昨天买的油画是临摹的版本。
   The picture which is displayed in the exhibition is a manuscript in facsimile.
   展览会展出的画是一张复制的手稿。

10. **simulate:** [ˈsimjuleit] *v.* 模仿；冒充

    分解记忆法：simul-(相似) + -ate(动词后缀) = 模仿；冒充

    【例句】A sheet of metal was shaken to simulate the thunder.
    用力抖动金属片以模仿雷声。
    The dolphin can simulate the sound of a baby.
    海豚能模仿孩子的声音。

    常用派生词：simulate → simulation → simulated → simulator

11. **simultaneous:** [ˌsiməlˈteiniəs] *a.* 同时的；同步的

    分解记忆法：simul-(相似) + -tane(时间) + -ous(……的) = 同时的；同步的

    【例句】There was a flash of lighting and a simultaneous crash of thunder.
    一道闪电出现，同时响起了雷声。
    There will be a simultaneous broadcast of the concert on TV and radio.
    电视和广播将同时对这场音乐会进行转播。

    常用派生词：simultaneous → simultaneousity

12. **resemble:** [riˈzembl] *v.* 像，类似

    分解记忆法：re-(回) + -semble(相同) =(回到相同的状态) 像，类似

    【例句】She closely resembles her mother.
    她和她妈妈长得很像。
    The plant resembles grass in appearance.
    这种植物的外形很像草。

    常用派生词：resemble → resemblance

Words in Use

1. The young man _____ the sadness and continues to work. Which of the following is the synonym of the underlined word?
   A. dissipates　　　B. dissembles　　　C. dissociates　　　D. dissolve

2. Mother brings the vegetables to a ____.
   A. sinew　　　B. silhouette　　　C. simmer　　　D. simile

3. The report highlights the _____ between the two groups. Which of the following is the antonym of the underlined word?
   A. dissuasion　　　B. difference　　　C. disservice　　　D. dissonance

4. The crowd soon ____ when the police arrived.
   A. dissuaded　　　B. dissented　　　C. dissipated　　　D. dissimulated

5. It looks quite nice from a ____, but when you get close you can see it is pretty awful.
   A. distance　　　B. dissolution　　　C. dissimilarity　　　D. disservice

6. Men must wear a jacket and tie; ____, women must wear a skirt or dress, not trousers.
   A. similar　　　B. similarly　　　C. sincerely　　　D. simultaneously

7. The meeting ended with ____ opinions.
   A. distant　　　B. dissipated　　　C. dissimilar　　　D. dissonant

8. The ____ of the Roman Empire directly leads to the fall in its literature.
   A. dissolution　　　B. dissonance　　　C. distance　　　D. dissipation

9. He was advised not to eat bread, cake and other ____ foods.
   A. sincere　　　B. simile　　　C. silly　　　D. similar

10. As for that miserable history, you have to ____ the facts, not just remember them.
    A. assess　　　B. assimilate　　　C. associate　　　D. assort

11. I was given some ____ in coming to my decision.
    A. assimilation　　　B. assistance　　　C. association　　　D. assortment

12. I ____ hope your father will be well soon.
    A. sincerely　　　B. similarly　　　C. simply　　　D. simultaneously

13. He ____ his large fortune in a few years of heavy spending.
    A. dissented　　　B. dissipated　　　C. dissimulated　　　D. dissolved

14. We ____ a day for our meeting.
    A. assisted　　　B. associated　　　C. assimilated　　　D. assigned

15. This doesn't ____ with his earlier statement.
    A. assure　　　B. assort　　　C. assimilate　　　D. assess

16. Opposition to the idea gradually ____.
    A. dissociated　　　B. dissimulated　　　C. dissuaded　　　D. dissolved

17. The picture we bought yesterday is a(n) ____ version.
    A. assiduous   B. assimilating   C. facsimile   D. simile
18. A sheet of metal was shaken to ____ the thunder.
    A. simulate   B. simmer   C. silent   D. silt
19. Her laugh ____ the tension in the air.
    A. dissimulates   B. dissipates   C. dissociates   D. dissents
20. The scientist spends much time designing the flight ____.
    A. simulating   B. simulation   C. similarity   D. simulator
21. Although he has been promoted, he is still ____ in his daily work.
    A. dissimulating   B. assistant   C. dissent   D. assiduous
22. This coat is made of ____ fur; it is not the real fur.
    A. simple   B. false   C. simulated   D. situated
23. You can't ____ yourself from the actions of your partner.
    A. dissent   B. dissociate   C. dissolve   D. dissimulate
24. There was a flash of lighting and ____ a crash of thunder.
    A. at the same time   B. in time   C. on time   D. beyond time
25. The old harbor ____ up years ago.
    A. silenced   B. silted   C. simulated   D. slipped
26. You have done a serious ____ to your country by selling military secrets to the enemies.
    A. disservice   B. dissident   C. dissimulation   D. dissipation
27. We booked early to ____ of good seats.
    A. assess   B. assimilate   C. assure   D. assort
28. I never tried to ____ her from the marriage.
    A. dissent   B. dissimulate   C. dissociate   D. dissuade
29. They ____ easily into the new community.
    A. assimilated   B. associated   C. assigned   D. assorted
30. Only one member ____ from the final report.
    A. dissembles   B. disagrees   C. dissents   D. dissipates

Key to Words in Use

1. B	2. C	3. B	4. C	5. A
6. B	7. D	8. D	9. D	10. B
11. B	12. A	13. B	14. D	15. B
16. D	17. C	18. A	19. B	20. D
21. D	22. C	23. B	24. A	25. B
26. A	27. C	28. D	29. A	30. C

第30章　表示"时间"的词根

Words in Context

The 60th Anniversary of the People's Republic of China

A grand ceremony starts on the National Day in Beijing to commemorate the 60th **anniversary** of the founding of the People's Republic of China (PRC). The celebrations which are also broadcasted **synchronally** via the Internet center on the Tian'anmen Square in the heart of Beijing, and Chang'an Avenue, the capital's main west-east thoroughfare. Immediately following a massive military parade, there is a civilians' parade comprising 36 formations and six performing groups involving about 100,000 citizens and 60 floats. It is complemented by 80,000 primary and middle school students in the Tian'anmen Square forming background patterns. Meanwhile more than 4,000 performers, including a 2,400 strong chorus, present a concert in the Tian'anmen Square. The civilians' parade begins with a formation of honor guards holding high the National Flag of the New China. And it has three themes: ideology, achievements and future prospects. "Ideology" is portrayed by formations holding high portraits of Mao Zedong, Deng Xiaoping, Jiang Zemin and Hu Jintao, and placards featuring slogans characteristic of their thinking. Nineteen floats display China's achievements in different sectors. What's more, three formations of teenagers will express the concept of wishing China a beautiful future. More than 5,000 children have been organized to fly and release colorful balloons and several tens of thousands of doves are free in the Tian'anmen Square Area.

Word Building

More Words with the Word Roots

词根	释义	例词
chron	时间	synchronous, synchronize
chrono		chronic, chronicle, chronology, chronometer, anachronism
ann	年	anniversary, annual, semiannual, biannual, annals, annalist, annuity, annuitant, superannuate
enn		biennial, perennial

1. **synchronous:** [ˈsiŋkrənəs] *a.* 同时的

   分解记忆法：syn- (一同) + chron- (时间) + -ous (……的) = 同时的

   【例句】He contributes himself to the development of the synchronous satellite navigation system.

   他对同步卫星导航系统的发展做出贡献。

   We can use synchronous satellite to explore the climate change.

   我们可以用同步卫星来探测天气变化。

2. **synchronize:** [ˈsiŋkrənaiz] *v.* 同步

   分解记忆法：syn- (一同) + chron- (时间) + -ize (动词后缀) = 同步

   【例句】You have to synchronize the soundtrack with the film.

   你必须使画面与声道同步。

   The sound track did not synchronize with the action.

   声音与动作不同步。

   常用派生词：synchronize → synchronization

3. **chronic:** [ˈkrɔnik] *a.* 慢性的，延续很久的

   分解记忆法：chron- (时间) + -ic (……的) = 慢性的，延续很久的

   【例句】The bad weather worsens his chronic bronchitis.

   恶劣的天气使他的慢性支气管炎加重了。

   The country has chronic unemployment problem.

   该国长期存在失业问题。

4. **chronicle:** [ˈkrɔnikl] *n.* 编年史

   分解记忆法：chron- (时间) + -icle (名词后缀) = (按时间顺序记载的历史) 编年史

   【例句】The newly published chronicle records the history in that historical period.

   这本新出版的编年史记载了那个时期的历史。

   Every time I visit her, she always gives me a chronicle of her complaints.

   每次我去看她，她总是向我述说她的委屈。

5. **chronology:** [krəˈnɔlədʒi] *n.* 年代学

   分解记忆法：chrono- (时间) + -logy (学) = 年代学

   【例句】He is interested in the chronology.

   他对年代学很感兴趣。

   He is editing a chronology of the past ten years.

   他正在编辑过去十年的大事年表。

   常用派生词：chronology → chronological

6. **chronological:** [ˌkrɔnəˈlɔdʒikəl] *a.* 年代学的

   分解记忆法：chrono- (时间) + logi- (学) + -cal (……的) = 年代学的

   【例句】We'll talk about the causes of the war in chronological order.

   我们将按照年代的顺序来讲述战争起因。

You can remember the historical event in chronological sequence.

你可以用年代的顺序来记历史事件。

7. anachronism: [əˈnækrənizəm] *n.* 年代错误；过时的人或风俗

分解记忆法： ana- (错误) + chrono-(时间) + -ism(名词后缀) = (将某事弄错历史时期)年代错误；过时的人或风俗

【例句】Some people believe that the British House of Lords is an anachronism.

有些人认为英国的贵族院是一种过时的东西。

We should abandon the anachronism to adapt to the new situation.

我们应该摒弃过时的思想以适应新的环境。

8. anniversary: [ˌænəˈvəːsəri] *n.* 周年

分解记忆法： anni - (年) + vers- (转) + -ary(名词后缀) = (时间转了一年)周年

【例句】They go for a holiday because of the wedding anniversary.

因为是结婚周年纪念日，他们度假去了。

It's the fiftieth anniversary of their country's independence today.

今天是他们国家独立五十周年纪念日。

9. annual: [ˈænjuəl] *a. & n.* 一年一次的；年鉴

分解记忆法： ann- (年) + -ual(……的) = 一年一次的；年鉴

【例句】Although he has little experience, he gets quite high annual salary.

虽然他没什么经验，但他的年薪却很高。

You can find the report about him in the Football Annual for 1987.

你可以在1987年的足球年刊上找到关于他的报告。

10. annuity: [əˈnjuːiti] *n.* 年金；养老金

分解记忆法： ann- (年) + -uity(名词后缀) = 年金；养老金

【例句】The old man lives on an annuity.

这个老人靠养老金过活。

You can have a high annuity if you work in this company.

如果你在这家公司工作，你可以拿到很高的年金。

11. superannuated: [ˌsuːpərˈænjueitid] *a.* 年老不能工作的；过时的

分解记忆法： super- (超) + annu- (年) + -ated(……的) = (超过一定年龄或年限的)年老不能工作的，过时的

【例句】Nobody recognized the superannuated rock star.

没人认出这个过气的摇滚歌星。

Please throw those superannuated thoughts and absorb more new ones from the books.

抛弃那些过时的思想，多从书里学习些新想法吧。

12. perennial: [pəˈreniəl] *a.* 终年的；永久的

分解记忆法： per- (贯穿) + -enn(年) + -ial(……的) = (贯穿一年的)终年的；永久的

【例句】I wish you perennial youth.
我祝愿您青春永驻。
The living condition of the immigrant workers is a perennial problem.
进城务工人员的住宿条件是一个长期存在的问题。

Words in Use

1. There is a ____ unemployment problem in this country.
   A. synthesis　　　B. chronic　　　C. chronicle　　　D. symptom
2. It is hard to ____ with her political opinions.
   A. sympathize　　B. synchronize　　C. synthesize　　D. syndicate
3. The new published ____ records the stories in that dark period.
   A. synchronic　　B. chronology　　C. chronicle　　D. chronic
4. The ____ doesn't appear until a few days after you're infected.
   A. sympathy　　B. symptom　　C. synchronization　　D. synthesis
5. Some people believe that the British House of Lords is a(n) ____.
   A. chronology　　B. anachronism　　C. synchronization　　D. chronicle
6. You need to ____ the soundtrack with the film.
   A. sympathize　　B. syndicate　　C. synchronize　　D. syncopate
7. The old lady had a miserable life and died of ____ depression.
   A. chromatic　　B. chubby　　C. chronicle　　D. chronic
8. The noisy traffic is a continual ____.
   A. annuity　　B. annoyance　　C. annals　　D. annual
9. I'm in ____ with her aims, but I don't like the way she goes about achieving them.
   A. symposium　　B. synchronization　　C. sympathy　　D. symphony
10. We ____ the enemy finally.
    A. superannuated　　B. annihilated　　C. annotated　　D. synchronized
11. After their meeting, the two leaders produced an ____ statement that didn't say anything at all.
    A. annul　　B. anodyne　　C. annual　　D. annuity
12. We should abandon the ____ to adapt to the new situation
    A. annuity　　B. anachronism　　C. anniversary　　D. annals
13. Please throw those ____ thoughts and absorb more new ones from the new condition.
    A. annual　　B. old-fashioned　　C. previous　　D. familiar
14. The medical care of the immigrant worker is always a(n) ____ problem.
    A. synchronal　　B. chronic　　C. annual　　D. perennial
15. I don't get much ____ from the doctor when I tell him about my pain.
    A. synchronization　　B. syndrome　　C. sympathy　　D. symposium

16. The captain orders his seamen in a ____ voice.
    A. perceptive　　　B. perfect　　　C. perennial　　　D. peremptory
17. His ____ comments win long-last applause.
    A. peremptory　　　B. perceptive　　　C. perennial　　　D. perfect
18. Their beliefs are a ____ of Eastern and Western religions.
    A. symptom　　　B. synchronization　　　C. synthesis　　　D. thesis
19. It is against the law that he doesn't get any ____ after his retirement.
    A. pension　　　B. annals　　　C. anniversary　　　D. chronicle
20. When he met me, a ____ smile appeared on his face.
    A. superhuman　　　B. superfluous　　　C. supercilious　　　D. superannuated
21. The oral ____ of the marriage has no legal power.
    A. chronicle　　　B. annulment　　　C. annuity　　　D. universe
22. We'll talk about the causes of the war in ____ order.
    A. chronicle　　　B. chronicle　　　C. synchronous　　　D. chronological
23. He had already been told, so our comments were ____.
    A. supercilious　　　B. superannuated　　　C. superfluous　　　D. superior
24. Their marriage was ____ after just six months.
    A. deleted　　　B. annulled　　　C. synchronized　　　D. annoyed
25. Their lifestyle is typical of the bored middle-aged housewife ____.
    A. synthesis　　　B. synchronization　　　C. syndrome　　　D. symptom
26. I was ____ with him because he kept interrupting.
    A. annoyed　　　B. annihilated　　　C. annotated　　　D. superannuated
27. You can have a high ____ after the retirement if you work in this company.
    A. chronic　　　B. annuity　　　C. annals　　　D. chronicle
28. It's the first ____ of that country's independence today.
    A. chronicle　　　B. anniversary　　　C. universe　　　D. annals
29. Let's ____ the watches before action.
    A. syncopate　　　B. syndicate　　　C. synthesize　　　D. synchronize
30. Every time I meet her, she always gives me a ____ of her complaints.
    A. synchronic　　　B. chronology　　　C. chronicle　　　D. chronic

Key to *Words in Use*

1. B	2. A	3. C	4. B	5. B
6. C	7. D	8. B	9. C	10. D
11. B	12. B	13. B	14. D	15. C
16. D	17. B	18. C	19. A	20. C
21. B	22. D	23. C	24. B	25. C
26. A	27. B	28. B	29. D	30. C

第31章　表示"方位"的词根

Words in Context

Rockefeller <u>Foundation</u>

Rockefeller's interest in philanthropy on a large scale began in 1889, influenced by Andrew Carnegie's published essay, *The Gospel of Wealth*, which prompted him to write a letter to Carnegie praising him as an example to other rich men. It was in that year that he made the first of what would become $35 million in gifts, over a period of two decades, to fund the University of Chicago. His initial idea to set up a large-scale tax-exempt **foundation** occurred in 1901, but it was not until 1906 that Senior's famous business and philanthropic advisor, Frederick T. Gates, seriously revived the idea, pointing **profoundly** that Rockefeller's fortune was rolling up so fast that his heirs would "dissipate their inheritances or become intoxicated with power," unless he set up "permanent corporate philanthropies for the good of Mankind." And in 1913 in New York State, Rockefeller Foundation was **founded** by John D. Rockefeller, along with Senior's principal business advisor, Frederick T. Gates, at 420 Fifth Avenue, New York City. Its **fundamental** mission is "to promote the well-being of mankind throughout the world." Some of its achievements **concentrate**.

Word Building

More Words with the Word Roots

词根	释义	例词
dexter-	右	dexterous, dexterity
dextr-		ambidextrous, ambidexterity
medi-	中间	mediate, mediator, medieval, mediocre
mid-		midday, midnight, amid, midway
cente-		concentrate, centrifuge, centrifugal, eccentric
later-	边	lateral, unilateral, bilateral, collateral, dilate, latitude
fund-	底	fund, fundament, fundamental
found		found, profound, foundation

1. dexterous: [ˈdekstərəs] *a.* 灵巧的；敏捷的

分解记忆法：dexter-（右）+ -ous（……的）=（右手比左手灵巧的）灵巧的；敏捷的

【例句】She untied the knots with dexterous fingers.

她用灵巧的手指解开了绳结。

Animals are usually dexterous by nature.

动物通常天生动作敏捷。

常用派生词：dexterous → dexterity

2. dexterity: [dekˈsteriti] *n.* 灵巧

分解记忆法：dexter-（右）+ -ity（名词后缀）= 灵巧

【例句】After long exercise, he has an obvious improvement in the dexterity of the fingers.

在长时间的练习后，他手指的灵活性有了明显的提高。

He is famous for the dexterity with which he plays the piano.

这个人以弹钢琴时娴熟的指法出名。

3. ambidextrous: [ˌæmbiˈdekstrəs] *a.* 两只手都灵巧的

分解记忆法：ambi-（两个都）+ dexter-（右）+ ity（名词后缀）=（左手和右手一样灵活）两只手都灵巧的

【例句】After much exercise, he is ambidextrous in playing the piano.

在大量练习后，他演奏钢琴时双手很灵活。

You need to practice more to get the ambidextrous level.

你要多加练习以达到双手灵活的水平。

常用派生词：ambidextrous → ambidexterity

4. mediate: [ˈmidieit] *v.* 调停

分解记忆法：medi-（中间）+ -ate（动词后缀）=（居中的位置）调停

【例句】The government mediates between the workers and the employers.

政府在工人和雇主之间斡旋。

The army leaders have mediated a cease-fire treaty.

军队领导人居间促成了一个停火协定。

常用派生词：mediate → mediation → mediator

5. medieval: [ˌmediˈi:vəl] *a.* 中世纪的

分解记忆法：medi-（中间）+ ev-（时代）+ -al（……的）= 中世纪的

【例句】The medieval age refers to the period between the 5th century and the 15th century.

中世纪指的是5世纪到15世纪这段时期。

The city is famous for the medieval architecture.

这座城市以中世纪的建筑闻名。

6. concentrate: [ˈkɔnsəntreit] *v.* 集中

分解记忆法：con（共同）+ centr-（中间）+ -ate（动词后缀）= 集中

【例句】This year the company concentrates on improving its efficiency.

这家公司今年把精力集中在提高效率方面。
Industrial development is being concentrated in the south of the country.
目前工业发展集中在这个国家的南部。

常用派生词：concentrate → concentration → concentrated

7. eccentric: [ikˈsentrik] *a. & n.* 古怪的；古怪的人

分解记忆法：ec-(离)+ centr-(中间)+ -ic(……的)=(离开中心的)古怪的；古怪的人

【例句】If you go to the party in tennis shoes, they'll think you're rather eccentric.
如果你穿网球鞋去宴会，人家一定会认为你很古怪。
The old lady is a bit of an eccentric.
那个老妇人有点古怪。

8. egocentric: [ˌiːgəuˈsentrik] *a.* 以自我为中心的

分解记忆法：ego-(自我)+ centr-(中间)+ ic(……的)= 以自我为中心的

【例句】I think you're egocentric by not letting her go.
我觉得你不让她离开这样很自私。
It is an egocentric behavior to choose the easy work.
挑简单的工作来做，这是一种自私的行为。

9. lateral: [ˈlætərəl] *a.* 侧面的；横向的

分解记忆法：later-(边)+ al(……的)= 侧面的；横向的

【例句】The lateral room has little sunshine.
侧面的屋子没什么阳光照进来。
We should develop staff's aptitude of the lateral thinking.
我们应该培养员工的横向思考能力。

10. collateral: [kəˈlætərəl] *a.* 并行的；平行的

分解记忆法：col-(一起)+ later-(边)+ -al(……的)= 并行的；平行的

【例句】A collateral aim of the government's industrial strategy is to increase employment.
政府工业战略的一个附带项目就是增加就业。
Cousins are collateral relatives but brothers are directly related.
表兄弟是旁系亲属，但兄弟是直系亲属。

11. dilate: [daiˈleit] *v.* 扩大；膨胀

分解记忆法：di-(分离)+ -late(边)=(边与边分离)扩大；膨胀

【例句】Her eyes dilated with terror.
她吓得瞪大了眼睛。
Red wine can help to dilate blood vessels.
红酒有助于扩张血管。

12. fund: [fʌnd] *n.& v.* 资金；提供资金

分解记忆法：fund 资金；提供资金

【例句】Part of school sports fund will be used to improve the football pitch.

部分学校运动会基金将用来整修足球场。

The scientists' search for a cure for this disease is being funded by the government.

科学家在研究治疗这种疾病的疗法，其资金是由政府提供的。

13. **fundamental:** [ˌfʌndəˈmentl] *a.* **基础的**

    分解记忆法：fund-(底) + ament(名词后缀) + -al(……的) = 基础的

    【例句】The changes will have to be fundamental if they are to have any effect.

    变革如果要起作用，就必须是根本性的。

    The fundamental purpose of the plan is to encourage further development.

    计划的主要目的是鼓励进一步发展。

14. **found:** [faund] *v.* **建立**

    分解记忆法：found(打底子) = 建立

    【例句】Her family founded the college in 1895.

    她的家族于1895年创办了这所学院。

    Their marriage was founded on love and mutual respect.

    他们的婚姻建立在爱情和相互尊重的基础上。

    常用派生词：found → foundation → founder

15. **profound:** [prəˈfaund] *a.* **深刻的**

    分解记忆法：pro-(向前) + found(底) = (伸向底部)深刻的

    【例句】Her father's death has a profound effect on her.

    她父亲的过世对她影响很大。

    He can always bring the readers profound creation.

    他总是能给读者带来意义深刻的创作。

    常用派生词：profound → profundity

Words in Use

1. She untied the knots with ____ fingers.

    A. adroit　　　　B. capable　　　　C. skilled　　　　D. devout

2. The temple was full of ____ praying.

    A. diagnosis　　B. diabetes　　　C. devotees　　　D. dexterity

3. You need practice more to get the ____ level.

    A. ancillary　　B. ancient　　　C. ambidextrous　D. ambitious

4. The government ____ between the employees and the employers.

    A. melts　　　　B. mellows　　　C. mediates　　　D. meditates

5. She is famous for the ____ with which she plays the violin.

    A. dexterity　　B. diabetes　　　C. diagnosis　　　D. devotion

6. Although it is a ____ story, she was moved deeply.
   A. meddlesome   B. mediocre   C. meditative   D. massive
7. There is no doubt that he can gain the award because he is ____ in the work all the time.
   A. conniving   B. dexterous   C. conscientious   D. conscious
8. I am only a ____ and want to have a common life like others.
   A. mediocrity   B. medium   C. media   D. mediator
9. The law includes special ____ for certain religious groups.
   A. condensation   B. conception   C. concession   D. concentration
10. A ____ aim of the government's industrial strategy is to accelerate the speed of the development.
    A. collusive   B. collective   C. collateral   D. collected
11. Part of school sports ____ will be used to improve the gym.
    A. fumes   B. funds   C. funnel   D. function
12. Most of our meetings were ____ to discussing the housing problem.
    A. diabolical   B. diabetic   C. devoted   D. dexterous
13. Do you have some ____ ideas about what we should do?
    A. concessive   B. concerted   C. concentrated   D. concrete
14. He interrupted my ____ upon the reason of that event.
    A. medium   B. media   C. meditation   D. mediation
15. Their marriage was ____ on love and the mutual respect.
    A. fount   B. founded   C. found   D. funded
16. The changes will have to be ____ if they are to have any effect.
    A. synchronous   B. fundamental   C. important   D. fervent
17. I think you're ____ by not letting her go.
    A. selfish   B. clever   C. dexterous   D. concentrated
18. After long exercise, he made obvious progress in the ____ of the fingers.
    A. diabetes   B. dextrose   C. devotion   D. dexterity
19. The army leaders have ____ a ceasefire treaty, which brought peace to the area.
    A. melted   B. mediated   C. mellowed   D. meditated
20. There is a ____ of industry in the south of the country.
    A. concentration B. conception   C. concession   D. conclusion
21. If you go to the party in tennis shoes, they'll think you're rather ____.
    A. unconventional B. ebullient   C. passionate   D. concentrated
22. They were very ____ for their children.
    A. conscientious B. conscious   C. ambitious   D. ambidextrous
23. I hear you're ____ giving up your job.
    A. mediating   B. considering   C. memorizing   D. melting

24. I can't ____ why you told her all the things.

    A. concern　　　　B. conceive　　　　C. concentrate　　　　D. concatenate

25. It's my ____ hope that he will never come back.

    A. dewy　　　　B. devout　　　　C. dexterous　　　　D. diabolical

26. This year the company ____ on improving its efficiency.

    A. conceals　　　　B. concedes　　　　C. concentrates　　　　D. conceives

27. The problem is that the factory is in lack of the ____ mechanic.

    A. dewy　　　　B. diabolical　　　　C. devout　　　　D. dexterous

28. Television can be a ____ for giving information and opinions, for amazing people, and for teaching them.

    A. medium　　　　B. mediation　　　　C. meditation　　　　D. medication

29. The skilled worker untied the knots with her ____ fingers.

    A. diabolic　　　　B. devout　　　　C. dexterous　　　　D. dewy

30. He ____ for two days before giving his answer.

    A. meditated　　　　B. mediated　　　　C. mergered　　　　D. meted

Key to Words in Use

1. A	2. C	3. C	4. C	5. A
6. B	7. C	8. A	9. C	10. C
11. B	12. C	13. D	14. C	15. B
16. B	17. A	18. D	19. B	20. A
21. A	22. C	23. B	24. B	25. B
26. C	27. D	28. A	29. C	30. A

第32章 表示"名字"的词根

Words in Context

Pseudonym

A pen name is a **pseudonym** adopted by authors or their publishers, often to conceal their identity. One famous example of this is Samuel Clemens writing under the pen name Mark Twain. A pen name may be used if a writer's real name is likely to be confused with the name of another writer or notable individual, or if their real name is deemed to be unsuitable. Authors who write in fiction and non-fiction, or in different genres, may use pen names to avoid confusing their readers, as in the case of mathematician Charles Dodgson, who wrote fantasy novels under the pen name Lewis Carroll. The Bronte family also used **pseudonyms** for their early works, so the local communities did not know their books were actually based on them. The Brontes used their neighbors' stories as inspiration for characters in many of their books. Anne Bronte published her poem "The Narrow Way" under the pseudonym Acton Belle. Charlotte Bronte wrote *Shirley* and *Jane Eyre* under the pseudonym Currer Belle. Emily Bronte wrote *Wuthering Heights* under Ellis Belle. Some female authors used male pen names, particularly in the 19th century, when it was **ignominious** and unacceptable for women to write novels.

Word Building

More Words with the Word Roots

词根	释义	例词
onym	名字	anonymous, homonym, pseudonym, synonym
nom		nominal, binominal, polynomial, misnomer
nomin		nominate, denominate, ignominious, ignominy

1. **anonymous**: [əˈnɔnɪməs] *a.* 无名的；匿名的

    分解记忆法：an-(无) + onym-(名字) + -ous(……的) = 无名的；匿名的

    【例句】The flowers were sent by an anonymous admirer.

    这些花是一位不具名的爱慕者送来的。

The writer of the article wishes to retain anonymous.

文章的作者希望不署名。

常用派生词：anonymous → anonymity

2. anonymity: [ˌænəˈnimiti] *n.* 无名；匿名

分解记忆法：an-(无)＋onym-(名字)＋-ity(名词后缀)＝无名；匿名

【例句】The defendants' anonymity was maintained until they were brought to court.

被告人的姓名一直不公开，直到他们被带上法庭时才予以披露。

He agreed to receive an interview on condition of anonymity.

他同意在不披露姓名的条件下接受采访。

3. pseudonym: [ˈsjuːdənim] *n.* 假名；笔名

分解记忆法：pseud-(假的)＋-onym(名字)＝假名；笔名

【例句】She writes under a pseudonym.

她用笔名写作。

In the 18th century many women published their novels in a pseudonym of a man.

在18世纪，很多妇女用男性的笔名来发表小说。

4. nominal: [ˈnɔminl] *a.* 名义上的；挂名的

分解记忆法：nomin-(名字)＋-al(……的)＝名义上的；挂名的

【例句】The old man is only the nominal head of the company, while his daughter makes all the decision.

这个老人只是这家公司名义上的老板，他女儿做出所有决策。

He is the nominal head of the company.

他是这家公司名义上的老板。

5. nominate: [ˈnɔmineit] *v.* 提名

分解记忆法：nomin-(名字)＋-ate(动词后缀)＝提名

【例句】I wish to nominate him for the president of the club.

我想提名他做俱乐部的主席。

The director nominated me as his official representative at the conference.

董事指定我作为他的正式代表出席会议。

常用派生词：nominate → nomination → nominee

6. nomination: [ˌnɔmiˈneiʃən] *n.* 提名

分解记忆法：nomin-(名字)＋-ation(名词后缀)＝提名

【例句】His nomination as chief executive was rejected by the board.

他被提名为行政总裁的事被董事会否决了。

Who will get the Republican nomination for president?

谁将被共和党提名竞选总统？

7. misnomer: [ˌmisˈnəumə] *n.* 误称；用词不当

分解记忆法：mis(错)＋nom-(名字)＋-er(名词后缀)＝误称；用词不当

【例句】Villa was something of a misnomer; that place was no more than an old farmhouse.

别墅一说有点不妥，那地方只不过是座旧农舍。

The misnomer of the phrase made quite a joke.

对这个短语的误用闹了很大一个笑话。

8. **denominate:** [diˈnɔmineit] *v.* 命名

   分解记忆法：de-（下）+ nomin-（名字）+ -ate（动词后缀）=（把名称定下）命名

   【例句】The meteor is denominated after the scientist who found it.

   这颗流星用发现它的科学家的名字命名。

   People denominate the meteor after his name to memorize his contribution in this field.

   人们用他的名字来命名这颗流星，以此来纪念他在这一领域的贡献。

   常用派生词：denominate → denomination → denominator

9. **denomination:** [diˌnɔmiˈneiʃən] *n.* 教派

   分解记忆法：de-（下）+ nomin-（名字）+ -ation（名词后缀）= 教派

   【例句】The service was attended by Christians of all denominations.

   这次礼拜仪式各教派的基督徒都参加了。

   She believes her denomination fervently.

   她虔诚地相信她的教派。

10. **ignominious:** [ˌignəˈminiəs] *a.* 丢脸的；耻辱的

    分解记忆法：ig-（没有）+ nomin-（名字）+ -ous（……的）=（没有好名字的）丢脸的；耻辱的

    【例句】He regarded it as an ignominious defeat.

    他把它看成是一次不光彩的失败。

    We should eliminate this ignominious behavior in order to build a harmonious society.

    为了建成和谐社会，我们应该杜绝这种不光彩的行为。

    常用派生词：ignominious → ignominy

Words in Use

1. The old man is only the ＿＿ head of the company, while his wife makes all the decision.
   A. nomad   B. normal   C. abnormal   D. nominal
2. The director <u>nominated</u> me as his official representative at the conference. Which of the following is the synonym of the underlined word?
   A. announced   B. appointed   C. illustrated   D. demonstrated
3. She received the prize with an air of <u>nonchalance</u>. Which of the following is the synonym

of the underlined word?

    A. nominal   B. unconcerned   C. nominative   D. noncommittal

4. The criminal agreed to receive an interview in the condition of ____.

    A. anniversary   B. annuity   C. anonymity   D. annoyance

5. The club agreed to all the committee's ____.

    A. nomination   B. information   C. confession   D. denomination

6. His ____ as chief executive was rejected by the board.

    A. ambition   B. nomination   C. administration   D. legislation

7. People ____ the meteor after the scientist's name to remember his contribution in this field.

    A. denude   B. denounce   C. denote   D. denominate

8. Names of people in the documentary were changed to preserve ____.

    A. anonymity   B. ambiguity   C. animosity   D. annuity

9. A smile often ____ the feeling of pleasure.

    A. defuses   B. denominate   C. denudes   D. denotes

10. The workers were kept in complete ____ of the company's financial situation.

    A. ignominy   B. ignorance   C. anonymity   D. misnomer

11. The excellent book attempts to ____ the whole subject of computers.

    A. demystify   B. denote   C. denominate   D. nomenclature

12. The author of the book wishes to retain ____.

    A. simultaneous   B. synchronous   C. ignominious   D. anonymous

13. We are all curious about this expensive but ____ gift.

    A. binomial   B. ignominious   C. anonymous   D. nominal

14. Wind and rain had ____ the mountainside of soil.

    A. denoted   B. denounced   C. denuded   D. denominated

15. We should remember the history when we were forced to sign so many ____ treaties with the foreign invaders.

    A. ignominious   B. abnormal   C. eccentric   D. anonymous

16. He regarded it as an <u>ignominious</u> defeat. Which of the following is NOT the synonym of the underlined word?

    A. departed   B. humiliating   C. shameful   D. ignoble

17. The noisy traffic is a continual ____.

    A. animosity   B. anodyne   C. anonymity   D. annoyance

18. The government would be unwise to ____ the growing dissatisfaction with its economic policies.

    A. demonstrate   B. nominate   C. ignore   D. identify

19. The president issued a tough ____ of terrorism.

    A. demonstration   B. denotation   C. denunciation   D. denomination

20. He regarded it as a (n) ____ defeat.
    A. identical	B. ignominious	C. idle	D. ignorant
21. She graduated from a ____ school and then she worked here as a teacher for about 20 years.
    A. demure	B. density	C. denotative	D. denominational
22. After the meeting, the two leaders produced an ____ statement that didn't really say anything at all.
    A. annual	B. anodyne	C. anonymous	D. animated
23. The service was attended by Christians of all ____.
    A. denunciation	B. denominations	C. connotation	D. denotation
24. People <u>denominate</u> the meteor after his name to memorize his contribution in this field. Which of the following is the synonym of the underlined word?
    A. name	B. recall	C. denote	D. notice
25. Villa was something of a ____; that place was just an old farmhouse.
    A. misdeed	B. mischief	C. misnomer	D. misleading
26. I wish to ____ him for the CEO of the company.
    A. legitimate	B. nominate	C. denominate	D. legislate
27. I ask him to vote for me but he was ____.
    A. ignominious	B. anonymous	C. abnormal	D. noncommittal
28. The life of the ____ in the desert is very mysterious for me.
    A. nomad	B. nominal	C. eccentric	D. abnormal
29. She writes under a ____.
    A. ignominy	B. pseudonym	C. homonym	D. anonym
30. The book was sent by an ____ admirer.
    A. animated	B. anonymous	C. anodyne	D. annual

Key to *Words in Use*

1. D	2. B	3. B	4. C	5. A
6. B	7. D	8. A	9. D	10. B
11. A	12. D	13. C	14. C	15. A
16. A	17. D	18. C	19. C	20. B
21. D	22. B	23. B	24. A	25. C
26. B	27. D	28. A	29. B	30. B

第四篇　英语其他构词法

第1章　复合法

复合法（compounding或composition）：也叫合成法，是把两个或两个以上的词按照一定的次序排列构成新词的方法，该方法构成的词叫合成词（compound words）或复合词，该方法可以构成复合名词、复合形容词、复合动词等。多数复合词可以通过其组成部分猜测到词义。例如，electrocardiograph这个词就是由electro（电）cardio（心）graph（图）三个部分复合而成的，这种复合词是理据词（motivated）。复合词往往使语言表达言简意赅，形象生动。只要稍加注意，就会发现复合词的使用比比皆是。如：greenhouse，homepage，breakthrough，blackboard，round-the-clock等。合成词的语义有的可以由结合的原词语义简单相加，如：black（黑色的）+board（木板）→blackboard（黑板）。但对于一些合成词来说，两个或两个以上的词一旦结合成合成词后，语义不是原来两个或几个词的语义简单相加，而是从中引出新的语义。例如:greenhouse（温室），looker-on（旁观者)等等。

第1单元　复合名词

复合名词是由两个或两个以上的词按一定的次序排列成的。复合名词词义简洁明了，往往能表达普通名词难以表达的概念，复合名词构成的方法有很多种。动词与副词直接相连，例如：blowup 爆炸，comeback 复原，复辟。动词、副词用连字符连接，例如：get-together联欢会。副词与动词用连字符连接，例如：by-pass 旁道，支流。动词 -ing 形式与副词分开，如：coming in 进入，开始。 动词 -ing 形式与副词由连字符连接，如：bringing-up 养育，抚养。副词与动词 -ing 形式直接相连，如：ingoing 进入。副词与动词 -ing 形式用连字符连接，如：out-clearing 票据交换额。（不规则）动词的过去分词与副词直接相连，如：leftover 剩余物，吃剩的饭。（不规则）动词的过去分词与副词用连字符相连，如：grown-up 成年人。副词与（不规则）动词的过去分词直接相连，如：upshot 结果，结局。副词与（不规则）动词的过去分词用连字符连接，如：by-gone往事。随着社会和语言的发展，还会有更多形式的复合名词出现。

Words in Context

Penguins

These cute seabirds have wings, but they cannot fly. They wear a black or blue-gray overcoat, and they have a white belly, a pair of short legs, and two wings that serve as flippers.

There are 18 species of them. We must look at their heads and necks to tell one species from another. Some have a pair of long, yellow eyebrows; some have a rock star hairstyle; some have lemon-yellow and orange markings on their cheeks, and some just have no special markings at all. When these seabirds walk on land, they look clumsy. Yet, when they dive into the water, they become excellent swimmers! Most of them live in places covered by snow and ice all year round in the Southern Hemisphere, but some are found in warmer areas near the equator. What are they? These cute seabirds are penguins!

King penguins and emperor penguins are the two largest types in their family. King penguins can reach a height of 38 inches, and emperor penguins can be 48 inches tall. The smallest penguin is the little blue penguin from Australia and New Zealand—when it stands straight, it is just about 16 inches tall. Big penguins have some advantages over their smaller relatives—big penguins can stay warm more easily so they can live in a colder climate; big penguins can dive deeper and stay underwater longer so they can catch food far below the surface.

Words in Use

I. Find the compound nouns in the above passage.

II. Find the compound nouns in the following sentences:
1. Alaska's state flower is the alpine forget-me-not. The best time to see the alpine forget-me-not is midsummer, from late June to late July.
2. The sunrise walk was just the beginning of a full day of games, concerts and a parade of old cars.
3. Some people believe that one's blood type determines one's character traits.
4. Unemployment has been the keynote of the conference.
5. He prefers green tea to coffee.
6. After years of quarrelling we at last sent our cousins a Christmas card as an olive-branch.
7. Factory managers understate their potential output.
8. Aspirin is a good stand-by for headaches.
9. They were scared by the sound of the gunshot.
10. Given goodwill on both sides, I'm sure we can reach an agreement.
11. Each person's fingerprints are unique.
12. These fig-leaves have all fallen down.
13. Finally, it discusses the remaining existing problems and their aftereffect of our policy.
14. I heard his footsteps in the hall.
15. The strain of his job led to the complete breakdown of his health.

Key to *Words in Use*

I.

seabird   overcoat   eyebrow   hairstyle

II.

1. forget-me-not   2. sunrise   3. blood type   4. keynote   5. green tea
6. olive-branch   7. output   8. stand-by   9. gunshot   10. Goodwill
11. fingerprint   12. fig-leaf   13. aftereffect   14. footstep   15. breakdown

第2单元　复合形容词

　　复合形容词（compound adjective）是复合词里的一类。它是由两个或两个以上独立的词复合而成的形容词。与普通形容词一样，在句子中通常起定语或表语的作用。
　　复合形容词的构成方法很多：
　　名词+形容词构成的复合形容词，例如：world-famous（闻名的）。形容词+形容词构成，例如：deep-yellow（深黄色的）。现在分词+形容词构成，例如：soaking-wet（湿透的）。形容词+名词构成，例如：first-rate（一流的）。名词+名词+-ed构成，例如：chick-hearted（胆怯的）。数词+名词构成，例如：a five-year plan（一个五年计划）。形容词+名词+-ed构成，例如：cold-blooded（冷血的）。数词+名词+-ed构成，例如：a one-eyed man（一个一只眼的人）。动词+名词构成，例如：break-neck（危险的)。名词+动词的过去分词构成，例如：poverty-stricken（贫穷的）。名词+动词的现在分词构成，例如：peace-loving（热爱和平的）。动词+连词+动词构成，例如：hit-or-miss（偶然的）。动词+副词（或介词）构成，例如：stand-up collars（竖领的）。形容词+现在分词构成，例如：strong-looking（看上去很强壮的)。副词（或形容词、名词）+现在分词构成，例如：ever-lasting（永久的）。动词+动词的过去分词（或形容词）构成，例如：get-ready（随时可……的）。副词+动词的过去分词构成，例如：well-known（很出名的)。

Words in Context

Starting of International Self-Employment

　　Motivation is the key factor in deciding on being self-employed or working in an international company.

　　Although most of the internationally placed candidates have the best of intentions to be self-confident and open-minded, the majority become depressed and apathetic. It can be a traumatic experience for some, to be in an environment so far removed from what you are accustomed to. The idea of not having a job or career to qualify your name with can be especially gloomy to some people.

　　It is important to remember to take small steps initially, and be pleased with each and every accomplishment you make, no matter how simple it might be. In some countries, everyday shopping can be exhaustive and time consuming. Opening a bank account or buying postage stamps on your own should be simple tasks, but often are complicated procedures in international countries.

Words in Use

I. Find the compound adjectives in the above passage.

II. Find the compound adjectives in the following sentences:

1. Today a twenty-year-old man was arrested.
2. Please accept my heart-felt thanks.
3. This raincoat is water-proof.
4. Success often goes to those who are hard-working.
5. That ordinary-looking girl is the ideal wife for him.
6. He often looked back upon his bitter-sweet days when studying abroad.
7. It is biting-cold today, so please put on more clothes.
8. The first full-length Disney film was *Snow White*.
9. The sweet witty soul of Ovid lives in mellifluous and honey-tongued Shakespeare.
10. He promised to buy his son a ten-speed bicycle as his birthday gift.
11. The woman was broken-hearted and close to tears.
12. Other animals and habitats under threat include the greater Asian one-horned rhinos, of which only 2,400 survive in the grasslands of northern India, Nepal and Bhutan.
13. I can see from the telltale look in her eyes that she loves him.
14. Now, Mr. Zhou Wenbin from Sanli Electronics is talking to Mr. Smith, director of a shoe-making enterprise in a small town.
15. The results of physical exercise test of the subjects were collected, including standing long-jump, 1500 meter long-distance running and 50 m×8 come-and-go running.

Key to *Words in Use*

I.
self-employed, self-confident, open-minded, time consuming

II.

1. twenty-year-old	2. heart-felt	3. water-proof
4. hard-working	5. ordinary-looking	6. bitter-sweet
7. biting-cold	8. full-length	9. honey-tongued
10. ten-speed	11. broken-hearted	12. one-horned
13. telltale	14. shoe-making	15. come-and-go

第3单元　复合动词

复合动词可以由两个词复合而成，例如dry-clean（干洗），ill-treat（虐待）等，但复合动词主要是通过转化法或逆生法从复合名词变来的，比如，复合动词 honeymoon（度蜜月）是由复合名词honeymoon（蜜月）转化来的；复合动词outline（画出……轮廓）是由复合名词outline（轮廓）转化来的。复合动词sightsee(观光）是由复合名词sightseeing（观光)逆生而成的；复合动词mass-produce（成批生产）是由复合名词mass-production（成批生产）逆生而成的。

Words in Context

Want to Live Longer?

　　If you want to live a long time, there are seven golden rules, say the experts. You should be married, live in a small town and have a job that requires physical activity. And you should not smoke. It is the most dangerous to chain-smoke. Nor should you become overweight. You should drive within the speed limits, wearing a safety belt, although you like overtaking. And you should have regular medical examinations.

　　It helps if you're a woman—on average they outlive men by six years—and your chances improve if your parents and grandparents each lived to a ripe old age. Currently the average lifespan for a man living within developed countries is 70 years; 76 is normal for a woman.

　　Want to live longer?

　　The number one killer in many countries is heart disease, caused by fatty deposits. Scientists have noticed that, while heart disease is the single biggest health problem in Britain and America, it is not a serious problem in Japan.

　　Yet the Japanese have the world's highest cigarette-smoking rate, high average blood pressure and lead stressful lives. The difference is that they eat a lot of fish and vegetables and very little meat and dairy products.

　　It is also true that heart problems are almost as uncommon in Mediterranean countries where they eat plenty of fish and less red meat.

　　High blood pressure makes a heart attack more likely, and one of the most common causes is being overweight. As a guide, scientists say you should not be more than four or five kilograms heavier than you were at 20—assuming that you were not then overweight. Obese people find it difficult to stop overeating. The only safe, sure way to lose weight is to cut the proportion of fat and added sugar in your diet, exercise and keep your calorie intake to a reasonable level. Some try to beat nature with treatments such as the injections of sheep cells, but there's no scientific evidence that they work.

Words in Use

I. Find the compound verbs in the above passage.

II. Find the compound verbs in the following sentences:

1. She emulously tried to outdo her elder sister.
2. Proofread the English Ad once a week by email.
3. They are honeymooning in Paris.
4. His critics say he is stalling for time to handpick a favored successor to run again if the first round is invalidated.
5. Low-income women may be more likely to breastfeed their infants if they get a little encouragement from their peers, a new study suggests.
6. Manna could baby-sit one night if your father has to work.
7. Cars have to be mass-produced in order to meet the increasing demand.
8. Can this fridge quick-freeze food?
9. They beat and ill-use me, and I am going to seek my fortune, some long way off.
10. Common goals can downplay differences.
11. It's going to be hard to take it down. Can you airdrop us anything?
12. After he double crossed his best friend, everyone gave him the cold shoulder.
13. I have started to learn how to ice skate and now I can even skate by myself.
14. As an organizer of this activity, how will you take them to sightsee?
15. They successfully trial-produced a new kind of hair-restorer.

Key to *Words in Use*
I.
chain-smoke   overtake   outlive   overeat
II.

1. outdo	2. Proofread	3. honeymooning	4. handpick
5. breastfeed	6. baby sit	7. mass-produced	8. quick-freeze
9. ill-use	10. downplay	11. airdrop	12. double crossed
13. ice skate	14. sightsee	15. trial-produced	

第2章　词类转化法

词类转化法（conversion, functional shift 或 transmutation）简称转化法，是指不改变词的形态，只是使词从一种词类转化为另一种词类，从而使该词具有新的意义和作用，成为一个新词，也有人把这种构词方法叫作"零位后缀派生法"（derivation by zero suffix），又简称"零位派生法"（zero-derivation）。零位派生法这个名称在一定程度上说明转化法只是派生法的一种特殊形式。例如：beauty n. + -fy →beautify v.； lovely a. + -ness →loveliness n.。后缀没有改变词的基本意思，只不过是改变了词类而已。转化法是用加"零位后缀"（即不加后缀）的方法，使一个词改变词类。

转化法是英语形成新词的重要方法之一，英语的实词不但多义，而且同一个词还可以属于一种以上的词类。各种词类的词经常转化，致使一个词往往可以用作几种词类。例如：name（名字）这个单词起初是名词，后来转化成动词，意思是命名、取名。此外，从一种词类又可以转化为另一种词类，其中以名词转化为动词、动词转化为名词以及形容词转化为动词，这三种最为普遍、最为生动。转化后的词具有该词基本的特性，因此转化名词有如真正名词，转化动词就像真正动词。英语中多数单音节名词都有与它相同形式的动词，例如：work, cup, deck, walk, grade 等。英语词类转化，最常见的是转成动词和转成名词。

第1单元　名词转化成动词

英语里的很多动词是由名词转化而来的。许多表示物件的名词可以转化为动词，意思也随之有些改变，例如：She had booked three seats on the plane.（她订了三个飞机上的座位。）The committee is chaired by General Lee.（委员会由李将军任主席。）表示身体某部分的名词也可用作动词，例如：His name headed the list.（他的名字列在名单之首）；He handed the glass of beer to Grandpa.（他把那杯啤酒递给了爷爷。）表示一类人的名词也可用作动词，例如：He is paid by the police to spy on other students.（他受警方雇用来监视其他学生。）It's hard to pilot a boat in rough waters.（在汹涌的水域中领航是困难的。）一些其他实物名词也可用作动词，例如：The library houses 600,000 books.（这个图书馆藏书60万册。）Cherry trees flower in the early spring.（樱桃树早春时开花。）甚至有些抽象名词也可用作动词，例如：The injustice of this angered him.（这事的不公平使他气愤。）I am hungering for news from you.（我渴望得到你的消息。）从以上可以看出，在现代英语词汇里，转化词很多。其中的名词转化为动词的趋势更为显著，原因是转化动词很有生气，极富吸引力。

Words in Context

Self-image

Do you have a self-image that can help you succeed or one that can make you fail? Let's work out what self-image is all about. Get a picture in your mind of two empty chairs. In the two chairs let's picture two visitors. In the first chair let's seat a young man who is deaf. In the second chair let's seat a young boy who was born with part of one foot missing.

The young man we picked for the first chair was a musician. He was a great artist. He composed many great songs. When he was a young man he lost his hearing. It is generally believed that a person cannot be a professional musician or compose music without hearing, but this man had a special driving force that enabled him to write some of the most beautiful music ever written. This man was Beethoven.

The visitor in the second chair was a young boy who was born with part of one foot missing. This young boy loved sports, especially football. As a young boy and later as a young man he had always dreamed of playing football with a major league football team. He had a thirst that could not be quenched. Finally, he made it into the New Orleans Saints football team and one day on the football field in New Orleans he kicked the longest field goal in football history. His name is Tom Dempsey.

If you try to find the special strength that turns an ordinary person into a hero it only exists in the heart or soul of man. It is called a positive self-image. A positive self-image is a great belief in yourself and your ideas.

Words in Use

I. Find the noun-to-verb conversions in the above passage.

II. Find the verbs conversed from nouns in the following sentences.

1. Be sure to lock your bicycle when you leave it outside.
2. These goals form the focus for a product's overall design, strategy, and branding.
3. They questioned her closely about her friendship with the arrested man but they found nothing.
4. She arrived at the interview armed with lists of statistics.
5. The police are investigating the murder shrouded in mystery.
6. I was trapped into telling the police all I had done to the dog.
7. When I arrived home from my shop, I flaked out on the sofa.

8. These criminals planned to go on a hunger strike, but they gave up the attention in the end.
9. He was trying to plant the seed of revolt, arouse that placid peasant docility.
10. Spatial organization of these within a pane or window is critical to minimizing extraneous mouse movements that, at best, could result in user annoyance and fatigue, and at worst, result in repetitive stress injury.
11. We order him to go out immediately.
12. Tell Juan to get the fix and log it right away.
13. Interaction designers often face the conundrum of whether to make their products user-customizable.
14. I saw him pedal to school every morning.
15. This again may point to the need to perform additional research directed at finding particular behaviors missing from your behavioral axes.

Key to *Words in Use*

I.

work, picture, seat, play

II.

1. lock	2. form	3. questioned	4. armed	5. shrouded
6. trapped	7. flaked	8. planned	9. plant	10. result
11. order	12. log	13. face	14. pedal	15. point

第2单元　形容词转化成动词

在第1单元我们谈到名词转化成动词的情况，除了名词可以转化成动词外，形容词也可以转化成动词，但不如名词转化成动词那样常见。形容词转化成动词大多数表示状态的变化。例如，形容词dry（干的），转化成动词dry（变干；使……变干）；形容词dirty（脏的），转化成动词dirty（变脏；使……变脏）；形容词warm（温暖的），转化成动词warm（变温暖；使……变温暖）。类似的形容词还有narrow, dim, empty, cool, slow等。

以上的形容词转化成的动词既能用作及物动词也能用作不及物动词。有的形容词只能转化成及物动词，例如:形容词free（自由的），转化成动词free（释放）；形容词humble（谦恭的），转化成动词humble（压低……的身份）。少数形容词转化成动词，表达的意思是以某种姿态或方式去做某事。比如：形容词brave（勇敢的），转化成动词brave（敢于……，冒着……）；形容词rough（粗糙的），转化成动词rough（粗暴地对待……）等。

Words in Context

The Hospice

The man whose hair has grayed sat quietly beside his dying wife's bed. He took meals on a tray and returned home only to sleep.

Several days later she was gone, and so was he. They had been married 55 years, the nurse said. Down the hall, two young men played loud music and watched video —it was a send-off party. The young men stayed deep into the night, as the night cooled. One brought his friend's dog to say goodbye.

The first hospice opened in the United States in 1974. Since then, hospice use has grown strikingly. As Americans get old, hospital costs rise sharply and patients decide that death, like birth, is a natural process rather than a medical procedure. Hospices neither accelerate nor lower the speed of death. Instead, they wish to give the patients and their families the most comfortable, painless, decent death possible.

"That really has been the feature of the hospice. Managing the emotional aspects of dying is as important as managing the physical pain of the patient," said Rosemary Crowley, head of the Illinois State Hospice Organization.

In the last five years, the number of US hospices jumped by nearly half, to 2510 last July from 1743 in 1990, according to the National Hospice Organization. In 1994, there were

340,000 patients, up 62 percent from 1990.

Most patients enter hospice care on a doctor's introduction when they have six months or less to live. Although 70 percent have cancer and most are elderly, hospices care for all ages and hopeless illnesses.

Words in Use

I. Find the verbs conversed from adjectives in the above passage.

II. Find the verbs conversed from adjectives in the following sentences:

1. Please warm up the dish over the stove before your father comes back.
2. Shelley was unable to calm her, so he asked his sister for help.
3. We must lower our expenses, otherwise we can't make ends meet.
4. Living conditions have bettered a great deal.
5. Don't idle away your precious time.
6. Language skills can be perfected by constant practice and regular reinforcement.
7. The hot weather soured the fresh milk.
8. How do you quiet a fretful child?
9. The man's muscles tensed as he saw the snake approaching him.
10. After a bath I dry myself with a towel.
11. It is easy to open a shop but hard to keep it always prosperous.
12. Clean out the bathtub when you are done.
13. Everything possible should be done to free them from the economic taint.
14. Altogether the situation was so unpleasant that Lucy determined to clear out.
15. The war might narrow the gulf.

Key to *Words in Use*

I.

gray, cool, open, lower

II.

1. warm	2. calm	3. lower	4. bettered	5. idle
6. perfected	7. soured	8. quiet	9. tensed	10. dry
11. open	12. Clean	13. free	14. clear	15. narrow

第3单元　动词转化成名词

　　由动词转化成的名词多数表示原来的动作或状态。例如：attempt（尝试），doubt（怀疑），desire（愿望），laugh（大笑），stroll（溜达）等等。这些由动词转化成的名词大多可以和have，take，give，make等动词连用，表示短暂的或一次性的动作。例如:have a look，have a swim，have a try，have a rest，have a glimpse，give a cry，give a howl，make a guess，make an attempt等。有一些由动词转化成的名词意思是动作的执行者，是从事某工作的人，例如：cook（厨师），coach（教练）等。还有一些由动词转化成的名词意思是动作的执行者，但带有贬义，指令人反感的人或物。例如：cheat（骗子），sneak（打小报告的人），bore（令人厌烦的人，烦人的状况或事情）等。有一些由动词转化成的名词意思是某工具，例如：catch（门闩，钩子），cover（盖子），cure（药剂）等。有一些由动词转化成的名词意思是动作的结果，例如：reply（回复），export（出口商品），catch（捕获物）等。有一些由动词转化成的名词表示某地点，例如：pass（关口），retreat（隐居处），divide（分水岭，分水线）等。

Words in Context

Changes

　　Change is a word that can bring either fear or excitement. It is human nature to oppose change because it requires us to cross into the unknown. As a result, most people are in a fight to keep from losing something they are familiar with than in seeking potential benefits from something new.

　　The workplace now is not just changing, but it is changing at an even faster pace. Technology is the thrust behind the appearance of the new economy. It is opening new opportunities for business to operate more efficiently and competitively.

　　Businesses aim at generating a profit instead of creating jobs. Those who take the greatest risks should be the ones who earn the most. That is the base of our enterprise system. We all need to assess what impact our efforts have on working favorably toward the bottom line. There is no inherent right to a job, especially if it has a negative impact upon growth.

　　Workers of all backgrounds should pay attention to the changes taking place throughout the economy. Communication skills, leadership abilities and an ability to work within a team will decide a person's value and ability to succeed in the new economy. People will be called upon to take ownership of their work. This requires new and mature thinking for those employees.

The sooner we embrace the inevitable situation of the new economy, the bigger jump we can have.

Words in Use

I. Find the nouns converted from verbs in the above passage.

II. Find the nouns converted from verbs in the following sentences:

1. If you have anything to discuss with me, don't hesitate to give me a ring.
2. I bought a bag of bird feed.
3. The father has the final say.
4. She passed her test at the first go.
5. It was a clever move.
6. She gave the girl a kiss.
7. Can I have a read of your paper?
8. You could make a guess at it.
9. This is for winter wear. Don't make it too tight.
10. The cause of unemployment was inadequate aggregate demand.
11. He had the grace to apologize to me for the insulting remark.
12. Tell Juan to get the fix and log it right away.
13. Famine came in the wake of the drought.
14. A visit to the Jurong Bird Park is a must for any tourist.
15. They have the same build.

Key to *Words in Use*

I.

change, fight, risk, jump

II.

1. ring	2. feed	3. say	4. go	5. move
6. kiss	7. read	8. guess	9. wear	10. demand
11. remark	12. fix	13. wake	14. visit	15. build

第4单元　形容词转化成名词

形容词转化为名词可分为两种：一种叫作部分转化（partial conversion），另一种叫作完全转化（full conversion）。

部分转化是指由形容词转化而成的名词未完全名词化，与名词尚有一定的区别，并受一定的语法结构的制约（如前面不能用不定冠词、指示代词、物主代词等）。如the rich，the dead，the unemployed，the sick等。这一类转化词前都带有定冠词，且不具有单复数形式，意思是表示一个整体。由于被转化的形容词种类不同，由此而来的名词也分为不同种类，大致如下：

1．表示抽象概念，指具有某种特点的东西。例如：

It is necessary to make a distinction between right and wrong.

In those days my father had to take the rough with the smooth.

2．表示类的概念，指具有某种特点的一类人，有集合意义。这种情况下，形容词前通常有the，而且没有复数结尾。例如：

This is a school for the deaf and the blind.

The poor were oppressed by the rich during pre-liberation days.

He had great sympathy for the oppressed and the exploited.

3．以-s，-se，-sh，-ch结尾，表示民族概念的形容词转化为名词，与定冠词连用，指整个民族。例如：

The Danish are a seafaring nation.

The Chinese are an industrious people.

4．最高级形容词转化为名词，其中有一些用在固定词组或习语词组中。例如：

I will give you a definite answer on Tuesday at the latest.

He is at his best in his description of college life.

5．由过去分词构成的形容词转化为名词。这类词如果前面加定冠词，则不指一般人，而指特定的人，如 the accused，the deceased，the departed，the deserted，the condemned等。（这些名词有时也用来指一群人或一类人。）

上述名词化形容词前均加上定冠词，但也有例外的情况。在表示两个相对概念的词并列时，定冠词可以省略。例如：

Both old and young took part in the run.

We will stand by you through thick and thin.

有些名词化形容词出现在固定词组中，也不用定冠词。例如：

He hoped that the repairs would stop the leak for good.

完全转化是指形容词完全转化为名词，并带有名词的一切特性。例如：形容词

native，转化为名词后，可以说a native, two natives, the native's personality, an industrious native。常见的例子有：

He is a natural for the job.（他是这项工作的天才人选。）

Tom is one of our regulars.（汤姆是我们的常客。）

表示有某种信仰、某一国籍或某些特征的人称名词很多来自形容词，例如：communist（共产主义者），Japanese（日本人），black（黑人），Christian（基督教徒）等。

现代英语中有相当一部分形容词已完全转化为名词，如mechanical（机械部件；机械结构；机械装置现亦指非主要任务或非主要角色），intravenous（静脉注射）， freebie或free bee（免费的东西或享受免费的人），dyslexic（诵读有困难的人），gay（同性恋者），disposable（指用后被弃的瓶子、罐头等），consumable（消耗品，特指提供宇航员使用的电力、氧气和水等消耗品），creative（具有创造性的人），crazy（傻子，疯子，生性怪僻的人）， nasty（讨厌的家伙，使人不愉快的事，卑鄙的事）等。

Words in Context

A Story about Tulips

This is a story that happened in Europe in the 17th century. Tulips were introduced into Holland before the 17th century, but it soon became popular among the upper classes. These beautiful and rare flowers became symbols of power and fortune and the rich did their utmost to get some to display in their gardens. It seemed that there was no alternative for tulips. When more people learned of this, they knew they had just found a gold mine.

By 1634, the whole country was so fascinated by tulips that all other activities almost stopped. It was reported that one rare bulb reached a price equivalent to ten tons of butter. As the tulip trade volume increased, markets were set up on the Stock Exchange of Amsterdam and other towns. That happened in the year 1636 when the mad situation was reaching its peak.

Many made a fortune in the beginning. As the prices moved in one direction, you only needed to buy low and sell high, buy high and sell higher. After the initial gains, confidence rose and many sold away their assets in order to put money in tulips, hoping to make more money. At that time, everyone thought that the high demand for tulips could go up forever.

When the prices of tulips reached such a high level, few bought them for planting in their gardens. The real demand for the flowers was exaggerated. This situation didn't last for long. The bubble finally burst in 1637. For some unknown reasons, tulips failed to keep the usual prices in a deal. Words spread and the market crashed. When confidence was destroyed, it could not be recovered and prices kept falling until they were one-tenth of those during the peak. Soon the nobles became poor. Cries of distress echoed everywhere in Holland.

Words in Use

I. Find the nouns converted from adjectives in the above passage.

II. Find the nouns conversed from adjectives in the following sentences:

1. The girl in black appears very beautiful.
2. The nurse is tending the wounded.
3. Poor innocents deserve our greatest sympathy.
4. He didn't want to disturb the quiet needed by patients.
5. Typically, convertibles cost more than the same make and model with a standard solid top roof.
6. There is only one black in my class.
7. He is a natural for the job.
8. They're running in the final.
9. Our six-year-old is at school.
10. When is your French oral?
11. It is necessary to make a distinction between right and wrong.
12. All of a sudden, the tire burst.
13. He's a dear.
14. This restaurant is his frequent.
15. She is investigating the ancients' conception of the universe.

Key to *Words in Use*

I.

the rich, alternative, long, nobles

II.

1. black	2. wounded	3. innocent	4. quiet	5. convertible
6. black	7. natural	8. final	9. six-year-old	10. oral
11. right, wrong	12. sudden	13. dear	14. frequent	15. ancient

第3章 缩略法

把词的音节加以省略或简化而产生的词统称为缩略词,这种构词方法为缩略法（abbreviation或shortening）。使用缩略词是世界上各种语言都存在的现象,如英语中的coed（coeducation,男女共校）；ob（weather observation,气象观察）；汉语中的"入世"（加入世界贸易组织）和"科技"（科学技术）等。科技英语中使用缩略词的现象更比比皆是,如plane取代了aeroplane；AIDS取代了Acquired Immune Deficiency Syndrome（获得性免疫缺损综合征）；SARS取代了Severe Acute Respiratory Syndrome（急性重症呼吸道综合征）等。20世纪30年代以后,特别第二次世界大战和战后的年代中,缩略语的使用尤为突出。缩略语的大量使用,其主要的原因是缩略语简单方便,节省时间,特别在现代英美文学作品、科技语体、计算机应用中使用更为广泛。此外,缩略语还有新奇、醒目的作用,在报刊中使用得也比较多。在当今时代,人们用语言进行交际,需要通过经济、高效的方式达到交换信息和交流思想的目的。缩略词符号少,信息量大,正好满足了现代人的这一需要。缩略词的大量产生和使用折射出现代社会的急剧变化,科学技术的飞跃进步和文化教育事业等的迅猛发展。英语中缩略词形式繁多,主要有四种类型：截短词（clipped word）、首字母缩略词（initialism）、首字母拼音词（acronym）、拼缀词（blend）。

第1单元 截短词

对原来完整的词进行加工,缩略其中一部分字母,构成新词,产生的词叫截短（缩短）词。主要以截取单词的词尾、词首、词腰为主。

截除词尾（apocope）,例如：fax—facsimile（电传）；lab—laboratory（实验室）；auto—automobile（汽车）；gas—gasoline（汽油）；tele—television（电视）；Hi-Fi—high fidelity（高保真）；dorm—dormitory（宿舍）；maths—mathematics（数学）；exam—examination（考试）；hippo—hippopotamus（河马）,等等。

截除词首(aphaeresis),例如：copter—helicopter（直升机）；dozer—bulldozer（推土机）；drome—aerodrome（飞机场）；quake—earthquake（地震）；scope—telescope（望远镜）；quake—earthquake（地震）；plane—aeroplane（飞机）,等等。

截除首尾（front and back clipping）, 有个别词截去首尾,保留不在首尾的重读音节。例如：flu—influenza（流行性感冒）；fridge—refrigerator（冰箱）；script—prescription（处方）,等等。

截除词腰（syncope），这样的情况很少见。有些词音节相当多，其中又含有读音相仿的章节，就可能截除一个音节。例如：fossilation — fossilization（化石作用）；fluidics— fluidonics（射流学）；pacifist — pacificist（和平主义者）等等。缩约形式（contractions）也可算作这一类，缩约形式是带有省略号的缩略词，如：gov't ← government（政府），rec'd ← received（收到），can't ← cannot（不能）等。有几个只用在诗歌中：e'en ← ever, ne'er ← never, o'er ← over。

截短词组，一种是留下词组成中的一个词，来表达整个词组的意思，如：daily ← daily paper（日报），weekly ← weekly paper（周报），finals ← final examinations（期终考试）。另一种是留下的词再经过截短，如：lube ← lubricated oil（润滑油），taxi ← taximeter cab（计程车）prefab ← prefabricated house（用预制件建造的房子），pub ← public house（小酒店），pop ← popular music（流行音乐），co-op ← co-operative store（合作商店），zoo ← zoological garden（动物园），perm ← permanent wave（烫发）。

截短词所指的事物或概念一般与原词一样，但也有个别截短词演变出新的词义，如fan(体育运动、电影等爱好者)来自fanatic（狂热者，盲信者）。miss现在指未婚女子，特别是未婚的青年女子，它的前身mistress却是"女主人"的意思。

有的截短词跟原词同时存在，但截短词是通用的词，而原词却不常用，甚至带有书卷气，例如：lunch（← luncheon午餐），movie（← motion picture 电影），pram（← perambulator童车）。也有的时候，截短词跟原词同时存在，但词义有分工，例如：cute ← acute, mend ← amend, spy ← espy, peal ← appeal。

Words in Context

Bicycles as a Means of Transportation

The bicycle has gone through one full circle already. It began as a toy for rich people. Then it was a means of transportation. Next it became a toy again. Now the bicycle is becoming popular than taxis and buses as a means of transportation once more.

There are several reasons for the new popularity of bicycles. The cost of fuel for cars is one reason. Another is the need to keep the environment clean. The third reason is a desire for exercise. Americans are one group of people who are leaving their cars at home. In fact, there are more than 100 million bicycles in the United States alone.

An institute called World Watch made a study about the future of the automobile. The researchers stated: "The bicycle is more convenient and saves more energy than the car." Furthermore, it is nearly as fast as the auto for short city trips. Many people, however, are still using their cars. Why? Time is one reason. It is still faster to drive a car than to ride a bicycle.

Another reason why people do not ride bikes is their lack of confidence. Some new bicycle riders do not trust themselves. If they are not completely certain that they can ride well enough, they decide to take their cars. New bicycle riders might be afraid of hurting themselves. They may lack confidence.

A more important reason is lack of knowledge about the vehicle. For example, the average person does not know how to shift the gears of the ten-speed bicycle. One shocking statistic indicates the bicycle riders' ignorance. Researchers say that 80 percent of the ten-speed bikes in the United States have never been shifted! If bike riders knew how to ride their bikes correctly, they would make better use of them.

Words in Use

I. Find the clipped words in the above passage.

II. Find the clipped words in the following sentences:

1. The adaptable Indian rhino is intermediate in size.
2. The commission cited Sept. 11 heroes as a group.
3. You'd better send the memo registered.
4. He sucked coke through a straw.
5. Today young people learn variations of disco dancing so complex that it would take hundreds of hours of observation to articulate the motions.
6. A cello prodigy at the age of four, he entered the prestigious Juilliard School in 1962.
7. The pilot quickly grabs a chute and jump out of the plane.
8. There are 100 cents in a euro, sometimes called euro cents.
9. It also established the Commodity Credit Corp., to make loans to farmers and to purchase and store crops in order to maintain farm prices. The program had limited success before it was declared unconstitutional in 1936.
10. I'll be feeding them info as soon as things break.
11. Zhongguancun High-Tech Park maintained rapid growth.
12. He disguised himself by wearing a wig.
13. Fast food, such as sandwiches or burgers, is customary.
14. The police hustled the thief into their van.
15. Prof. Jackson plays an important role in the scientific world.

Key to *Words in Use*

I.

taxis, bus, bike, auto

II.

1. rhino	2. Sept	3. memo	4. coke	5. disco
6. cello	7. chute	8. euro	9. Corp	10. info
11. High-Tech	12. wig	13. burger	14. van	15. Prof

第2单元　首字母缩略词

利用词的第一个字母代表一个词组的缩略词，就叫作首字母缩略词。缩略后不可以拼读，只能按照字母的读音来读。随着社会的进步和现代生活节奏的加快,首字母缩略词的数量急剧增加。例如：GEM是Ground-Effect Machine（气垫船）的首字母缩略词，B.A. 是Bachelor of Arts degree（文学学士）的首字母缩略词，AP 是Associated Press (美联社)的首字母缩略词。

有一些首字母缩略词的构成是用词组里每个单词的首字母代表整个单词，例如：UN ← United Nations（联合国），GMT ← Greenwich Mean Time（格林威治标准时间），IOC ← International Olympics Committee（国际奥委会），ABC← American Broadcasting Corporation(美国广播公司），CBS ← Columbia Broadcasting System（哥伦比亚广播公司），CPA ← Certified Public Accountant（注册会计师），CIA← Central Intelligence Agency（中央情报局)等。首字母缩略词后面是否加圆点，一般是约定俗成的，用法各异。英国人经常不加圆点，美国人经常加圆点，可是总的倾向是不加圆点。

有一些首字母缩略词的构成是用字母代表词的一部分，例如：MTV ← music TV（音乐电视），TB ← tuberculosis（肺结核），GHQ ← General Headquarters（总司令部），ID-card ← identity card（身份证）等。

有的缩略词还可以和其他词连用构成新的单词，例如：E-business ← electronic business（电子商务），A-bomb ← atom bomb（原子弹），V. J. Day ← Victory over Japan Day（战胜日本纪念日）等。

衡量单位的缩略词多用小写字母来表示，如：m ← metre（公尺/米）；cm← centimeter（厘米）；g ← gram（克）等。

日常生活中也有不少首字母缩略词，例如：VIP ← very important person（大人物），CEO ← Chief Executive Officer（首席执行官），asap ← as soon as possible（尽快），ILY ← I love you（我爱你），CU ← See you（再见）等。

专有名词也多有缩略词，例如：CIS ← Commonwealth of Independent States（独联体），GATT ← General Agreement on Tariffs and Trade（关贸总协定），OAU ← Organization of African Unity（非洲统一组织），ISBN ← International Standard Book Number（国际标准书号），EEC ← European Economic Community（欧洲经济共同体），VOA← Voice of America（美国之音）等。

来自拉丁语的字母缩略词，在英语的书面语中已必不可少，例如：e.g. ← exampli gratia（例如），i.e. ← id ext（即），etc. ← et cetra（等等），viz ← videlicet（也就是说），v. ← vide（参见）等。

金融方面的缩略词常遇到的有：ATM ← automated teller machine（自动取款机），

GDP ← gross domestic product（国内生产总值），GNP ← gross national product（国民生产总值）等。

总而言之，首字母缩略词几乎遍及所有领域，这里不能一一提及。

Words in Context

Public's Attitude Toward Human Cloning

What's the public's attitude toward the issue of human cloning? The fact that an unknown scientist could become the attention of the media by announcing he was ready to create a human clone showed how much this issue has fascinated and scared the whole world.

"It's not a fear of science but of how to control the technology," said Anne Figert, a professor in the Department of Sociology at Loyola University in Chicago. The idea also had a strong appeal because it touched on a central subject throughout civilization: the search for immortality, added Kenneth Howard, a professor of psychology at NWU in Chicago.

Richard Seed, a Harvard-educated physicist, said cloning a human could happen within 18 months if he could get financial backing. His first products would be cloned babies for infertile couples.

Within hours Seed was condemned by the White House and attacked in the US Congress. He was also put on ABC's Nightline last week under the wave of media publicity. There, he even offered to clone Ted Koppel, the host of the program. The University of Illinois at Chicago said the 69-year-old Seed had used the space there for three years to do small-scale experiments on the immune systems of mice. His space had neither a desk nor a file cabinet.

A university spokesman said Seed had published more than 20 scientific papers including an article in the Journal of the American Medical Association in 1994. He was involved in human embryo transplant research 20 years ago.

Words in Use

I. Find the initialisms in the above passage.

II. Write out in full the following words and translate them into Chinese:

1. IMF _____
2. CAAC _____
3. M.A. _____
4. ABS _____
5. GDP _____
6. GNP _____

7. DNA _____
8. H-bomb _____
9. PVC _____
10. UPI _____
11. CAD _____
12. IDD _____
13. OAU _____
14. V-Day _____
15. LP _____

Key to *Words in Use*
I. NWU, ABC, US

II.
1. International Monetary Fund 国际货币基金
2. Civil Aviation Administration of China 中国民航
3. master of arts 文学硕士
4. anti-lock braking system 防抱死装置
5. gross domestic product 国内生产总值
6. gross national product 国民生产总值
7. deoxyribonucleic acid 脱氧核糖核酸
8. hydrogen bomb 氢弹
9. polyvinyl chloride 聚乙烯
10. United Press International 合众国际社
11. computer assisted design 计算机辅助设计
12. international direct dial 国际直拨电话
13. Organization of African Unity 非洲统一组织
14. Victory Day 第二次世界大战胜利日
15. long-playing records 密纹唱片

第3单元　首字母拼音词

　　首字母拼音词是一种新的构词方法，把用首字母组成的缩略词拼读成一个词，就是首字母拼音词。例如："托福"就是根据首字母拼音词TOEFL（←Test of English as a Foreign Language）音译而来的，其他常见的例子还有，非典型肺炎SARS←Severe Acute Respiratory Syndrome。

　　过去运用首字母的缩略得到的词只按字母读音，而现在越来越多的科技术语、组织名称、产品名称等等都拼成一个词来读，例如：NATO ← the North Atlantic Treaty Organization（北大西洋公约组织），ASEAN ← the Association for South-East Asian Nations（东南亚国家联盟），UNESCO ← the United Nations Education, Science and Culture Organization（联合国教科文组织），sofar ← sound fixing and ranging（声发），radar ← radio detection and ranging（雷达）等。

Words in Context

UNESCO's History

　　UNESCO is the United Nations Educational, Scientific and Cultural Organization. It contributes to peace and security by promoting international cooperation in education, sciences, culture, communication and information. UNESCO promotes knowledge sharing and the free flow of ideas to accelerate mutual understanding and a more perfect knowledge of each other's lives. UNESCO's programmes contribute to the achievement of the Sustainable Development Goals defined in the 2030 Agenda, adopted by the UN General Assembly in 2015.

　　As early as 1942, in wartime, the governments of the European countries, which were confronting Nazi Germany and its allies, met in the United Kingdom for the Conference of Allied Ministers of Education (CAME). World War II was far from over, yet those countries were looking for ways and means to rebuild their education systems once peace was restored. The project quickly gained momentum and soon acquired a universal character. New governments, including that of the United States, decided to join in. Upon the proposal of CAME, a United Nations Conference for the establishment of an educational and cultural organization (ECO/CONF) was convened in London from 1 to 16 November 1945. Scarcely had the war ended when the conference opened. It gathered together representatives of forty-four countries who decided to create an organization that would embody a genuine culture of peace. In their eyes, the new organization was to establish the "intellectual and moral solidarity of mankind" and thereby prevent the outbreak of another world war.

Words in Use

I. Find the acronyms in the above passage.

II. Write out in full the following words and translate them into Chinese:
1. AIDS _____
2. TEWT _____
3. SALT _____
4. hipar _____
5. UFO _____
6. SAM _____
7. NANA _____
8. MOSS _____
9. CAR _____
10. BADGE _____
11. CORE _____
12. ROM _____
13. RAM _____
14. Vera _____
15. scuba _____

Key to *Words in Use*

I. SARS, AIDS

II.
1. acquired immune deficiency syndrome 艾滋病
2. tactical exercise without troops 没有军队参加的军官战术演习
3. Strategic Arms Limitation Talks 限制战略武器会谈
4. high power acquisition radar 高功率探测雷达
5. unidentified flying object 不明飞行物
6. Surface to Air Missile 地对空导弹，萨姆防空导弹
7. North American Newspaper Alliance 北美报业联盟
8. Manned Orbital Space Station 载人轨道空间站
9. Central African Republic 中非共和国
10. Base Air Defense Ground Environment 空军基地防空地面设施
11. Congress of Racial Equality 争取种族平等大会
12. read-only memory 只读存储器
13. random access memory 随机存取内存
14. vision electronic recording apparatus 电子录像机
15. self-contained underwater breathing apparatus 水肺〔潜水者用的水下呼吸器〕

第4单元 拼缀词

组成复合词的各词中,一个词失去部分或者各个词都失去部分音节后连接成一个新词,这样的构词方法叫作"拼缀法"(blending)。用这种构词方法构成的词叫作"拼缀词"或"合成词"(blend),也叫作"混成词"(telescopic word)或"行囊词"(portmanteau word)。根据形态结构,拼缀词有以下四种:

1. 第一个词的词头 + 第二个词的词尾,例如:
brunch ← breakfast + lunch (早午餐)
camcorder ← camera + recorder (摄录机)
chunnel ← channel + tunnel (海底隧道)
autocide ← automobile + suicide (撞车自杀)
motel ← motor + hotel (汽车旅馆)
Japlish ← Japanese + English (日式英语)
Oxbridge ← Oxford + Cambridge (牛津与剑桥)
positron ← positive + electron (正电子)

2. 第一个词 + 第二个词的词尾,例如:
workfare ← work + welfare (工作福利)
videophone ← video + telephone (可视电话)
moonmark ← moon + landmark (月球地标)
travelogue ← travel + catalogue (旅游介绍)

3. 第一个词的词头 + 第二个词,例如:
astrospace ← astronautical + space (太空空间)
helipad ← helicopter + pad (直升机机坪)
telediagnosis ← television + diagnosis (远程诊断)
hi-rise ← high + rise (高层建筑)
medicare ← medical + care (医疗,医治)
Eurasia ← European + Asia (欧亚)

4. 第一个词的词头 + 第二个词的词头,例如:
Amerind ← American + Indian (美洲印第安人)
comint ← communications + intelligence (通讯智能)
diamat ← dialectical + materialism (辩证唯物论)
interpol ← international + police (国际警察)
moped ← motor + pedal-cycle (电动自行车)
psywar ← psychological + warfare (心理战)

Words in Context

Buying a Camcorder

When buying a camcorder, you have to decide which format of machine you want. There are several: VHS (though these aren't common anymore), VHS-C (little tapes that, with an adapter, play back on a VHS VCR), 8mm, and the new digital format. There are also high resolution versions of the VHS and 8mm formats, called SuperVHS (or S-VHS), S-VHS-C and Hi8mm. Digital beats them all for picture quality, but the average consumer can write it off for a few more years until the price comes down to earth.

Each format has its advantages and disadvantages. Full size VHS camcorders are the most stable without technological intervention (the little camcorders can have "image stabilization" doohickeys built in) and the tapes are completely compatible with any VHS VCR. They're also bigger and bulkier than the little guys, so they take up more room when traveling and weigh more heavily on your shoulder. On the other hand, you can rent a movie on vacation (if you run out of landmarks to visit) and play it in the motel room.

Words in Use

I. Find the blends in the above passage.

II. Please tell the words from which these blends come from and translate them into Chinese:

1. comsat _____
2. smog _____
3. paratroops _____
4. meld _____
5. breathalyse _____
6. fantabulous _____
7. dawk _____
8. lansign _____
9. medichair _____
10. medevac _____
11. lunarnaut _____
12. slurb _____
13. nightglow _____
14. multiversity _____

15. spork _____

Key to *Words in Use*

I. camcorder，motel

II.
1. communication + satellite 通讯卫星
2. smoke + fog 烟雾
3. parachute + troops 空降部队
4. melt + weld 熔焊
5. breath + analyze 对……作呼吸的测醉分析
6. fantastic + fabulous 极出色的
7. dove + hawk 介于鸽派和鹰派之间的中间隔派
8. language + sign 语言符号
9. medical + chair 医疗用椅
10. medical + evacuation 医疗性疏散
11. lunar + astronaut 探月宇航员
12. slum + suburb 贫民郊区
13. night + airglow 夜光
14. multiple + university 综合大学
15. spoon + fork 勺叉

第4章　逆生法

英语中，去掉一个现存的词的词缀以构成新词的方法叫逆生构词法(back-formation)。逆生法的构词程序与派生法的构词过程恰好相反。如动词televise 由名词television 逆构而成，动词peddle 由peddler 逆构而成。 逆生法只改变词性，不改变词的基本含义。逆生法构成的词绝大多数都是动词，主要有四种方式：

（1）以 "-ion" 结尾的名词逆生而成，如 automation → automate, association → associate, stagflation → stagflate , valuation → valuate。

（2）以 "-ing" 结尾的名词逆生而成，如 gangling → gangle, merrymaking → merrymake, bookkeeping → bookkeep, banting → bant。

（3）以 "-ar, -or, -er" 结尾的名词逆生而成，如 typewriter → typewrite, editor → edit, loafer → loaf, laser → lase。

（4）以其他后缀结尾的词逆生而成，如 tongue-tied → tongue-tie, reminiscence → reminisce, hand picked → hand pick, fluorescence → fluoresce。

Words in Context

"No" to the Shopping Center

While the proponents of the plan to build a large shopping center in my community believe that it will aid economic development, I think that it will possibly do irreparable harm to our neighborhood. The proposed shopping center will damage existing businesses, provide inferior products, and the environment of our peaceful community will self-destruct.

Research indicates that companies with less than 50 workers employ more people and generate more revenue as a percentage of a nation's GDP than large-scale corporations. This is true in America, where small businesses are considered the engine of the economy, as it is in our community where many people own and operate small shops. Large stores can buy large quantities of goods at wholesale prices. While local grocery, that cannot buy products in bulk, will be unable to compete. Once the competition is gone, the large store can raise its prices and lower its employees' wages. They enthuse about this. This classic example of exploitative monopoly capitalism impoverishes a community while enriching a small number of people.

The goods sold at the shopping center would be mass produced and necessarily of inferior quality to the handcrafted local goods and freshly grown local produce. Cheap products like plastic furniture would lack the character and local flavor of traditional wooden furniture made right here in our town. Cheaply mass-produced food, laden with pesticides and chemical preservatives, would crowd out the healthier, fresher, and tastier local produce on the shelves of the large shopping center. Low prices from the large store might tempt local consumers to eat less healthy food, endangering the health of local people as well as harming the incomes of local farmers and shopkeepers.

Lastly, I must point out that a large shopping center might bring unwelcome development to our small community. Ugly and noisy roads and parking lots would need to be constructed. The volume of people wanting to buy things at the new shopping center would worsen the traffic situation, which is already bad. Pollution from cars and trucks already has a notably degrading effect on the local air-quality and this is also bound to become worse as the traffic to and from the shopping center increases. People in the neighborhood would be peeved for this rather than be pleased.

Words in Use

I. Find the back-formations in the above passage.

II. Find the back-formations in the following sentences:

1. We should know not only the phenomenon and result, but also the reason, so that we can valuate the influence and decide our policy.
2. It's impossible to legislate for every contingency.
3. The game will be televised live on ABC tonight.
4. Those who wished a favor of the emperor had to grovel on hands and knees before him.
5. I babysit for Jane on Tuesday evenings while she goes to her yoga class.
6. They are not given hearing aids or taught to lip-read.
7. The invention of machinery to mass-produce footwear.
8. An investigation is underway after a missile self-destructed shortly after it was launched.
9. These products are generally peddled (from) door to door.
10. He did not enthuse over the purchases.
11. Miss Crawford proposed their going up into her room, where they might cose comfortably.
12. He was peeved because we didn't ask him what he thought about the idea.
13. They used the swimming-pool, rode, lazed in the deep shade of the oaks in the heat of the day.
14. Melissa had chain-smoked all evening while she waited for a phone call from Tom.
15. Those who loaf all day and do nothing are social parasites.

Key to *Words in Use*

I.
self-destruct, enthuse, mass-produce, peeve

II.
1. valuate   2. legislate   3. televise   4. grovel   5. babysit
6. lip-read   7. mass-produce   8. self-destructed   9. peddled   10. enthuse
11. cose   12. peeved   13. lazed   14. chain-smoked   15. loaf

第5章 拟声法

拟声法(onomatopoeia)指借助语音或声音相似的词描写自然现象或事物的构词法。主要分为以下四种方式：

一、模仿走兽的叫声，如：

1. 狮子 (lion) roar, howl

2. 老虎 (tiger) roar, howl

3. 豹子 (panther) howl

4. 大象 (elephant) trumpet

5. 豺 (jackal) howl

6. 狼 (wolf) howl

7. 狗 (dog) bark, yap, yelp, howl, growl, snarl

8. 狐 (fox) bark

9. 猫 (cat) mew, miaow, meow

10. 鼠 (mouse) squeak, cheep, peep

二、模仿虫子的叫声，如：

1. 青蛙 (frog) croak

2. 蟾蜍 (toad) shriek

3. 蛇 (snake, serpent) hiss

4. 蜜蜂 (bee) buzz, hum, bumble, drone

5. 黄蜂 (wasp) hum

6. 蟋蟀 (cricket) chirp

7. 甲虫 (beetle) drone, boom

8. 苍蝇 (fly) hum, buzz, drone

9. 蚊子 (mosquito) hum, buzz, drone

三、模仿飞禽的叫声，如：

1. 公鸡 (cock) crow

2. 母鸡 (hen) cackle, cluck

3. 小鸡 (chicken) cheep

4. 鸭 (duck) quack

5. 鹰 (eagle) scream

6. 鹅 (goose) cackle, hiss, creak, gaggle

7. 鸽子 (dove, pigeon) coo

8. 燕 (swallow) chirp, twitte

9. 鸠 (stock-dove) murmur
10. 布谷 (cuckoo) cuckoo

四、模仿其他各类物体的响声，如：

1. 金属磕碰声，当啷 clank, clang
2. 形容金属的响声，当当 rattle
3. 金属、瓷器连续撞击声，丁零当啷 jingle, jangle, cling-clang
4. 鼓声、敲门声，咚咚 rub-a dub, rat-tat, rat-a-tat
5. 鞭炮爆炸声，噼啪 pop
6. 敲打木头声，梆梆 rat-tat
7. 重物落下声，咕咚 thud, splash, plump
8. 东西倾倒声，哗啦 crash, clank
9. 风吹动树枝叶声，飒飒 sough, rustle
10. 树枝等折断声，嘎巴 crack, snap

Words in Context

Ostrich Logic (Yan Er Dao Ling)

At the time when Fan, a nobleman of the state of Jin, became a fugitive, a commoner found a bell and wanted to carry it off on his back. But the bell was too big for him. When he tried to knock it into pieces with a hammer there was a loud clanking sound. He was afraid that someone would hear the clang and take the bell from him, so he immediately stopped his own ears.

To worry about other people hearing the rattling is understandable, but to worry about himself hearing the rattling (as if stopping his own ears would prevent other people from hearing) is absurd.

Words in Use

I. Find the onomatopoeias in the above passage.

II. Find the onomatopoeias in the following sentences:

1. Crack! The stick broke into two.
2. Only the ventilators in the cellar window kept up a ceaseless rattle.
3. Round the corner of Croscent Bay, between the pile-up masses of broken rocks, a flock of sheep came pattering.
4. The cock in the yard crowed its first round.

5. He felt as if he must shout and sing, he seemed to hear about him the rustle of unceasing and innumerable wings.
6. They splashed through the mire to the village.
7. The logs were burning briskly in the fire.
8. "Impertinent!" snorted Imalds.
9. Then a dog began to howl somewhere in a farm house far down the road, a long, agonized wailing, as if from fear.
10. I seldom opened my door in a winter evening without hearing it; Hoo hoo hoo, hooner hoo, sounded sonorously, and the first three syllables accented somewhat like how deardo; or sometimes hoo hoo only.
11. The manual affordances of the door scream "Pull me."
12. Ducks go "quack."
13. He could hear the hum of the bees in the garden.
14. Birds have begun to chirp and twitter among the trees.
15. Powerful searchlights snap on and scan the area.

Key to *Words in Use*

I.

clanking, clang, rattling

II.

1. crack	2. rattle	3. pattering	4. crowed	5. rustle
6. splashed	7. briskly	8. snorted	9. howl	10. hoo
11. scream	12. quack	13. hum	14. chirp, twitter	15. snap

第6章　专有名词普通化

专有名词普通化（antonomasia or words from proper names）：是指专有名词的代用，即人名、地名、物名有时作普通名词和动词，借以丰富词汇。当代英语有大量的词汇来自于专有名词的普通化，主要包括以下四种情况：

1. 来自人名，如：maverick: an independent individual who does not go along with a group or party "不服从的人；持不同意见的人"。源自未在自己的小牛身上打烙印的美国德州牧场主人之名。boycott: refuse to handle or buy（goods）；refuse to take part in（e.g. a meeting）"联合抵制"。源自查理斯·C. 博伊考特（1832—1897），爱尔兰的英国土地独家代理商。还有一些来自神话中的人名，如cherub（一小天使名）现意为"胖娃娃"。还有来自文学作品中的人名，如 shylock (莎剧中人物)现意为"高利贷者"。

2. 来自地名，如：Hollywood：a flashy, vulgar atmosphere or tone, held to be associated with the U.S. film industry 与美国电影工业有关的艳丽花哨的作风或氛围。limousine "豪华小轿车" 源自法国此地。

3. 来自书名，如：Utopia: an imaginary perfect society "乌托邦，理想的社会" 源自英国空想社会主义者托马斯·莫尔所作《乌托邦》一书。Odyssey: long adventurous journey "长途的冒险行程" 源自《奥德赛》，荷马史诗中记述了奥德修斯在特洛伊失败后的漂泊生活。

4. 来自商标名，如：nylon (尼龙), dacron (涤纶), rayon (人造丝)，orlon (奥伦纤维)都来自商标名。

Words in Context

The Chic Jeans

Hollywood types like Will Smith and Courtney Cox might be shocked to learn their chic Agave jeans are designed at the edge of a rural industrial park in southwest Washington, overlooking horses, barns and wetland.

But the secret will soon be out in the Portland area, as Agave opens its first outlet store Saturday at the company's new Ridgefield headquarters. Upscale denim, slacks and shirts will sell for 40 to 60 percent off—bringing Agave within reach for non-celebrities who can't afford $200 jeans.

Jeff Shafer, owner and designer, says he always envisioned a place to market last season's leftovers, chat about his work and offer the occasional custom fitting. After moving his family and company from California, he also wanted to welcome their adopted community.

Armed with an eye for design, a psychology degree and an MBA, Shafer launched a clothing company called BC Ethic in 1992. The laid-back look took off, growing to $25 million-a-year sales in less than a decade.

Frustrated by doing so much management and so little design, Shafer felt like "babysitter extraordinaire." He felt like a cynic. He asked his partners to buy him out.

In 2002 Shafer started Agave, vowing to hire an executive if the company got big enough to need one.

A few years ago, Shafer began to fantasize about getting out of Southern California. They found their new home during a road trip by limousine through the Pacific Northwest.

The family moved to Camas three years ago. Agave opened its 16,000-square-foot warehouse and 6,500-square-foot office in Ridgefield this winter, leaving just the production in California.

The move has been a thrill for some local shops.

A couple of years ago, Dawn Stanchfield turned down a sales representative pitching Agave at her women's boutique in downtown Camas. Lily Atelier didn't need any more denim.

Soon, Stanchfield ran into a woman wearing amazing-looking jeans. Turned out the pants were Agave—and the woman was Lauren Shafer, the owner's wife (and an Agave designer). "Send your rep back," Stanchfield implored.

Since then, she's restocked again and again. Stanchfield says shoppers love the stylish look, which fits body types from tiny to curvy.

Despite its success, Agave faces an uphill climb in an economy that skewers luxury brands.

Rick Soberanis, a local business consultant who spent time at Nautilus and Levi Strauss, has worked with Agave informally. He says Shafer is smart about tailoring clothing to his demographic, from style to price.

Staying nimble will help Shafer thrive, says Soberanis—who regularly wears Agave. "He's got the right brain and the left brain," Soberanis says. "He's not going to be an ostrich who buries his head in the ground, although he is a bit of maverick."

Words in Use

I. Find the antonomasia in the above passage.

II. Find the antonomasia in the following sentences:
1. Politically, she's a bit of a maverick.
2. Athletes from several countries boycotted the Olympic Games.

3. Dame Archer brought the cherub down to master in the house, and his face just began to light up.
4. Hollywood jeans.
5. Parisian nights.
6. Santa Ana winds.
7. Camembert cheese.
8. The hotel has a fleet of limousine to take guests to the airport.
9. Have you ever danced the Charleston?
10. Even hardened cynics believe the meeting is a step towards peace.
11. People liked seeing their friendly local bobby on his beat.
12. At half past 12 the guillotine severed her head from her body.
13. You Judas!
14. A few years ago this factory was still regarded as the Cinderella of the printing trade, but now it is very famous.
15. Your mackintosh looks better belted.

Key to *Words in Use*

I.

Hollywood, cynic, limousine, maverick

II.

1. maverick	2. boycotted	3. cherub	4. Hollywood	5. Parisian
6. Santa Ana	7. Camembert	8. limousine	9. Charleston	10. cynics
11. bobby	12. guillotine	13. Judas	14. Cinderella	15. mackintosh